The Third Citizen

Stephen G. Nichols, Gerald Prince, and Wendy Steiner

SERIES EDITORS

The Third Citizen

Shakespeare's Theater and the Early Modern House of Commons

Oliver Arnold

The Johns Hopkins University Press
Baltimore

Printed in the United States of America on acid-free paper
9 8 7 6 5 4 3 2 1

The Johns Hopkins University Press
2715 North Charles Street
Baltimore, Maryland 21218-4363
www.press.jhu.edu

Library of Congress Cataloging-in-Publication Data

Arnold, Oliver, 1962–
The third citizen : Shakespeare's theater and the early modern House of Commons / Oliver Arnold.
p. cm. — (Parallax)
Includes bibliographical references and index.
ISBN 0-8018-8504-3 (hardcover : alk. paper)
1. Shakespeare, William, 1564–1616—Political and social views. 2. Politics and literature—Great Britain—History—16th century. 3. Politics and literature—Great Britain—History—17th century. 4. Political plays, English—History and criticism. 5. Shakespeare, William, 1564–1616—Knowledge—Rome. 6. Rome—In literature. 7. Great Britain—In literature. I. Title. II. Series: Parallax (Baltimore, Md.)
PR3017.A48 2007
822.3′3—dc22 2006010567

A catalog record for this book is available from the British Library.

To my parents, Patricia Arnold and Maxwell Arnold

Contents

Acknowledgments

I am grateful to Princeton University for several grants and fellowships that allowed me to pursue research in England; the kind and helpful librarians and staff at the British Library, the Print Room of the British Museum, the Society of Antiquaries, and the John Rylands University Library of Manchester helped me make the most of my time.

The Johns Hopkins University Press has been a generous and supportive partner in this project: Stephen Nichols, Michael Lonegro, Courtney Bond, and Juliana McCarthy have been unfailingly encouraging and patient; the anonymous readers offered productive criticism; and Peter Dreyer's careful attention and wise judgment purged the manuscript of many errors, opaque sentences, and other infelicities.

This book has been a long time in the making; its publication is a happy event in no small measure because I now have the opportunity to acknowledge debts of such long standing. It is rare that I read a Renaissance play without thinking of Janet Adelman, Stephen Booth, and Jonas Barish. Before the project had really taken form, Harry Berger and I had several conversations that have stayed with me for years and helped to lay the foundations of this book. Had I not dedicated this book to my parents, I would have dedicated it to the late Julian Boyd; the three of them taught me how to read.

Princeton's early modernists—past and present—have been wonderful colleagues: Lawrence Danson, Michael Goldman, Tom Roche, and the late Earl Miner all read substantial portions of the manuscript and made many excellent and challenging suggestions. I am especially grateful to Victoria Kahn—it was wildly lucky for me that she was at Princeton when I arrived—and Joanna Picciotto, whose exceptionally keen reading of the penultimate draft of the manuscript led to dozens of improvements, large and small. I am very grateful to J. K. Barret and Abigail Heald for their invaluable help and good humor.

My sisters Caroline and Jane, my parents, Thomas Garrity, Dorothy Hale, Jeff Nunokawa, Michael Wood, Claudia Johnson, Uli Knopflmacher, Eduardo Cadava, Esther Schor, Deborah Nord, Larry Danson, and Martin Harries have given me the kind of intellectual and emotional support that can be repaid only with love.

This book would never have been finished without the encouragement and support of three people. At several moments when the project was foundering, Jeffrey Knapp rescued it and me. Jeff has an uncanny knack for seeing the misalignments, gaps, and disorders in the deep structure of an argument; showing someone how to fix those problems requires both a high gift and an awful lot of hard work. If I have made a contribution to the scholarship on the Elizabethan and Jacobean Parliament, it is only because I fell in love with Susan Maslan, who just happened to be a brilliant historian. In countless conversations, she supplied the gear I was missing—and badly needed—to understand what I most wanted to say about everything from Habermas to new historicism to the Third Citizen's account of power. More than that, she stuck with the book through thick and thin and never let me give up on it. Stephen Greenblatt's intellectual generosity has meant everything to me: every rough idea that I ever bounced off him always bounced back higher—transfigured into something more ambitious and exciting, something that I had to stretch for. His friendship has meant everything and more: among many kind, expansive, and loyal acts and gestures I will recall just one—one night, at a bar in Princeton, he willed me to write the chapter on *Julius Caesar* and finish the book.

Note on References and Abbreviations

Citations from manuscripts and early printed books generally follow the original spelling, but I have modernized in the cases of *u/v, i/j,* and *f/s* and silently amended early modern spellings, contractions, and punctuation that might cause confusion. References to and quotations from *Julius Caesar* follow T. S. Dorsch's Arden edition; unless otherwise noted, all other references to and quotations from Shakespeare's plays follow the Oxford edition of *The Complete Works,* edited by Stanley Wells, Gary Taylor, John Jowett, and William Montgomery. I have occasionally restored contractions where the Oxford editors spell out words, made some small changes to punctuation, and omitted a few of the stage directions that do not appear in early modern editions. All significant departures from the Oxford are noted and discussed.

Abbreviations

APC	Great Britain, *Acts of the Privy Council of England, 1542–1631,* ed. J. R. Dasent et al.
BB	*The Black Book of Warwick,* ed. Thomas Kemp
CDL	Samuel Schoenbaum, *William Shakespeare: A Compact Documentary Life,* rev. ed.
CJ	Great Britain, *Journals of the House of Commons*
D'Ewes	Simonds D'Ewes, *Journals of all the Parliaments during the Reign of Queen Elizabeth*
EJ	J. E. Neale, *Elizabeth I and Her Parliaments*
HC	J. E. Neale, *The Elizabethan House of Commons*
OED	*The Oxford English Dictionary*
1HIV	Shakespeare, *King Henry IV,* Part 1
1HVI, 2HVI, and 3HVI	Shakespeare, *King Henry VI,* Parts 1, 2, and 3

PPE	T. E. Hartley, ed., *Proceedings in the Parliaments of Elizabeth I*
PP 1610	Elizabeth Read Foster, ed., *Proceedings in Parliament, 1610*
PP 1614	Maija Jansson, ed., *Proceedings in Parliament 1614 (House of Commons)*
SPV	Annabel Patterson, *Shakespeare and the Popular Voice*
SR	Great Britain, *Statutes of the Realm*
WS	Gerald Eades Bentley, *Shakespeare: A Biographical Handbook*

The Third Citizen

1 Introduction

Le peuple anglais pense être libre, il se trompe fort: il ne l'est que durant l'élection des membres du parlement; sitôt qu'ils sont élus, il est esclave, il n'est rien. Dans les courts moments de sa liberté, l'usage qu'il en fait mérite bien qu'il la perde.

Jean-Jacques Rousseau, *Du contrat social*

The two great points of difference between a democracy and a republic are: first, the delegation of the government, in the latter, to a small number of citizens elected by the rest; secondly, the greater number of citizens, and greater sphere of country, over which the latter may be extended.

The effect of the first difference is . . . to refine and enlarge the public views, by passing them through the medium of a chosen body of citizens, whose wisdom may best discern the true interest of their country. . . . it may well happen that the public voice, pronounced by the representatives of the people, will be more consonant to the public good than if pronounced by the people themselves.

Publius (James Madison), *New York Packet*, November 23, 1787

In his speech to Queen Elizabeth at the closing of Parliament in 1598, Christopher Yelverton, the speaker of the House of Commons, celebrated the English subject's unique freedoms:

> If that comon wealth (most sacred and most renowned Quene) was reputed in the world to be the best-framed, and the most likely to flourishe in fe-

> licitie, where the subjects had there freedom of discourse, and there libertie of likeing, in establishing the lawes that should governe them; then must your Majestie's mighty and most famous realme of England . . . acknowledge it self the most happie of all the nations under heaven, that possesseth this favour in more frank and flowing manner than any kingdome doth besides. Singuler was the commendation of Solon that set lawes among the Athenians; passing was the praise of Licurgus that planted lawes among the Lacedemonians; and highly was Plato extolled that devised lawes for the Magnesians: but neither yet could the inconveniences of the state be so providently forseene, nor the reason of the lawes be so deeply searched into, were they never so wise, nor the course of them be so indifferent, or so plausible; nor the people be so willing to put themselves under the dutie of them, as when the people themselves be agents in the frameing of them. (*PPE* 3:197)

Yelverton's "most sacred" queen would seem an unlikely audience for an encomium to legal codes established by popular consent: before he began his oration, after all, the speaker had "made . . . 3 reverences" to his sovereign, who claimed to rule by divine right (*PPE* 3:241); he ended it by begging Elizabeth "to geve full life and essence" to the bills that had passed both the House of Lords and the Commons but remained "emptie and sencelesse shaddowes" (198). In his youth, Yelverton had tried his hand at poetry and playwriting, and he dusted off his old skills for a final flourish that must have pleased the queen: when Elizabeth's royal assent transformed dead parchment into living statutes, she would be like "Jupiter" when he "inspired breath" into "the picture of Pigmalion" (198–99).[1]

The mystical trappings, symbolic displays, and lush rhetoric of sacred monarchy have long captivated the new historicist imagination. The scene of legislation Yelverton conjures up so poetically, however, defined Englishness for many Elizabethans, not because a queen was enthroned at its center, but because she was only one person in a sovereign trinity, a "mixed estate" composed of a divinely anointed monarch, a hereditary House of Lords, and a popularly elected House of Commons. England was a monarchy, to be sure, but English subjects were not like other subjects, because "[t]he English monarch," as James Morice reminded his fellow members of Parliament in 1593, was not like other monarchs:

> No Spartane kinge, or Venetian duke, but free from accompt and cohercion of anye . . . requiringe taxe and tribute of the people, yet not causeless, nor without comon assent.

> Wee agayne the subjects of this kingdome are borne and brought upp in due obedience, butt farre from servitude and bondage, subject to lawfull aucthoritye and commaundment, but freed from licentious will and tyrannie; enjoyinge by lymitts of lawe and justice oure liefs, lands, goods and liberties in great peace and security, this our happy and blessed estate. (*PPE* 3:35)

The replanting of the true church in English soil convinced Spenser and like-minded Protestants that England was God's chosen nation; Yelverton and Morice believed that England was "the most happie of all the nations under heaven" and "blessed" because the people of the realm consented to the laws that governed them and to the taxes that they paid.

Consent, assent, freedom, liberty: these are the stirring terms of Yelverton and Morice's exceptionalist political theology, but the liberties that happily distinguished the English from the woeful slaves of other nations were complicated by political representation. English laws are supremely wise, impartial, and good, and English subjects supremely law-abiding, Yelverton reasons, because "the people themselves [are] agents in the frameing" of law, but he then allows that the people's agency is mediated by representatives:

> [W]here the rules of government in some comon wealths have been setled only by some fewe magistrates, there divers varieties of mischeifes have allso many times befallen them. . . . According therefore to . . . the ancient and well-ruled freedome of the subjectes of England, hath the whole state of your kingdome (represented here by Parliament) assembled, consulted, and resolved uppon some fewe petitions, thought fitt for lawes to them by your Majestie to be established. (*PPE* 3:197–98)

The "people themselves" did not consent directly to the laws that bound them; they enjoyed instead the "ancient . . . freedome" of electing the 450 or so MPs who sat in the House of Commons: "in the Knights . . . and Burgesses," according to John Hooker's *The Order and usage of the keeping of a Parlement in England* (1572), "are represented the Commons of the whole Realme, and every of these giveth not consent onely for him self . . . but for all those also for whom he is sent" (182). The English subject's special freedoms, then, depended absolutely on political representation. Early modern MPs and the Whig scholars who have lionized them often figure political representation as nothing more than a "structural device," through which the people expressed their concerns and gave their consent. The mediation of political representatives, however, distinguishes republicanism and representative democracy from direct democracy—makes a difference, in other words, that political philosophers from Locke to Rousseau to the Founding Fathers considered no less profound than the difference between democracy and monarchy.

Recovering the advent of political representation as an effective ideology should radically change our understanding of both early modern political culture and Shakespeare's political art, and of the way Anglo-American critics, for whom representative democracy is second nature, construe them. The new practices and theories of parliamentary representation that emerged during Elizabeth's and James's reigns shattered the unity of human agency, redefined the nature of power, transformed the image of the body politic, and unsettled constructs and concepts as fundamental as the relation between presence and absence. Shakespeare believed that political representation produced (and required for its reproduction) a new kind of subject and a new kind of subjectivity, and he fashioned a new kind of tragedy to represent the loss of power, the fall from dignity, the false consciousness, and the grief peculiar to the experiences of representing and of being represented. Representationalism and its subject mark the beginning of political modernity; Shakespeare's tragedies of political representation greet them with skepticism, bleakness, and despair.[2]

The Alchemy of Political Representation

In Yelverton's conflation of "the people themselves" and their parliamentary representatives, we can just begin to glimpse the secular magic that Elizabethan and Jacobean antiquarians, political philosophers, legal theorists, and MPs routinely attributed to political representation. At times, theories of representation matched the mysticism of divine kingship. In 1593, for example, Francis Bacon argued that every man in England was present in the Commons' chamber in St. Stephen's Chapel. The occasion for this extraordinary claim was mundane enough: during the Commons' consideration of a bill to settle the countess of Cumberland's jointure, Sir Thomas Heanage reported that Francis Clifford, a party with an interest in the proposed settlement, had assured him that he "was contented" that it pass. A few MPs objected that Heanage's *report* of Clifford's speech was immaterial, but Bacon successfully persuaded the House that reported speech introduced into Commons' proceedings could not be considered hearsay:

> Mr. Francis Bacon in this pointe shewed there was a difference betwixt this Courte where we are all judges appointed of recorde and other inferiour courtes where there are judges appointed of record: for there they are not to credit report or information, but the party to be bound must be brought

> *coram* and be present. But in this Court representatively all men are present, wherfore this scruple needs not that the party to be bound should be here seene, for all men are here present representatively. So this bill passed currant. (*PPE* 3:122)

We seem to have caught the genius Bacon on an off day, or, at least, on a day when he put his genius to the base purpose of improvising an embarrassingly flimsy argument in order to spare the Commons the bother of tracking down Francis Clifford. How can the claim that "all men are here present representatively" answer the charge of hearsay? The juridical "scruple" of disregarding hearsay rests entirely on a distinction between actual presence and representative presence.[3]

Bacon leaps right over the seemingly insurmountable distinction between direct testimony and reported speech because the magic of political representation has brought tumbling down the even more absolute difference between being present in one's own person (*coram*) and being "present representatively." Bacon does not exempt Parliament from hearsay rules; he claims that such rules are irrelevant to Parliament because political representation produces something like the "real presence" of the people of the realm in their parliamentary representatives. Bacon's construction of representation is an extreme, but by no means singular, expression of the foundational orthodoxy of the early modern House of Commons. The monarch and the lords made themselves present in Parliament; the common people of the realm, "the whole flower and power of [the] kingdom," as the authors of the Commons' Apology to James I styled them in 1604, "amounting to many millions of people, are representatively present in us of this house of Commons" (Petyt 235). The tripartite Parliament was omnicompetent and its statutes sovereign, because, as Sir Thomas Smith reasoned in *De republica Anglorum* (1583), "the Parliament of England representeth and hath the power of the whole realm": "[f]or every Englishman is intended to be there present, either in person or by procuration and attorneys. . . . from the prince (be he king or queen) to the lowest person in England. And the consent of the Parliament is taken to be every man's consent." Unlike Bacon and the authors of the Apology, Smith treats the presence of the people in Parliament as a legal fiction: because "every Englishman *is intended* to be there present, either in person or by procuration and attornies. . . . the consent of the Parliament *is taken to be* every man's consent" (78–79). The first statute of James's reign similarly acknowledges an ontological—though not a legal—difference between actual presence and representative presence: "in this Highe Courte of Parliament . . . all the whole Bodie of the Realme, and everie p[ar]ticular Member thereof, either in p[er]son or by Rep[re]sentation (upon their own free Elections) are by the Lawes of this Realme *deemed to be* p[er]sonallie p[re]sent" (*SR* 2:1017–18; emphasis added).

Legal fictions won't do for Bacon, because early modern rules of evidence reject the conflation of an agent speaking for himself or herself in person and a representation of his or her speech. Why not simply fetch Mr. Clifford, then? Why should so modest a matter as the countess of Cumberland's jointure move Bacon to spin out instead such an absolute construction of representative presence? Bacon recognized that the objection to Heanage's attempt to report Clifford's *assent* put intolerable pressure on all of the claims the MPs made for the efficacy of political representation and thus on all of the claims they made for their own authority, power, and usefulness. Other courts could acknowledge in hearsay rules the insufficiency of representation, the difference between direct testimony and mediated testimony, because other courts were wholly juridical in function; but the High Court of Parliament was both a juridical and a legislative institution. To call Francis Clifford to the bar in St. Stephen's Chapel would be to acknowledge that "intending" him present was insufficient; but if that were so in the matter of a private bill that affected only a few subjects, how could the MPs claim to speak for the whole commons of the realm in debates about public bills for taxes, religious reforms, provisions for the monarch's safety, and other great matters? If Clifford's physical absence meant that he could not be "bound" to the terms of the private bill for the countess of Cumberland's jointure, how could Parliament give consent on behalf of every subject in England and thus bind them to the statutes of the realm? Bacon recognized that *everything,* at least in theory, was at stake in the debate over Heanage's reporting of Clifford's "assent": the MPs' usefulness to the crown and lords, their power in Parliament, and their authority over the people they represented all depended on their claim to fashion through representation a political subject who understood himself to be self-fashioned—that exceptional subject who was "willing" to obey laws because he had "frame[d]" them himself.

Political representation, on Bacon's account, is an act of faith, a belief in things unseen: it was not necessary that Clifford "should be . . . *seene*" in the House of Commons, Bacon argues, not because his presence was unnecessary; he *was* present, but he was invisible. The legal fiction of the people's presence in Parliament may be more conservative than Bacon's claim of "real presence," which we might think of as a political fiction—a fiction that has forgotten or occluded its fictiveness; but the open secret of the legal fiction does not negate its fictiveness or the cognitive operations fictions require. "[E]very Englishman is *intended* to be there present": the technical sense of "intend" here—"to understand as in the view or sense of the law; to construe, or hold legally" (*OED*, s.v., IV.16)—follows logically and historically from a cluster of meanings that turn on the power of the mind: "to exert the mind" (III.8); "To turn one's thoughts to, fix the mind on (something)" (III.12); "to understand or apprehend that something is" (IV.13). The legal fiction of the people's presence makes its own remarkable demand: that we intend presence in the absence of extension; that we pretend that the people themselves are in the Parliament. Bacon is driven beyond legal fiction to a claim of real presence, not because the legal fiction of presence asks too little of the imagination, but because it asks too much.

Even the literalism of Baconian representation left the imagination a vast role to play in the culture of representationalism. The very structure and mechanisms of political representation made the artificial, the fictional a necessary category for ideology and political thought: the same beehive might be interpreted as the natural (and hence divine) sanction for monarchy, oligarchy, or democracy, but even the cleverest of political philosophers would search God's First Book in vain for a natural model of political representation. Political representation is more clearly, more wholly feigned than all other modes of governance. Elizabeth's and James's subjects—at least the good ones—believed that God had chosen their rulers to be his regents in England; through his grace, their natural bodies had been wedded to (and perfected by) a mystical body invested with profound powers. The ideal subject of the House of Commons had to hold far more counterintuitive beliefs, and he attributed miraculous properties—some of which the state religion denied even to the Son of God—not only to the knights and burgesses but also to himself. Elizabethan and Jacobean representationalism posited a subject who believed not only that he was representatively present at the political center (that he was at once home in Shropshire, for example, and present in St. Stephen's Chapel in London), but also that he empowered himself by empowering others; that he attained a political voice by allowing others to speak for him; and that his representatives subordinated their particular interests to the general good by conceiving of themselves as artificial persons.

These were leaps of faith that Shakespeare could not make, flights of fancy he refused to take. Shakespeare rattles the faith and beggars the imagination that representationalism requires by asking us to see through political representation, to see, that is, what is—or rather what is not—before our eyes at the moment of representation: in *Titus Andronicus,* the tribune Marcus Andronicus repeatedly speaks for the people and solicits their voices as if they were present, but "the people" are not on stage, and Marcus alone answers his own calls for great general acclamations; in *Henry VI, Part 2,* the people, seeking Suffolk death, manage to push their way into Henry's presence and onto Shakespeare's stage, but before they can speak, Salisbury dismisses them back to the wings ("Sirs, stand apart. The King shall know your mind" [3.2.244]) and takes their place ("Dread lord, the commons sends you word by me" [3.2.244]); in the first scene of *Julius Caesar,* the tribunes, who recognize that the presence of the people in their own persons renders political representation superfluous, chase the people from the stage ("I'll about / And drive away the vulgar from the streets;" Flavius advises Marullus, "So do you too where you perceive them thick" [1.1.69–71]); in *Coriolanus,* the citizens speak 137 of the first 212 lines of the play, but from the moment Coriolanus announces the creation of the tribunate, the citizens virtually disappear.[4] "They are dissolv'd" (1.1.202): so Coriolanus describes the moment when the people give up their armed rebellion in exchange for political representation. In Shakespeare's bluntly mimetic critique, the magic of political representation makes the people disappear.

To figure the subjectivity peculiar to representationalism and to embody its tragic articulation, however, one needs subjects, and Shakespeare's most ambitious political art reaches its most profound expression in characters who appear on his stage, but only as ghosts of themselves, as half selves unable to fashion themselves in relation to others because they themselves are fashioned though representation. The tongueless Lavinia, who, like the people of Rome, must depend on Titus and Marcus to speak for her, is a literal figure for the political condition of being represented, of being absent even when present. After the creation of the tribunate, the citizens of *Coriolanus* do not suffer physical deformation, but they are curiously like Lavinia: remarking Coriolanus's refusal to submit himself to the tribunes' commands, the First Citizen warns, "He shall well know / The noble tribunes are the people's mouths, / And we their hands" (3.1.270–72). (Coriolanus himself has just reviled "the tribunes of the people, / The tongues o'th' common mouth" [3.1.22–23].) In the first scene, before the people have tribunes to speak for them, the First Citizen's quick tongue stings the patrician Menenius into frustrated sputtering; now he believes, even as he speaks, that his tongue is alienated from him—the only words he has left himself declare that he has no other words, that he no longer has a tongue. When he is still in possession of his own tongue, the First Citizen wonderfully mocks Menenius's image of a body politic in which an altruistic patrician belly eats and eats only in order to nourish the plebeian "members";

in a last act of (now unwitting) wit, he imagines a newfangled body politic in which he nonetheless still plays the role he has always played—that of speechless member. Nothing could signal subjection to the new order more wistfully, nothing could signal the genius of the new order more neatly, than the First Citizen's recycling of Menenius's political anatomy, an anatomy in which he is the "great toe" rather than the smart mouth.

Lavinia figures the people of Rome because she shares their condition; but the people in *Titus Andronicus* and the citizens in *Coriolanus* willingly—or, at least, without physical coercion—make themselves tongueless. The perfect form of symbolic violence under representationalism is self-inflicted: "He's to make his requests by particulars, wherein every one of us," the Third Citizen tells his fellows as they prepare to bestow the consulship on Coriolanus, "has a single honour in giving him our own voices with our own tongues" (2.3.44–46). In Shakespeare's England, participants in parliamentary elections typically expressed their preferences by shouting a candidate's name: "voice" was a synonym for "vote"; and when they voted for a parliamentary representative, the inhabitants of a borough or shire authorized him to be their voice, to speak for them, to bind them to statutes. After the creation of the tribunate in *Coriolanus,* the "tribunes are the people's mouth." The dreadful modesty of the Third Citizen's boast signals the triumph of the new ideology: to believe that one attains honor by giving up one's voice with one's own tongue is to misrecognize the loss of power as the achievement of personal distinction. Perhaps, however, we can also register a tickle of unconscious enlightenment in the Third Citizen's anxious assertion of the obvious: a subject might well brag that he is going to give his voice with his own tongue, if he *almost* realizes that he has already lost it.

I have not named this book for the Third Citizen in order to suggest that Shakespeare subversively endowed him with forceful historical agency even though early modern theatrical decorum required that he languish anonymously far down the list of dramatis personae. We should consider the Third Citizen a tragic protagonist precisely because he is so self-effacing and so radically alienated from his own agency. The citizens elect Coriolanus in a kind of fog: they know that he is their enemy, but they give him their voices anyway. That fog is the psychic state peculiar to representationalism. As they wait for Coriolanus, the newly enfranchised citizens debate the nature and limits of their new power. The First Citizen claims that he and his fellow plebeians "ought not to deny" Coriolanus their voices (2.3.1–2), but the Second Citizen disagrees: "We may, sir, if we will" (2.3.3). The Third Citizen proposes an improbable synthesis, a third way: "We have power in ourselves to do it, but it is a power that we have no power to do" (2.3.4–5). The Third Citizen does not think of himself as powerless. Rather, he believes that he is powerful but powerless to retain his power; he recognizes that his power is constituted precisely as—and only as—the power to yield his power to others. The play begins with an armed plebeian uprising against patrician oligarchy: for a few fleeting moments, the people have power in themselves—a power coextensive with their persons—and they exercise that power in their own persons. When they give up their assault on the Capitol in exchange for the creation of the tribunate, they transform a power proper to themselves into a power that can only be exercised by others, into a symbolic capital whose value depends absolutely on its alienation. The Third Citizen thus misrecognizes his powerlessness as power and his power as powerlessness, and that misrecognition is not only an ideological effect of political representation and the enabling condition of its reproduction but also the wonderfully prosaic expression of a tragic fall: with the climb up the Capitoline hill behind them, with the steps to the Capitol itself right before them, with power just at their fingertips, the citizens turn fortune's wheel with their own hands and cast themselves down before masters of their own creation. What makes the Third Citizen's loss of power so moving, and so different from, say, Lear's, I suggest in both Chapter 5 and the Epilogue, is the concomitant loss of the capacity to articulate loss and, perhaps, even the loss of a selfhood sufficiently integrated to register loss as loss.

Shakespeare's Tribunes

Shakespeare's interest in political representation was unparalleled among Elizabethan and Jacobean literary artists. His first historical tetralogy—*Henry VI, Parts 1*, *2*, and *3* and *Richard III* (1591–93)—is by far the most ambitious Tudor-Stuart attempt to stage the English Parliament: in each of the three *Henry VI* plays, a long scene is set in Parliament, where Henry's bungling helps to bring about his own disaster; and the structure and effects of representation and surrogacy integrate the political imagination of the entire trilogy. We briefly glimpse the English Parliament in the second tetralogy (*Richard II, Henry IV, Parts 1* and *2*, and *Henry V* [1595–99]), but after 1592, Shakespeare pursued his critique of political representation in a series of idiosyncratic works about republican Rome. (This turn to Rome, as we shall see, tells us something important about the early modern parliamentary politics that shaped Shakespeare's representation of the tribunate.) The political culture of the Roman Republic had been enormously important, of course, to the Italian Renaissance but struck very few sparks for English Renaissance dramatists and poets. Shakespeare's predecessors and contemporaries scarcely mention the tribunate, the first institution of popular political power in Europe. By contrast, Shakespeare's compact history of the rise and fall of the republic turns on the people, their tribunes, and representational politics: *The Rape of Lucrece* (1594), to be sure, gestures only briefly at the popular revolt that chased the Tarquins through the gates of Rome and gave birth to the consulate and the primitive republic, but in *Titus Andronicus* (1592–93), Shakespeare's juxtaposition of election scenes—speaking for the people, Marcus acclaims first Saturninus and then Lucius emperor—and Titus's attempts to speak for the maimed Lavinia refashion Livy's history of Lucrece into a mythic treatment of the violence of political representation; in *Coriolanus* (1608), the founding of the tribunate and the development of representational politics shape the actions of the eponymous protagonist; and *Julius Caesar* (1599), unlike the many Tudor-Stuart character studies of the would-be king, is principally concerned with the threat Caesarism poses to the tribunate, strife between the people and their tribunes, Brutus's belief that he speaks as the people and enacts their will, and the collapse of republicanism.

The unruly plebeians of *Julius Caesar* and *Coriolanus* and the riotous butchers and tailors of *Henry VI, Part 2* have convinced legions of critics that Shakespeare loathed the lower orders of Rome, Lancastrian England, and his own London. Recently, however, a group of Whiggish critics have discovered a prescient, progressive Shakespeare who believed that the common people had a legitimate right to participate in governance. *Coriolanus* is the great text for the Whigs: the play's famous first scene of popular protest against aristocratic grain hoarding and other oppressions demonstrates, according to Vivian Thomas, "that the people are in desperate need of representation" (180) and, according to Annabel Patterson, commends the establishment of a "constitution that provided, through the tribunate, for popular representation" (Patterson, *Shakespeare and the Popular Voice,* 123). The republican cure that Shakespeare recommends for the ills suffered by his fictional Roman plebeians is also his prescription for the beleaguered commons of England: Shakespeare "belie[ved]," Patterson argues, "that Jacobean England desperately needed to borrow from the strengths, as well as learn from the difficulties, of republican political theory" (ibid., 122).

The Whigs' attempt to make Shakespeare our liberal contemporary is misguided.[5] The people of Shakespeare's England were not "in desperate need of representation"; they already had it in the House of Commons. Patterson claims that *Coriolanus* nonetheless had something subversive to teach James I's subjects, because the Roman franchise was wider than the franchise in early modern England. The Jacobean franchise—roughly, one-sixth of adult males—was not as narrow as Patterson suggests, but bringing the liberal assumption that all the defects of representative democracy can be cured with more democracy to bear on the Jacobean mixed estate misfires here for a simpler reason: to Shakespeare's way of thinking, the franchise is no boon. In *Coriolanus,* for example, political representation contains and diminishes the people's power and serves the interests of the Senate and the newly created tribunes, who aspire to tame and rule over, rather than empower, the people. In Shakespeare's plays, the tragedy of political representation turns not on the exclusion from power of the unenfranchised but on the powerlessness enfranchisement produces (and mystifies), not on the subjection of the unenfranchised but on the deforming effect of representation on the enfranchised subject. In Shakespeare's canon, there is not a single exception to this rule: when they invest representatives with their voices, the people lose both power and their capacity to articulate cogently their aims and desires. Nor does a system of benignly paternalistic political representation benefit the people even as it marginalizes them; political representation is almost always a catastrophe for Shakespeare's "people."

Titus Andronicus pulls down so many woes on his own head that we may hardly notice that his cynical manipulation of representational politics nearly destroys Rome and its people into the bargain. *Titus* begins with Saturninus and Bassianus vying for their dead father's throne: Saturninus appeals to his fellow patricians to uphold primogeniture; his younger brother Bassianus urges all of Rome to "let desert in pure election shine" (1.1.16). Titus's brother Marcus seems to dash the hopes of the imperial brothers when he announces "that the people of Rome, for whom we stand / A special party, have by common voice / In election for the Roman empery / Chosen Andronicus, surnamed *Pius*" (1.1.20–23). Marcus, the people's "tribune and their trust" (1.1.181), invests Titus with the people's voices; Titus designates Saturninus the new emperor; and Marcus acclaims him: "With voices and applause of every sort, / Patricians and plebeians, we create / Lord Saturninus Rome's great emperor, / And say, 'Long live our Emperor Saturnine!'" (1.1.230–33). As Marcus "elects" Saturninus emperor, the people for whom he acts and speaks are eerily, palpably absent. The people themselves must be absent precisely because creating Saturninus emperor—even before he proves himself a lurid tyrant—is a perverse betrayal of the people: Saturninus, after all, opposes popular election and threatens to plunge Rome into a civil war if Titus, the people's choice, prevails. The unhappy precedent of the Andronici's responsibility for electing this Tarquin, an enemy of the people, makes it hard indeed to hail the election of Lucius—who is himself implicated in the disastrous scheme to make Saturninus emperor and has led an alien army to Rome's gate—as the rebirth of Rome. Framing the rape of Lavinia between these elections, Shakespeare haunts his play with invocations of Lucrece and Virginia, even as he turns the republican rape topos on its head. In Livy, autocracy reaches its extreme expression in rape, which, in turn, sparks the violent institution (or reestablishment) of republicanism; for Livy, of course, republicanism is the cure for tyranny. In Chapter 3, I argue that in *Titus,* political representation is the disease rather than its remedy.

Titus and Marcus are close kin to the English kingmakers Warwick and Salisbury, who bring down Suffolk in the people's name: "They say," Salisbury reports to Henry, "by him the good Duke Humphrey died; / They say, in him they fear your Highness' death" (*2HVI* 3.2.250–51). Warwick and Salisbury do in Suffolk neither to reform the realm nor to secure Henry's safety but, quite the contrary, to pave the way for a bloody civil war that will devastate the commons and win the crown for the sons of Richard Plantagenet, duke of York. With the expectation that the grateful Saturninus will take Lavinia for his wife, Titus throws the people's voices to the elder imperial brother in order to make himself the great patriarch of a secure line of emperors; smooth succession seems a distant dream in fifteenth-century England, but when Warwick abandons the Yorkist cause to support Henry, his quid pro quo has all of Titus's optimism: his service in exchange for a marriage that will make him, through his daughter, the grandfather of the next heir. Marcus, an aristocratic tribune, and Warwick, a noble spokesman for the commons, may strike us as peculiar embodiments of the defects and hazards of popular political representation, but many members of the early modern House of Commons were powerful men of high birth; indeed, St. Stephen's was so thick with the sons of great men that the renegade MP Arthur Hall described the Commons as a kind of preparatory academy for the House of Lords (see Hall Ei^{v}). The self-serving ends to which great magnates such as Marcus and Warwick put their status as popular spokesmen might, then, suggest a limited, reformist critique of political representation, but Shakespeare *invariably* represents the relation between representative and represented as hierarchical and antagonistic. Jack Cade is as humbly born as his followers, but when he proclaims that his "mouth shall be the parliament of England," he translates the most resonant sign of monarchic tyranny in the English tradition—the collapsing of *lex* and *rex*—into the form of political representation. In the *Henry VI* plays, I argue in Chapter 2, oppression typically takes the form of representation, and representation is always oppressive and violent.

In *Julius Caesar* and *Coriolanus,* the tribunes are plebeian by birth, but their status as representatives has made them part of Rome's governing class, and they devote themselves to managing, controlling, bamboozling, and pacifying the plebeians. They are, in fact, as zealous as the patricians in limiting the people's power. In the first scene of *Caesar,* the tribunes suppress the people's celebration of Caesar's triumph over Pompey. In Plutarch, the people hate Caesar and exalt their tribunes for braving Rome's most powerful man; Shakespeare makes Caesar the people's darling and the tribunes their scourge. As we shall see in Chapter 4, Shakespeare's Flavius and Marullus recognize Caesarism as a double assault on their power: Caesar's desire to usurp all political authority and the people's unmediated participation in Caesar's mode of power pose equally devastating threats to the function and authority of political representation. The tribunes, who care only for their offices and privileges, oppose Caesar not because he threatens the people's power but because his invitation to the people to exercise their power directly would eliminate the need for tribunes. Caesarism, as Shakespeare elaborates it, collapses the particular kind of mediation political representation institutes between the subject and governing authority. By contrast, in *Coriolanus,* the subject of Chapter 5, the people and their tribunes share a hatred for Coriolanus, but the tribunes delight in their new status as "masters of the people," express contempt for those who have elected them, plot to demonize the people in the eyes of the Senate in order to shore up their own credit with the ruling elite they seek to join, and congratulate themselves for transforming the rebellious people into docile subjects "singing in their shops and going / About their functions friendly" (4.6.8–9). Here, again, Shakespeare departs from Plutarch, who neither sets Brutus and Sicinius up as shining examples of virtue nor demonizes them as deceitful schemers. If Shakespeare hoped to convince his audiences that they needed more representation than they already enjoyed, he left it to them to imagine what a good representative would look like.

The House of Commons and the Ideology of Political Representation

Shakespeare's representations of the Lancastrian Parliament and the Roman tribunate recast the popular politics of the past in an early modern mold. The fifteenth-century House of Commons Shakespeare encountered in the great chronicle histories must have struck him as quite alien, and he introduces distinctly Elizabethan notions about parliamentary representation into Henry VI's England. The tribunes of Livy's and Plutarch's histories and Shakespeare's tribunes would recognize one another only as distant cousins. In the Shakespearean republic, tribunes attribute their power and authority both to elections and to their status as representatives. The Roman tribunes were elected by the plebeians, but political representation does not figure—is not even a recognized structure—in Livy and Plutarch. Reflecting on a postclassical world in which a fallen humanity could dream no better dream of freedom than the English Parliament, Rousseau scoffs, "[l]'idée des représentants est moderne. . . . Dans les anciennes Républiques . . . jamais le peuple n'eut de représentants: on ne connaissait pas ce mot-là" (*Du contrat social,* 190).[6] Like generations of MPs before them, Elizabethan and Jacobean knights and burgesses were elected to their seats in the Commons, but the claims they made to represent and speak for thousands of people were "modern" and unprecedented. Shakespeare's Roman plays are histories of the present, dramas of the modern ideology of representation that was being born.

Representationalism is an ideology that grew up around, but need not have followed from, parliamentary elections.[7] Why should Elizabethan and Jacobean MPs have developed such an ideology? The claim to represent was, in part, a strategy for establishing the Commons' position in relation to the lords and monarch: in 1601, Edward Coke argued that the members of the House of Commons could hold their own with the lords and the queen, because "[her] Majesty and the Nobles being every one a great person, represented but themselves; but . . . [the] Commons though they were but inferior men, yet every one of them represented a thousand of men" (D'Ewes 515). In this economy of power, the magic of representation raises "the inferior man" to the stature of "a great person." When they wanted to oppose particular royal policies, lift the dignity of "the nether house," or assert their competence to discuss religion and other great affairs of state, some MPs were quick to play the representation card: "the voice of the people in the things of their knowledge," the authors of the Apology warned James, is "the voice of God" (Petyt 243); the MPs were, of course, the "voice of the people." James liked to tell the MPs that kings were "God's lieutenants" (*PP 1610* 1:45); the MPs claimed to be His representatives once removed.

Revisionist historians, who assign the Commons a very passive role in Elizabethan and early Jacobean political culture, have ignored the politics of representation, but my purpose here is not to revive Whiggish visions of an oppositional House of Commons heroically protecting the ancient liberties of free Englishmen from overbearing monarchs. The advent of representationalism owes as much to the MPs' desire to establish power over the common subject as it does to their aspirations for an equal share of parliamentary power. The story I tell in Chapter 1 has remained outside established historiography: the emergence of a Commons that disciplined and formed subjects in a distinct and novel way, the rise of a Commons whose authority over the people—as well as its authority in relation to the crown and the lords—was predicated on its being recognized as the representative of the people. Elizabethan and Jacobean MPs never challenged the primacy of the subject's relationship to the monarch: that every man and woman was the monarch's subject went without saying. In any society, however, agents—especially those far down the social ladder—recognize themselves as subjects of multiple authorities (religious, political, economic, and so on) without experiencing all of those authorities as embodiments of a foundational, unified "highest authority" (such as a monarch) and without fully integrating their multiple relations to authority into a coherent subjection to a foundational, unified "highest authority." In Chapter 1, I argue that Elizabethan and Jacobean MPs increasingly sought to subject the commons of the realm—already the subjects of a monarch, a church, landlords, masters—through representation, to produce subjects, that is, who were interpellated, in part, by an institution that claimed to represent them and to be empowered by them.

Early modern MPs occasionally describe the House of Commons as if it were nothing more than a primitive public sphere: "a vehicle of public opinion [to] put the state in touch with the needs of society" (Habermas 30–31). The House of Commons had been created, according to an MP in 1566, to put the monarch in touch with every part of the realm "absent from the king's eye and eare" (*PPE* 1:129–30): the king could not "be in every corner of his kingdome and dominions at one instant to view and hearken out the benefittes or inconveniences" his people needed or suffered, but the knights and burgesses could set the faces of the people before his eyes and make their voices sound in his ears. The MPs were not, in fact, private persons constituting themselves as a representative public, as "addressees of public authority," who, in turn, "compel public authority to legitimate itself before public opinion" (Habermas 18). The MPs were public persons, and the House of Commons was itself a public authority, a state institution that traded in decisions rather than opinions, that addressed itself—and its decisions—to the public, and to which the public increasingly addressed its opinions. Early modern MPs exercised power over many aspects of the common subject's life: statutes—the legal instruments by which taxes were levied, many freedoms granted and restricted, and important aspects of religious life established and regulated—could not be passed without the Commons' consent.[8]

In John Hooker's founding myth of Parliament, the ancient British kings had established an elected, representative body not simply to help them hear the voices of the people but to help them govern:

> the benefit thereof grew so much in short time, that there was as it were a Metamorphoses of the state of the publique weale in those daies, for what Sedition and contention had disordred: good order and concord recovered. What loosenes and dissolutenes of life had marred: honest behaviour restored. What disobedience had decayed: loiable obedience ammended. And finally what soever by any disorder was amiss: was by these means reformed and redressed . . . as that the people beeing better governed. . . . Lo, suche are the frutes which grew of the Parlements. (118)

Better governed, more orderly, reformed, and obedient because he was shaped and restrained by laws that he had framed himself (through representatives), the subject Hooker and Yelverton extol was the "fruit" of Parliament.

Early modern representationalism promises a willing subject, a subjected sovereign who fashions his own restraints, but the House of Commons also played a role in policing the realm: in Hooker's riff on the body politic topos, the knights and burgesses "are as it were one body, having many eyes to se, many feet to go, and many hands to labour withall, and so circumspectt they are for the government of the commonwelth: that they se all things, nothing is hid or secret, nothing is straunge or new" (117). Consenting subjects, then, still needed careful watching and, even, coercive correction. The many MPs who served the crown as justices of the peace would have been involved in trying and punishing those who transgressed statutes, but the MPs also performed many disciplinary actions in their capacity as elected representatives. The MPs frequently punished members of the public who were thought to have defied the authority and dignity of the Commons. The MPs were quick to suppress both published accounts of their proceedings and any description of Parliament that they considered heterodox or irreverent: printers, authors, and booksellers were arrested by the serjeant-at-arms, made to kneel at the bar of St. Stephen's Chapel, fined, and sometimes incarcerated in the Commons' own prison. During Elizabeth's and James's reigns, hundreds of private subjects were escorted to St. Stephen's for a variety of other offenses: bringing legal proceedings against MPs or their servants during parliamentary sessions; disseminating rumors about Commons' proceedings; making obscene gestures at MPs; and, even, telling jokes about the pace of parliamentary business. The first pictorial representation of the House of Commons in St. Stephen's (fig. 1)—a broadside printed in 1624—almost certainly represents a member of the public submitting himself to his representatives. MPs spoke from the benches; petitioners stood at the bar: the figure we see kneeling has assumed the traditional posture of punishment and submission. This scene of discipline is especially resonant because private subjects were not allowed to enter the Commons' chamber while the MPs were sitting, and transgressors were punished in the usual fashion. "[N]othing" the people did could be "hid" from the MPs, but nearly everything the MPs did was "hid and secret." The engraving seems to warn those who gaze upon it that if they attempt to see the MPs in the flesh, they will find themselves in the position of the kneeling figure whose perspective they share.

My aim is not to chastise the early modern House of Commons for falling short of the standards of representative democracy maintained by modern representative assemblies. The contexts I posit for Shakespeare's tragedies of political representation—the experience of parliamentary elections (Chapter 5), the disciplinary practices of the House of Commons (Chapter 1), theories of and attitudes toward parliamentary representation (Chapters 1, 2, and 4)—are contemporaneous with those tragedies, and the Shakespearean critique of parliamentary politics that I elaborate turns on ideological contradictions, fissures between rhetoric and practice that are internal to early modern representational politics. To be sure, primary evidence—here, more than a hundred parliamentary speeches, borough and county records of elections, and dozens of treatises, tracts, and letters about Parliament and parliamentary politics—must be interpreted, but I strive to attribute to Elizabethans and Jacobeans only those ideas and beliefs that they themselves clearly articulated. Early modern representationalism does not, of course, announce itself as an ideology, and to anatomize it as such would seem to require that we stand outside of its operations. Historical distance is not, however, the positive condition of such a perspective: key aspects of my history of the House of Commons and my critique of the ideology of parliamentary representation are anticipated by—indeed, are based upon—Elizabethan and Jacobean demystifications of representationalism. When it served their purposes, James or Elizabeth scolded the MPs for behaving as if they had magically merged with the people they represented and knew their minds and desires; from an entirely different perspective, the sometimes quite radical Elizabethan MP Robert Snagge questioned whether the MPs could really consent on the people's behalf.

Indeed, early modern observers, for whom political representation was both relatively novel and only one of three quite distinct, if constitutionally reconciled, bases of legislative authority, may have something disquieting to tell us, the subjects of a representationalism so entrenched as to seem virtually natural and inevitable. Early modern parliamentary representation is neither formally analogous to nor, in any simple way, the mother of our own systems of representation, but we may want to consider whether the most fundamental contradictions and ideological misrecognitions of political representation in its primitive form have been exorcised from, or simply work more effectively in, its perfected form.

Shakespeare and Parliament

The MPs' dangerous touchiness begins to explain why, after 1592, Shakespearean scenes of malicious political representatives duping, marginalizing, and tyrannizing over "the people" unfold in the streets, marketplace, and Senate House of Rome. Several episodes in Tudor parliamentary history had plenty of dramatic potential, but plays treating Henry VIII's Reformation Parliaments or the Commons' fiery role in the tragedy of Mary, Queen of Scots, would have been doubly doomed: the master of the revels would have made quick work of plays that made the greatness of the queen, her father, or even her mortal enemy too "familiar"; and had he taken up such recent episodes in parliamentary history, Shakespeare might well have found himself kneeling at the bar of St. Stephen's Chapel before the subjects of his art. There were serious impediments, then, to representing the English Parliament in its proper shape, but the Roman Republic was much more than a safely alien screen for Shakespeare's critique of parliamentary rhetoric and practices. Roman greatness in almost every kind of endeavor loomed large in the Elizabethan and Jacobean imagination, and Shakespeare's contemporaries had a lively awareness of the nearly four centuries during which their island had been under the Roman yoke. John Hooker, for example, posited a historical relation between Roman institutions and the House of Commons:

> For by the ancient orders and prescribed lawes of this land: onely such are to be elected and to have place [in the House of Commons] as for gravitie, wisdome, knowledge and experience, are reputed and knowen to be the moste chosen and principall personages of the whole land and Realme. . . .

> The order . . . among the Romains was that none should be received or allowed to be of their Senat house: unlesse he were grave in yeeres, and wel experienced in common affaires of the publique welth. . . . The like order also was and is within this Realm, the same being derived and taken cheefly from the Romains, among and under whome: divers of tholde and ancient Kings of this Realm, have ben bred and brought up. (116)

For Hooker, the legend of Brutus founding England after the fall of Troy gives way to a legend of the Roman Republic as the mother of Parliaments. The Roman yoke was a path to liberty: like Shakespeare's own Cymbeline, Hooker's "ancient Kings" had been "bred and brought up" by the Romans; they had learned the system of governance that would make English freedom unique in the modern world from direct observation of the ancient world's master state. On this account, to represent the Roman Republic was to recover English history.

For most commentators, the similarities between the Roman Republic and England's mixed estate were merely formal rather than historical, and by the time Shakespeare wrote *Titus Andronicus,* analogies between plebeians and the English lower orders, tribunes and MPs, senators and peers, and the consuls and speakers of the House were already commonplace in histories, political philosophy, parliamentary speeches, and tracts addressed to Parliament.[9] Shakespeare turns the necessity of obliqueness to account: assimilating the Roman tribune to the shape of the early modern MP, he imagines the failings of parliamentary representation as corruptions already present in the original and surpassingly prestigious form of political representation (pace Rousseau). In Shakespeare's hands, the creation of the tribunate in *Coriolanus* becomes a primal fraud, a Machiavellian bamboozlement that suppresses and usurps the people's power at the very moment of its first flowering.

If the repressive measures the House of Commons took to control its public image help to explain Shakespeare's turn to Rome, they would also seem to scuttle my project: how could Shakespeare have known enough about the House of Commons to develop the sophisticated critique of parliamentary representation that I attribute to him? That critique is astonishingly sophisticated, but it depends not on an intimate knowledge of the Commons' proceedings—though Shakespeare was certainly in a good position to know far more about Commons' business than the vast majority of his contemporaries—but instead on a more general familiarity with the fundamental propositions of parliamentary representation and the institutional culture of the House of Commons.

Early modern MPs succeeded almost entirely in preventing their debates from circulating in print, but dozens of books and tracts that treated the Commons' role in governance, the nature of political representation, and parliamentary procedure and customs were published during Shakespeare's lifetime. Indeed, Elizabethan and Jacobean MPs themselves clearly believed that books and tracts might help to establish and maintain the ideology of political representation: several MPs wrote about the Commons; in debates, conferences with the House of Lords, and petitions to the crown, MPs occasionally appealed to the authority of treatises on Parliament; and the Commons suppressed with customary zeal books and tracts they deemed to be heretical challenges to their authority and their claims to represent the people.

The 1587 edition of Holinshed's *Chronicles* was a particularly important chapter in the writing of the English Parliament. In 1572, fresh from representing Exeter in the Parliament of 1571, John Hooker published his treatise *The Order and usage of the keeping of a Parlement in England* and his translation of the *Modus tenendi Parliamentum;* fifteen years later, Hooker helped himself to a larger readership by republishing *The Order and usage* in his 1587 edition of the *Chronicles.* The same edition begins with William Harrison's *Description of England,* which includes a lengthy discussion of the Commons. Certain details of parliamentary rhetoric and practice—claims for Parliament's antiquity; prohibitions on bearing arms in the House of Commons; the role of the speaker—that find their way into Shakespeare's plays suggest a familiarity with *The Order and usage* and the *Description,* and in these same works Shakespeare would also have discovered both the grand rhetoric of political representation and the exclusionary practices that seemed to contradict it. Hooker and Harrison, for example, both claim that MPs make the people of the realm "present" in the Commons: "our Parliament House . . . is the head and body of all the realm and the place wherein every particular person is intended to be present, if not by himself, yet by his advocate or attorney" (Harrison 149–50). Hooker, however, repeatedly stipulates that the people must be excluded from the Commons: "if any forain person doo enter into that house, the assembly therof beeing sitting, he ought . . . to be punished" (Hooker 170); "every person of the Parlement ought to keep secret and not to disclose the secrets and things spoken and doon in the Parlement house" (187). In what was surely one of the most dog-eared books in his possession, Shakespeare, I believe, encountered the defining contradiction between early modern representationalism's rhetoric of radical presence and its practices of secrecy and exclusion.

Shakespeare's literacy opened up a library of writings about Parliament, but his success as a London theatrical entrepreneur, star status in a playing company with royal patronage, and position as a prominent Warwickshire property owner would have opened more exclusive doors to St. Stephen's Chapel. In Warwickshire, Coventry and Warwick each returned two burgesses to Parliament; residents of rural areas and smaller towns were eligible to participate in the election of two knights of the shire if they possessed "free tenement to the value of forty shillings by the year at least, above all charges" (Hirst 25). Shakespeare's holdings in Warwickshire would have entitled him to vote in the parliamentary elections of 1597, 1601, 1604, and 1614; his father, John, would have enjoyed the franchise in 1563, 1571, 1572, 1575, and 1578. Mark Kishlansky, an eminent authority on early modern elections, argues that *Coriolanus* "so accurately portray[s] the process by which officeholders were selected in the early seventeenth century that one must conclude that Shakespeare had firsthand experience, either of wardmote elections to the London Common Council or of parliamentary selections themselves" (5).[10] The franchise itself was hardly an entrée to the inner workings of the House of Commons, but Shakespeare knew and did business with Warwickshire men who had served in the Commons, and his life in London would certainly have brought him into the orbit of men who knew MPs and, perhaps, of MPs themselves.[11]

Shakespeare's experience of parliamentary politics, then, was relatively privileged, but the condition of being represented by political agents was nearly universal, and Parliament was a quite routine and not insignificant part of many early modern subjects' lives: with the exceptions of the monarch and the lords temporal, every member of the laity—the enfranchised and the unenfranchised, the literate and the illiterate—was either an MP or represented by an MP;[12] between Shakespeare's birth and death, there were ten elections; Parliament sat for a total of roughly sixty months; eleven subsidies were levied and collected by order of Parliament; and, at the end of every session, with the exception of 1614, Parliament enacted and published statutes that affected almost every aspect of life. Moreover, many Elizabethans and Jacobeans were also represented in local government by members of town or city councils. Local representation typically reproduced many of the contradictions of parliamentary representation: borough franchises were often quite limited, but council members claimed to speak and act for all residents; town councils treated many matters of public concern, but council proceedings were secret. In Stratford, for example, the town corporation—of which John Shakespeare had once been a member—agreed in 1593 to expel any alderman or burgess who discussed the proceedings of the corporation outside the council chamber (Fox 13).

Parliament time would have been especially hard to ignore in London: a session brought to the city hundreds of MPs and their servants, as well as many private persons with an interest in parliamentary legislation; despite the MPs' best efforts to suppress public discourse, news of Parliament's business did occasionally become the talk of the town; and the opening of Parliament began with a spectacular public procession—"the full Court in motion" (Neale *HC,* 336), almost every member of the House of Lords to boot, and Elizabeth herself in "an open chariot . . . [a] chair, carried between two white horses . . . like a throne, with two silver pillars at the back supporting a crown of gold, and another with two at the Queen's feet, on which were a lion and a dragon" (Neale *HC,* 337). When the vanguard of court messengers reached Westminster Abbey, the tail of this great snake of ceremony—the captain of the guard and his men—must still have been waiting to leave the Palace of Whitehall; after a sermon at the Abbey, the procession traveled to Westminster Palace.

In the shires and boroughs outside of London, most people would have heard little of Parliament's doings until word of subsidies and new laws began to spread, but the elections that marked the beginning and end of the typical voter's active participation in parliamentary politics were, perhaps, even more remarkable than the opening procession. Few occasions—fairs, market days, the mustering of troops, riots, plays—brought so many people together in one place: at Warwick, just eight miles from Stratford, nearly two thousand voters participated in shire elections; in York, six thousand people gave their voices; borough electorates were far smaller but could exceed five hundred.[13] At the vast majority of elections, to be sure, behind-the-scenes power brokers and town councils had seen to it that the number of candidates matched the number of places: voters simply appeared to give a ritual assent. Even uncontested elections were, however, events sufficiently compelling to attract substantial numbers of the unenfranchised: ale paid for by candidates flowed freely; the entire electorate, high and low, assembled in the same place, at the same time; standing on scaffolds, candidates were required, for a moment, to submit themselves to the approval of both their peers and their tenants and inferiors; and a gentleman might bristle because "fellows without shirts challenge[d] as good a voice as" his (qtd. in Kishlanksy 61). On those rare occasions when a genuine contest pitted humble voters against shire magnates or municipal grandees, elections seemed less like empty festive rituals of popular power than moments of carnivalesque disorder.[14] We should, however, regard even those rebellious electorates that actually prevailed with a Bakhtinian squint rather than the wide eye of Whiggery: as we shall see in Chapter 5, after their voices transformed candidates—some of them bona fide reformers, some of them true rabble-rousers, most of them "politically" indistinguishable from their rivals, all of them well-to-do, not a one of them a boy bishop or lord of misrule—into new MPs, the voters went home; their power, such as it had been, was exhausted. More than a few Jacobean playgoers who had given their voices at an election might well have identified with the Third Citizen's uncharacteristic moment of enlightenment after Coriolanus flees the scene of his own election in the plebeian marketplace for the familiar surroundings of the Senate House: "When we granted [him our voices], / Here was 'I thank you for your voices, thank you. / Your most sweet voices. Now you have left your voices / I have no further with you.' Was not this mockery?" (2.3.170–73).

Treatises on parliamentary procedure and hot news about Commons proceedings were beyond the ken of the humbler sort in Shakespeare's audience, but the subjective and sensory experiences of representational politics were familiar enough that they could be recognized even when they were embodied in antique Romans. Witnessing the astoundingly anomalous spectacle—astounding even when it was nothing more than spectacle—of the high submitting themselves to the low (landlords to tenants, sons of dukes to the cobblers who made their shoes, mayors to tradesmen just free of their apprenticeships); exercising a power so fleeting that it seemed to disappear in the very moment one shouted out "Yelverton" or "Morice" or "Bacon"; alienating one's voice, one's power, one's very agency: figuring these experiences and the mockery of representationalism was the most ambitious aim of Shakespeare's political art.

Historicism, Theatrical Monarchy, and the Ideology of Consent

Shakespeare's republican dramas are his most rigorously political works, but they have been marginal, at best, to new historicist studies of theater and power in Elizabethan and Jacobean England; the participation of a popularly elected representative assembly in the raising of taxes and the making of statute law was the most distinctive aspect of Elizabethan and Jacobean governance, but the new historicist map of early modern political culture has very seldom stretched beyond crown and court; the condition of being represented by political agents was nearly universal among Shakespeare's contemporaries but does not figure at all in new historicist constructions of early modern subjectivity. For twenty-five years, inquiries into Shakespeare's "high politics" have hewn very closely to the corpus of plays, historical contexts, and interpretive problems established in the early 1980s by the seminal work of scholars such as Jonathan Goldberg, Louis Montrose, Stephen Orgel, Richard Helgerson, Leah Marcus, and, of course, Stephen Greenblatt: the English histories, *Lear, Macbeth,* and *Cymbeline;* Renaissance theories of kingship and the practices of Renaissance monarchs; the representation of the subjectivity, ideology, and culture peculiar to monarchy.[15]

Why did the legions of critics who followed in the footsteps of these pioneers never take up the House of Commons? It would be hard to imagine a more tantalizing mingling of the spheres traditionalists oppose and new historicists superimpose, of agents who make history and those who make culture: politicians and poets, courtiers and historians, power brokers and theologians, advocates of New World empire and rhetoricians, privy councilors and philosophers, bureaucratic time-servers and quintessential Renaissance men. Many of the 450-odd members in any session were unremarkable lawyers or members of the country elite, but during (or just a bit beyond) the span of Shakespeare's life, Thomas Norton, Walter Ralegh, Francis Vere, John Lyly, John Donne, Inigo Jones, George Herbert, George Gascoigne, Christopher Brooke, Edwin Sandys, Thomas Wilson, John Davies, Philip Sidney, John Stubbes, Fulke Greville, Edward Coke, Peter Wentworth, Richard Grafton, Job Throckmorton, Robert Cecil, William Fleetwood, William Hakewill, Thomas Smith, Henry Spelman, Francis Drake, William Lambarde, Arthur Gorges, and Robert Cotton all sat in St. Stephen's Chapel. Revisionist historians often treat the MPs with weirdly personal scorn, but these stars and dozens of lesser lights sustained a level of political discourse we can scarcely imagine: well-crafted and rigorous arguments, learned scriptural exegeses, long quotations in Latin and Greek, and allusions to classical literature and philosophy were commonplace.[16] The millions of words left behind by Elizabethan and Jacobean MPs, all of whom seem to have had the oratorical stamina of Fidel Castro, were pretty fine, but they were not merely pretty: the knights and burgesses engaged in serious debates about the duty of the rich to the poor, the Eucharist, the nature of Englishness, trade policy, foreign affairs, and the characteristics of good ministers—not to mention the pernicious effects of starch on English fashions and morals. They also talked endlessly about themselves and the institution in which they served, about the proper relation between a representative and those he represented, about the role of the Commons in relation to the crown and the lords, about the history of the institution and the institution's place in history, and about the Commons' shaping force in

English national identity. New historicism has discovered the crackle of art and psychic complexity in Elizabeth's speeches and James's many writings, but this ocean of parliamentary discourse remains unexplored.

The rhetoric of "the strangely neglected" always invites sneering: Elizabeth and James *were* the titanic figures of their times, and the literature of kingship fills many more shelves than the literature of representational politics. The near effacement of Parliament from new historicist studies of early modern England, however, does tell us something important—and something quite germane to the largest concerns of this book—about historicism and the hegemony of representationalism in contemporary Anglo-American culture. The degree zero of that effacement is "Invisible Bullets: Renaissance Authority and Its Subversion" (1981), Stephen Greenblatt's epochal analysis of the "poetics of Elizabethan power." Elizabeth I, Greenblatt argues, was "a ruler without a standing army, without a highly developed bureaucracy, without an extensive police force, a ruler whose power [was] constituted in theatrical celebrations of royal glory and theatrical violence visited upon the enemies of that glory" (64).

Elizabeth's own words provide a now famous cornerstone of the theatrical power thesis: "We princes are set as it were upon Stages, in the Sight and view of all the World." Greenblatt's brilliant reading of Shakespeare's representation of monarchy turns on the apparent homology between Elizabeth's mode of power and theater: "the charismatic authority of the king, like that of the stage" (63), Greenblatt claims, depends on "the imaginary forces of the spectators" (64). "'Tis your thoughts now must deck our kings": theatrical monarchy shares, but occludes, the imaginative economy that the Prologue of *Henry V* acknowledges so openly, for while Elizabeth's "play of authority depends upon spectators," her "performance is made to seem entirely beyond the control of those whose 'imaginary forces' actually confer upon it its significance and force" (65).

Greenblatt treats Elizabeth's figure of the player-prince as a general axiom about the queen's relationship to her subjects, but the queen delivered her celebrated line during an extremely complex performance on a very particular occasion. On November 12, 1586, a delegation from the Lords and Commons presented Elizabeth with a petition urging her to execute Mary, Queen of Scots; before reading the petition, Elizabeth assured the peers and the MPs that she would proceed with great care, lest either foreigners or her own subjects impeach the justness of her course: "we princes . . . are set on stages," she well knew, "in the sight and view of al the worlde duly observed. Th'eyes of many behold our actions, a spott is sone spied in our garments, a blemish quickly noted in our doings. It behoveth us therefore to be carefull that our proceedings be just and honorable" (*PPE* 2:251). Members of the House of Commons had long been agitating for action against Mary: "Warninge hath alredy ben given her by statut," Robert Snagge reminded the House in 1572, "and no good folowed of it, and therfore the axe must give the next warninge" (*PPE* 1:324). Bold words. If, however, Elizabeth sometimes bristled at parliamentary pressure to bring down the ax, she also knew that the same pressure, especially in the form of a petition claiming to express the will of "the universall state of [her] whole people of all degrees" (*PPE* 2:245), could put at least a thin veil between her own hand and Mary's neck and help to legitimate a regicide.[17]

Greenblatt, then, unmoors Elizabeth's utterance from its context: the role the Lords and Commons played in shaping, augmenting, and limiting Elizabeth's power and in mediating her relationship to her subjects. In the most influential text of the new historicism, Parliament lies buried beneath an argument about monarchy so powerful and attractive that subsequent critics have never been moved to challenge or complicate it. In the wake of "Invisible Bullets," dozens of new historicists and cultural historians repeated Greenblatt's provocative thesis about Elizabethan political culture as if it were a simple fact:

> Elizabeth, of course, was a brilliant actor, as perhaps she had to be in the absence of effective instruments of coercion . . . her rule could be—and in her case perhaps could only be—celebrated and confirmed theatrically. . . . Elizabeth's use of pageantry and progress enabled her to transform her country into a theatre and, in the absence of a standing army, create an audience, troops of loyal admirers, to guarantee her rule. (Kastan 365)

> Lacking a professional army and even the rudiments of a paid bureaucracy, Elizabeth wielded little real coercive force. She could maintain her throne only by devoting herself to the arts of political persuasion and performance. . . . Royal power depended upon its "privileged visibility," in Stephen Greenblatt's excellent phrase, and as Greenblatt especially has shown, such visibility was theatrically constituted and theatrically maintained. (Mullaney 24)

> The Tudors, who ruled without a standing army or an extensive police force, had their power "constituted in theatrical celebrations of royal glory," in Stephen Greenblatt's words. (Levin 24)

On the one hand, Greenblatt's argument is merely transmitted rather than tested or developed; on the other hand, the argument is silently but significantly altered. Greenblatt carefully limits the claim he makes for theatrical power (theatricality is "*a* primary expression of Renaissance power," "*one* of power's essential modes," and "*one* of the crucial agents of royal power" [65, 46, 50; emphasis added]); for subsequent critics, theatrical power is total—there is nothing outside of theatrical power. More striking, more telling is the fate of the double role that Greenblatt assigns to theatricality: Elizabeth's power is "constituted in theatrical celebrations of royal glory and theatrical violence visited upon the enemies of that glory." Greenblatt's Elizabeth uses theatricality both to secure her subjects' willing support and to cow the many who would resist her authority by subjecting a few to lurid displays of coercion. For Greenblatt, then, theatricality is a point of intersection between what Althusser calls the Ideological State Apparatus and the Repressive State Apparatus. Theatrical celebrations "function massively and predominantly by ideology, but they also function secondarily by repression, even if ultimately, but only ultimately, this is very attenuated and concealed" (Althusser 145): Elizabeth's "performance is made to seem entirely beyond the control of those whose 'imaginary forces' actually confer upon it its significance and force" (65). Theatrical violence "functions massively and predominantly by repression (including physical repression), while functioning secondarily by ideology" (145).

Greenblatt distinguishes "theatrical celebrations" from "theatrical violence," but he is always keenly attuned to the coercive dimension of ideological celebration and to the ideological dimension of coercive, repressive violence. By contrast, later scholars not only adduce the necessity of theatrical power from the absence of particular "instruments of coercion" but assume an absolute opposition between theatricality and coercion per se: with no "standing army," "highly developed bureaucracy," or "extensive police force" to compel obedience, Elizabeth won her subjects over with pageants and progresses, "the arts of political persuasion and performance," and other forms of political, ideological theatricality. As we shall see, the refashioning of Greenblatt's continuum of theatrical celebration and theatrical violence into an opposition between theatrical power and coercion tells us something far more important about historicism and representationalism than the translation of a speech made to a parliamentary committee into an abstract dictum about monarchy.

What do new historicists after Greenblatt mean by "theatrical power"? Theatrical power is not a way of strategically publicizing (and thereby augmenting) an already constituted power; it is not what Habermas calls "representative publicness": the public display of powers that the ruler already possesses. Nor, on the other hand, does theatrical power mask or mystify a real order of coercive power: theatricality is, after all, precisely what Elizabeth has instead of coercion. Nor, even, is theatricality a technique of ideology: theatricality, that is, is not a means by which belief in the divine right of the monarch is generated. Theatrical power is the reality at the end of new historicism's archaeology of ideology: while monarchs attributed their authority to God and natural order, their power derived from "persuasion," "an audience . . . of loyal admirers," and their subjects' "imaginary forces."

The missing term in the new historicist account of Elizabethan power is *consent.* "Missing" is not quite right: consent is immanent but never named in the theory of theatrical power; it is, indeed, its sublimated foundation. In the closing pages of *The Tudor Regime* (1979), the historian Penry Williams remarks that Henry VIII and his children lacked many of the instruments of control at the disposal of their fellow rulers: the tsars' "secret police, the Oprichniki, 6,000 in number, sustained a reign of terror"; "[t]he rulers of France and of the Spanish Kingdoms were subject to certain laws, but the state machines were vastly more powerful than in England"; and "[t]he Valois and Habsburgs maintained large standing armies and considerable bureaucracies" (464). Served by "institutions of government" so "slender and inadequate," how, then, did the Tudors "maintain a stable regime and impose their will, albeit incompletely, upon important areas of national life?" (462). Through "government," Williams answers, "by the informal mechanisms of consent" (464). The same set of facts that leads new historicists to theatrical power leads historians to consent. Thus, in his survey *The Age of Elizabeth* (1983), D. M. Palliser rehearses Williams's conclusion in a form now very familiar to us, but for one crucial difference: "The Tudors had no standing army or state police (though Secretary Walsingham employed paid agents or spies in the 1570s and 1580s) and only a rudimentary bureaucracy. Monarchs needed the cooperation of their nobles and gentry, who in turn had to rely on the acquiescence of lesser folk. It made for a situation of 'government by the informal mechanisms of consent'" (302). Greenblatt's "theatrical power" is the literary critic's translation and displacement of "consent" into a construct that fuses the political and the aesthetic. Thus redescribed, the truth new historicists reveal about Elizabethan power is suspiciously similar to contemporary Anglo-American political culture's chief article of faith: power is a function of popular consent.

The "dilemma of any 'historicism,'" according to Frederic Jameson, "can . . . be dramatized by the peculiar, unavoidable, yet seemingly unresolvable alternation between Identity and Difference" (150). The theatrical power thesis seems to follow the stricter logic of difference that defines historicism's ideal rather than its dilemma: lacking the institutions of state power so familiar in the critics' own culture (a standing army, police, and a highly developed bureaucracy), Elizabeth exercised a kind of power that distinguishes early modern monarchies from modern representative democracies. The theatrical power thesis, however, emerges from failures of both distinction and identification. On the one hand, critics who affirm "theatrical celebrations" as the "real" basis of Elizabeth's power often give scant attention to the function of alien ideologies such as the divine right of kings.[18] Moreover, to privilege "theatrical celebrations" while neglecting "theatrical violence" is to mystify early modern forms of coercion that are alien to us. Elizabeth could and did deprive particularly uncooperative subjects from York to Penzance of their ears, hands, and lives. The stars of these horrific spectacles of coercion were discovered only because the state also maintained more mundane mechanisms for monitoring, controlling, and discouraging dissent, and for apprehending the unruly. Penry Williams argues that Tudor government depended on "informal mechanisms of consent," but he also finds that every Tudor monarch increased the government's power over the subject. Under Elizabeth in particular, "the pressures of government increased markedly, sometimes alarmingly": "It seems indisputable that by the end of the 16th century England was more intensely governed than before. . . . more compulsion was being applied and more elaborate machinery employed for th[at] purpose by a government which knew more about its subjects than had any of its predecessors" (128). In the final twenty years of her reign alone, Elizabeth created thousands of paid offices both to enhance the crown's control over civilian affairs and to bring the management of military personnel more formally under the control of the central government.

Tudor monarchs governed through "informal mechanisms of consent"; Elizabeth Tudor enjoyed unprecedented powers of compulsion: Williams can make both claims because, like Greenblatt, he never argues that consent and compulsion are mutually exclusive—or even opposed—in early modern governance. After all, if Elizabeth, acting alone, could order the maiming or execution of rabble-rousing reformists, clandestine Jesuit priests, and other enemies, many of her government's most important actions could only be accomplished by parliamentary statutes, which required the consent of the monarch, the lords, and the people of the realm acting through their representatives in the Commons. We have finally come back round to the other hand, to the new historicism's failure of identification: for new historicists, Elizabethan political culture is defined by—owes much of its historical difference and particularity to—an exotic mode of power that secretly depended on "the people" (redescribed as an audience), but many Elizabethans thought that England was special because of its House of Commons, an institution whose members were popularly elected and openly attributed their power and authority to the consent of the people, an institution whose status as a "representative body" enabled Elizabeth and then James to claim, when it suited them, that their people were willing and loving subjects rather than the slaves of a tyrant. An institution, that is, that in certain respects does not seem especially alien to our own political culture.

The relation between early modern and modern representationalism that I am entertaining here is not a Whiggish betrayal of historicism but, instead, a critical and historical identification entirely appropriate to a peculiarly historicist approach to ideology critique. Such a critique would see ideology at work not only in certain identifications, the traditional obstacle to historicism, but also in certain reflexive assumptions of difference. For example, to assume an absolute opposition between coercion and consent—because Elizabeth lacked instruments of coercion, she was compelled to cultivate consent—is to refuse uncomfortable points of intersection between early modern England and our own culture: our standing armies, police forces, and massive bureaucracies are all funded and controlled by political agents who figure the consent of the governed as the fundamental source of all state power, legitimacy, and authority. One might avoid the categorical problem here—either consent and coercion are opposed or they are not—by historicizing the putatively categorical: coercion and consent can be reconciled in modern representative democracies because their instruments of coercion are empowered and approved by the people through acts of consent; coercion and consent were opposed in early modern England because the executive authority that administered coercion was not empowered by the consent of the governed. But this would be bad history. Early modern England's mixed estate did not reconcile discrete orders of coercion and consent in, respectively, a crown and a Commons that did uneasy business together in Parliament; a blurry continuum of consent and coercion internal to the practices and rhetoric of the House of Commons defines early modern representationalism. As we have already seen, the MPs sometimes pitched themselves to the monarch as useful assistants in policing and controlling the realm: the MPs have "many eyes to se, many feet to go, and many hands to labour withall, and so circumspectt they are for the government of the commonwelth: that they se all things, nothing is hid or secret, nothing is straunge or new" (Hooker 117). The convergence of coercion and consent under the order of representationalism was even deeper, even more complex when the MPs exercised a discrete power over the people they represented: when a private subject allowed the serjeant-at-arms to escort him to St. Stephen's, make him kneel before the MPs, or incarcerate him in the Commons' prison, we see the birth of one version of political modernity; we glimpse a new mode of power.

I have discovered very few attempts between 1559 and 1614 to resist the Commons' authority to investigate and discipline private persons. The accused sometimes disputed the charges made against them, but when they were hailed by an agent of the Commons, they answered and submitted. If monarchy depends in part on the subject's fear of external coercion, representationalism is a politics of repression, of disciplining oneself. The coercive dimension of representationalism-as-ideology can be internalized because its subject is also its agent: "the people," Yelverton tells his queen, are never "so willing to put themselves under the dutie of [the lawes], as when the people themselves be agents in the frameing of them." The subject of representationalism, then, shares something with Michel Foucault's "subjected sovereign," the fulfillment of "humanism," that "totality of discourse through which Western man is told: 'Even though you don't exercise power, you can still be a ruler. Better yet, the more you deny yourself the exercise of power, the more you submit to those in power, then the more this increases your sovereignty.' Humanism . . . is everything in Western civilization that restricts *the desire for power*" (221). Better still: the subject of representationalism constructs the empowering of others as power and is never more sovereign than when he makes himself obedient. Obeying oneself in representational culture is a special pleasure: it is a rare moment when one's agency is not alienated, a moment when one acts in one's own person rather than through representatives. Even when discipline is embodied in external form, when the subject hears the Commons' serjeant-at-arms call out, "Hey, you!" he hears his own voice. To tussle with the serjeant-at-arms—to make him the agent of discipline, to treat him as other rather than as a manifestation of one's own will—would spoil the moment.

All systems of governance depend on both the willing participation of those who help to govern and the willing submission of at least some of those who are governed. Representative democracy is, however, distinct from monarchy, dictatorship, oligarchy, and so on, both because it institutes more formal and more widespread mechanisms for the positive expression of consent and because it explicitly identifies the consent of the governed as the foundation of political power and legitimacy. Shakespeare's England was, of course, a monarchy rather than a representative democracy, but the "mixed estate" that materialized during parliamentary sessions made representationalism and acts of consent vital aspects of an unusually complex political culture. The Elizabethan and Jacobean subject's relation to power was correspondingly complex and mixed: subject to a monarch who claimed to be God's anointed and whose "power," James VI wrote in *The Trew Law of Free Monarchies* (1598), "flowes always from him self" (*Political Works*, 75), he believed himself to be powerless; the ruler's "performance is made to seem entirely beyond the control of those whose 'imaginary forces' actually confer upon it its significance and force" (Greenblatt, "Invisible Bullets," 65). By contrast, representationalism, as it is instantiated both in early modern parliamentary politics and in modern representative democracies, explicitly locates the source of the representative's power and legitimacy in "the people." Representationalism, then, seems to acknowledge a universal and fundamental truth that other political ideologies occlude, and many of Shakespeare's contemporaries recognized—believed in and accepted as legitimate—its economy of power: as we shall see in Chapter 5, Elizabethans and Jacobeans who sought to secure the franchise in municipal elections and to play a more significant role in parliamentary elections often believed that they were pursuing political power. Why, then, call representationalism an ideology? Why would political agents who openly acknowledge that "the people . . . [are] the whole flower and power of [the] kingdom" require an ideological account of the people's relation to power?

Representationalism does not transcend but instead advances ideology a quantum leap precisely because it does not disguise the "real" source of the power to govern: representationalism turns truth to account because the subject's consciousness of his power helps to render him powerless. Representationalism makes the truth of power safe by shifting the work of ideology from mystifying the source of state power to redefining power itself. The rhetoric of representational politics redistributes power from public persons to private persons, from those who govern to those who are governed, but as power migrates, it is also transformed: power is voting for, choosing, consenting to the authority of those who govern. I speak of power, still the fashionable thing to do after so many years, but early modern representationalism functioned, in part, by deemphasizing power, by blurring the distinction between power and rights, by elevating "liberty" above power as the subject's highest good. Elizabethans and Jacobeans—including Elizabeth I and James I—frequently spoke of the monarch's power and, occasionally, even of the House of Commons' power, but they typically attributed "freedom" rather than power to the subject. The subject's freedom, in turn, was defined as the right to consent, through representatives, to the laws he obeyed and the taxes he paid.

How does the subject of early modern representationalism know that he is free? He knows that he is free *because* he consents: the right to consent does not help the subject to secure freedom; the right to consent *is* the state of freedom. Prizing the right to consent *as* freedom per se joins liberty and subjection in a novel political-psychic calculus: because the subject consents to the laws, he must obey them; the subject knows that he is free because he obeys. The right to consent is, for representationalism, the black hole of critique: consent liberates us from bondage; we know that we are not slaves because we consent to the government that rules us; we are free because we willingly obey, because we are not violently coerced (unless we disobey). Consent and freedom—and their conflation—subsume power in the discourse of representationalism: whether the system of governance that the subject's acts of consent perpetuate and legitimate actually empowers the subject is a consideration suppressed by the ideology of consent. Consent is the great idol of representationalism: faith in the value of consent and the system of representation it enables secures adherence to a system that diminishes the people's power precisely by telling them that they are powerful because they are free.

The Hazards of Analogy: Resisting a Theatrical Parliament

The critique of theatrical monarchy that I have been developing would seem to lead inexorably (and disappointingly) to a new, improved analogy: theater is like political representation. Out with "we princes are set as it were upon Stages, in the Sight and view of all the World"; in with John Hooker's description of the House of Commons in St. Stephen's Chapel: "The lower house . . . is made like a Theater, having four rowes of seates one aboove an other round about the same" (163). My interpretations of Shakespeare's plays and early modern parliamentary politics reject the analogy between theater and political representation—an analogy that has appealed to philosophers from Hobbes to Bourdieu—but playing that analogy out will reveal something telling about its temptations, defects, and dangers.

Elizabethan and Jacobean MPs often anticipated aspects of the Hobbesian association of theatricality and the kind of artificial personhood required by political representation: "We must laye downe the respectes of our owne persons," William Hakewill urged his fellow MPs in 1601, "and put on others' and their affections ffor whome wee speake, ffor they speake by us. If the matter which is spoken of touche the poore, then thincke me a poore man. He that speakes, sometymes, he must be a lawyer, sometymes a paynter, sometymes a marchante, some tymes a meane artifycer" (*PPE* 3:432–33). Conceiving representation as impersonation was, as we shall see in Chapters 1 and 3, a novel strategy for promoting MPs' capacity to serve interests that diverged from their own. In a 1542 tract, the reformer and polemicist Henry Brinklow expressed what was already a long-standing skepticism about the likelihood of wealthy MPs ameliorating the plight of the poor: "it is hard to have it redressed by parlament, because it pricketh them chiefly. . . . And wold to god thei [the people] wold leave their old accustomed chosing of burgessys: for whom do thei chose, but such as be rych" (B2^{r}).

If Bacon's construction of representation as incarnation demands an act of faith, Hakewill's wonderful declension of roles suggests that political representation requires a twofold act of imagination: at a particular moment, one must "think" that the representative is not himself but someone else (a painter); and, over the course of a session, one must "think" that the representative is not just the one person he seems but many persons. The Prologue's appeal to the audience of *Henry V,* then, is an apt catechism not only for Elizabeth's subjects but for the House of Commons as well:

> Piece out our imperfections with your thoughts:
> Into a thousand parts divide one man,
> And make imaginary puissance.
> Think, when we talk of horses, that you see them,
> Printing their proud hoofs i'th' receiving earth;
> For 'tis your thoughts that now must deck our kings. (23–28)

The double act of imagination solicited here suggests that theatrical representation finds its closest political analogue in parliamentary representation rather than monarchy: decking out a bricklayer's son as Henry V, a weaver as Pyramus, Elizabeth Tudor as the sacred Elizabeth I, or William Hakewill as a mean artificer demand roughly the same kind of "thoughts," but dividing one actor into a thousand parts and believing that every MP in the House of Commons "represent[s]," as Edward Coke put it, "a thousand of men" (D'Ewes 516) have no corollary in the imaginative experience of monarchy.

A mystified spectator-subject is the willing but unwitting source of monarchic power: Elizabeth's "performance is made to seem entirely beyond the control of those whose 'imaginary forces' actually confer upon it its significance and force" (Greenblatt, "Invisible Bullets," 65). If Elizabeth and James were empowered by their audiences, they were not about to acknowledge it: "The King," the earl of Salisbury admonished the Commons in 1610, "takes himself to be beholding to no elective power, depends upon no popular applause" (*PP*

1610 2:49). Parliament's authority similarly depends on the subject's beliefs, on his willingness to credit the representative's performances and acts of consent as his own, but, as we have already begun to see, the subject's power in the economy of representationalism is not a secret revealed only by ideology critique but instead a chief article of ideological faith and the foundation of false consciousness: unlike the monarch, the knights and burgesses of the House of Commons loudly proclaimed that a consenting public had invested them with their authority. From platforms in courtyards and common halls all over England, candidates for Parliament solicited the voices of often enormous crowds; when they arrived at Westminster, they would often claim that their authority derived from free elections by the residents of the shires or boroughs they represented. Theatrical monarchy, according to new historicists, prevents the agents who empower it from recognizing their power; the House of Commons disempowers its subjects even as it tells them that they are powerful.

The economy of theatrical power—like the imaginative structure of theatrical representation—seems, then, to model representational rather than monarchic politics. From the stages of London's theaters, Prologues and Epilogues addressed their audiences as both the imaginative and the economic engine of theatrical representation. Remarking the power of paying audiences of commoners, John Cocke (1615) seems to warn new historicists away from the analogy between theater and monarchy: "the player . . . pretends to have a royall Master or Mistresse, [but] his wages and dependence prove him to be the servant of the people" (Chambers 4:256). London's players might be the liveried servants of great patrons, but the theater was, in fact, a market enterprise rather than a courtly institution. As we shall see in Chapter 4, the theater's economic dependence on a mass audience of common patrons rather than the patronage of the monarch or great nobles could be redescribed in political language: Prologues and Epilogues begged their audiences' "suffrages," "voices," and "generall consent." The rhetorical assimilation of theatrical audiences to electorates is all the more compelling because it can be reversed: at some hustings, support was expressed by "applause."

The theatrical audience became, not surprisingly, a potent figure for popular power in early modern culture. Even the reform-minded ministers who wrote *A Lamentable Complaint of the Commonality, by way of supplication to the High Court of Parliament, for a learned ministery* (1585) embrace the theater—hardly a typical school for the godly—as a model for the proper relationship between shepherds and their flocks. Railing against the practice of picking and confirming ministers in secret, the anonymous authors argue that their brethren should not be appointed without the approval of the sheep they will tend:

> How requisite were it, that such a man as should have the bringing up & government of the sonnes and daughters of the glorious king of heaven . . . should rather come unto a publicke place of trial, as it were into an open Theater, that after publicke prayer and fastinge he might be seene and viewed of all men, that if the beholders had as many eies as thei saine that Argos had, they shuld use them all, to sift & try out that man. . . . Moreover, seeing we know that there be many subtile workers, transforming themselves into Angels of light, who seeke craftily to creepe in to devour the flocke: is it not to be feared, that they will more easily slide in through the hands of one then of many? (A8[r])

Open "election" by a body of believers, the authors argued, was sanctioned again and again in Scripture and had been practiced in the "primitive" church, but it was disdained in the English church that promised to restore early Christian ways. In the parliamentary session of 1584–85, MPs incorporated these and similar complaints against insufficiently reformed church leaders into petitions sent by the Commons to the House of Lords: "they make and ordeine ministers without a sermon in private places as in their chambers and chappells, where skarse anie at all are present but their owne servauntes" (*PPE* 2:46); "when they have . . . extorted a confession out of [ministers suspected of Puritanism] . . . they proceade uppon the same unto suspencion and deprivacion, which is not don in a publyke place where there is free accesse, but in a private chamber where the dore is kept shutt" (*PPE* 2:46). John Whitgift, archbishop of Canterbury, rejected with special vigor all proposals to make the selection and disciplining of ministers more public and subject to the parishioners' will: "the petition we could not yeelde unto because . . . yt savoureth of popular elections longe agoe abrogated in the Church for diverse inconveniencies therof" (*PPE* 2:50). Remaking the church in the image of the House of Commons was not in the cards.

That is not quite right: Whitgift was objecting to a form of church government that would have been more transparent and democratic than parliamentary representation, a form of government closer to the theater than political representation. Why didn't our would-be lobbyists make a comparison between parliamentary elections and the choosing of ministers? What better way to remind men who owed their seats in the Commons to "popular elections" that they should have ears to hear the *Lamentable Complaint*? Our authors not only forgo this seemingly irresistible appeal, they draw an implicit, invidious comparison between theater and the House of Commons. The tract's authors claim that they have long tried to bring their concerns to the attention of Parliament, but all their efforts have been frustrated by the MPs' seclusion in their own "private chamber." These spokesmen for "the commonality" have taken up their pens as a last resort: "Because our desire was, that this our complaint should be communicated to every one of the honorable Parliament, and finding no other waies to performe the same we desire that it might be done by the way of printing" (A1^{v}). Printing itself is only half the battle; with the heavy doors of the House of Commons shut against them, the authors imagine a textual siege on St. Stephen's: "finding no other way, we uncover the tiles of your house of Parliament, & let them down with cordes before you, to stirre up your bowels of compassion" (A3^{v}).

The impenetrable House of Commons stands in stark opposition to an open theater of judgment in which a minister "might be seene and viewed of all men," every one of them an Argos. Even parliamentary elections fall far short of the ministers' ideal of massive scrutiny: in many boroughs, town councils—some elected, some not—appointed MPs on behalf of the freemen of the city; in some boroughs, town councils allowed local magnates to handpick one of the burgesses; and the vast majority of shire elections were closely managed affairs that afforded voters little or no opportunity "to sift & try" candidates. Once the knights and burgesses took their seats, only a tiny percentage of the people they represented had any access to them, and a tinier percentage still ever laid two eyes—much less a thousand—on them while they were in session. By contrast, the authors of the *Lamentable Complaint* and MPs who sympathized with their aims advocated meaningful public participation both in the choice of ministers and in the evaluation of their performance during their tenures.

At the end of their long *Complaint,* the authors seem to dream of a theatrical House of Commons; how much easier it would be to "stirre up . . . compassion" in the MPs if they performed before the millions of people they represented:

> Looke upon us; lift up your eies & behold a great multitude gathered about you, which are in the wildernes & have nothing to eate. Be moved with compassion towardes us, for we are as sheepe wanting a shepheard. . . . Oh, that you were caried in a vision into some great high mountaine, and could behold the huge army of people of the land spiritually slaine of Sathan. . . . Then would you shed teares aboundantly with our Saviour Christ, who standing upon mount Olivet, beheld that stubburne city of Jerusalem &

> wept for them, because thei refused the doctrine of salvation then offered them. (D5^{v}–D7^{v})

Milton's Adam weeps for the wretched and degraded creatures Michael reveals to him on "a hill / Of Paradise the highest" (*Paradise Lost* 11.377–78) because they are his flesh. To become secular shepherds, to assume the heady role of saviors offered them, the MPs must feel compassion for *others* through acts of imagination. Secluded from the public, the MPs can neither see nor be seen by the people whom they represent: "looke," "lifte up your eies," and "behold" are exhortations to see with the mind's eye, to conjure a "vision" of the "great multitude" who, even in the metonymic form of a gallery audience, were barred from entering St. Stephen's. The burden of imagination shifts, then, from the persons represented—from lowly commoners who must believe that gentlemen will protect the interests of "mean artificer[s]" by playing them in the House of Commons—to their representatives. Unable to make themselves visible to the MPs, the authors of the *Lamentable Complaint* must hope that words will "carry" their readers "in a vision" and paint for them the suffering of their charges. Hakewill's model of representation offers an alternative imaginative path to compassion: one MP plays for all his fellows the "huge army of people" who look to them for comfort; if they "deck" him a lost sheep with their thoughts, if they "think" him a "mean artificer," then, like spectators at a play, they may be moved by an embodied representation.

Hakewill's version of political theater is deeply peculiar to the culture of early modern representationalism: the only audience to an MP's attempts to speak for painters and mean artificers were his fellows MPs, his fellow performers. To be sure, MPs sometimes invoked the people as an audience to their proceedings: "The eyes of the poore are upon this parliament," an anonymous MP warned the House in 1597 (*PPE* 3:220). The best this MP could do, however, was to "play" a scrutinizing public, to articulate for his fellow representatives what he imagined the poor would say if they could witness Commons proceedings: even MPs who represented the people in good faith participated in the usurpation of their voices and judgment. In Chapters 1 and 3, we shall see that trying to be an Argos to oneself has its limits and hazards.

The Politics of Presence

If theater does not model early modern monarchy or political representation, what is it like? Shakespeare's answer is elusive—perhaps, in part, because he would not ask the question, at least not in a form that assumes that *the* theater has *a* politics or that any theater has a politics (only) because it is "like" a political system or institution. In *Julius Caesar,* however, the distinction between theater and representationalism is so primal that we may begin to see in Shakespeare's assertion of what theater *is not like* a flicker of what he thinks theater *is.* The conspirators themselves persistently link theater and the plot to restore the republic: Brutus tells his comrades to conceal their bloody thoughts by emulating "Roman actors"; Brutus and Cassius prophesy that dramatizations of their salvation of the republic will be greeted with rapturous applause; and the conspirators begin to plot their plot in Pompey's theater. The actor as arch deceiver; passive audiences approving violent actions; a subversive cabal finding cover at a theater: this is the stuff of Elizabethan and Jacobean antitheatricalism. The conspirators' conception and exploitation of theater, however, is overshadowed and overwhelmed by an alternative idea of theater: for many early modern observers, the theater's aesthetics, social effects, and politics were, for good or ill, shaped by its openness, by the presence of a large, paying, public audience to performance. In *Julius Caesar,* Shakespeare does not draw an analogy between theater and representationalism; rather, he conflates republicanism and conspiracy and opposes both to a radically *public* theater.

Conspiracy and a theater defined by its publicness are, on the face of it, ill suited to each other: a conspiracy is not theatrical because it is, well, a conspiracy, a plot hatched and executed out of the public eye. Yet Pompey's theater is one of the two most resonant sites in the symbolic topography of the conspiracy against Caesar; the other is Brutus's private orchard—a fine place for secrets. The meeting at the theater is Shakespeare's invention, and it prejudices the audience against the conspiracy precisely because it reveals a chasm, rather than sympathy, between theater and conspiracy. The conspirators meet at Pompey's theater "after midnight" (1.3.164), when "there is no stir or walking in the streets" (1.3.126). The conspirators plot in an *empty* theater, a structure so haunted by the absence of an audience that it functions as a sign of theater's antithesis. Hooker's analogy between St. Stephen's and a theater is merely architectural: empty, the two structures resemble each other; in full swing, however, a theater and the House of Commons could hardly be more different. The empty theater is Shakespearean shorthand for the betrayals of political representation.

We do not see the meeting in Pompey's theater: we see it planned; we hear reports of it; but Shakespeare does not stage the meeting itself, as if such a perversion of theater would pollute his stage. We see instead a scene that unfolds while the conspirators are meeting in the theater: Brutus, in his orchard, resolving to join the plot. Shakespeare's special genius for rich dramaturgical insteads—for showing us one scene while another event, to which he has drawn our intense attention, transpires offstage, in an imaginative elsewhere—is at its zenith here. As he so often does in the Roman plays, Shakespeare makes us aware of a crucial event that he withholds from theatrical representation whose meaning depends on its being withheld. At the end of act 1, Cassius twice urges Cinna and Casca to join him and other conspirators at "Pompey's theatre" (1.3.152). Shakespeare thus whets our appetite for this momentous meeting, but act 2 opens with the orchard scene. Alone in his orchard, in the middle of the night, Brutus reads an anonymous letter—forged, we know, by Cassius—that implores him to "*awake,*" to "[*s*]*peak, strike, redress!*" (2.1.46–47). Hakewill suggests that every MP must be a Bottom, ready to play not just Pyramus but Thisbe and the Lion, too, not just a lawyer but a painter and a mean artificer as well. As he reads and ponders the letter, Brutus enacts an even more radical artificial personhood: he does not simply quote the other ("*Brutus, thou sleep'st; awake, and see thyself. / Shall Rome, etc.*"); exceeding the letter's text, he begins to speak *as the other to himself:* "'Shall Rome, et cetera.' Thus must I piece it out: / Shall Rome stand under one man's awe?" In a dialogic monologue, Brutus speaks as Rome and listens as Brutus. All the popular spokesmen in Shakespeare's plays, save only Brutus, are in complete possession of themselves when they cynically fabricate the people's voice to serve their own ends. Brutus hears voices, hears another voice, which he speaks: if the Third Citizen suffers a tragic loss of integrated identity, Brutus's (ultimately fatal) delusion that Rome hails him as its liberator is the other side of the tragedy of political representation, the enabling and disabling schizophrenia, the self-aggrandizing yet self-sacrificing effacement of discrete, integrated selfhood that the "sincere," if willful, representative must perform.

The orchard scene, then, repeats the hermetic gesture of the meeting at Pompey's theater: at a time and place meant to cloak them from a scrutinizing audience, the conspirators decide to kill Caesar in the people's name; speaking in the voice of Rome, Brutus hails himself as Rome's liberator. At the moment Brutus plays Rome, Shakespeare is defining his own theater against political representation: Brutus can convince himself that Rome wills him to strike down Caesar only because "Rome" is not present to speak for itself, but the theatrical audience are, of course, present, and they know that the conspiracy is a flat betrayal of the people's will; Plutarch's Caesar has lost the people's affection, but the very first scene of Shakespeare's play establishes Caesar's unflagging popularity. Turning theater's openness, its plenitude of presence, its staging of all things private against the opacity of political representation is always central to Shakespeare's critique.

The presence of Shakespeare's audience intensifies the complicated bad faith of Brutus's solitary hailing of himself and the rather more straightforward bad faith of the offstage cabal in Pompey's theater, but these usurpations of the people's agency are also haunted by another audience. Before Cassius invites Cinna and Casca to Pompey's theater, before Brutus meditates in his orchard, we hear Casca report a bit of real political theater: Anthony offering a crown to Caesar before the great crowd assembled to watch the Lupercalia. Caesar, of course, hopes that the people will insist that he take the crown. His audience is uncooperative: Antony offers the crown three times; Caesar rejects it each time; and the crowd roars its approval of each refusal of kingship. Caesar does not get his crown, but he retains the people's affection: when he offers them his throat, they decline and console him. Brutus hears Casca's report, questions him doggedly, carefully verifies the key facts: a few minutes later, we watch Brutus convince himself that all of Rome wants him to kill Caesar. Brutus's refusal of knowledge here is consistent with his absolute isolation from the people whose agent he claims to be: prior to his speech in the Forum, we never see or even hear a mention of any actual contact between Brutus and the people. Brutus in his orchard; the conspirators in the empty theater; the MPs in St. Stephen's Chapel: the positive condition of political representation, of speaking for and as the people, is always the absence of the people themselves.

Caesar never claims to speak for Rome or know its will. Instead, he simply *presents* himself and his desires to Rome for approval or rejection. Submitting himself in his own person to the people themselves, in the absence of any mediation, Caesar is, at least in Casca's mind, like an actor, and the people are like an audience: "If the tag-rag people did not clap him and hiss him, according as he pleased and displeased them, as they use to do the players in the theatre, I am no true man" (1.2.258–61). Casca is just Casca, just one of the play's more than thirty characters, and his status as a "true man" is in some doubt, but, unlike his co-conspirators, he knows that theater is not like political representation or conspiracy. The scene Casca paints for Brutus and Cassius reminds us that Shakespeare's theater shares the fundamental dynamic, the basic economy upon which are built all those politics of presence that political representation suppresses: popular revolution, fascism, Caesarism, and, of course, democracy.

Shakespeare's theater was not, in any strict sense, the House of Commons' rival: theater audiences were not parts of the sovereign and did not vote on legislation; they passed judgment on dramatic performances and thus exercised some influence over the fortunes of theater companies, theatrical entrepreneurs, actors, playwrights, and, perhaps, the evolution of English dramatic literature. But plays about "issues" that were debated in the Commons—wardship (*A Yorkshire Tragedy*), the Spanish match (*A Game at Chess*), alien laborers (*Thomas More, The Shoemaker's Holiday*), monopolies (*Westward Ho*), impositions (*The Ghost of Richard III*)—created a plebeian public sphere in which opinions might be shaped and political effects achieved. In the 1640s, many observers attributed the closing of the theaters not to Puritan moralizing but rather to a widespread desire among MPs to suppress the publicizing of parliamentary politics: "there lay they open truth and falshood in their naked colours, and scourge Iniquity untill he bleeds againe," according to an anatomy of the Parliament's antipathy to theater in the *Mercurius Melancholicus* of January 22–29, 1648; "there you may read the Parliament in print . . . therfore Players and Pamphleters, they must, they shall come down, the Parliament playhouse is sufficient to lead the Kingdom a dance without these" (136). During Shakespeare's lifetime, to be sure, most playgoers had few opportunities to bring the political opinions that they might have formed at the theater directly to bear on parliamentary politics—there were no newspapers or coffeehouses and MPs did not hold town hall meetings back home; we do know, however, that MPs not infrequently expressed anxiety about parliamentary affairs becoming the subject of "vulgar opinion" and talk in the streets.

Topical matters that fell under the House of Commons' purview figure in several of the plays that I discuss in this book: in *Henry VI, Part 1,* the effect of enclosure on small farmers and agricultural laborers—a central issue in the Parliaments of the 1580s and 1590s—turns the commons against Suffolk; the price of grain, poverty, and the conditions under which money was borrowed, the causes of rebellion in *Coriolanus,* were the subject of much debate in James I's first Parliament (1604–10). Unlike the topical plays mentioned in the previous paragraph, however, the first tetralogy, *Titus Andronicus, Julius Caesar,* and *Coriolanus* also stand in a primal, fundamental relation to parliamentary politics because they are about political representation per se. Shakespeare's critique of political representation is, moreover, doubly fundamental because it was staged for audiences who were experiencing precisely the kind of authority in the theater that political representation, on Shakespeare's account, denies its subjects in the political field proper. On Shakespeare's stage, political representatives invariably usurp the people's power to judge and decide, to turn their thumbs up or down; in the theater, of course, playgoers never alienate their right to judge the dramatic representations performed before them. As they watched the political power of Shakespeare's citizens ebb and evaporate under the bamboozlement of representation, their own power was undiminished. Would Shakespeare's audiences have *consciously* registered the difference between their power in the theater and the powerlessness of the citizens of Shakespeare's Roman world? Perhaps not, but wherever political representation conspicuously excludes the people, Shakespeare supplies his own audience, makes them subversively, intensely present to the way representatives displace and even efface the people they represent. At such moments, Shakespeare's audience can only identify with those people by feeling their absence. A theater overflowing with people is the most resonant place to play out the tragedy of political representation, because, for a few hours, it embodies its radical alternative.

PART ONE

Parliament in Shakespeare's England

1 “An epitome of the whole realme”

Absorption and Representation in the Elizabethan and Jacobean House of Commons

The House of Commons did not have a permanent meeting place until 1549, when Edward VI granted the knights and burgesses the use of St. Stephen's Chapel in Westminster. One of the earliest descriptions of the Commons in St. Stephen's comes to us from John Hooker's *The Order and usage of the keeping of a Parlement in England* (1572): the Commons' chamber, according to Hooker, was “made like a Theater, having foure rowes of seates one aboove an other round about the same. At the higher end in the midle of the lower rowe is a seat made for the Speaker, in which he alwaies sitteth; before it is a table boord, at which sitteth the Clark of the house and there upon [he] layeth his Books, and writeth his recordes” (163).

As an MP, Hooker had, of course, seen the Commons' chamber himself, and the first pictorial representations of the MPs in St. Stephen's, broadside engravings dating from 1624 (fig. 1) and 1628 (fig. 2), confirm his architectural analogy.[1] The engravings, moreover, seem to embrace theatricality as a strategy for representing political representation by staging St. Stephen's itself: the whole of the chamber and the MPs in intense activity have been thrown open to the viewer's scrutiny. The Commons we see here, however, is an entirely mythic place, not only because St. Stephen's was very often nearly empty but also because it was entirely closed to public inspection. Although the MPs figured their new home as a *public* structure—a place where all matters of public interest could be openly and freely debated and where the people themselves were “deemed personally present” (*SR* 2:1018), they used St. Stephen's to secure unprecedented isolation from the public and to maintain secret proceedings.[2]

Hooker's analogy between a theater and the Commons, then, is remarkably infelicitous. Although St. Stephen's was constructed like a theater, the House of Commons lacked the definitive feature of theater: it had no room for spectators. The elevated benches were filled entirely with performers, and where the stage and parterre should have been, there was a void. The closest the public ever came to seeing the inside of St. Stephen's was as an audience to *representations* of the Commons.

The fate of those few members of the public who surreptitiously entered St. Stephen's during parliamentary sessions tells us volumes about the relationship the MPs sought to create between themselves and the people they represented. Consider, for example, a lurid scene from the House of Commons' session of November 28, 1584. The day, to be sure, got off to a stirring start: Sir Walter Mildmay, chancellor of the Exchequer, and Sir Christopher Hatton, vice-chamberlain of the Household, made long, impressive speeches about the mortal threat that both foreign and domestic enemies posed to Elizabeth and England. In his diary, William Fleetwood, the recorder of London, allows that these speeches made even his very experienced ears tingle: "Befor this tyme I never herd in Parliament the lyke matters uttered. . . . They were *magnalia regni*" (*PPE* 2:66). When the MPs rose for their noon recess, they were deeply disturbed to discover an intruder in their midst:

> One being no Member of this House, being found to have sit here this present day by the space of two hours, during the whole time of the Speeches delivered by Mr. Chancellor and Mr Vicechamberlain, as aforesaid, did upon Examination confess his name to be *Richard Robinson,* and that he was by occupation a Skinner, and dwelt at the *Harts Horns* in *Gracious-street London,* the house of one *Mark Fryer* a Skinner also his Father-in-law: Whereupon himself having been stripped to his shirt, and his pockets all searched, the Custody and further Examination of him was by this House referred to Mr. Recorder of *London,* Mr. *Topcliffe,* Mr. *Beale,* and another. (D'Ewes 334; cf. *PPE* 2:66)

The MPs were understandably nervous in the fall of 1584: in 1583, several plots against Elizabeth had been thwarted; in July, William of Orange had been assassinated; relations with Spain had collapsed over the Throckmorton plot; and always there was the terror inspired by Mary, Queen of Scots. But can the MPs really have supposed that Robinson was an assassin? Elizabeth, after all, never set foot in St. Stephen's while the House was sitting. The MPs must instead have feared, somewhat more plausibly, that Robinson was a spy for Mary or Spain: thus, they ordered a search of Robinson's lodgings and a "further Examination of him" (D'Ewes 344).

Richard Topcliffe, a notoriously vicious inquisitor, determined that Richard Robinson had nothing more than his name to confess: he was a skinner who had wandered into St. Stephen's to satisfy his curiosity.[3] This was happy news, but Robinson "was brought to the Bar, and was there censured by the House, having taken the Oath (as it should seem of Allegiance and Supremacy) to suffer Imprisonment in the Serjeants Ward until *Saturday* next, and then having swore to keep secret what he had heard, to be relesed" (D'Ewes 334). Topcliffe made his report on Tuesday, November 30, and John Puckering, the speaker of the House, rendered judgment the same day: Robinson, then, spent four nights in prison *after* he had been cleared. The skinner of Gracious Street was neither an assassin nor a spy, but his very presence in the House of Commons had been criminal: "if any forain person doo enter into that house, the assembly therof beeing sitting," Hooker stipulates in *Order and usage,* "he ought . . . to be punished" (170). The specter of Catholic plots perhaps explains the MPs' unusually severe treatment of Robinson, but the dozen or so "strangers" who found their way into the Commons' chamber during Elizabeth's and James's reigns were invariably punished.

Robinson's reckoning at the bar is a surpassingly odd spectacle of discipline and punishment: the MPs who commanded Robinson to kneel before them claimed that he and millions of other commoners had consented to and thus legitimized the Commons' *authority;* and the MPs' *power*—including the power to punish "forain persons" who entered the House—derived precisely from their capacity to make Robinson and millions of other commoners present in the House of Commons. According to one of the foundational myths of early modern political representation, Richard Robinson was "representatively present" in the Commons' chamber before, during, and after the "actual" visit to St. Stephen's that landed him in such hot water. The coercive gag order—Robinson was released only after he "swore to keep secret what he had heard"—is equally perplexing and revealing. Robinson may have heard "*magnalia regni,*" but he had not learned anything especially sensitive: Mildmay and Hatton had not reported on English naval strategy or Walsingham's spy network. Rather, in the early days of the new Parliament, these important officers of the crown delivered a very general state of the state address: economy humming, religion sound, the nation blessed in its queen; but Mary, Spain, and the pope were mortal threats, and Parliament had been called to take measures for the queen's safety. Robinson was sworn to secrecy because all but a very few Elizabethan knights and burgesses wanted to keep *all* of their proceedings entirely secret: thus, the MPs themselves were enjoined never to speak of Commons business outside of the council chamber.[4] "I wish that whatsoever is here spoken may be buried within these Walls," Robert Cecil, Elizabeth's chief minister, declared after a spate of leaks in 1601. "Let us take Example of the Jewish Synagogue, who would always *Sepelire Senatum cum honore,* and not blast their own Follies and Imperfections" (D'Ewes 653). During precisely the same period when the Commons began to institute and enforce its secrecy rules, the MPs were also increasingly claiming that they spoke in the "voyce of the people" (*PPE* 1:58) and functioned as "the mouthes of the moste grave and religious commons of this realme" (*PPE* 3:368).[5] Robinson was punished in part for hearing what in theory were his own words, and he was forced to swear that he would not repeat to the "grave and religious commons" what their surrogate "mouthes" were saying on their behalf.

In Robinson's ordeal, we see both the emergence of the Commons as a public authority that directly exercised power over the subjects of the realm and the contradictions between ideological rhetoric and institutional practice that defined Elizabethan and Jacobean political representation.[6] As we shall see, the early modern Commons established itself as a representative body and a public authority not by effacing the boundaries between itself and the people but by rhetorically absorbing the public within the narrow walls of the Commons' chamber. The sorts of issues that I have begun to raise here fall far outside of the scholarly literature on Elizabethan and early Jacobean parliamentary politics. The debate between Whig and revisionist historians has largely turned on two questions: How much power did the Commons possess? What was the nature of the political relationship between crown and Commons? David Loades has recently summarized the Whig narrative of the post-Henrician Tudor Parliaments: "The anti-clerical and 'patriotic' Commons, who had . . . legislated a Protestant reformation under Edward, and proved such an unmanageable handful for the reactionary Mary, developed logically into the House which forced the Protestant pace in 1559, and strove thereafter to impose their own agenda upon a reluctant Queen" (74).

In the 1970s, G. R. Elton and Conrad Russell began a sweeping revision of, respectively, sixteenth- and early seventeenth-century English political history. In 1987, Elton, confident that the historiographical battle had been won, wrote a revisionist epitaph for the Whigs' misguided fantasy of an increasingly powerful House of Commons: "we have heard so much about the rising power of the Lower House . . . that it comes as something of a surprise to discover how little real power the Commons especially possessed" ("Parliament," 86). Once revisionists had burst the illusion of power, the Whig dream of a confrontational Commons collapsed as well: "I now wonder," Elton muses after critically revisiting Sir John Neale's evidence for an organized Puritan opposition in the Elizabethan Commons, "whether the institution—one of the Crown's instruments of government—ever really mattered all that much in the politics of the nation, except perhaps as a stage sometimes used by the real contenders over government and policy" (*Parliament,* ix).

Freed of Whig delusions, revisionist historians claimed to recover the real early modern England: a "one-party state" in which the House of Commons was merely a department of the crown rather than an independently powerful institution (Russell, *Crisis,* 219).[7] In place of the Whigs' oppositional, "crisis-ridden past," the revisionists "emphasize[d] . . . business . . . [and] the essential harmony of King, Lords, and Commons" (Loades 74) and "played down the importance of progressive movements" (Haigh 16). Revisionists have thus replaced the teleological character of Whig historiography with synchronic functionalism: "in early modern England," Mark Kishlansky has argued, "political activity took place within the context of a hierarchical social structure and . . . was guided by concern for maintaining the order of the social structure and the harmony of the universe" (ix). Kishlansky's powerful reappraisal of early modern parliamentary elections posits an electoral process "that when it worked *as it was supposed to work* precluded electoral contests" (58; emphasis added). Elton's seminal "Points of Contact" essays are explicitly founded on the notion that "one of the functions of government is to preserve in contentment and balance that society which it rules" (183). When Elton and other revisionists applied this principle to parliamentary politics, the orderly transaction of business not surprisingly emerged as the "purpose of parliament." Any "talk of . . . the rise of the House of Commons . . . into political prominence," Elton concluded, "is balderdash" (*Parliament,* 378).

This somewhat ungracious eulogy was premature. In 1992, R. W. Davis and J. H. Hexter tellingly chose a volume of essays about *Parliament and Liberty from the Reign of Elizabeth to the English Civil War* to launch a new series of scholarly publications on "The Making of Modern Freedom," which will, according to Davis and Hexter, explain "the way in which freedom, as it is generally understood in the modern world, came into being in the West, or a small part of it, and then was realized elsewhere across the globe" (v).[8] "Modern freedom" is, for Hexter especially, inseparable from representative government: religious freedom, for example, begins in England because the Henrician, Edwardian, and Marian revolutions in the church were, for all their turbulence, "achieved by statute law with the consent of the people of England as represented in Parliament" (5). Political representation also protected property rights, the basis of secular freedom: parliamentary subsidies "made lawful [the monarchs'] taking of the property of their English subjects . . . because by their representatives in Parliament those subjects had consented to the taking" (6). According to Hexter, "every English subject had already consented to whatever levy a subsidy bill imposed through his representatives to whom, as all recognized, he had given *plena potestas,* full power, to speak for him in Parliament" (7–8). When a Commons committee produced the Humble Answer and the Apology (1604), a cogent defense of this system of government by consent against James's incipient absolutism, we have reached "the starting point in the making of modern freedom" (Hexter 51–52).

Hexter's claim that "every English subject" empowered and consented to the Commons' actions sounds suspiciously like the ideology of political representation developed by Elizabethan and Jacobean parliamentary theorists and MPs: "the Parliament of England . . . hath the power of the whole realm," Sir Thomas Smith reasoned in *De republica Anglorum* (1583), "[f]or every Englishman is intended to be there present, either in person or by procuration and attornies. . . . from the Prince (be he King or Queen) to the lowest person of England. And the consent of the Parliament is taken to be every man's consent" (78–79). During the Commons' proceedings, the knights and burgesses similarly claimed that what was enacted by their consent was, as Robert Atkinson said in a 1563 speech, enacted "by consent of the whole realme in high court of Parlement" (*PPE* 1:96). During Shakespeare's lifetime, however, only one-sixth of the adult male population were qualified to vote in parliamentary elections: the legal fiction that "the consent of Parliament is taken to be *every man's consent*" itself rested on the political fiction that every man had the right to choose representatives to consent on his behalf, but I am more interested here in the fiction of representation per se. Hexter claims that "all recognized" that "every English subject had already consented to whatever levy a subsidy bill imposed through his representatives to whom . . . he had given *plena potestas,* full power, to speak for him in Parliament" (7–8). In fact, not even all early modern MPs believed that they were fully empowered to speak and act *as* their constituents. During the 1572 debates over the fate of Mary, Queen of Scots, Robert Snagge proposed that the government should canvass the entire realm: "He would have every man which is absent likewise to declare their consent as we have don, and therefore requireth a generall oath" (*PPE* 1:392). Snagge almost always had a few fellow travelers on the radical path he walked, but not a single MP seconded this proposal. To acknowledge that the consent of the MPs and the consent of the people themselves were distinct, to acknowledge that the people were "absent" rather than "representatively . . . present," in Bacon's words, was to acknowledge that political representation fundamentally did not work.[9] To neglect Snagge's contemporary critique of the legal and political fiction of "representative presence" is to choose ideology over ideology critique and historical analysis.

Revisionists, on the other hand, have hardly been more critical of the crown than the Whigs have been of their heroes. Elton's account of the Elizabethan Commons, for example, is very much shaped by a profoundly romanticized vision of Tudor monarchy: "In that age of a strong monarchy wisely using the inherited institutions of government, the Lords and Commons, with the agreement and toleration of the Crown, formed a convenient and really rather ingeniously devised instrument for raising supply by consent and for making laws binding upon the agencies of enforcement" (*Parliament,* 379). Elton accepts, in passing, the myth that the people of the realm consented to subsidies, but his notion of the Commons' proper role in England's mixed estate sounds distinctly monarchic.[10]

Revisionists, moreover, take the crown's dim view of any "improper" defiance by the MPs, which they tend to attribute not to substantive political motives but to irrationality and pettiness. For example, the Commons' protracted debate over the crown's 1604 Union proposal earns James I the sympathy of Kevin Sharpe and R. C. Munden: although "James showed remarkable patience with the petty, selfish vacillations of the Commons" (Sharpe 36), the MPs ultimately engineered the "emasculation of the scheme" (Munden 62). According to Elton, the realm's need for efficient parliamentary proceedings was forever being undermined by "the whims of private members promoting private causes, or [by] those sudden rushes of blood to the head for very small reasons to which the House of Commons has always had an inclination—a not unnatural result, perhaps, of those 'idle heads' (to use Elizabeth's description) in close proximity and only half aware in all that to-and-fro of what was going on" ("Parliament," 90).[11] Elton's repeated willingness to "use Elizabeth's description[s]" of the House of Commons is everywhere evident in—and significantly compromises—his enormously influential work.[12]

Whigs and revisionists have together produced a monumental history of the Commons' relationship to the crown and its role in great affairs of state. My aim, however, is to tell the story of the Commons' relationship to the people it claimed to represent. The alternative history of the Commons I develop here is shaped by Shakespeare's treatment of political representation in the first Henriad, *Titus Andronicus, Julius Caesar,* and *Coriolanus.* The historical moments Shakespeare chose to dramatize certainly afforded him the opportunity to explore struggles between political authorities who claimed to derive their power from the people and political authorities who claimed a power independent of the people. In the Roman plays and in the English histories, however, Shakespeare turns again and again to the violent effect of political representation on the enfranchised, on the putative beneficiaries of political representation. To understand why the representative operations of the early modern House of Commons inspired Shakespeare's relentless critique of political representation, we need to recognize that the knights and burgesses disciplined Richard Robinson not in spite of but because of their claims to speak for him and to make him present.

◇◇

On March 3, 1593, Edward Coke, the speaker of the House of Commons, scolded some of his fellow MPs for whispering: "Mr. Speaker, perceiving some men to whisper together, said that it was not the manner of the House, that any should whisper or talk secretly, for here only publick Speeches are to be used" (D'Ewes 487). Covert speech disturbs Coke because it undermines the Commons' status as a distinctly *public* institution. Private speech might, on the one hand, suggest that members were pursuing personal rather than public ends.[13] On the other hand, whispering might signify an even more damaging timidity: MPs afraid to speak their minds could hardly maintain the Commons' claim that no matter of public concern would ever be sacrificed to restrictions on speech. On February 22, Coke's first official act as speaker had been to "make unto [Elizabeth] three peticions in the names of your Commons": "First, that libertie of speech and the auncient priviledge of the parliament may be graunted unto your subiectes. That we may have accesse to your royall person to present those things that shalbe [considered] of amongst us. That your Majestie will give us your royall assent to the thinges that are agred uppon" (*PPE* 3:66–67). The order of the speaker's requests was hardly arbitrary. According to the institutional ideology articulated in the "Petition of Right" the MPs sent to James I in 1610, the Commons' most fundamental liberty was "to debate freely al matters, which do properly concerne the subject, and his right, or State: which freedome of debate being once forclosed, the essence of the libertie of Parliament is with all dissolved."[14]

Freedom of speech was the necessary condition of "the libertie of Parliament"; "the libertie of Parliament," in turn, was the necessary condition of the subject's liberty and felicity. When, for example, John Puckering, the speaker of the House, informed the MPs in 1585 that Elizabeth insisted that they cease debating religious matters, the distraught MPs identified this attack on their freedom of speech as an attack on the people's liberty:

> With this message the House found them selves so greatlie moved and so deeplye wounded as they could not devise which way to cure themselves agayne, for so theire case stoode, as either theie must offende their gracious soveraigne towardes whom, in respecte of their singuler benefittes that they received by hir most blessed and happie governmente, theie durst not so muche as to lifte up one evill thought or imagination, or else to suffer the liberties of their House to be infringed, whereby theie shoulde leave their children and posteritie in thraldome and bondage, they themselves by their forefathers beinge delivered into freedom and libertie. (*PPE* 2:183)

The notion that English subjects consented to the laws that bound them depended not merely on their ancient right to representation but also on the parliamentary freedom of speech that made their representatives truly efficacious.

The freedom of speech the MPs sought to preserve, however, was strictly circumscribed by the walls of St. Stephen's Chapel.[15] For the publicness of the Commons was threatened, not only by members who whispered in Parliament, but also, paradoxically, by members who reported Commons proceedings to the public. The day after Coke admonished the whisperers, Sir Henry Knyvet "moved that for the freedom of the House it might be concluded amongst them a matter answerable at the Bar, for any man to report any thing of any Speech used, or matters done in this House" (D'Ewes 487). Coke preserves the liberty of the English subject by suppressing the whispered speech of the MPs; Knyvet wants to protect "the freedom of the House" by concealing all speech within the chamber from the outside world—by reducing it to a whisper. Knyvet's circumspection was typical: Parliament men of all dispositions routinely supported the enforcement of the institution's prohibitions on breaching the secrecy of proceedings. Thus, the walls of St. Stephen's functioned as a boundary marker of public discourse: within the walls, all speech was public; but nothing spoken within the walls could be reported to the public itself.

MPs routinely claimed that secret proceedings, far from signaling a contradiction in the Commons' status as a public institution, were the positive condition of its capacity to function as the representative body of the people of the realm. According to the Commons' own quasi-official history, the knights and burgesses' desire to protect the public interest from the oppressive influence of the lords and the crown precipitated an internal division of the ancient Parliament. Once upon a time, Coke told his colleagues in 1597, all the estates of the realm had assembled together:

> At the first we were all one House and sat together, by a precedent which I have of a Parliament holden before the Conquest by *Edward* the Son of *Etheldred.* For there were Parliaments before the Conquest. This appeareth in a Book which a grave Member of this House delivered unto me, which is Intituled *Modus tenendi Parliamentum;* out of that Book I learn this, and if any man desire to see it, I will shew it him. And this Book declareth how we all sat together, but the Commons sitting in preference of the King and amongst the Nobles disliked it, and found fault that they had not free liberty to speak. And upon this reason that they might speak more freely, being out of the Royal sight of the King, and not amongst the great Lords so far their betters, the House was divided and came to sit asunder. (D'Ewes 515)

The Commons' creation myth, enshrined in a sacred book, figures seclusion as the founding condition of a Commons empowered by free, open, public speech.[16] To maintain that enabling privacy, all members were enjoined never to communicate to the lords or crown the business of the Lower House. "The providence of God," an anonymous MP claimed in 1567, "hath ordeined by lawe that in this House every one hath free speech and consent"; thus, "he doth iniury to the whole realme that makes any thing knowne to the prince that is here in hand without consent of the House" (*PPE* 1:130).

The specter of a royal and noble audience to the debates and speeches in St. Stephen's Chapel turns out to be something of a red herring.[17] The physical absence of the great may indeed have put the members more at ease, but no modestly experienced MP imagined that the proceedings of the Lower House could be kept secret from the Upper House and crown. The Commons was full of knights and burgesses whose elections had been secured with help from privy councilors, peers, and courtiers who expected, in return for their patronage, to be well provided with information about parliamentary business.[18] Indeed, many privy councilors and other royal advisers were themselves MPs. Let me give two telling examples of the crown's knowledge of Commons proceedings. In 1572, Thomas Wilson, Elizabeth's master of requests and an MP, reported to the House that during a conference with the queen "it pleased her to demaunde of me what matters were now in the Howse. I desired pardon, for that the same were matters of secrecy. Shee was important" (*PPE* 1:379). T. E. Hartley suggests that Thomas Cromwell meant to record "importunate" in his diary (1:379n), but "important" neatly suggests the difficulty of Wilson's position: he told his important and importunate queen everything. Although it would be a long time yet before an MP would face down a direct request from his sovereign, the relative ease with which the lords and the monarch apprised themselves of Commons business does not mean, as some revisionists argue, that the Commons was merely a department of the crown. The efforts of the lords and crown to monitor the Commons in fact often betray anxiety about the Commons' independence. For example, the earl of Essex warned his friend Sir Henry Unton that Elizabeth was incensed by speeches he had made in 1593 against Robert Cecil and in defense of the integrity of the House: "She startles at your name, chargeth you with popularity, and hath every particular of your speeches in Parliament. . . . , as the anatomy, the pots and pans, and such like" (qtd. in *EP* 2:306; cf. *PPE* 1:163). Sir Henry, I suggest, could not have been startled to learn that Elizabeth had intelligence about speeches in St. Stephen's; nonetheless, he cannot, one imagines, have been entirely sanguine about Elizabeth's startled reaction to his particular performance.[19]

Imagining their speeches being rehearsed for Elizabeth undoubtedly made some MPs nervous, resentful, and, even, fearful,[20] but royal monitoring was an open secret; only a very few MPs actively sought to eliminate the activities of the "tale tellers," as Wentworth called the men who served as the crown's ears and eyes in St. Stephen's.[21] By contrast, the Commons, as a corporate body, vigorously sought to prevent the development of a *popular* audience to their proceedings and punished members for speaking of Parliament's business in public. In 1572, just a few months before one of Wentworth's attacks on tale tellers fell on deaf ears, the Commons forced Arthur Hall to recant "sundry lewd Speeches, used as well in this House as also abroad elsewhere" in which he had both mildly defended Mary and Norfolk and insisted that the Commons should leave their fates up to Elizabeth (D'Ewes 207).[22] Defending Mary and disparaging the Commons' competence was certainly provocative: the MPs hawked and stamped their feet while Hall spoke.[23] But the Commons' handling of Hall's case focused on the words he spoke "abroad elsewhere" and turned on the way the institution defined its relationship not to royal power but to the public.

William Fleetwood's distinction between freedom of speech within and outside of St. Stephen's shaped the debate on Hall's case:

> in all cases the tyme, place and person ought to bee considered. . . . We have nowe greate matters in hande and the arreignement of a queene; and therefore he would have speech to be more liberalie suffered within the Howse.

> Let them aledge for her what thay can, they shalbe answered. But here is mencion of speech without the Howse: nowe the case is changed. . . . words tollerable in this Howse are not sufferable at Blunte's table. (*PPE* 1:360)

Fleetwood was not worried about Elizabeth learning of Hall's speech: Blunte's table was a tavern, not a royal council chamber. Thus, when Fleetwood recommended that "Hall be put to aunswere sutch speach as he used out of the House, and be suffered to explaine his minde for his speach within the House" (*PPE* 1:327), he was concerned about *publicity.* Fleetwood does not dispute Hall's right to say what he said in St. Stephen's, although he asserts the Commons' right, as a deliberative body, to understand Hall's meaning. By contrast, Fleetwood suggests that the Commons can hold Hall legally accountable for—can make him answer to the charge of—speaking of the Commons' business in a public place.[24]

Francis Alford concurred with Fleetwood's sense of decorum: it was, he said, "worthie of consideracion where the wordes were spoken." But he wanted to make it even clearer that Hall, like any MP, could speak his mind within the House: "Surelie he would have much borne within the Howse. Kings' titles have been here examined and a bill preferred against a king in possession. . . . He is jeleous of the liberties of the Howse. If the wordes were spoken out of the Howse, let him be called to answer" (*PPE* 1:361). For Alford, then, the Commons' liberty of free speech within the House was, remarkably, no more important than keeping the Commons' proceedings occluded from the public. Alford's principal concern was that Hall's speech "sholde be keapt in the secretes of the House" (327).[25]

In the end, Hall participated in an elaborate show trial in which he venerated the Commons and confessed his folly. Thomas Cromwell's journal reports that Hall pleaded with "the Howse to thinke that it amazeth him to be brought to answere in such an assemblie and that it takes away his harte. . . . He spake he knewe not what, the disturbance [the MPs' hawking and shuffling] offered moved him to anger and he was *homo* and knewe not certainlie what he had said" (*PPE* 1:366). Hall's performance was deemed satisfactory and he escaped serious punishment.[26] To his cost, Hall never learned to stop discussing politics in the "abroad elsewhere" beyond St. Stephen's Chapel. In 1576, Hall published a book of two pamphlets—*An Account of A Quarrel between Arthur Hall Esq. and Melchisidech Mallorie, Gent.* and *An Admonition by the Father of F.A. to him being a Burgesse of the Parliament for his better Behaviour therein*—in which he both rehearsed speeches made during the parliamentary sessions of 1576 and belittled the Lower House. When the MPs next assembled in 1581, they took the extraordinary step of "dismembr[ing]" Hall, who was again sitting for Grantham, called for a new borough election to replace him, and disabled him from any future parliamentary service (*PPE* 1:536).

The great MP and statesman Thomas Norton introduced the complaint against Hall's book on February 4, 1581:

> he declared that some person of late had caused a Book to be set forth in print, not only greatly reproachful against some particular good Members of this House of great Credit, but also very much slanderous and derogatory to the general Authority, Power and State of this House, and prejudicial to the validity of the Proceedings of the same, in making and establishing of Laws, charging this House with Drunkenness as Accompanied in their Councils with *Bacchus,* and then also with Choler, as those which had never failed to *Anticyra,* and the Proceedings of this House to be *opera tenebrarum.* (D'Ewes 291)

In Chapters 3 and 5, I take up some of the particulars of Hall's attempt to demystify the Commons' authority, but my concern here is the Commons' outrage over publicity per se. Hall's characterization of the Commons' proceedings as "*opera tenebrarum,*" Norton charges, is "slanderous" and "prejudicial." It was also accurate: the Commons' unhappy discussions of the pamphlets and their author's own several retractions confirm that perhaps Hall's principal crime was bringing the MPs' labors out of the darkness and into the light. After all the sticky spots that Hall had wriggled out of, it was "publish[ing] the conferences of the Howse in print" that did him in (*PPE* 1:509).

The House appointed "Mr. Vice-Chamberlain, Mr Chancellor of the Exchequer, Mr. Secretary *Wilson,* Mr Treasurer of the Chamber" and four other prominent MPs to "send for the Printer of the said Book, and to examine him" (D'Ewes 291). Two days later, Wilson reported to the House that the commission's interrogation of the printer, Henry Bynneman, had been quite fruitful. Bynneman disclosed that a scrivener named John Wells had delivered Hall's manuscript and provided an inventory of the initial printing: one copy had been sent to a Henry Shirland, another had been delivered to Hall's servant, and twelve had been handed over to Hall himself. Bynneman was then "brought to the Bar, [where he] affirmed in all things as Mr. Secretary *Wilson* before reported; and further, that he had printed fourscore or an hundred of the said Books, and was thereupon sequestred" (D'Ewes 292). Shirland next appeared at the bar and "confessed that Mr. *Hall* did write a Letter unto him, and sent the said Book unto him, willing him to get it Printed. And thereupon he delivered the Book to the said *Bynnyman* to have it Printed, *Wells* the Scrivener being present with him; and so he was then sequestered" (D'Ewes 292). Wells at the bar; Wells implicates his master Mr. Dalton; Wells sequestered (D'Ewes 292).

The House enlarged the commission "for the further proceeding to the Examination of the matter touching Mr. *Hall,* the Printer, the Scrivener, and all other persons, Parties or privy to the publishing of the said Book" (D'Ewes 292). On February 14, Christopher Hatton, speaking for the committee, charged Hall "with divers Articles of great importance selected by the said Committees out of the said Book; as *first,* with publishing the Conferences of this House abroad in Print" (D'Ewes 295; emphasis added). In the end, the other parties to the case were set free, but Hall was "by the whole House without any one negative voice, . . . committed to the Prison of the *Tower,* as the Prison Proper to this House . . . until himself should willingly make a Retractation of the said Book to the satisfaction of this House" (D'Ewes 296). After nearly two months, Hall finally won his release by producing a groveling confession: he proclaimed his "reverence" for all those aspects of the Commons' mythology that he had so carefully debunked and repented having "published the conferences of the Howse in printe" (*APC* 14:9).

The MPs' motives for suppressing Hall's subversive attacks on their power and legitimacy are transparent enough; but why should publishing the Commons' proceedings or discussing parliamentary affairs at Blunte's table have been taboo? Or, to put the question more sharply, why were the private citizens of the realm—the very political subjects who supposedly empowered the Commons—denied access to information about what the MPs said and did in their names? Many MPs shared parliamentary news with their own professional and social peers in London and with the important men (and, occasionally, women) of the boroughs and shires they represented, but they withheld the same intelligence not only from the unenfranchised millions they claimed to represent but also from the vast majority of the tens of thousands of voters who had elected them.[27] Thus, the anonymous publisher of *A Record of some worthy Proceedings; in the Honourable, wise and faithfull Howse of Commons in the late Parliament* (1611) humbly suggested that even the literate, book-buying public would have much to learn from a slim volume of excerpts from the proceedings of 1610: "I am not (in deed) in any such eminent place, as where I may be sure to have a perfect relation of all remarkable affaires: yet by my diligent indevour, I obteyne (in time) more probable intelligence, than many of you doe" (A2^{r}). To my knowledge, during the thirty-five years that separated the appearance of *A Record* in 1611 and the publication of Hall's tracts in 1576, a handful of printed works reproduced only a few speeches from the Commons' proceedings. Perhaps Hall's fate explains why *A Record* was printed in Amsterdam and dedicated from a safe distance "To all true hearted Englishmen dwelling in their native soile" (A2^{r}).[28]

The MPs' motives for maintaining secrecy and thus preserving the Commons' exclusive right to define public debate are fully revealed by the outrage some members expressed over leaks during the 1601 debates about the queen's right to grant commercial and manufacturing monopolies to her favorites. Robert Cecil was incensed by breaches of secrecy during these contentious sessions, but not, obviously enough, because he feared that Elizabeth and the powerful patent-holders would prematurely discover the Commons' assault on their privileges. After all, Sir Walter Ralegh, sitting for Cornwall, heard for himself the stinging attacks on his tin patent and defended himself in the House (*PPE* 3:375–77).[29] Cecil admonished his fellow MPs for allowing the common people—perhaps the chief victims of the monopolies[30]—to learn of the Commons' proceedings:

> I ffeare we are not secrett amonge our selves. Then muste I needes give yow this for a ffuture caution, that whatsoever is subject to a publique expectacion cannot be good. Whie, Parleament matters are ordinarye talke in the streetes. I have hearde my self, being in my coache, these words spoaken alowde: "God prosper those that further the overthrowe of these monopolies. God send the prerogative touche not our libertyie." I will not wronge anye so muche as to ymagine he was of this Howse, yett lett me give yow this note, that the tyme was never more apte to disorder and make ill interpretacion of good meaneinge. I thincke those persones would be glad that all soveraignitye were converted into popularitye, we beinge here, are but the popular branche and our libertye, the libertye of the subjecte. (*PPE* 3:398)

Cecil's anxiety turns on a link between power and knowledge: publicizing the Commons' business will end in popular sovereignty because it will make the MPs themselves "subject to public expectation."[31] Publicity enables power: once the people know who is for and who is against the monopolies, they, not God, will prosper those who please them.[32]

Cecil's horror of sovereignty devolving into popularity is somewhat out of place in the House of Commons. MPs and parliamentary theorists did not, of course, figure popularity as the sole basis of sovereignty, but they did claim that the sovereign legislative authority of the monarch-in-Parliament depended, in part, on the Commons' status as a popularly elected representative body: "for the lawfull power of making laws to command whole politic societies of men," Richard Hooker reasoned,

> belongeth so properly unto the same entire societies. . . . Laws they are not therefore which public approbation hath not made so. But approbation not only they give who personally declare their assent by voice sign or act, but also when others do it in their names by right originally at the least derived from them. As in parliaments, councils, and the like assemblies, although we be not personally ourselves present, notwithstanding our assent is by reason of other agents there in our behalf. And what we do by others, no reason but that it should stand as our deed. (93)

Only the House of Commons, early modern MPs routinely argued, provided such "public approbation" of England's laws: "the whole realm," an anonymous MP claimed in 1563, "hath chosen us to sitt here diligently to enquire what is beneficiall or hurtfull for the same, and to provide accordinglie" (*PPE* 1:130). Thus, at the close of Parliament, the speaker of the House could represent the bills before the monarch as the embodiment of the people's will: "according to the ancient and well-ruled freedome of the subjects of England," Speaker Yelverton assured Elizabeth in 1598, "hath the whole state of your kingdome (represented heere by Parliament) assembled, consulted, and resolved uppon some fewe petitions, thought fit for lawes to them by your Majestie to be established" (*PPE* 3:197–98). Making sovereignty a function of popularity, then, is precisely what the Commons claimed to do, but for Cecil, shut up in his private coach, the Commons ceases to function properly precisely when it threatens to fulfill its own rhetoric.[33] Cecil, to be sure, was a councilor to the queen, but almost every Elizabethan and early Jacobean MP shared Cecil's "wish that whatsoever is here spoken may be buried within these Walls" (D'Ewes 653). The occasion of Cecil's outrage reminds us, of course, that when it suited their purposes MPs did indeed leak information about parliamentary deliberations: without such leaks, "parliament matters" could not become "ordinary talk in the street." But publicizing the Commons' business beyond a very small circle of citizens of substance was widely condemned, and the Elizabethan and early Jacobean Commons never authorized a formal or even informal canvassing of public opinion.[34]

The Commons' prohibition on disclosing the secrets of the House was the foundation of a much broader effort to inhibit the development of an informed, effective political public. The Commons, for example, aggressively disciplined and silenced private persons who attempted to subject the Commons to publicity, or, what is much the same thing, public judgment. The

MPs routinely investigated subjects who wrote, published, or simply read accounts of any kind of parliamentary activity. On November 16, 1601, for example, Henry Doyley, a barrister of Lincoln's Inn and a burgess for Wallingford, "made a Motion and said, Mr. Speaker, I think myself bound in Conscience to certifie you of an Infamous Libel that is newly Printed and spread abroad since the beginning of this Parliament; Saving your presence, Mr. Speaker, It is called *An Assembly of Fools*. . . . The House wondered much at this Motion, and great murmurring there was" (D'Ewes 639).

Doyley asked the speaker to call the printer to the bar, but Coke instead dispatched the serjeant-at-arms to pick up John Baker, the owner of the "libellous book" (*PPE* 3:354). At the bar, Baker insisted that the book was entirely innocuous, and the serjeant returned to Baker's lodgings, collected the book, and delivered it to the Privy Council: "after yt was . . . well scanned by the Privy Councell, it was ffound to be a meere toye and an ould booke entitled 'The Second Parte of Jack of Dover', a thinge both stale and ffoolishe, ffor which the said Mr Doyley was well lawghed at" (*PPE* 3:355).[35] As Hall's case amply demonstrates, there can be no doubt that had *An Assembly of Fools* indeed existed, the Commons' consequent investigation would have been no laughing matter.[36]

We have been considering the Commons' use of its juridical authority to suppress both internal and external criticism, but the MPs also used their legislative powers to punish private subjects who discussed parliamentary affairs. After learning in 1610 that the "act"—a candidate's defense of his thesis—at Oxford and Cambridge had become an occasion for ridiculing the Commons, the MPs sent letters to both universities warning them to "give the House satisfaction" or face the revocation of their exemption from subsidies (*PP 1610* 2:384; see also 2:278). What may strike us as an extremely trivial matter clearly preoccupied the MPs, even as they simultaneously debated the Great Contract, which, had it been adopted, would have entirely transformed the Commons' role in raising revenues. In a letter of July 14, 1610, Dudley Carleton interrupted his discussion of the Contract to inform Sir Thomas Edmondes, a fellow MP, of the assault on the Commons' honor: "You must know, by the way, that we of the lower House do find ourselves much scandalized by both universities, for some public speeches used by men in chief place amongst them, in disgrace of our proceedings" (*PP 1610* 2:278). The MPs' rather fragile dignity had for a long time made them quick to punish even absurdly inconsequential offenses: in 1559, an unlucky man by the name of Thrower was committed to the serjeant's custody because an MP had overheard him joking that "if a Bill were brought in for Womens Wyers [i.e., supports for elaborate hair styles]," the members "would dispute it and go to the Question" as if a matter of great import were before them (D'Ewes 54).[37]

The Oxbridge dons' "public speeches," Hall's pamphlets, the phantom satire *An Assembly of Fools,* and, of course, the antimonopoly talk in the streets signal the emergence of public opinion about parliamentary affairs. These low and high, elite and popular responses to the Commons are early modern precursors of both Habermas's "classical" bourgeois public—a "public sphere in the political realm evolved from the public sphere in the world of letters" (30–31)—and a "*plebeian* public sphere": that is, "a public sphere stripped of its literary garb" whose "subject was no longer the 'educated strata' but the uneducated 'people'" (viii).[38] The MPs' outrage over these quite different expressions of the public's interest in the Commons suggests that many MPs were determined to suppress or at least manage the very manifestations of public opinion that helped the Commons establish itself as a public authority.

Shakespeare's life spanned an important stage in the evolution of the Commons' relation to "the public." In many respects, the medieval Commons fulfilled neither of the functions that, for Habermas, define the public sphere: a "vehicle of public opinion [to] put the state in touch with the needs of society" (30–31); a structured medium that turned "the principle of publicity against the established authorities" (56).[39] Early modern MPs wanted the House of Commons to play both parts: "vehicle of public opinion" and "established authorities." On the one hand, the Elizabethan and Jacobean Commons—despite its permanent home in Westminster and its quite secure role in constitutional theory and practice—occasionally represented itself as a public sphere. Many MPs and theorists claimed that the Commons' defining institutional mission was to articulate the voice of the people and address that voice to regal authorities: "I think it time to speak plainly and to let his Majesty understand the voice of his loving and loyal commons," Thomas Lewknor told his fellow MPs in a 1610 speech against James's impositions; "They complain that they are already . . . fallen into a gulf of misery and poverty. . . . They say they have already . . . given to his Majesty more in time of peace than ever they have to any of his predecessors in so few years in time of war" (*PP 1610* 2:402). On the other hand, many Elizabethan MPs also wanted to establish the Commons as a public authority, a maker of decisions rather than a conduit of opinions. In 1572, the MPs debated how best to communicate to Elizabeth their desire that Mary, Queen of Scots, and her proposed husband, the duke of Norfolk, be executed: should the House deliver an "opinion" to the queen or should it issue a formal "request" for the executions? The privy councilors and conservatives in the House successfully urged an "opinion" (*PPE* 1:357–58), but Thomas Cromwell's journal shows that more independent parliamentarians such as William Fleetwood were reconceiving the Commons' role: "There was talke also of opinion. Opinion he thinketh is nothing; may change every day . . . He misliketh this word 'opinion', and would have it brought to a resolucion, for that the gravitie of this Howse is not to deale with opinions but to make conclusions" (*PPE* 1:383). Fleetwood argued in vain, but later Elizabethan and Jacobean MPs would increasingly figure "opinion" as something fit for the streets rather than "the gravitie" of St. Stephen's Chapel.

The Commons' capacity "to make conclusions" was, of course, still very much circumscribed by its constitutional relations with the crown and the lords, but both Whig and revisionist historians neglect how important the Commons' relation to the public was in the evolution of its power. The emergence in Elizabethan and Jacobean England of a public that turned to the Commons for redress and sought to influence the MPs' decisions established the Commons as a public authority—the addressee, that is, of the public's demands and opinions.[40] Thus, for example, in the 1570s and 1580s important tracts advocating religious reform were addressed to Parliament or the House of Commons; in 1601, "a multitude of people who said they were commonwealth men and desired [the House] to take compassion of their griefs" gathered outside of St. Stephen's (qtd. in Williams 135); in 1610, "A packet of letters directed to the House was found at the parliament House door and brought by the finder to Mr. Speaker" (*PP 1610* 2:381); in 1610, "A clamorous woman, pressing Mr. Speaker with petitions and receiving no answer, ordered if she delivered any more petitions to be sent to the bridewell [i.e., Bridewell prison]" (*PP 1610* 2:385).

The value and the burden of this sort of attention is deliciously at play in the overtures the crank and genius John Dee made to the House in 1604. Dee arranged for the printing of a broadside addressed "To the honorable Assemblie of the COMMONS *in the present Parlament.*" Dee laments that he has for fifty years been slandered as a "Conjurer" and calls on the knights and burgesses, "by your Powre, so great and sure," to pass "An Act generall against sclaunder, and a speciall penall Order for John Dee his case." Dreadful verses exalting the MPs and reviling slander follow. Dee, "Mathematician to his most Royal Majestie," asks the Commons—not James, not the lords, not Parliament—to censor his detractors. In this particular context, Dee recognizes the House of Commons as a public authority in virtue precisely of its "great and sure" power to suppress public opinion. The Commons undoubtedly benefited from such recognition, but the MPs were also distressed by its inevitable by-products: public expectations, to borrow Cecil's phrase, and public opinions about how felicitously those expectations were fulfilled. Elizabethan and early Jacobean knights and burgesses, with very few exceptions, wished to *usurp* all public debate about Commons' affairs. To the extent that they suppressed the information necessary to the development of an effective public sphere, the MPs were free not only to act in the name of public opinion but to define the public opinion they sometimes claimed merely to ventriloquize.

◇◇

Any state institution—even one claiming to articulate the voice of the people—must regulate the public's access to its offices, records, and day-to-day operations, but the Elizabethan and Jacobean Commons maintained St. Stephen's as a fortress against invaders and aliens from the "abroad elsewhere" of London and the realm. Securing the boundaries of the chamber was necessary, in the first instance, to prevent the direct publicizing of the Commons' business: enjoining MPs not to disclose details of the proceedings would be pointless if members of the public witnessed the proceedings for themselves. Thus, John Hooker stipulates that the serjeant-at-arms must "not suffer any to enter into thise house during the time of the sitting there, unlesse he be one of the house" (173). But "if any forain person doo enter into that house, the assembly therof beeing sitting . . . he ought . . . to be punished" (Hooker 170). The exclusion of nonmembers was clearly linked to the desire to keep the Commons' business secret. In *Order and usage,* for example, a prohibition on tale-telling is interposed between two injunctions against admitting "forain person[s]":

> Also no manner of person beeing not one of the Parlement house: ought to enter or come within the house, as long as the sitting is there: upon pain of imprisonment or suche other punishment, as by the house shalbe ordered and adjudged.
>
> Also every person of the Parlement ought to keep secret and not to disclose the secrets and things spoken and doon in the Parlement house, to any manner of person unlesse he be one of the same house: upon pain to be sequestred out of the house, or otherwise punished, as by the order of the house shalbe appointed.
>
> Also none of the Parlement house ought to departe from the Parlement: without speciall leave obteyned of the Speaker of the house, and the same his licence be also recorded.
>
> Also no person beeing not of the Parlement house: ought to come into the same, during the time of the sitting. (Hooker 186–87)

Hooker's admonition about absenteeism, as we shall see, fell on very deaf ears, but his ideal of a hermetic Commons nicely conjures up a vision of St. Stephen's as an epitome of little England "bound in," in John of Gaunt's dying words, "with the triumphant sea, / Whose rocky shore beats back the envious siege" (*Richard II* 2.1.61–62). No foreigners get in; no natives get out.

The Commons' justification for these exclusionary measures deploys a familiar rhetoric: St. Stephen's must be impregnable against spies of the crown and the lords who would eavesdrop on the Lower House's business and thus undermine the "freedom of the house." As we have seen, the lords and crown had plenty of "spies" among the members themselves. It is thus not surprising that the MPs were generally quite calm on those rare occasions when a "forain person" with connections to the Upper House was discovered in St. Stephen's. The MPs, for example, expressed no *special* alarm when they realized that the earl of Northumberland's servant John Legg was present during some rather sensitive debates over a proposed subsidy (D'Ewes 486).

Parliamentary records do, however, reveal considerable concern about the dozen or so ordinary people who managed to make their way past the serjeant-at-arms. These "strangers to the House" were not factors of great lords; they were the sort of people who, when they were not trying to sneak a glimpse of the Commons, might have gone to the theater: students at the Inns of Court, apprentices, craftsmen, modestly prosperous merchants, minor gentry. For example, on November 6, 1584, Edmund Moore, a tallow-chandler, and John Turner, a butcher, were discovered in the House of Commons and committed to "the Serjeants Custody for presuming to come into this House (sitting the House) and being no Members of the same; it is, upon opinion that they did it of ignorance and meer simplicity, and not of any pretended purpose. . . . Agreed by this House, that they shall be discharged and set at Liberty, taking first the Oath of Supremacy openly in this House" (D'Ewes 394). It seems improbable that the knights and burgesses were afraid that a tallow-chandler and a butcher would report the proceedings of the Commons to the queen or the lord chancellor; the members, I suggest, instead feared that Moore and Turner might tell other tallow-chandlers, butchers, and the like what they had seen inside St. Stephens.

Moore and Turner were comparatively lucky: swearing the oath of supremacy was very light punishment.[41] For if the Commons' treatment of Richard Robinson was especially nasty, most intruders were committed to the Serjeant's Ward or the Gatehouse, which William Lambarde described as "a prison to this House," for several days or more; required to pay fees to the serjeant and his assistants; and made to kneel at the bar.[42] Perhaps, then, the earliest engravings of the Commons are disciplinary: in the broadside engravings from 1624 (fig. 1) and 1628 (fig. 2), the viewer shares the perspective of a figure kneeling at the bar.[43] It is shocking to discover how much time the MPs devoted to disciplining private persons: the cases we have discussed are a tiny tip of the iceberg. We have not even considered, for example, transgressors of the laws protecting MPs' and their servants from arrest and legal action during parliamentary sessions: hundreds of private citizens were brought to the bar of the Elizabethan and Jacobean Commons for violating these privileges.[44]

The punishment of illicit visits to the Commons' chamber is uniquely strange: displays of coercive power and an obsession with inscrutability might be consistent with monarchic government, but the practices of figuring members of the public as "strangers" and "forain person[s]" and barring them from St. Stephen's seem extraordinarily inappropriate for an institution that claimed to be empowered by the people. In fact, the Commons instituted its secrecy rules and exclusionary procedures during precisely the same period when many members began routinely to attribute the Commons' share of sovereign authority to its capacity to make the people "representatively . . . present" in Parliament.[45] The notion that the Commons represented the people was itself relatively novel: "the idea of Parliament as a representative body," according to Elton, did not really take hold until well into the sixteenth century ("Body," 25). It was still, judging from Elizabeth's response to a Commons' petition, somewhat unfamiliar in 1563: "I have hard by yow the commen request of my commons, which I may well terme (me thinketh) the wholl realme because, they geve, as I have hard, in all these matters of Parliament their commen consent to such as be here assembled" (*PPE* 1:94).

During Shakespeare's lifetime, there was nothing like a uniform, settled construction of political representation among either political theorists or MPs. According to one view, the people's presence in Parliament was a legal fiction: "the Parliament of England," Sir Thomas Smith argued, "representeth and hath the power of the whole realm, both the head and the body. . . . For every Englishman is intended to be there present, either in person or by procuration and attornies. . . . from the Prince (be he King or Queen) to the lowest person of England. And the consent of the Parliament is taken to be every man's consent" (78–79). Smith recognizes that the doctrine of consent is based on a legal convention: Parliament "hath the power of the whole realm" because "every Englishman *is intended to be there present*" and because "the consent of Parliament *is taken to be* every man's consent."[46] William Harrison's *Description of England,* which was included in the 1587 edition of Holinshed's

Chronicles, preserves Smith's careful language: "To be short, whatsoever the people of Rome did in their *centuriatis* or *tribunitiis comitiis,* the same is and may be done by authority of our Parliament House, which is the head and body of all the realm and the place wherein every particular person is intended to be present, if not by himself, yet by his advocate or attorney" (149–50). A generation later, we encounter the same rhetoric in the statute for the "juste Recognition of the imediate lawfull and undoubted Succession" of James I: "Wee your Majesties loyall and faithfull Subjects . . . agnize our most constant Faithe, Obedience and Loyaltie to your Majestie . . . in this Highe Courte of Parliament, where all the whole Bodie of the Realme, and everie p[ar]ticular Member thereof, either in p[er]son or by Rep[re]sentation (upon their own free Elections) *are by the Lawes* of this Realme *deemed to be* p[er]sonallie p[re]sent" (*SR* 2:1017–18; emphasis added).

The Succession Statute reveals the peculiar nature and limits of legal fictions: "Lawes" do not simply make it possible for human agents to construe, for legal purposes, the people as "p[er]sonallie p[re]sent"; rather, it is in the imagination of the Law itself that the people are personally present in Parliament. In another parliamentary document from James's first Parliament, we can see the translation of a legal fiction into a political fiction. During the sessions of 1604, James I expressed several rather Scottish notions of Parliament's proper role; the alarmed knights and burgesses charged a committee to draft a response to James. The committee's work resulted in the famous "Form of Apology and Satisfaction"—a kind of tutorial in the ways of Tudor England's mixed estate. The common people, the authors of the Apology cautioned James, are "the whole flower and power of your kingdom": "with their bodies your wars, with their purses your treasuyres, are upheld and supplied. . . . All these, amounting to many millions of people, are representatively present in us of this house of Commons" (Petyt 234–35).[47] The context of this claim is very broad: the MPs were not addressing the legal status of acts of consent made by proxies; in the "Apology," the representative presence of the people is a political fiction rather than a legal fiction. As we shall see, political fictions, unlike legal fictions, tend to forget their own fictionality.

◇◇

The knights and burgesses barred the people from St. Stephen's to secure the secrecy of their proceedings, but eyewitnesses also posed a profound threat to the rhetoric of representative presence. The fiction of the people's presence could be maintained only by excluding the people from St. Stephen's, for illicit eyewitnesses discovered that the MPs, far from magically filling St. Stephen's with a plenitude of presence, frequently left the chamber virtually empty. In 1584, Speaker Puckering created a commotion when he revealed to the MPs that John Bland, a London currier, had publicly reported

> that this house passing the Bill of the Shoomakers had proceeded contrary to an Order taken in the same House, which he [Bland] said was, that the Shoomakers Bill should not be further read till the Curriers Bill were first read before; and hath likewise reported, that the Curriers could have no Justice in thise House; and also that this House passed the said Shoomakers Bill when there were scantly fifty persons in the House. . . . And further reported, that the Bill for the Tanners lately read in this House was not all read out, but some leaves thereof left unread. . . . Which Speeches being very slanderous and prejudicial to the State of this House . . . it was thereupon resolved, that Bland . . . be examined. (D'Ewes 366)

Reporting minor deviations from parliamentary practice—considering bills out of order, reading only portions of a bill—hardly undermined the fundamental integrity of the Commons, but publicizing the fact that only 50 out of the more than 450 members were sitting during a session did. The absence of members rendered St. Stephen's doubly empty: empty of the representatives themselves, and, consequently, empty of the millions of people those representatives, according to the most important institutional myth of the Commons, made present at the center of governance. But Bland's report slandered the Commons, above all, because it demonstrated not only that the people were neither personally nor representatively present in St. Stephen's, but also that the Commons continued to act despite their absence.

Absenteeism in the Elizabethan and Jacobean Commons was high: Neale, Elton, David Dean, and Jennifer Loach have shown that throughout the reigns of Elizabeth I and James I, the House was frequently only half full, and that it was not at all unusual for only one quarter of the members to be present during business.[48] On many occasions, the Commons' chamber was almost empty: one recorded vote in 1610 lists 15 ayes and 15 nays (*PP 1610* 2:277); on July 1, 1607, Robert Bowyer's diary entry indicates that a bill was read with only 20 MPs sitting.[49] On those days, over 400 MPs were absent. (We can now justly call the engravings of the Commons—with the members crowding St. Stephen's Chapel—propaganda.)

In theory, absenteeism was discouraged and could be punished. William Lambarde's tract on Parliament warns that "no Knight or Burgess should depart without license of the House or of the Speaker, to be entered with the

Clerk upon pain to lose their wages" (66).[50] Sporadic practical efforts were made to curb absenteeism: during the 1581 session, "it was Ordered that the House should be called on *Wednesday* next . . . that so it might appear who did diligently intend the business of the House, and who did negligently absent themselves" (D'Ewes 283); at end of the session, fines were levied against members who had been absent for the whole session (*PPE* 1:546).[51] These measures, however, produced absolutely no sustained improvement during Elizabeth's or James's reigns. More important, the MPs very seldom expressed any real concern over the effect absenteeism might have on the day-to-day operations and efficacy of the Commons. By contrast, leading members of the House were acutely aware of the threat *the public discovery* of absenteeism posed to the mythology of the Commons.

Despite the especially severe absenteeism of 1606, Sir Thomas Holcroft argued against a proposal to send shire and borough officials letters recalling the many absent members. While Holcroft agreed that the missing members should be contacted, he nonetheless "misliked the Course, for he wished no Writing to be" (Bowyer 96–97). Holcroft argued that recording the Commons' emptiness in letters risked damning publicity: "it will be a Scandal, to shew, what we have done [during the session] is done with so small a Number."[52] Holcroft recognized that absenteeism was scandalous not because it revealed a dysfunctional Commons but because it demonstrated, on the contrary, that the Commons could meet, debate, and act when the people were neither actually nor representatively present.[53] And if the people had not, through their representatives, consented to the bills passed in the Commons, how could the three estates of the Parliament claim that the English people were uniquely free because they bound themselves to the laws of the land?

For some MPs and theorists, the solution to this problem was simply a different and more powerful conception of representation. As we have already seen, Francis Bacon dismissed an objection to admitting hearsay into Commons' debates on the grounds that everyone in the realm was really present in St. Stephen's while the MPs were sitting. There can be no hearsay in the House of Commons, Bacon argued, because being present in one's own person (*coram*) and being "present representatively" were, because of the magic of parliamentary representation, one and the same (*PPE* 3:122). During the 1606 debates about absent MPs, Robert Bowyer elaborated a Baconian answer to Holcroft's anxiety about publicity. He argued on philosophical grounds that absenteeism per se in no way diminished the Commons' capacity to represent the people and that it was therefore unnecessary to recall absent members in the first place: "[I] could wish the Company full in regard of the business which is expected, yet will I not soe narrowly impound the Discretion and Sufficiency of those that remaine, as to think them unable to proceed in such matters as they shall have in hand, and for that which remaineth, it will suffice that all that are absent, Yea all the realme is intended present" (Bowyer 97).

The Commons, whether full or nearly empty, constituted "all the Realme." Thus, Bowyer suggested, it makes no sense to argue that the Commons requires the presence of all its members, for if some members are physically outside of St. Stephen's, they, like everyone else in England, are representatively inside St. Stephen's (97).[54] Bowyer's rejection of the "problem" of massive absenteeism is, in some sense, the inevitable theoretical solution to the pressure *any* absenteeism puts on the basic arithmetic of representation. In one of his subversive pamphlets, Arthur Hall challenged the fundamental plausibility of political representation: "your number of Parliament men . . . are fewe to the huge multitude" of the whole (*A letter,* Eii[r]). But once one allows for the efficacy of representation per se one can argue that the representative operations of 472 MPs can be achieved by 236 MPs or 118 MPs or 59 MPs. Or by one: Bowyer's *absolutist* construction of representation defines an MP not as the representative of the residents of the particular shire or borough from which he was returned but as a supersufficient body capable of representing the entire realm. Bowyer, then, does not diminish the importance of representativeness; rather, he conceives of the Commons' powers of representation in almost mystical terms.

Bowyer does qualify the presence representation produces: "All the realme is *intended* present." But I suggest that despite this familiar modification, Bowyer's elaboration of representative presence has passed from legal fiction to political fiction—a fiction, that is, that no longer fully acknowledges its fictiveness. After all, Bowyer's gesture at the fictionality of representative presence is largely undone by his earlier claim that representation empties out absence as a category. Bowyer's elaboration of the Commons' "sufficiency" has a Derridean quality: those who are absent are present in virtue of their absence. Thus, "absence" is a kind of impossibility: if the people of the realm are not absent from the Commons, their presence there must be "real" rather than "fictional." The most familiar early modern adjective to describe this kind of representation was not, of course, "deconstructionist" but "incarnate."

It is telling that several of the most powerful claims for the Commons' capacity to produce something like the "real presence" of the people were made by theologians.[55] In his 1559 response to John Knox's attacks on female rule, John Aylmer—later bishop of London—had occasion to give his opponent a basic civics lesson: "The regiment of Englande is not a mere Monarchie, as some for lacke of consideracioun thinke, nor a meere Oligarchie, nor Democratie, but a rule mixte of all these wherein ech one of these have or shoulde have authoritie. Th[e] image whereof, and not the image, but the thinge in dede, is to be sene in the parliament house, wherin you shal find these 3. estats" (H2^{v}–H3^{r}). If one were to see the queen and lords in the Upper House of Parliament, image and thing would be identical in a fairly uninteresting way: the queen herself constituted the monarchy; the lords themselves constituted the oligarchy. To imagine that the knights and burgesses constitute the demos—to imagine that the Commons is no longer a metonymy for a greater but absent whole because it is the whole—is to collapse image and thing.

Richard Hooker even more boldly claimed that Parliament, through the representative operations of the Commons, became not a reflection of the body of the realm but instead the body itself: "The *Parliament* of *England* . . . is that whereupon the very *ESSENCE* of all government within this kingdom doth depend. It is even the body of the whole Realme; it consisteth of the *King* and of all that within the *Land* are subject unto him, for they all are there present, either in person or by such as they voluntarily have derived their personal right unto" (192). Like Robert Bowyer, Hooker retreats to the traditional language of fictive presence—"either in person or by such" as represent them—*only after* he has asserted that Parliament is not the image or shadow of the body but the body itself. Hooker's belated qualification of real presence can't get the theoretical toothpaste back into its tube.

The knights and burgesses themselves occasionally made wholly unqualified claims for the capacity of political representation to produce the real presence of the people in the House of Commons. In June of 1572, the Commons considered a momentous provision in a bill against Mary, Queen of Scots: in the event of an insurrection, anyone who murdered Mary would "not be any kinde of wayes troubled or impeached for the same" (*PPE* 1:315).[56] Francis Alford, a cautious MP whose wife was a practicing Catholic, was troubled by a bill that would absolve the lowliest commoner of regicide; Mary was, he reminded the House, "a queene still *in esse*" (*PPE* 1:316). But even Alford acknowledged the Commons' power to take such a step: "We that deale against her are the Queene's Maiestie, whom God longe preserve, and the whole bodie of the realme assembled in the high court of Parliament" (*PPE* 1:316). The representative "we" here speaks not *for* an absent body but *as* the body itself "assembled in the high court of Parliament."

It is beyond the scope of this book to explore the intersections between early modern theological and political constructions of representation, but one might begin such an inquiry with Hans-Georg Gadamer's theory that "in light of the Christian idea of the incarnation and the mystical body [representation] acquired a completely new meaning. Representation now no longer means 'copy' or 'representation in a picture' . . . but 'replacement' . . . what is represented is present in the copy" (513–14n53). English political theorists and practitioners developed the concept of "representative presence" during a period marked by intense theological debate about the Eucharist.

The incarnationist construction of the Commons is seemingly contradictory: by transforming the Commons from a body that represents the whole realm into the body of the whole realm itself, representational ideology excludes the people from the political institution that they supposedly empower. The members of the Commons no longer stand for but take the place of the people of the realm. In even the most charitable and generous hands, this ideology disturbingly transforms the representatives' accountability to the people beyond St. Stephen's into an internal accountability. During the 1597 debates over enclosure, for example, MPs invoked the desires of the various groups interested in land management even as they effectively effaced those interest groups by imaginatively relocating them inside St. Stephen's. On November 26, an anonymous speaker warned that "the ears of our great sheepmasters do hang at the doors of this House" (*PPE* 3:220): the MPs, he feared, would be tempted to protect their own private interests by gratifying the desires of those rich men. But our MP pleaded with his colleagues to preserve for small farmers the land those wealthy husbandmen coveted for grazing:

> A lawe framed out of the private affeccions of men wil never tend to the generall good of all; and if every one may putt in a caution to save his owne particuler it will never prove a lawe of restraint, but rather of loosenes and libertie. The eyes of the poore are upon this parliament, and sad for the want they yet suffer. The cryes of the poore doe importune much, standing like reedes shaking in every corner of the land. This place is an epitome of the whole realme: the trust of the poore committed to us, whose persons we supplie, doth challenge our furtheraunce for theire releife. This hath bene the inscripcion of mayne bills. If our forwardnes procede from singlehartedness we can noe waye effect this so well as by leadinge their handes to the plough and leaving the success to God. We sitt now in judgment over ourselves. (*PPE* 3:220–21)

The speech is quite beautiful; it is also, I think, heartfelt. And yet it is precisely as he articulates a politics of selflessness that our MP's construction of representation becomes disturbing. Because he and his fellow MPs supply the persons—an extraordinary phrase—of the people of the realm, they assume an enormous accountability, but an accountability they can feel only to themselves.[57] Thus, the odd self-reflexiveness of the speaker's final admonition ("We sitt now in judgment over ourselves"), which should, one feels, recall the poor: the eyes of the poor are upon us and they sit in judgment over us. The displacement of the poor by a representative "we" fulfills the figure of the Commons as "an epitome of the whole realme." If the Commons rather than metonymically representing the realm simply is the whole realm in miniature, there is nothing outside it which is not also in it. Thus, even as the speaker articulates the Commons' moral and political accountability to the public, that public is relocated within the Commons itself. What remains, after political representation, is an "abroad elsewhere"—an insubstantial, otherworldly place inhabited by the ghostly people, the shadows of the body.

◇◇

The representative operations that I have been recovering here establish the House of Commons as both representative body and a representation. That is, it is not merely a collection of representative agents who speak for the absent people they represent; rather, the House of Commons is itself a representation of the realm: "This *place,*" our anonymous MP claims, "is an epitome of the whole realme." We can understand what kind of a "place" the House of Commons was by comparing the 1624 and 1628 engravings of the MPs in St. Stephen's (figs. 1 and 2) with figures 4 and 5, licensed broadsides of the House of Lords. These representations are *theatrical* in Michael Fried's sense of the word: here, the great display themselves, turn themselves toward the viewer; here, many eyes seem to solicit and return the viewer's gaze. The engravings of the Commons (figs. 1–3), by contrast, depict MPs whose absorption in their own activity renders them oblivious to the viewer's presence. Their gazes are directed in every direction but ours. These representations of the House of Commons refuse to acknowledge the presence of any potential viewer; the viewer is absorbed by the MPs' absorption. The Commons' authority, according to its ideology, rested on its capacity to make all England present within its walls. Thus, we see in the engravings the MPs busy at the business of representing: the MPs are absorbed in the activity of absorption. The representational strategy of the engravings—absorption—repeats the representational strategy of the House of Commons: absorption. The reason, in short, that the MPs do not return the viewer's gaze is that there simply is, according to the Commons' rhetoric, no viewer to gaze.

2 Cade's Mouth

Swallowing Parliament in the First Tetralogy

Henry VI's reign was so crowded with cruel misfortunes and gross miscalculations that it would seem impossible to identify any particular event or royal shortcoming as the cause of the king's downfall. In the first Henriad, however, Shakespeare makes Henry's mismanagement of Parliament the positive condition of the Yorkist triumph over the House of Lancaster: in the Parliament at London in *Henry VI, Part 1,* Henry restores Richard Plantagenet to his lands and titles (3.1); in the Parliament at London in Part 3, Henry bars his son Edward from the succession in favor of Richard and his sons (1.1).[1] The Parliament at the Abbey of Bury St. Edmunds in Part 2 is the king's Waterloo: here, according to Andrew Cairncross's somewhat overheated headnote to the scene, "the holocaust begins" (62n).[2] Henry allows the duke of Suffolk to arrest Humphrey, duke of Gloucester, the king's most loyal and powerful protector, on trumped-up charges. After Gloucester is led away under guard, the king himself, who knows that his uncle is innocent, leaves the Parliament: "My lords, what to your wisdoms seemeth best / Do or undo, as if ourself were here" (*2HVI* 3.1.195–96). Henry's parliamentary abdication is Shakespeare's invention and the font from which all of the first tetralogy's elusive political narratives and complex representations of power flow and to which they all return.

Henry's fate at the hands of those who represent him in the Parliament at Bury is the fate suffered by all Shakespearean characters who are the subjects of political representation. As Henry takes leave of his lords, he explicitly laments the imprisonment of Gloucester: "His fortunes I will weep, and 'twixt each groan / Say 'Who's a traitor? Gloucester, he is none'" (*2HVI* 3.1.221–22). Henry's last words are still echoing in Parliament when Queen Margaret, Suffolk, York, and Cardinal Beaufort conspire to murder Gloucester (223–81). The cardinal then encourages York to lead a military campaign against an Irish rebellion. Even York seems to assume that only Henry could authorize him to undertake such an enterprise:

> CARDINAL: My lord of York, try what your fortune is.
> Th'uncivil kerns of Ireland are in arms
> And temper clay with blood of Englishmen.
> To Ireland will you lead a band of men
> Collected choicely, from each county some,
> And try your hap against the Irishmen?
> YORK: I will, my lord, so please his majesty.
> SUFFOLK: Why, our authority is his consent,
> And what we do establish he confirms.
> (*2HVI* 3.1.309–17)

After the Parliament concludes its business, York stands alone on stage and gloats over the foolishness of the peers who have just armed his ambition for the crown: "'Twas men I lacked, and you will give them me. / I take it kindly. Yet be well assured / You put sharp weapons in a madman's hands" (*2HVI* 3.1.345–47). York is prophetic: the troops he leads to victory in Ireland will indeed form part of the army that eventually defeats the Lancastrian forces. Henry, then, "consents" to the act that ultimately brings about his own downfall at the hands of York and his sons.[3]

As Henry leaves the Parliament at Bury, of course, these fatal consequences lie far in the future, but his departure shocks even Margaret, who typically encourages her husband to cede policy and command to her: "What, will your highness leave the Parliament?" (*2HVI* 3.1.197). Henry is a serial abdicator, and it is not immediately clear why this particular flight from kingly responsibility should be remarkable. Indeed, it is Henry's belief that Parliament can continue as if he were present, rather than his tearful exit itself, that is so striking: "My lords, what to your wisdoms seemeth best, / Do, or undo, as if ourself were here." Henry's use of the royal plural here fundamentally misconceives the monarch's unique relation to Parliament. When he resigns the disposition of his own interests to the wisdom of others and allots himself only a fictive presence in Parliament, Henry transforms himself into a mere commoner. Later in the play, Henry will muse "was never subject long'd to be a king / As I do long and wish to be a subject" (*2HVI* 4.8.5–6); Henry longs for a transformation he himself has already effected. Whereas the monarch attended Parliament in person and gave consent only for him- or herself, the commoners of the realm were made "representatively present" by their MPs: "in the Knights, Citizens, and Burgesses," according to John Hooker's *Order and usage* (1572), "are represented the Commons of the whole Realme, and every of these giveth not consent onely for him self . . . but for all those also for whom he is sent" (182). The monarch, by contrast, neither represented anyone in Parliament nor could be represented by anyone.[4] Elizabeth and James might speak to the Lords or Commons through various spokesmen, but not even the lord chancellor could consent on the monarch's behalf.[5]

When Henry empowers Suffolk and the other lords to act in his place, he undermines a fundamental Tudor construction of royal authority.[6] To imagine that Parliament can continue to act as if the king were present despite his physical absence is to imagine either that the king's body politic—his divinely invested authority—can be represented (and thus alienated from his body natural) or that Parliament can act without the king. But Parliament can act—can do and undo—only when the monarch joins with the other degrees or estates of the realm: in England's mixed estate, Hooker writes, "the first [degree] is the King, who in his personage is a ful and whole degree of him self, and without whome nothing can be done" (152). In the absence of the monarch—and Elizabeth and James were routinely absent from the House of Lords[7]—the Lords and the Commons could debate, draw up bills, and form committees, but doing and undoing required the royal presence: "[God] hath ordeined by lawe," according to an anonymous MP in 1567, "that all things agreed upon by the Parliament are dead and noe lawes, until she hath quickened them and given them life by her royall assent" (*PPE* 1:130).[8] In 1598, Speaker Christopher Yelverton, who knew his queen well, elaborated an analogy for Elizabeth's quickening role in parliamentary legislation:

> The picture of Pigmalion, though by art it were never so curious and exquisite, and that in all the liniamentes (almost) it had overcome nature and enticed the artisan himself, through the finenes of the faitures, to be fondly enamoured with his owne creature, yet had it not the delight of life untill Jupiter, assuming some pittie of his wofull state and travell, inspired breath into it.
>
> So these our petitions, howe fitt soever they be framed, and howe commodious soever they be imagined for your kingdome, yet be they but emptie and sencelesse shaddowes untill your Majestie takeing compassion on the common wealth . . . shall instill your most high and royall assent, to geve full life and essence unto them. (*PPE* 3:198–99)

Perhaps not even Elizabeth could live up to Yelverton's vision, but the sight of England's Jupiter enthroned in the Upper House before a joint assembly of the Lords and Commons must have been impressive. William Harrison's chapter on Parliament in *The Description of England*—available to Shakespeare in the 1587 edition of Holinshed's *Chronicles* he often had at hand while he worked on the first tetralogy—describes the crowning scene of England's mixed estate:

> [A bill is] not holden for law till the prince have given his assent. Upon the last day, therefore, of the Parliament or session, the prince cometh in person . . . into the house. . . . Where. . . . one readeth the title of every act passed in that session, and then it is noted upon them what the prince doth allow of, with these words, *Le roy veult.* If the prince like not of them, it is written upon them, *Le roy advisera.* And so those acts are dashed, as the other from thenceforth are taken and holden for law. (153–54)

The laws of England were enacted not simply by the queen-in-Parliament but, quite literally, by the queen in the Parliament House.[9]

No surrogate could blow life into the "emptie and sencelesse shaddowes" of parliamentary bills. The "king's power," Fortescue argues in *The Governance of England,* is not like a subject's power:

> it is no power to be able to alienate and put away; but it is a power to be able to have and keep to himself. . . . the holy spirits and angels, who are not able to sin, grow old, be sick, or hurt themselves have more power than we, who may harm ourselves with all these defects. So the king's power is greater, in that he may not put from himself possessions necessary for his own sustenance, than if he might put them from himself, and alienate the same to his own hurt and harm. (95)

In Shakespeare's England, the monarch's unique relation to legislation was understood to be an attribute not of her body natural but of her body politic—that is, the "mystical body" that "contains the Office, Government, and Majesty royal."[10] The properties of the body politic, unlike a common subject's consent, could not be alienated and invested in representatives. For the king's body natural, the Elizabethan jurist Edmund Plowden explained,

> is conjoined [to] his Body politic, which contains his royal Estate and Dignity and the Body politic includes the Body natural. . . . So that he has a Body natural, adorned and invested with the Estate and Dignity royal; and he has not a Body natural distinct and divided by itself from the Office and Dignity royal, but a Body natural and a Body politic together indivisible; and these two Bodies are incorporated in one Person, and make one Body and not divers. (qtd. in Kantorowicz 9)

Only at the king's demise did the two bodies finally come asunder: "Demise is a word signifying that there is a Separation of the two Bodies; and that the Body politic is conveyed over from the Body natural, now dead or removed from the Dignity royal, to another Body natural. . . . So that it signifies a Removal of the Body politic of the King of this realm from one Body natural to another."[11]

When Henry leaves the Parliament, he divides his living body natural from what Plowden terms "the Office . . . royal," and this objectification of the king's office from his person proves a fatally attractive invitation to a succession of other natural bodies eager to host the body politic Henry has left hovering in the Parliament at Bury. Warwick and Clarence hope to rule as Henry's representatives; York and Edward seek the crown itself, and they express their monarchic ambitions as a desire to reverse Henry's division of himself from the law. Thus, York, contemplating the weak king he would topple, admires his own strength: "Here is a hand to hold a sceptre up, / And with the same to act controlling laws" (*2HVI* 5.1.102–3). Edward lacks his father's Marlovian confidence, but he occasionally musters slightly defective imitations of York's vaunting rhetoric. When his brothers question one of his first royal acts, he does his best to act the *lex loquens*: "it was my will and grant; / And for this once my will shall stand for law" (*3HVI* 4.1.48–49).[12] Suffolk occasionally sounds like these usurpers—"I have been a truant in the law / And never yet could frame my will to it, / And therefore frame the law unto my will" (*1HVI* 2.4.7–10)—but he settles for the role he plays at Bury: the royal shadow.

None of the great nobles who wage the War of the Roses can begin to match the lowly soldier-artisan Jack Cade's response to Henry's parliamentary abdication. One act after Henry leaves the Parliament at Bury, Cade and a "rude multitude" from Kent take up arms to redistribute England's wealth and to eradicate literacy. Indeed, when Cade first addresses his followers and promises that "all the realm shall be in common" if they succeed (*2HVI* 4.2.70), they seem equally motivated by their desire to kill anyone who can write: the rebels' first violent act is to apprehend the clerk of Chartham because he can "write and read" (81). When the rebels, as one, condemn the clerk as a "villain and a traitor" (107), Cade orders his execution: "Away with him, I say: hang him with his pen and ink-horn about his neck" (108–9). Cade himself figures literacy as a kind of Fall, a perversion of native culture: "Thou hast most traitorously corrupted the youth of the realm," he admonishes Lord Say, "in erecting a grammar-school; and whereas, before, our forefathers had no other books but the score and the tally, thou hast caus'd printing to be us'd" (*2HVI* 4.7.30–34). Cade's solution to the nation's corruption is not merely purgative—"pull down the Savoy; others to the Inns of Court: down with them all" (4.7.1–2); he aims to replace England's culture of writing with an Edenic economy of presence and orality. When Dick the Butcher proposes to Cade that all "the laws of England may come out of [his] mouth" (5–6), Cade grandly accepts with a foundational proclamation for the new order: "I have thought upon it; it shall be so. Away! Burn all the records of the realm. My mouth shall be the Parliament of England" (12–13). In a trenchant aside, the rebel John contemplates the prospect of Cadeian legislation: "Then we are like to have biting statutes, unless his teeth be pull'd out" (4.7.15–16). Henry VI leaves Parliament and Cade swallows it: the Kentish tailor imagines an absolutist reunification of king and Parliament, *rex* and *lex*, body natural and body politic.

Dick's suggestion that Cade become a *lex loquens* is cribbed from Holinshed's narrative of the 1381 rising led by Wat Tyler, who promised his followers that "within foure daies all the lawes of England should come foorth his mouth" rather than Richard II's (Grafton 2:740).[13] But Cade's elaboration of Dick's proposal—his figure of incorporating Parliament and thus law itself—is inspired not only by Tyler's subversive usurpation of authority but also by one of Richard II's own most famous tyrannies. The account of Richard's deposition in the *Rotuli Parliamentorum* sums up the king's many affronts to Parliament and constitutional process in a remarkable charge: "Dixit expresse . . . quod Leges sue erant in ore suo, et aliquotiens in pectore suo" (3:426).[14] Grafton, Hall, and Holinshed produced nearly identical transcriptions of the "xxxv solempne articles" Parliament brought against the king, but their Richard's absolutist boast is not quite as deliciously Cadeian: "Item, he said that the lawes of the realme were in his head, and sometime in his brest, by reason of whiche fantasticall opinion, he destroied noble men and empoverished the pore commons" (Hall 10).[15] "Head" and "brest" will do. The Parliament was seeking to persuade "the commons" that Richard "was an unjust and unprofitable Prince and a tiraunte over his subjectes, and worthy to be deposed" (Hall 9): Richard was a tyrant precisely because he made no distinction between *rex* and *lex*, his own body (his head, mouth, and breast) and the body of the law. In *Henry VI, Part 2,* John's aside—"we are like to have biting statutes, unless his teeth be pull'd out"—reminds the audience that to incorporate Parliament is to be a *lex animata.* Cade is not a would-be king but a would-be tyrant.

Cade's "fantasticall" usurpation of Parliament is a precise reversal of Henry's notion that Parliament can act without the king. Elizabeth, like Richard II before her, enjoyed certain prerogative powers, but by the beginning of her reign, the sovereignty of the monarch-in-Parliament was an almost universally accepted constitutional principle.[16] In the Commons' own origin myths, English government became truly and distinctly English only after Henry III recognized that law made by the king-in-Parliament was superior to law made by the king alone. Such was the history lesson Speaker Bell recited to Elizabeth at the opening of Parliament in 1572:

> Your Highnes' noble progenitors kings of this realme not many yeares after the Conquest did publish and set forth diverse ordinances and constitucions. But the same was not confirmed by Parliament, and therefore proved perillous as well in not sufficiently providing for those which deserved well nor sufficient authoritie for punishment of them which deserved contrarie. Whereupon King Henrie the Third finding noe such perfection therein as he did desire, by the mature deliberacion and grave advise of his lordes and councell did condiscende to walke in a newe course of government, in which he determyned that all things should be provided for by authoritie of Parliament. (*PPE* 1:339)

Henry III liberates England from the legal legacy of the Norman yoke when he recognizes that parliamentary statute is superior to royal proclamation.[17] Elizabeth saw that there was little to be gained from disputing the sovereignty of the queen-in-Parliament. By contrast, James occasionally indulged himself in Richardian flights of fancy: "you all know," he told a joint deputation of the Lords and Commons in 1607, "that *Rex est lex loquens;* And you have oft heard me say, That the Kings will and intention being the speaking Law, ought to be *Luce clarius*" (*Political Works*, 161). But James's MPs didn't know this at all: in 1610, Nicholas Fuller flatly stated that "the King by his charter cannot change or alter the laws of the land in anything but by parliament" (*PP* 1610 2:154).

Cade's conflation of *lex* and *rex* would have confirmed for an Elizabethan audience the charge so many critics have laid at his door: beneath the rebel's populist rhetoric, his utopian talk of abolishing meum and tuum, lurk not only the kingly ambitions of his aristocratic sponsor the duke of York but his own desire for tyrannical power. But if Cade's translation of Tyler's rebel yell into absolutist proclamation jars with the Kentish revolt against aristocratic privilege, his Ricardian usurpation of Parliament simultaneously conjures up the tyranny both of absolute monarchism and of absolute representation. The incarnational model of political representation that I recovered in Chapter 1 suggests that Cade's seemingly ironic collapsing of a representative institution into one-man rule fulfills the ideology of representation as Elizabethan MPs themselves routinely articulated it. The representational logic elaborated by MPs such as Robert Bowyer is an absolute logic: if 50 MPs can take the place of the 450 MPs who have taken the place of three to four million people, then one MP can stand for 50 and simply become the whole commons of the realm.[18]

Why should Cade articulate his most radical bid for power by invoking Parliament, and why should the most disturbing and damaging of Henry's many abdications be constituted by his withdrawal from Parliament? I yoke these large questions together at the beginning of this chapter because I want to argue that the political concerns of the entire Henry VI trilogy emerge out of the movement from Henry's parliamentary abdication to Cade's mouth, out of the tension between Henry's spectral presence in his own kingdom and Cade's incarnation of Parliament. Stanley Wells and Gary Taylor have argued persuasively that Shakespeare wrote *Henry VI, Part 2* in 1591 and then composed the rest of Henry's sad story in a little circle: Part 3 in early 1592 and Part 1 later the same year. At the center of *Henry VI, Part 2,* Cade's double dream of absolute monarchy and absolute representation briefly fills up the vacuum Henry leaves when he flees his own Parliament. In the rest of the Henry trilogy, Cade's conjoined fantasies of power divide and are diversely reincarnated in York and Edward, who would usurp the body politic Henry leaves floating in the Parliament at Bury, and in Suffolk, Warwick, and Clarence, who seek to replace Henry not by usurping him but by representing him absolutely.

◇◇

I want to begin to trace the orthodoxy of Cade's seemingly "fantasticall opinion" that his mouth can constitute the Parliament of England by positing a third source for this image of embodiment. In *The Description of England,* Harrison gives a brief account of the House of Commons' first order of business in every Parliament: the knights and burgesses of the Lower House of Parliament "choose a Speaker, who is as it were their mouth" (151). Harrison may be borrowing here from *De republica Anglorum* (1583): the knights and burgesses, Smith warns, should "choose an able and discrete man to be as it were the mouth of them all, and to speake for and in the name of them" (51). The inevitable figure of the speaker as the mouth of the Lower House had become, by Shakespeare's time, a commonplace in political theory and parliamentary rhetoric: every speaker in the last nine Parliaments of Elizabeth's reign—from Thomas Williams in 1563 to John Croke in 1601—referred to himself at least once as the mouth of the Commons.[19] Shakespeare was certainly familiar with this aspect of the speaker's office: "God speed the parliament," Joan goads the commanders of the defeated English forces as they confer amongst themselves before the gates of Rouen, "who shall be the Speaker?" (*1HVI* 3.5.20).

The figurative relation of the speaker to the knights and burgesses is a metonymy of a metonymy: the MPs for whom he speaks are themselves, as Sir Francis Darcy styled them in 1601, "the mouthes of the moste grave and religious commons of this realme" (*PPE* 3:368). Thus, the speaker is the mouth of virtually the whole realm: "How great a charge this is," Coke confessed to Elizabeth in 1593, "to be the mouth of such a bodye as your whole commons doe represent" (*PPE* 3:65). The humbling burden of representing millions of people could also, of course, be deployed as a rhetoric of power. Charged with the unenviable task in 1563 of urging Elizabeth to marry, Thomas Williams sought strength in numbers: "We again . . . are in most humble manner come to your Majestie's presence. . . . And I, the mouth appointed for them, together with and in the name of all your most loving, naturall and obedient subjectes do present unto yow our most lowly sute and peticion" (*PPE* 1:92; cf. *PPE* 3:20). Williams is humble, the subjects are loving and obedient, and the suit is lowly; but the Commons' petition that the queen marry expresses the will of millions of people.

Not all claims for the speaker's power were so scrupulously balanced by gestures of submission. In 1601, the great parliamentarian Edward Hoby objected to Secretary Cecil's suggestion that Speaker Croke attend the lord keeper in his examination of witnesses to a disputed parliamentary election:

> Me thinckes under ffavor the motion Mr Secretarye made was good, but the fforme therin (I speake with all reverence) [was] not fittinge the state of this Howse, ffor he said Mr Speaker should attend my Lord Keeper. Attend. It is well known that the Speaker of this Howse ys the mouthe of the whole realm and that the whole . . . cominaltye of a kingdome should attend any person I see noe reason. I referre yt to the consideracion of the Howse; onlye this position I hould, that our Speaker ys to be comaunded by none, neyther to attend any but the Queene onlye. (*PPE* 3:321)

Hoby conflates being "the mouthe of the whole realm" and being "the whole cominaltye of [the] kingdome": the speaker embodies the MPs, who embody millions of people.

In Chapter 1, I argued that an incarnational model of representation helped to produce the early modern MPs' authority over the subjects they represented. Hoby deploys the same ideology to shape the MPs' political relations with the lords and the crown. For even as Hoby backs away from his pronouncement that the speaker "ys to be comaunded by none," he admits "the Queene onlye" as an exception. The economy of power Hoby posits here depends, in part, on the sheer force of numbers: the great lord keeper is one person; the "knight of any shire here," an MP boasted in 1593, "representeth many thousands" (qtd. in Loach 148). The MPs' power, then, is a function of representative multiplicity: the knights and burgesses, according to Hooker's translation of the *Modus tenendi Parliamentum*, "represent the whole communalties of England wheras th'other estates doo represent but their owne persons" (142).

"But their owne persons": the lords were keenly aware of the disabling import of representationalism for the nonrepresentative body sitting in the Upper House. In 1572, they were scandalized when they learned that Robert Snagge, one of the most radical MPs of his time, had claimed that the members of the House of Lords "had not to doe with the common wealth, but that we in the common howse had onely the care thereof; they cam for their owne persons only. . . . Hereuppon he sheweth that he declared as it were the state of Parliament, that in the same the Queene and the noble men represented their own voices only, the knights and burgesses of the lower house represented all the commynalty of the realme" (*PPE* 1:403). One might have expected the lords, who came to Parliament in their own august persons, to disparage the MPs as mere shadows of the absent and lowly commons. Instead, the lords' fury over Snagge's speech indicates the increasing political capital of representativeness: those great lordly bodies who "represent[ed] but their owne persons" complained to the Commons that in the "state of parliament" elaborated by Snagge "they were made shaddowes, unable to deale in matters of common weale" (403).

Even Elizabeth was subject to invidious comparisons between representative and nonrepresentative persons. The monarch, as we have seen, was the indispensable foundation of Parliament: "The first [degree] is the King, who in his personage is a ful and whole degree of him self, and without whome nothing can be done" (Hooker 152). But in 1593, Coke claimed that the Commons could hold their own not only with the lords but with the monarch as well: his "Majesty and the Nobles being every one a great person, represented but themselves; but . . . [the] Commons though they were but inferior men, yet every one of them represented a thousand of men" (D'Ewes 516). The monarch's unequalled sufficiency—"the King . . . is a ful and whole degree of him self"—was also a deficiency.[20]

During Elizabeth's reign, the natural limitations of the royal body became a staple of Commons origin myths. In 1571, for example, an anonymous MP argued that the House of Commons was a necessary supplement to Elizabeth's imperfect knowledge of her own country: "Howe may her Majestie or howe may this court knowe," he asked his fellow MPs,

> the state of her frontiers, or who shall make report of the portes, or howe every quarter, shiere, or countrey is in state? Wee who nether have seene Barwicke or St Michaelle's Mount can but blindly guess at them, albeit wee looke on the mapps that come from thence, or letters of instructions sent from thence: some one whom observacion, experience and due consideracion of that countrey hath taught can more perfectly open what shall in question thereof growe, and more effectually reason thereuppon, then the skillfullest otherwise whatsoever. And that they should bee the very inhabitors of the severall counties of this kingdome who should bee here in tymes certaine imployed, doubtles it was the true meaninge of the auncient kings and our forfathers who first began and established this court might be founde. (*PPE* 1:227)

This vision of the Commons as a living map of England reaches a kind of pictorial fulfillment in figure 3, a beautiful engraving of the Commons from 1640. On all sides, the MPs are surrounded by maps: on the right and left, bird's-eye-view plans of England's enfranchised boroughs; in the lower left corner, a map of the shires; and in the lower right corner, an elaborate map and view of London. The MPs we see busy at work inside St. Stephen's make the absent places we see depicted on the borders present in the Commons' chamber. By contrast, the armorial borders of Ronald Elstrack's 1604 engraving of James I in the House of Lords (fig. 4) function simply as a key to the persons we see inside the House of Lords.

The borders of the 1640 engraving make it more provocative than earlier representations of the Commons (figs. 1–2): the knights and burgesses, rather than Charles I, embody England. It would be a Whiggish mistake to construct the 1571 speech as proto-revolutionary, but our MP's blunt claim that "her Majestie" is incapable of knowing the state of the entire realm is daring enough: Henrician MPs did not volunteer inventories of their king's natural defects. If our MP's assertion of Elizabeth's natural weaknesses was novel and radical, his account of the Commons' representative operations was, by contrast, quite conservative. The occasion of his speech was a debate about the rise of carpetbagging in borough elections: of the 352 burgesses elected in 1571, 82 resided in the boroughs they represented; 125 lived in the county; 138 lived outside the county altogether.[21] When our MP reminded his colleagues that "the old president of Parliament writtes doe teach us that of every . . . burroughe their owne burgesses, should bee" (227), he was swimming against a flood tide.[22] Big social and political players were now accustomed to using boroughs, typically beholden to lords of the manor and other powerful figures, to place favorites, cousins, younger sons, and valued servants of the crown. Moreover, our MP's theory of parliamentary representation was fossilized: indeed, set against the mystical claims for representation made by so many of his fellows, it seems positively antirepresentational. Maps and reports, he worries, are wholly inadequate representations of shires and boroughs because they are, well, representations—mere signs of absent terrains and towns. Only a man who comes from and knows a place can represent it, and the same principle extends to the representation of persons: "And I meane this wholly to noe other end," he concludes, "but since wee deale universally for all sortes and all places, that there bee here of all sortes and all countreyes" (*PPE* 1:228).

This literalist construction of representation—the Commons can represent all sorts of people and places only if all sorts of people from all sorts of places serve as MPs—lost out to the absolute construction of representation discussed at the end of Chapter 1: according to Robert Bowyer, a mere handful of men could, through the secular magic of representation, make the entire realm and its far-flung inhabitants present in the House of Commons. The crusader against carpetbaggers does not attribute magical properties to his fellow MPs: the monarchic body is limited because single; the Commons can do what the queen cannot only because it is a body comprised of 438 bodies.

Theorists of absolute representation, by contrast, argued that the monarchic body was limited—perhaps even defective—because it could not represent other bodies, and the representational inadequacies of the royal body were the point of departure for the radical theorists' own institutional origin myth. In 1566, an MP defending the Commons' competence to propose a successor to the queen acknowledged that Elizabeth was the supreme, if slightly detached, head of the nation:

> The office of the head consisteth in these two pointes: first, carefullie to devise and put in execucion all things most commodious for the whole bodie and every member therof; then, wisely to forsee and prevent the evills that may come to any part therof. . . . This king, this head, with the consent of the whole bodie and through the providence of God, weying that his eye and eare cannot be in every corner of his kingdome and dominions at one instant to view and hearken out the benefittes or inconveniences that might growe to the head, bodie, or any member therof, hath established this honorable counsell of everie part of the same absent from the king's eye and eare, the which is termed a parliament. (*PPE* 1:129–30)

Because the monarch's natural constitution is merely human, the nation's political constitution supplements it with a political body: "Certaine it is that *the law hath made* this counsell the eyes, the eares, and the tongue of the prince and realme" (*PPE* 1:136; emphasis added).

To this point, our two critics of the princely body seem in complete harmony, but the MP arguing for a succession bill eventually claims that the individual representative possesses precisely the powers he claims are absent from the regal body. In his peroration, he articulates the needs not of his home shire or borough but of "every corner of [the] kingdom" from Barwick to St. Michael's Mount:

> I speake for all England, yea, and for the noble English nation. . . . Therfore noble England, being now in great distresse (as is before sayd) it crieth out in most solefull wise by me, the poor and simple advocate therof, sayinge: "Helpe, o yee my noble, faithfull counsellors and subiectes inheritors, help this my feeble and weake estate that I may long live and be preserved to your use"—Mr Speaker, oh that noble England should intreate us here to performe it to our owne uses—"for I have noe meane to help me but you, and to that you were especially borne; and there is no time and place to heale my sicknes but this." (*PPE* 1:137, 138–39)

"I speke for all England": our speaker's mythology of the Commons' origins begins in the insufficiency of the natural body and ends in the infinite capacity of the representative body. The argument from the limitations of the royal natural body—because even a monarch's "eye and eare cannot be in every corner of his kingdome and domains at one instant," the Commons must supplement his deficiency—is ironically supplanted by an absolutist account of representation according to which a single MP might claim, after Jack Cade, "My mouth shall be the Parliament of England."

The monarch cannot "be in every corner of his kingdom and dominions at one instant," because he is not God. The political representative achieves a version of omnipresence neither divinely nor naturally but artificially: he is everywhere in the realm at once because he makes the entire realm present in himself. The notion of artificial personhood is implicit in the distinction between private and public persons that MPs routinely invoked when defending their privilege of freedom from arrest: in 1571, for example, George Carleton protested the arrest of William Strickland on the grounds that "hee nowe was not a private man but to supply the roome, person and place of a multitude especially chosen and therfor sent" (*PPE* 1:238). To arrest Strickland was to arrest the "multitude" his public person made present in the Commons. We find, however, the richest Elizabethan anticipations of Hobbes in elaborations of the MP's capacity to speak for the absent people. In his natural person, the knight or burgess can speak as himself and, perhaps, for his country or town and for his "sort." But when the knight or burgess speaks as thousands or millions of men and women—who may or not share his "place" or "sort"—he does so as an artificial person, as a species of actor. Thus, in 1601, William Hakewill spoke against a bill to limit credit even though its provisions suited his "perticular" financial interests.

> the safest course this bill offers to me ffor my perticuler. But the greate mischeife that will redound by it to the commons is that which makes me speak. . . . We must laye downe the respectes of our owne persons, and put on others' and their affections ffor whome wee speake, ffor they speake by us. If the matter which is spoken of touche the poore, then thincke me a poore man. He that speakes, sometymes, he must be a lawyer, sometymes a paynter, sometymes a marchante, some tymes a meane artifycer. (*PPE* 3:432–33)

Because the bill offers "the safest course" for Hakewill himself, he will speak against the bill not in his own voice but in the voice of the "meane artifycer" whose personal interests would be damaged by restrictions on debt and credit. We are worlds away from the champion of residency requirements, who concluded his speech in 1571 by suggesting that an MP can play only himself: "Since we deale universally for all sortes and all places, there [should] bee here all sortes and all countrys" (*PPE* 1:228). To his old-fashioned mind, a lawyer could no more "play" a painter than a resident of Warwick could represent Rutland.

Elizabeth I never, to my knowledge, directly challenged the MPs' claims to speak for and as the common people of the realm; perhaps her confidence in her constitutional powers and in the power of her own rhetorics—Virgin Queen, Mother of the Realm, and so on—made her less likely to dispute the developing ideology of the House of Commons. It is telling both that James I was less sanguine on this point and that he often chose to attack the ideology of representation rather than try to trump it with some aspect of monarchic ideology.[23] In a speech delivered to both Houses on March 31, 1607, James turned a biting critique of parliamentary speechmaking—too rhetorical, too crafted, smacked too much of university training—into an attack on the MPs' status as public persons. James's own speech, he assured the MPs, would be substantive if inelegant: "I am forced hereunto by necessitie, my place calling me to action . . . my thoughts busied with the publique care of you all, where every one of you having but himselfe, and his owne private to thinke of, are at more leisure to make studied speeches" (*Political Works,* 160). James could be far more direct. In 1607, he chastised the MPs for speaking as if they knew the minds of their constituents: "Impossible it was for them to know all that would be propounded here; much more all those answers that you would make" (qtd. in Kenyon 21). In 1610, an even more frustrated James admonished the MPs that they did "not so represent the whole commons of the realm as the shadow doth the body but only representatively." James was behind the curve: Hooker, Bowyer, Bacon and others had long been figuring the Commons not as a perfect shadow of the body but as the body itself. The people were the shadows of a body that had taken their place.

James should have turned to an early work by the playwright who was now his liveried servant: in *Henry VI, Part 2,* the king would have found a far more effective and rather wittier attack on artificial personhood and political representation. During the very few moments Jack Cade silently considers Dick the Butcher's suggestion that the laws of England come out of his mouth, John Holland and Smith the Weaver are pondering it too:

> JOHN (*aside to his fellows*): Mass, 'twill be a sore law then, for he was thrust in the mouth with a spear, and 'tis not whole yet.
> WEAVER (*aside to John*): Nay, John, it will be a stinking law, for his breath stinks with eating of toasted cheese.
> CADE: I have thought upon it; it shall be so. Away! Burn all the records of the realm. My mouth shall be the Parliament of England.
> JOHN (*aside to his fellows*). Then we are like to have biting statutes, unless his teeth be all pulled out.
> CADE: And henceforward all things shall be in common.
> (*2HVI* 4.7.7–17)

Many critics have argued that Shakespeare sets up Cade's followers as a mob of unthinking, easily swayed buffoons.[24] But Holland and Smith toss off as comic asides a thoroughly devastating debunking of the fiction of the artificial person. The entire ideology I have been recovering here and in Chapter 1 hinges on artificial personhood, on the notion that the representative can speak as the other. But the rebels know that Cade will speak neither as a butcher nor a weaver—nor as "a lawyer . . . a paynter . . . a marchante . . . [or] a meane artifycer"—but in his own "perticuler" person. The statutory products of Cadeian legislation will be bloody, biting, and cheesy materializations of his all-too-natural body. Cade, that is, is now an epitome of the Parliament he has swallowed: he is what he ate.[25]

◇◇

Cade's usurpation of parliamentary legislation is the tyrannical answer to Henry's abdication of the monarch's special role in Parliament. But Cade's reduction of Parliament to a single person is also an epitome of Shakespeare's own very curious representation of the Lancastrian House of Commons. By the time of Henry VI's reign, the Commons had become a regular partner in Parliament. In the Tudor chronicles of Henry VI's reign, "Parliament" almost always designates a gathering of the king and the three medieval estates—that is, prelates, the lords temporal, and the commons. (John Hooker and other post-Reformation parliamentary theorists reconceived the three parliamentary estates as king, lords, and commons.) In Hall's *The Union of the two noble & illustre famelies of Lancastre & Yorke* (1548), for example, the duke of York hopes to legitimize the terms of Henry's surrender at St. Albans by calling "a great assemble of thre estates, commonly called a Parliament" (233).[26] In Shakespeare's version of this event, there is no mention at all of the third estate (*3HVI* 1.1), nor do we see or hear anything of the Commons when Parliament restores Richard Plantagenet to his titles (*1HVI* 3.1.149–77).[27]

Shakespeare's omission of the Commons' participation in the Parliament at Bury is especially puzzling. Between the end of the Parliament (*2HVI* 3.1.330) and the beginning of the Cade rebellion (4.2.1), Shakespeare tells the story of Suffolk's fall: Suffolk's men murder Gloucester (3.2.1–14); the next day, Henry and his court discover that Gloucester has died (3.2.15–33); the common people of Bury demand an account of Gloucester's death (3.2.122–35), and, set on by Warwick and Salisbury, threaten to rush in and murder Suffolk if Henry will not comply with their demand that he be executed or banished (236–90); Henry banishes Suffolk (297–99), who is murdered by wonderfully patriotic pirates (4.1.140). In Shakespeare's sources, the House of Commons, reprising the role it had played in bringing down Richard II's "caterpillars," takes the lead in prosecuting Suffolk.[28] In both Grafton's *Chronicle at Large* (1569) and Hall's *Union,* the common people blame Suffolk for their beloved Gloucester's death, but the House of Commons presses the case against the great duke: "the Commons of the nether house put up to the king and Lordes, many articles of treason, misprison and misdemeanour agaynst the Duke of Suffolke" (Hall 217; cf. Grafton 1:638).[29]

Shakespeare retains the popular unrest sparked by Gloucester's death but entirely omits the House of Commons' role in Suffolk's downfall. As Henry laments his uncle's death, Warwick, Salisbury, and the people burst into the court:

> *Noise within. Enter the Earls of Warwick and Salisbury with many commons.*
>
> WARWICK: It is reported, mighty sovereign,
> That good Duke Humphrey traitorously is murdered

By Suffolk and the Cardinal Beaufort's means.
The commons, like an angry hive of bees
That want their leader, scatter up and down
And care not who they sting in his revenge.
Myself have calmed their spleenful mutiny,
Until they hear the order of his death.
KING: That he is dead, good Warwick, 'tis too true.
But how he died God knows, not Henry.
Enter his chamber, view his breathless corpse,
And comment then upon his sudden death.
WARWICK: That shall I do, my liege. —Stay, Salisbury,
With the rude multitude till I return.
(*2HVI* 3.2.121.sd–135)

Shakespeare elides the House of Commons from his history, but the people's participation in Suffolk's banishment is hardly unmediated. Even when the commoners are on stage, Warwick speaks for them. The "rude multitude," moreover, never quite return to the stage after Warwick sends them off under his father's supervision. While the people wait in the wings, Warwick examines Gloucester's corpse and then challenges Suffolk to try their dispute by sword. As Warwick and Suffolk's duel moves on- and offstage, the people become restless and twice shout "Down with Suffolk! Down with Suffolk!" (236, 243). After the second cry, Salisbury returns to the stage but orders the commoners to remain outside the royal presence: "Sirs, stand apart. The King shall know your mind" (244).

Dread lord, the commons sends you word by me,
Unless Lord Suffolk straight be done to death,
Or banished fair England's territories,
They will by violence tear him from your palace
And torture him with grievous ling'ring death.
They say, by him the good Duke Humphrey died;
They say, in him they fear your highness' death;
And mere instinct of love and loyalty,
Free from a stubborn opposite intent,
As being thought to contradict your liking,
Makes them thus forward in his banishment.

. . . .

And therefore do they cry, though you forbid,
That they will guard you, whe'er you will or no,
From such fell serpents as false Suffolk is,
With whose envenomed and fatal sting

> Your loving uncle, twenty times his worth,
> They say, is shamefully bereft of life.
> (*2HVI* 3.2.245–55, 266–71)

Salisbury styles himself the representative of the people of Bury—"the commons sends you word by me"—and in virtue of his representation the people themselves are reduced to an offstage chorus: "An answer from the King, my lord of Salisbury!" (272); "An answer from the King, or we will all break in!" (281–82).

Annabel Patterson has argued that Salisbury is a scrupulous spokesman for the commons of Bury:

> The rhetorical "They say" formula identifies Salisbury as a ventriloquist, while the dramatic situation ensures his recognition as the people's sincere advocate. Their protest is, therefore, both morally authoritative and, as petitioning from strength, effective. . . . With this conditional approval of popular protest in the play—conditional, that is, on rightful motives, a basic loyalty to the crown, and a proper spokesman—we can now turn to the . . . Cade uprising. Compared to Salisbury, Cade fails every test for the proper popular spokesman. (*Shakespeare and the Popular Voice,* 48)

Patterson's generous account of Salisbury rests on her concept of "ventriloquism": "the most important evidence, finally, of the popular voice raised in articulate protest has come down to us by way of ventriloquism, in the texts of the dominant culture"; even a hostile "ventriloquist must himself utter, in order to refute them, ethical and pathetic claims whose force may linger beyond his powers of persuasion" (41–42), and a sympathetic ventriloquist brings us closer still to the voices of the voiceless.[30] As she translates epistemological representationalism—historians can discover the people's words on the mediating tongues and pens of their ventriloquists—into the political field, Patterson makes representation by "a proper spokesman" a necessary condition of legitimate popular protest as Shakespeare defined it.

Casting the earl of Salisbury in the role of "proper popular spokesman" would seem to hitch paternalism and liberalism in an unlikely marriage, but paternalism, at least in Shakespeare's plays, is always either a cause or an effect of representation, the defining political structure of liberalism. Salisbury is typical of Shakespearean characters, high and low, who speak for the commons: deceitful, ambitious, self-serving, and contemptuous of the people he represents. Salisbury claims that the people demand Suffolk's death or banishment because they loved Gloucester and want to save King Henry (246–47):

"They say, by him the good Duke Humphrey died; / They say, in him they fear your highness' death" (250–51).[31] Salisbury and Warwick bring down Suffolk in the people's name, but they shed no tears for good Duke Humphrey, and they aim to overthrow Henry rather than protect him: with Gloucester out of the way, Suffolk is now the most formidable obstacle to their plot to set Richard, duke of York, on the throne.[32] In act 2, scene 2 of *Henry VI, Part 2,* Salisbury and Warwick listen approvingly to York's genealogical case for his title to the throne (1–51); declare him king ("Long live our sovereign Richard, England's king!" [63]); and express no concern when York gleefully anticipates the moment when his "sword [will] be stain'd / With heart-blood of the house of Lancaster" (2.2.65–66). Warwick and Salisbury may genuinely believe that Richard's claim is just, but their own ambitions surely move them to foreswear their loyalty to Henry:

> WARWICK: My heart assures me that the Earl of Warwick
> Shall one day make the Duke of York a king.
> YORK: And Neville, this I do assure myself—
> Richard shall live to make the Earl of Warwick
> The greatest man in England but the king.
> (*2HVI* 2.2.78–82)

When he wrote the other parts of his trilogy, Shakespeare was unsparingly harsh in his treatment of Warwick: in *Part 1,* Warwick is the first to pluck a white rose for York, even though he clearly knows that Richard's ambition may spell civil war and Henry's violent overthrow (2.4.36, 116–27); in *Part 3,* Warwick eventually abandons York's son Edward, whom he has made king, and throws his support back to the Lancastrian cause. Warwick's reward for this flip-flop is a marriage match between his daughter and Henry VI's son. In the context of the entire cycle, then, Warwick's original decision to support York looks even more like a base quid pro quo.

Suffolk *is* an enemy of the people: he snarls at a humble petitioner who seeks relief "Against the Duke of Suffolk, for enclosing the commons of Melford" (*2HVI* 1.3.22–23);[33] plots the murder of the people's beloved Duke Humphrey; and sneers at the "rude unpolished hinds" of Bury. Salisbury and Warwick, however, manipulate the people's passionate hatred of Suffolk for their own self-interested ends: the civil war the Nevilles foment will consume thousands of lowly commoners, but, on Shakespeare's account, it is fought only to gratify noble ambition and to firm up or resettle the distribution of power among the great. Shakespeare's audience would not have expected the welfare of the commons to precipitate or shape a dynastic struggle such as the Wars of the Roses, but the lowly people and their troubles keep bubbling up into the space of grand history: enclosure sparked popular protest in both fifteenth-century England and Shakespeare's own time; Simpcox's wife assures Henry that she and her husband staged their miracle play "for pure need" (2.1.159); and Cade's rebels rehearse a litany of complaints about their "gentleman" oppressors. On the one hand, the commoners and their troubles never figure in the motivations or even in the rhetoric of the great magnates who wage the Wars of the Roses: neither the Yorkists nor the Lancastrians invoke reform or the common good. On the other hand, Shakespeare makes much of the conflict's dire consequences for the commoners.[34] Of all the tableaux of death and grief that it produces, two common soldiers—one grieving over his fallen father, the other over his fallen son—act out the cycle's greatest spectacle of loss and, despite the lowliness of the protagonists, tragedy. In this entirely gratuitous scene in *Part 3,* Shakespeare figures the civil war as a pointless disaster for the common people. As Henry, who has left the field, looks on from a "molehill," one of the king's soldiers discovers that he has slain his own father:

> Ill blows the wind that profits nobody.
> This man, whom hand to hand I slew in fight,
> May be possessed with some store of crowns;
> And I, that haply take them from him now,
> May yet ere night yield both my life and them
> To some man else, as this dead man doth me.
> [*He removes the dead man's helmet*]
> Who's this? O God! It is my father's face
> Whom in this conflict I, unwares, have killed.
> O, heavy times, begetting such events!
> From London by the King was I pressed forth;
> My father, being the Earl of Warwick's man,
> Came on the part of York, pressed by his master.
> (3*HVI* 2.5.55–66)

The operatic discovery of parricide depends, of course, on the anonymity of common soldiers ("This man," "some man else," "this dead man"), who bear no legible signs—no crests, insignias, or coats of arms—of their identities; by contrast, the great men who meet so often on the field of battle in the Henriad always recognize each other. The highly personal combats between opposing nobles remind us of how personal the stakes of the Wars of the Roses are for them: when York and Clifford square off, the one hazards his life for a crown, the other to maintain his position as one of the most powerful men in the realm. The unfortunate son figures the spoil of a few crowns, rather than a particular settlement of crown and kingdom, as the only interest that the war might hold for a man such as himself. His even bleaker conjecture that "some man else" may soon be rifling his pockets suggests that this woeful grain of cannon fodder—"food for powder, food for powder," Falstaff says of the men he "press[es]" into service (*1HIV* 4.2.65–66 and 4.2.10–14)—recognizes that the war is a meaningless plague for the commons. This deadly circulation—a few coins endlessly passing back and forth between Henry's soldiers and York's, each exchange marking a death—is immediately embodied through an imaginative displacement. Still atop his hillock, Henry watches a second "piteous spectacle": a soldier enters with a body, and, as he searches the corpse for "gold," discovers that he has killed his own son (2.5.79–93). "Ill blows the wind that profits nobody": it seems at first that the son cites the aphorism to justify robbing a corpse, but he is condemning the Wars of the Roses.

Small wonder that the great magnates on both sides must compel the service of their troops: "From London by the King was I pressed forth; / My father, being the Earl of Warwick's man, / Came on the part of York, pressed by his master." Cade has no power to press men into his service; his followers flock to him willingly because he promises a war that will profit them:

> All the realm shall be in common . . .
> (*2HVI* 4.2.70)
>
> And you that love the commons, follow me!
> Now show yourselves men—'tis for liberty.
> We will not leave one lord, one gentleman—
> (4.2.181–83)
>
> And henceforward all things shall be in common.
> (4.7.17)

We don't have to take it on faith that Cade felicitously represents the desires of his followers: they greet his proclamations with ringing acclamations; and before we ever lay eyes on Cade, some of the rebels anticipate the leveling that he will promise:

> FIRST REBEL: I tell thee, Jack Cade the clothier means to dress the commonwealth, and turn it, and set a new nap upon it.
> SECOND REBEL: So he had need, for 'tis threadbare. Well, I say it was never a merry world in England since gentlemen came up.
> (*2HVI* 4.2.5–10).

Warwick and Salisbury claim that the commons of Bury are on the verge of revolt because Suffolk has done in Gloucester. Perhaps this is true, though all the commons say is "down with Suffolk." Cade's communist rhetoric and the rebels' exchange reminds us of a different basis for the commons' hatred of Suffolk: he is an encloser and no friend of the commons. It takes Cade, that improper popular spokesmen, to address such issues.

Cade, of course, betrays the populist, communist rhetoric that so excites the rebels: "All the realm shall be in common. . . . And when I am king, as king I will be. . . . there shall be no money. All shall eat and drink on my score, and I will apparel them all in one livery, that they may agree like brothers, and worship me their lord" (*2HVI* 4.2.70–77). Cade, then, is a precursor of Gonzalo: "the later end of his commonwealth forgets the beginning" (*Tempest* 2.1.158). After Cade swallows Parliament, he reaffirms his foundational promise: "henceforward all things shall be in common" (4.7.16). All things will be in common, but always just a little more in common for Cade: "there shall not a maid be married, but she shall pay to me her maiden-head" (4.7.118–20). This "biting statute" bears the mark of Cade's tyrannical teeth: on the other side of communist liberation from meum and tuum lies the "droit du seigneur," the Tarquinian lord's rejection of any distinction between public and private, of the subject's right to any private property. Unlike the noble spokesmen for the commons, however, Cade hides little or nothing from his followers: Cade doesn't boast loudly about his ties to the duke of York, but neither does he make much effort to deny them. More to the point, Cade seems to have forgotten that he is York's trial balloon: when a messenger informs Henry that "Jack Cade proclaims himself Lord Mortimer . . . And calls your grace usurper, openly, / And vows to crown himself in Westminster" (4.4.27–30), we must wonder whether Cade now seeks power for himself.

We never have to ask ourselves if Jack Cade accurately represents the will and the words of his followers, because he is not a ventriloquist. Cade's power rests entirely and openly on the people's support, but he never claims to speak for them, never silences them, never pushes them offstage. Even when, as the rebellion's leader, Cade addresses the Staffords, Lord Saye, and Buckingham, he neither explicitly styles himself the representative of the people nor speaks in the grammar of representation ("they say," "by me," "we").[35] Cade's relation to the people is transparent: he articulates his aims, proposes plans of action, and submits himself in his own person to the people in theirs. If they don't like what they hear, they are free to abandon him, and eventually they do. Cade practices a politics of total presence. What happened, then, to Cade's incorporation of Parliament? Cade reveals the contradictions of parliamentary representation, but he also transcends them: incorporating Parliament into his own person, Cade effaces any mediation between himself and the people he leads. As we shall see in Chapter 4, certain aspects of Cade's politics find their way into the Shakespearean Caesar's brand of popular dictatorship: as with that titanic figure from antiquity, Cade's power resides in the people, and he never hesitates to put his fate in their hands.

PART TWO

Political Representation in Shakespeare's Rome

3 "Their tribune and their trust"

Political Representation, Property, and Rape in *Titus Andronicus* and *The Rape of Lucrece*

Shakespeare framed the lurid revenge plot of *Titus Andronicus* (1594)—the rape and maiming of Lavinia and her father Titus's subsequent destruction of Rome's imperial family—with two popular elections: at the beginning of the play, the people's "voices . . . create / Lord Saturninus Rome's great emperor" (1.1.230–32); the play ends when "the common voice" hails Lucius Andronicus as Saturninus's successor (5.3.139).[1] *Titus* has never been taken very seriously as a political play, but these imperial elections, for which Shakespeare seems to have had no specific source, are quite remarkable: at the very moments Saturninus and Lucius are empowered by the "voices and applause of every sort, / Patricians and plebeians" (1.1.230–31), the stage is haunted by the silence of the people.[2] In both scenes, tribunes and patricians solicit the people's voices and proceed as if their appeals have been greeted by thunderous general acclamations, but, in fact, the people never utter a word. To be represented in Titus's Rome is not to gain a voice in state affairs but to lose one's tongue. Muteness, it goes without saying, is deeply resonant in *Titus:* Lavinia's rapists rip out her tongue. In *Titus,* then, muteness is the shared condition of the victim of rape and the victims of political representation, and, as we shall see, the elections anticipate and repeat Lavinia's rape and make her awful plight fully intelligible.

The political narrative of the play has been dismissed on two grounds: some critics find the young Shakespeare's representation of Roman politics a hopelessly incoherent amalgamation of historically distinct institutions and practices; others argue that the first election scene is irrelevant to Titus's tragic fall, the rape of Lavinia, and the play's intersecting revenge plots.[3] C. L. Barber and Richard Wheeler partially synthesize these positions: Shakespeare, they suggest, "does not succeed in projecting a Roman state . . . because his interest is so intensely on family matters" (127). I will return to the notion that Shakespeare's first real stab at representing Roman political culture is a haphazard mix of emperors, senators, and tribunes, but I want to begin by addressing Barber and Wheeler's claim that *Titus* is an immature tragedy because it lacks "the sort of complex interpenetration of social with family and sexual action which [Shakespeare] could control so marvelously later" (136).[4] Shakespeare's interweaving of public matters and "family matters," which Barber has so brilliantly explored, is undoubtedly more deeply moving in the later histories and tragedies, but the social and the familial, the political and the sexual, the public and the private are bound together as completely and complexly in *Titus* as they are in *Hamlet, Lear,* the second tetralogy or any other of Shakespeare's mature plays.

The rape of Lavinia—the very event that seems to jolt our attention away from affairs of state and to plunge us into a world of sexual violence, patriarchal oppression, misogyny, and private revenge—leads us back to, not away from, "high" politics. Indeed, the logic of interpenetration shapes the action of *Titus:* private considerations move Titus to engineer the election of Saturninus; the election of Saturninus is the positive condition for the rape of Lavinia; and the rape of Lavinia precipitates Saturninus's downfall and the subsequent election of Lucius. Shakespeare's narrative inspiration here is "the republican rape topos," in Stephanie Jed's fine phrase, in Roman historiography: in a tradition established principally by Livy and well known to Elizabethans, the rape of a chaste Roman woman by an autocrat sparks popular outrage and occasions a transition from monarchy or dictatorship to emergent or resurgent republicanism.[5] In Shakespeare's own *Rape of Lucrece* (1594), for example, Sextus Tarquinius reproduces his father Lucius's political tyranny as sexual tyranny when he rapes Lucrece, whose heart, beating under Sextus's oppressive hand, is a "poor citizen" (465).[6] After Lucrece commits suicide, the public display of her raped body "so moved" the people that "with one consent and a general acclamation the Tarquins were all exiled, and the state government changed from kings to consuls" (*Rape of Lucrece,* "The Argument," 33–36). In a later episode in Roman history, the autocratic Appius, one of the *decemviri* who suspended republican institutions from 451 to 449 B.C., instructs his crony Marcus Claudius to claim that Virginia, the daughter of a republican-minded centurion, is the child of one of Marcus's household slaves and thus his property. Appius plans to rape Virginia as soon as Marcus takes possession of her. To prevent this defilement, Virginius murders his daughter; Virginius and Virginia's betrothed, Icilius, then lead a popular uprising that restores the tribunate and republican freedoms.

In *The Rape of Lucrece,* Shakespeare introduces a fundamental and very English paradox into the heart of the republican rape topos. According to Livy and the early modern writers who closely followed his *Ab urbe condita,* Sextus's rape of Lucrece is a figure for Lucius Tarquinius's political tyranny: the father reigns without the people's consent; the son penetrates Lucrece without her consent.[7] Under the Tarquins, all Romans are Lucreces: subject to the unrestrained desires and unfettered demands of their tyrant master, they are nothing more than slaves. In William Painter's *The palace of pleasure* (1566), for example, Lucius Junius Brutus suggests to the people that in "the abominable Rape of *Lucrece,* committed by *Sextus Tarquinius*" they should recognize their own condition: "the pride and insolent behaviour of the kyng, the miserie and drudgerie of the people, and how thei, which in tyme paste were victors and Conquerours, were made men of warre, Artificers and Labourers" (Biii[r]). The popular revolt begins when the people "abrogate . . . and depose . . . Tarquinius" (Biii[r]) and ends when the people's consent is established as the basis of legitimate sovereignty: in the new republic, popularly elected consuls replace kings. Shakespeare, I believe, had his doubts about the ideological relation Livy seems to posit between Lucrece's rape and the winning of republican liberties: women, after all, did not vote in consular elections.[8] In *Lucrece,* Shakespeare intensifies this irony when he translates Livy's liberation politics into the materialist idiom of English political discourse: when Elizabethan and Jacobean MPs invoked the subject's freedoms and liberties, they were speaking, more often than not, about the subject's right to own property and to consent to its alienation. In Shakespeare's poem, Lucrece's very Elizabethan husband and father cannot conceive of Sextus's assault as a violation of her freedom of choice: Collatine and Lucretius instead treat both Sextus's sexual violation of Lucrece and her subsequent suicide as crimes against their property. Kings become tyrants, on Collatine and Lucretius's account, when they ignore distinctions between public and private, meum and tuum. The republican revolution Shakespeare's Brutus instigates is a defense of property rights; it is a defense, more particularly, of slavery.

The critique of republican historiography Shakespeare develops in *Titus* is still more radical. And yet the republican rape topos would not seem to be Shakespeare's concern in *Titus:* several characters identify Lavinia as a type of Lucrece or Virginia, but the political context of Lavinia's rape is all wrong.

Tarquin ascends the throne without soliciting the people's voices: "Lucius Tarquinius, for his excessive pride surnamed Superbus, after he had caused his father-in-law Servius Tullius to be cruelly murdered, and, contrary to the Roman laws and customs, not requiring or staying for the people's suffrages . . . possessed himself of the kingdom" (*Rape of Lucrece,* "The Argument," 1–5). Saturninus, by contrast, is elected by the people's voices. Shakespeare's circular narrative—an election leads to a rape that leads to an election—is an imaginative and ideological critique of the republican rape topos rather than a variation on source materials. In Livy, election is the logical antidote to a tyranny that is defined by its contempt for consent: tyrannical rule in the absence of consent expresses itself as rape and is remedied by the institution of elected authority. Shakespeare interposes Lavinia's rape between two elections to demonstrate that elective politics—like rape and autocratic tyranny—can deprive the "poor citizen" of voice. The Livian remedy for Tarquinism, Shakespeare suggests in *Titus,* is another form of the disease.[9]

◇◇

Titus begins with a cataclysmic political conflict: Rome's emperor has died, and his sons Saturninus and Bassianus both seek their father's crown. This fraternal rivalry does not resemble the kinds of succession struggle familiar to us from Shakespeare's English histories: Bassianus is not a bastard pretender; he does not base his challenge on an interpretation of succession law; nor does he scheme to eliminate relatives who stand between him and the crown. Instead, Bassianus questions the legitimacy of lineal succession itself. Saturninus, the eldest son, predictably claims the throne according to the laws of hereditary monarchy and primogeniture:

> SATURNINUS: Noble patricians, patrons of my right,
> Defend the justice of my cause with arms.
> And countrymen, my loving followers,
> Plead my successive title with your swords.
> I am his first-born son that was the last
> That ware the imperial diadem of Rome.
> (1.1.1–6)

Bassianus, by contrast, appeals not to "noble patricians" and genealogical credentials but to all Romans and merit: "let desert in pure election shine, / And, Romans, fight for freedom in your choice" (1.1.16–17). The contest to succeed the old emperor, then, turns on a debate between two radically divergent accounts of legitimate political authority.[10]

That debate is resolved almost as soon as it begins: immediately after Saturninus and Bassianus stake their respective claims to the throne, the tribune Marcus Andronicus makes it clear that the people of Rome will determine who will wear the crown he tellingly holds in his hands. The people's choice, according to Marcus, is neither of the royal heirs but his own brother Titus:

> [*Enter*] *Marcus Andronicus* [*aloft*] *with the crown*
> MARCUS: Princes that strive by factions and by friends
> Ambitiously for rule and empery,
> Know that the people of Rome, for whom we stand
> A special party, have by common voice
> In election for the Roman empery
> Chosen Andronicus, surnamed *Pius*
> For many good and great deserts to Rome.
> (I.I.18–24)

Marcus's invocation of "the people of Rome" is remarkably effective: Saturninus and Bassianus quickly submit themselves to Marcus and dismiss their followers (I.I.46–64). But if Marcus's assertion of the people's authority resolves the conflict between the politics of lineal succession and the politics of election, it opens up a contradiction within representational politics. For as the scene develops, Marcus's claims to speak and act on behalf of the people make the absence and silence of the people themselves extraordinarily palpable, even as the efficacy of those claims confirms the dominance of popular politics in Rome.

Shakespeare first makes Marcus's representation of the people a matter for our scrutiny by making it a subject of some scrutiny among Rome's other political players. When Marcus assures Titus "thou shalt obtain and ask the empery" (I.I.201), his revealing inversion of the normal sequence of elective politics—one first asks for and then obtains an office—is not lost on Saturninus: "Proud and ambitious tribune," he demands, "canst thou tell?" (I.I.202). Marcus can indeed "tell" the outcome of the election: he can *predict* the people's choice because there is nothing to predict, for whatever he *speaks* will *count* as the votes of the people.[11] When Saturninus dismisses his faction, he thinks that he is submitting himself to Rome:

> SATURNINUS: Friends that have been thus forward in my right,
> I thank you all, and here dismiss you all,
> And to the love and favour of my country
> Commit myself, my person, and the cause.
> *Exeunt his soldiers and followers*

Rome, be as just and gracious unto me
As I am confident and kind to thee.
(1.1.56–61)

When Marcus preemptively promises Titus the empery, Saturninus discovers that Marcus *is* Rome.

Saturninus's anxiety is misplaced: it is precisely Marcus's capacity to "be" all of Rome that secures Saturninus's improbable election. Just as Saturninus's and Bassianus's factions are filing off the stage, Titus returns to Rome, trailed by his army and the human trophies of his victory over the Goths. Marcus greets his brother with the news of his imminent election, but Titus refuses the people's will: after forty years of fighting Rome's battles and after burying twenty-one of his warrior sons, the old general, in so many ways a prototype of Lear, is ready to retire, to turn to his daughter Lavinia, "the cordial of [his] age" (1.1.166). But Titus is happy to broker the people's political capital:

TITUS: People of Rome, and people's tribunes here,
I ask your voices and your suffrages.
Will ye bestow them friendly on Andronicus?
TRIBUNES: To gratify the good Andronicus
And gratulate his safe return to Rome
The people will accept whom he admits.
TITUS: Tribunes, I thank you, and this suit I make:
That you create our emperor's eldest son
Lord Saturnine, whose virtues will I hope,
Reflect on Rome as Titan's rays on earth,
And ripen justice in this commonweal.
Then if you will elect by my advice,
Crown him and say, "Long live our Emperor!"
MARCUS: With voices and applause of every sort,
Patricians and plebeians, we create
Lord Saturninus Rome's great emperor,
And say, "Long live our Emperor Saturnine!"
(1.1.217–33)

When Titus asks the people for their voices and suffrages, he invokes ghostly tongues: there are no "people" on stage to respond, and the acclamations seemingly suited for great general cries—"Long live our emperor!"; "Long live our Emperor Saturnine!"—are pronounced by Titus and Marcus alone.[12] The "voices and applause of every sort"—that is, of every rank of person—have been swallowed up by Marcus and transmuted into his own powerful speech act: "we create / Lord Saturninus Rome's great emperor." Marcus absorbs the people into a "we" that, neither precisely royal, nor plural, nor collective, but all three and more, effaces them as it represents them.

Titus, to be sure, addresses himself to "the people of Rome, and people's tribunes here" as if both the people and their representatives were present, but the oddly emphatic deixis of "here" opens a rift in representational rhetoric, not only because it stages the distinction between the merely rhetorical presence of the people and the actual presence of their tribunes, but also because it implies a "there" occupied by the people. But that political "elsewhere," to borrow one Elizabethan MP's appellation for the world beyond St. Stephen's Chapel, is emptied out precisely by representation: when the tribunes speak *as* "the people," when Marcus speaks *as* patrician and plebeian rather than *for* patrician and plebeian, "the people," as a political entity, cease to exist anywhere but in the representative and representational practices. This absorption is already evident in Marcus's first speech:

> MARCUS: Princes that strive by factions and by friends
> Ambitiously for rule and empery,
> Know that the people of Rome, for whom we stand
> A special party, have by common voice
> In election for the Roman empery,
> Chosen Andronicus, surnamed *Pius*
> For many good and great deserts to Rome.
> (1.1.18–24)

Neither Saturninus nor Bassianus has said anything to suggest that Titus is a factor in the struggle for the throne: Marcus's imperious announcement is news to them. It seems fair to assume, then, that Marcus has just come from the primal scene of representation—a gathering where the people designated Titus as their choice for emperor and authorized Marcus to articulate and enact their will.[13] That space offstage is the elsewhere of political representation, the "there" implied by Titus's "here," but as soon as Marcus identifies himself as the people's representative, there's no there there: "Know that the people of Rome, for whom *we* stand / A special party, have by common voice. . . . Chosen Andronicus." Why is Marcus "we"? In the ideological grammar of representation, the presence of the people in Marcus makes him plural: "the people of Rome" *disappear* into a representative "we" that incarnates and replaces them.[14]

The absolute character of Marcus's representation is signified by the absence of all whom he claims to represent: just as Cade politically incorporates and theatrically figures Parliament, Marcus "stands for" the people both politically and theatrically.[15] The absence of the people, moreover, confirms the efficacy of absolute representation. Marcus's power—both when he quashes the dispute between the royal brothers and when he creates Saturninus emperor—does not depend on the physical presence of the people: he faces down Bassianus, Saturninus, and their *armed* followers with a few words; he declares Saturninus emperor and in virtue of his utterance Saturninus *is* emperor. The power of Marcus's speech act, of course, is not inherent in the words he speaks but derives instead from what Pierre Bourdieu calls the "alchemy of representation": "the mystery of performative magic is . . . resolved in the mystery of ministry . . . in the alchemy of *representation* (in the different senses of the term) through which the representative creates the group which creates him" (106).[16] The power of the representative's "words resides in the fact that they are not pronounced on behalf of the person is only the 'carrier' [*porte-parole*] of these words: the authorized spokesperson is only able to use words to act on other agents and, through their action, on things themselves, because his speech concentrates within it the accumulated symbolic capital of the group which has delegated him and of which he is the *authorized representative*" (*Language*, 109–11).[17]

I am not suggesting that Bourdieu's account of representation either confirms or is confirmed by Shakespeare's—neither claim, in any event, would be particularly interesting. I turn to Bourdieu because Shakespeare's critique of political representation illuminates and is illuminated by the ways in which Bourdieu's *theoretical construction* of representation is indistinguishable from an *ideology* of political representation. Bourdieu's recursive model—"the representative creates the group which creates him"—mystifies representation (see chaps. 4 and 5 below), but my interest here is in his claim that the representative's speech is powerful because it "concentrates within it the accumulated symbolic capital of the group which has delegated him." The circularity of Bourdieu's analysis here is unmistakable if uncharacteristically implicit: before delegation, the group has no symbolic capital to invest—indeed, according to Bourdieu, the group does not exist *until* it delegates its power; thus, the symbolic capital the group invests in a representative is created by and only at the moment of delegation.[18] Political representation, then, creates the very symbolic capital that enables political representation, just as "the representative creates the group which creates him."[19]

Bourdieu figures the foundational moment of representation as alchemy: before representation, there are only mere individuals; at the institution of representation, some of the individuals become "the group," one becomes the "authorized representative," and this immaterial transformation of individuals into group and representative produces "symbolic capital" out of nothing other than the immaterial transformation itself. The "symbolic capital" generated by the reflexive creation of representative and group is simultaneously the positive condition for founding representation and the surplus product of representation. But the genesis of symbolic capital is, I suggest, reverse alchemy: the mysterious creation of nothing out of something. Before representation, the group—or the individuals who will become "the group" or "the people"—possess the highly literal power of their own bodies; representation transforms that physical power and its potential for violence and action into an always already alienated and contained symbolic capital. For the group's symbolic capital can only be registered in the moment it is spent, in the moment it is invested in a representative: in the economy of political representation Bourdieu posits, symbolic capital exists only in an *alienated* form. Bourdieu's model, then, occludes the way in which representational politics, rather than creating power out of nothing, instead refigures physical power as symbolic power and, in the process, disjoins the people from the very power it apparently creates in them.

The alienating effect of representation that Bourdieu's elaboration of symbolic capital both suggests and obscures is neatly encompassed in Marcus Andronicus's account of his relationship to the people he represents:

> MARCUS: Titus Andronicus, the people of Rome,
> Whose friend in justice thou hast ever been,
> Send thee by me, their tribune and their trust,
> This palliament of white and spotless hue,
> And name thee in election for the empire
> With these our late-deceased emperor's sons.
> (1.1.179–84)

Editors assign "trust" a very general meaning ("trusted one" [Maxwell 13n], "the representative in whom their trust is placed" [Bate 139n]), but "trust" was a familiar term of law (*fiducia*) in Shakespeare's England and it figured significantly in early modern conceptions of political representation.

The trust—a mid-sixteenth-century innovation that F. W. Maitland regards as the "most distinctive achievement" of English lawyers (2:272)—was not a political covenant but a legal contract: a trust, according to an Elizabethan translation of Littleton's *Tenures* (1574), is a "feoffment made uppon confidence to perfourme the will of the feoffour" (97[r]). In a typical trust, one party (*cestui que trust*) transferred the legal ownership of his property to another party (the trustee or trust), who yielded the profits from that property back to the *cestui que trust* or his designated beneficiaries.[20] Thus, the trust, like the older enfeoffment to use, enabled a landowner to convey the value of property, rather than the property itself, to his heirs; because the property itself did not descend to the heirs, no feudal dues were owed the king or queen.[21] Early modern voters did not, of course, enfeoff property to their MPs, but Elizabethan MPs frequently figured themselves as trusts of the subject's property.[22] In *An Admonition by the Father of F.A. to him being a Burgesse of the Parliament for his better Behaviour therein* (1576), the MP Arthur Hall's fictional alter ego defines for his son the particular kind of trust electorates repose in their representatives:

> The lower or common house of Parliament standeth of 442 persons . . . who are chosen by the whole commons of the Realme. . . . Now thinke with your selfe what confidence these persons have in you, when they appointe you in this Ro[o]me of enacting and disanulling. . . . They commit unto your considerations their libertyes, not only of person but of living, their goods, their lands, their lives, their attainders of bloud, all that they have, shall have, or can have . . . they yeelde into your hands, and not only to bind them hereafter to stand to your doome and decree from time to come . . . but also submit themselves and all before recited, unto what you shall dispose of it, without a loking backe consideration whereby you may nerely touche them: the confidence placed in you is so great a trust. (Eii^{r-v})

The "libertyes" subjects entrust to MPs are, above all, the liberties of property: "their goods, their lands, their lives, their attainders of bloud, all that they have, shall have, or can have . . . they yeelde into your hands." For Hall, "trust" always signifies a material relationship between subjects and their representatives: "see what the commons of England *put in your handes,* when you are chosen a spokesman for them" (Eiv^{v}; emphasis added). Even Hall's references to the voters' "confidence" in their MPs, far from asserting a relation of trust in its nontechnical sense, take us right back to property relations: in Elizabethan legal discourse, "confidence" is a synonym for a legal trust.

The knights and burgesses were, as one MP put it in 1593, "the stewards of many purses" (qtd. in Loach 148), and they routinely allowed the monarch to loosen the strings of those purses. Elizabethan and Jacobean voters, who were so often ignorant of the Commons' business, could be certain of at least one thing: a session of Parliament would result in taxes assessed against the value of their property. Indeed, it was under Elizabeth that the parliamentary subsidy became a regular rather than an extraordinary instrument of royal revenue; in nine of the ten Parliaments of her reign, Elizabeth requested at least one subsidy; she got them all.[23] It is an odd kind of trust that pays money out to a third party rather than back to the *cestui que trust* or his kin. The MPs themselves were sensitive on this point: in 1593, they were still gnashing their teeth over Hall's jibe, then nearly twenty years old, that the knights and burgesses "were assembled for graunting of subsidyes only" (*PPE* 3:153).[24] The MPs, of course, claimed that Parliament served the economic interests of both crown and people: a strapped monarch might call a Parliament principally to secure a subsidy, but the MPs, once assembled, could use the occasion to promote legislation—for roads, dams, improvements in trade policy, restrictions on enclosure, poor relief, forestry management, and so on—that benefited their constituents.[25] More important still, the MPs were the best defense against the crown's various attempts to profit from the subject's labor or property in the absence of his consent. The rhetoric of Elizabethan and Jacobean political representation amply anticipates Locke's philosophy of government: "the People . . . [reserve] to themselves the Choice of their *Representatives* as the Fence to their Properties" (413).

The wolves threatening to leap over the fence are, of course, the monarch, enclosers, and other great ones, but, like Locke, Arthur Hall feared that the MPs' desire to enrich and empower themselves compromised the protection they claimed to provide.[26] In Hall's tract, the father repeatedly warns his son not to emulate the many MPs who are "corrupted with brybes of the great ones" (Eii^{v}) and who "play the hireling" (Eiii^{r}): "If you go a trewanting, if you play Legerdemayn, if you will be bridled, if you gape for ambition, if you play the Mongrel, if fayre words abuse you . . . hereof will proceede not only to your trusters and theirs now borne and unborne, (I use the word still, bycause I knowe not how so rightly to hit the minde of your choosers who commit trust in you) . . . but the same to you and yours" (Fi^{r}).[27] The typical MP, Hall suggests throughout his tract, is a wolf in sheep's clothing, a confidence man rather than a conscientious trust, an open gate rather than a fence: the "trusters" of such an MP are nothing more than gulls.

Marcus Andronicus, like most of Shakespeare's political representatives, is just such a confidence man. Marcus identifies himself as the people's "trust" but he "play[s] Legerdemayn" with the capital his "trusters" invest in him: when the people endow Marcus with their voices, they expect him to advance Titus's candidacy for the empery; but Titus and Marcus perform something like a bait-and-switch when they, in turn, bestow the people's voices on the decidedly unpopular and antipopulist Saturninus. Saturninus, we recall, assumes that an election will thwart his succession, but Titus reassures him that popular politics will put him on the throne: "Content thee, prince; I will restore to thee / The people's hearts, and wean them from themselves" (1.1.210–11). Titus's own account of representation, then, fully reveals its alienating effects: Titus speaks here not of some postelection attempt to reconcile the people to Saturninus's victory; weaning the people from themselves *enables* the election. Indeed, weaning the people from themselves *is* the election.[28] The election of Saturninus is a cautionary tale about the hazards of political trusts: the alienation of power from persons—the positive condition of political representation—makes it possible not only to exclude the people from the political field but also to manipulate their own "voices" against them.

Marcus and Titus's betrayal of the people's trust could hardly be more naked. After Saturninus claims the throne as his hereditary right, two progressively democratizing prospects unfold: the election of Bassianus; and the election of Titus, who claims no kinship with the previous emperor and thus represents a more radical challenge to lineal succession. Titus not only refuses the people's mandate but settles Rome's imperial succession in the most retrograde fashion imaginable. Rather than confer power on Bassianus, Titus and Marcus perversely put elective politics at the service of hereditary monarchy: the last emperor's eldest son is "elected" emperor. In *Titus,* moreover, representational politics devolves into something very like the kingmaking so familiar to us from the English histories. Saturninus himself understands that Titus seeks power even as he refuses the "palliament of white and spotless hue": "Sly frantic wretch that holpst to make me great, / In hope [he] should govern Rome and me" (4.4.59–60). But Saturninus also recognizes that a kingmaker—especially a great general who commands a vast army—must have his due:

> SATURNINUS: Titus Andronicus, for thy favours done
> To us in our election this day
> I give thee thanks in part of thy deserts,
> And will with deeds requite thy gentleness.
> And for an onset, Titus, to advance
> Thy name and honourable family,
> Lavinia will I make my empress.
> (1.1.234–40)

Saturninus's economy of "desert" is very different from the elective meritocracy Bassianus advocates ("let desert in pure election shine" [1.1.16]): Titus resigns his sword—the symbol of his command—and pledges fealty to the new emperor only *after* Saturninus designates Lavinia his empress. There is more than a hint here of quid pro quo: in exchange for delivering up the people's voices, Titus and Marcus will become the patriarchs of Rome's dynastic family.[29] The most fundamental legal principle of the trust bound the trustee to use the property in trust not for his own benefit but for the benefit of *cestui que trust,* but the people of Rome get a disastrous return on the voices they invest in trust: an emperor who seeks to rule in the absence of the people's "suffrages"; an emperor who is prepared to oppose popular election with patrician violence (1.1.203–5); an emperor who knows they hate him. They get, in other words, an elected Tarquin.[30]

This is sharp dealing indeed, but there is a small measure of dramatic justice in the almost immediate collapse of the Andronican settlement of Rome's political estate. Kingmaking in Rome, like kingmaking in fifteenth-century England, turns out to be a dicey business: just as Saturninus is preparing to celebrate his good fortune with "trump and drum" (1.1.275), Bassianus objects that he has a prior claim to Lavinia and lays hold of her.

> BASSIANUS: Lord Titus, by your leave, this maid is mine.
> TITUS: How, sir, are you in earnest then, my lord?
> BASSIANUS: Ay, noble Titus, and resolved withal
> To do myself this reason and this right.
> MARCUS: *Suum cuique* is our Roman justice;
> This prince in justice seizeth but his own.
> LUCIUS: And that he will and shall, if Lucius live.
> TITUS: Traitors, avaunt! Where is the Emperor's guard?
> Treason, my lord! Lavinia is surprised.
> SATURNINUS: Surprised, by whom?
> BASSIANUS: By him that justly may
> Bear his betrothed from all the world away.
> *Exeunt Bassianus, Marcus, Quintus and Martius with Lavinia*
> MUTIUS: Brothers, help to convey her hence away,
> And with my sword I'll keep this door safe.
> (1.1.276–85)

As it happens, Bassianus and Lavinia's betrothal is an unexpected boon for Saturninus: freed from a political match with the daughter of Rome's power broker, he can instead marry Tamora, the captured Gothic queen and the object of his genuine desire. Saturninus nevertheless pounces on Bassianus's (fortuitous) defiance—a repetition of his bid for the crown—and accuses him of treason:

SATURNINUS: Traitor, if Rome have law or we have power,
Thou and thy faction shall repent this rape.
BASSIANUS: "Rape" call you it, my lord, to seize my own,
My true betrothed love, and now my wife?
But let the laws of Rome determine all;
Meanwhile am I possessed of that is mine.
(1.1.400–5)

The language of property in these disputes over Lavinia is strikingly pervasive: Bassianus repeatedly figures Lavinia as his possession; Marcus recognizes Bassianus's "seiz[ing]" of Lavinia as the execution of a legal title to property; Lucius approves Marcus's judgment; and Mutius urges his brothers to "convey" his sister.[31] This universal commodification of Lavinia reaches its grimmest expression in the name Saturninus gives to Bassianus's treasonous affront: the first mention of "rape" in *Titus* refers not to sexual violation (*OED* 2) but to an illegal seizure of property (*OED* 1).

In the very next scene, Aaron establishes sexual rape as the point of identification between Lavinia and Lucrece: "Lucrece was not more chaste," he warns Tamora's sons Demetrius and Chiron, "Than this Lavinia"; thus, if the brothers are to have their "snatch," Aaron counsels, they must rape her rather than woo her (2.1.96–117). Even before Aaron posits Lavinia's Lucrecean chastity as an argument for sexual violence, Bassianus's alleged rape and the property dispute it occasions conjure up Lucrece—or, to be more precise, the Lucrece Shakespeare fashioned at roughly the same time that he wrote *Titus.*[32] In both *Lucrece* and *Titus,* Shakespeare's critique of the republican rape topos turns on the commodification of the tragic heroine. In *Lucrece,* the victim's father and husband construct her as property after she commits suicide. Standing over his daughter's corpse, Lucretius stakes the first claim: "'Daughter, dear daughter,' old Lucretius cries, / 'That life was mine which thou hast here deprived'" (1751–52). The father's proprietary tears rouse the husband—"By this starts Collatine as from a dream / And bids Lucretius give his sorrow place" (1772–73)—and an unspeakably queasy battle over "who should weep most" ensues:

The one doth call her his, the other his;
Yet neither may possess the claim they lay.
The father says, "She's mine." "O mine she is,"
Replies her husband: "do not take away
My sorrow's interest; let no mourner say
He weeps for her, for she was only mine,
And only must be wailed by Collatine."

> "O," quoth Lucretius, "I did give that life
> Which she too early and too late hath spilled."
> "Woe, woe," quoth Collatine, "she was my wife;
> I owed her, and 'tis mine that she hath killed."
> (1793–1803)

Lucrece was one of the great tragic heroines of the Renaissance, but Shakespeare makes her family's mourning a spectacle of childish self-absorption. The assumptions that motivate this unsavory contest are, moreover, deeply unsettling: when both Collatine and Lucretius figure Lucrece's suicide as dispossession (1752, 1803), we have passed into the language of slavery. Shakespeare's Brutus may not think of the revolt against the tyrannical Tarquins as a defense of bondage, but his two principal partners in the establishment of republican liberty construct Lucrece's very life as *their* property.[33]

Livy and earlier English authors define Sextus's crime as a transgression of the private—even as a violation of the *domus*—but never explicitly define Lucrece as property. Transforming Sextus's assault into a crime against property, Shakespeare assimilates Roman tyranny to an English model. Tyranny typically assumed two terrifying shapes in the minds of Shakespeare's contemporaries: a Catholic ruler who would subject the English to a foreign yoke; or an English ruler who would seize and tax property without seeking authorization from the people's representative in parliament.[34] Protecting the subject's property was the MPs' highest charge: "the knightes, citizenes and burgeses," Speaker Fulke Onslow told Elizabeth at the opening of Parliament in 1567, were "fitte men to whome the commones have comitted the care and charge of them selves, wives and children, landes and goodes, and soe in their behalfe to forsee and take ordere in and for all thinges necessarye" (*PPE* 1:168). In the early modern rhetoric of freedom, "landes and goodes" seldom yielded pride of place to women and children. Even the most poetic, passionate, and high-minded defenses of the subject's liberties typically celebrated neither freedom of speech nor freedom of conscience but instead the right to consent to the alienation of one's property.[35] According to Hall, we recall, MPs shouldered the daunting burden of guarding the people's "libertyes, not only of person but of living, their goods, their lands, their lives, their attainders of bloud, all that they have, shall have, or can have" (Eii[v]). Speaking in the House of Commons in 1593, James Morice even more fully conflated liberty and secure property rights: "the subjects of this kingdome are borne and brought upp in due obedience, but farre from servitude and bondage, subject to lawfull aucthoritye and commaundment, but freed from licentious will and tyrannie; enjoyinge by lymitts of lawe and justice oure lifes, lands, goods and liberties in greate peace and security" (*PPE* 3:35).

Elizabeth's and James's occasional attempts to raise revenue through extra-parliamentary means were often greeted with invocations of "tyranny" and "bondage." In 1601, Francis More argued that monopolies—which limited a producer's freedom to profit from his labor and property and, in some cases, inflated consumer prices—enslaved the subject: "'Mr. Speaker, I know the Queene's Prerogatyve is a thinge curyous to be dealt withal, yett all grievances are not comparable. I cannot utter with my toungue or conceive with my harte the great grievances that the town and country for which I Serve, suffer by some of these monopolies: It bringeth the general profit into a private hand; and the end of all, is beggary and bondage to the subject" (*PPE* 3:374–75).[36] In a remarkable speech in 1610, Thomas Hedley warned that James I's practice of authorizing impositions on merchandise "without the assent of parliament" (*PP 1610* 2:188) threatened the very identity of the English nation:

> But once take this ancient liberty from the commons, so that they perceive their lands and goods not absolutely their own but in the absolute power and command of another, they will neither have nor care for that wealth and courage that now they have . . . for seeing their liberty and condition no better than the bondmen or the peasants in other places, their courage will be no better than theirs; for it is not the nature of the people or climate, though I know they are not utterly without their operation and influence, that makes this difference; but it is the laws, liberties, and government of this realm. (*PP 1610* 2:196)

Hedley's theory of English exceptionalism is based entirely on the common subject's unique relation to property. England's greatness and its "difference" from other nations rests in the common subject's "liberties," the chief of which, Hedley suggests again and again, are property rights. Between that defining liberty and James I's alleged designs on absolute power—this is Hedley's own resonant term—over his subjects' property stand the knights and burgesses.[37]

As he transplants the Lucrece story to English soil, Shakespeare leans on the paradox he produces: the righteous outrage of Lucrece's family, their recognition that they are slaves, and their revolt against the Tarquins depend on their belief that Lucrece is their property. Sextus himself tellingly adduces Lucrece's lack of property in herself as a *cause* of his assault: "I'll beg her love: but she is not her own" (241). Because Lucrece does not own herself—and therefore could not, even if she so desired, consent to Sextus's appeals—Sextus "must" force her.[38] Sextus, moreover, regards Collatine's property in Lucrece as a challenge to his family's claims to absolute power, as a spur, that is, to a specifically tyrannical desire:

> Her breasts like ivory globes circled with blue,
> A pair of maiden worlds unconquered,
> Save of their lord no bearing *yoke* they knew,
> And him by oath they truly honoured.
> These worlds in Tarquin new ambition bred,
>   Who like a foul usurper went about
>   From this fair throne to heave the owner out.
> (407–13; emphasis added)

If Collatine can be an "owner," if he can be the enthroned king of Lucrece's "maiden worlds," then Sextus and his father are not the *absolute* rulers of Rome. Sextus's ambition is the ambition of an English tyrant.

In *Titus,* Shakespeare reverses the movement I have just traced in *Lucrece:* Lavinia's family and betrothed construct her as property—as a possession that can be illegally seized (that is, raped)—*before* she is sexually assaulted (that is, raped). Moreover, Saturninus and Bassianus's dispute over Lavinia at the end of act 1 models Demetrius and Chiron's dispute over which of them is most entitled to woo or rape Lavinia: indeed, act 2 virtually begins with the Gothic brothers, who are present during the first "rape," mimicking the imperial brothers' struggles for the crown and Lavinia. The relation between the two rapes of Lavinia blurs the opposition between Gothic barbarism and Roman civility that is, as we shall see, so important to the rhetoric of the Andronici, but the commodification of Lavinia also radically undermines the apparent opposition between the tyrannical Saturninus and his republican-minded brother. Bassianus, to be sure, rejects Saturninus's charge of theft but shares his brother's assumption that Lavinia is property. Indeed, Bassianus's claim that a man cannot rape his betrothed—cannot steal what he already owns—suggests that he cannot conceive of sexual rape at all: if a woman has no property in herself, if she can be owned, she has, on this account, no consent to give or withhold. If Bassianus had outlived the sexual violation of Lavinia, he would surely have charged Chiron and Demetrius with a crime against his property.

Bassianus's domestic politics, then, apparently diverge from his public politics. We should recall here Bassianus's first speech and the strong impression it must have made on Shakespeare's audiences. Elizabethans would have found nothing remarkable in Saturninus's theory of legitimate authority (1.1.1–10), but Bassianus's attack on genealogical kingship would have struck them as heterodox and alien: "let desert in pure election shine, / And, Romans, fight for freedom in your choice" (16–17). Bassianus, however, understands "freedom in . . . choice" as a quite limited right: when he challenges the betrothal of Saturninus and Lavinia, he never directly asks Lavinia to declare her own desire, nor does he, in his appeals to Titus and Saturninus, invoke her right to choose a husband. Rather, Bassianus rests his case *entirely* on the claim that Lavinia belongs to him: his rhetoric of free choice has turned into a rhetoric of slavery.

Shakespeare begins *Titus* by setting up what seem to be absolute oppositions between succession and election, Saturninus and Bassianus. By the end of the act 1, these oppositions have proved illusory: the putative difference between Saturninus and Bassianus—the very distinction that made Titus's choice of Saturninus seem such a perverse betrayal of the people—has blurred, but this apparent irony is itself emptied out—or intensified—by the related and more radical collapse of the opposition between succession and election. Even before we fully recognize that he is training his plot along the framework established by Livy, Shakespeare has already undermined the very possibility of an orthodox fulfillment of the republican rape topos: republican salvation—the remedy for tyrannical rape—has already been compromised by the bankrupt election that produces succession. Put another way, Shakespeare jumbles together tribunes, senators, and emperors not because he is a poor student of history but because he thinks political representatives and emperors, Brutuses and Tarquins, are doubles rather than opposites.

◇◇

The historiographical motive of the republican rape topos is to posit a relation between coercive political authority and rape. But what kind of political tyranny does the rape of Lavinia express? Let me begin to answer my question by suggesting that Lavinia's silence figures the alienation of the people's voices. The silence of the people in act 1 must be read in the context of the extraordinary significance of muteness in *Titus.* Shakespeare withholds the maiming of Lavinia from theatrical representation but then endlessly stages its result: Lavinia's silence is profoundly, disturbingly, inescapably present to us for most of the play. Her loss of voice, moreover, seems nothing less than a loss of identity: when he encounters his niece fleeing through the woods, Marcus asks, "Who is this?" (2.4.11); later, when he first brings Lavinia to her father, Marcus registers the totality of Lavinia's loss by warning Titus, "this *was* thy daughter" (3.1.62; emphasis added). The catastrophic loss of identity itself is, for Marcus, the inevitable result of losing one's tongue:

MARCUS: O, that delightful engine of her thoughts,
That blabbed them with such pleasing eloquence,
Is torn from forth that pretty hollow cage,
Where, like a sweet melodious bird, it sung
Sweet varied notes, enchanting every ear.
(3.1.82–86)

If Lavinia's tongue was the "engine of her thoughts" (3.1.82), then her body can no longer signify her self. Lavinia must now depend on her father and uncle to articulate her thoughts and feelings, and, as we shall see, they represent her no more felicitously than they do the people.

Chiron and Demetrius's brutal violence transforms Lavinia into the people's double. This is not quite right: rather, the Gothic brothers horribly fix an identity Lavinia *already* shares with the people, for Marcus's own telling analogy between Lavinia's tongue and a caged bird reminds us that while Saturninus, Bassianus, and Titus argue over her marital fate, she remains silent. Her thoughts have always been opaque. Lavinia and the people, then, are identified *before* the rape: Lavinia's silence as Titus decides her fate repeats the people's silence as Titus elects Saturninus in their name; in the pursuit of his political schemes, Titus delivers both Lavinia and the people's voices into Saturninus's hands. Chiron and Demetrius make Lavinia's body into a literal figure for her silence and the alienation of the people's voices.[39]

Once Lavinia has lost her tongue, everyone perversely urges her to speak: "Speak, Lavinia, what accursed hand / Hath made thee handless in thy father's sight?" (3.1.66–67); "Speak, gentle sister, who hath martyred thee?" (3.1.81). These futile invitations to speak, as we might expect, turn into offers to speak for Lavinia. The problem of representing Lavinia becomes the problem of the play, for she, of course, possesses the information her family requires to avenge her terrible loss. Marcus, to be sure, knows that Lavinia has been raped and, indeed, immediately suggests that Philomela's fate models his niece's. But the mystery of the rapists' identity bedevils the Andronici: "Shall I speak for thee?" Marcus asks Lavinia, "O, that I knew thy heart, and knew the beast, / That I might rail at him to ease my mind!" (2.4.33–35); "O, say thou for her," Lucius implores his uncle, "who hath done this deed?" (3.1.87); "Thou hast no hands to wipe away thy tears," Titus laments, "Nor tongue to tell me who hath martyred thee" (3.1.106–7). The problem of solving the crime, then, is articulated as a problem of representation: "Shall I speak for thee?"; "say thou for her."

The chief task of anyone who endeavors to speak for Lavinia is to name her assailants; her grief is inexpressible. When Titus first sees his ruined child, he marvels that the affective powers of the maimed body itself so exceed the capacity of any representation of the body to express agony, tragedy, loss: "Had I but seen thy picture in this plight / It would have madded me: what shall I do / Now I behold thy lively body so?" (3.1.103–5). Despite—or, perhaps, because of—the overwhelming power of the body to express Lavinia's plight, Titus wants almost immediately to reproduce Lavinia's "lively body": "Give me a sword, I'll chop off my hands too" (3.1.72). Titus, however, soon rethinks his poignant, paternal impulse to share his daughter's condition:

> TITUS: . . . shall we cut away our hands like thine?
> Or shall we bite our tongues, and in dumb shows
> Pass the remainder of our hateful days?
> What shall we do? Let us that have our tongues
> Plot some device of further misery,
> To make us wonder'd at in time to come.
> (3.1.130–35)

Titus considers *replicating* Lavinia's plight because he recognizes the impossibility of adequately *representing* her plight. But reproducing Lavinia's muteness would allow only for "dumb shows"; plotting "some device of further misery"—that is, a terrible revenge against Lavinia's assailants—will require "tongues."

Plotting, for Titus, is bound up with representing: indeed, from the moment he decides to retain his tongue in order that he might plot, Titus devotes himself to speaking for Lavinia. When, for example, Lavinia appears to refuse food and drink, Titus reads her bodily motions as he would linguistic signs:

> TITUS: Hark, Marcus, what she says.
> I can interpret all her martyr'd signs:
> She says she drinks no other drink but tears,
> Brew'd with her sorrow, mash'd upon her cheeks.
> Speechless complainer, I will learn thy thought.
> In thy dumb action will I be as perfect
> As begging hermits in their holy prayers:
> Thou shalt not sigh nor hold thy stumps to heaven,
> Nor wink, nor nod, nor kneel, nor make a sign,
> But I of these will wrest an alphabet,
> And by still practice learn to know thy meaning.
> (3.2.35–45)

Titus seems to retain his ideal of replication as the basis for his mode of representation: he will function as a prosthetic tongue, a mere instrument that transmits Lavinia's thoughts. Even as Titus describes this fantasy of wholly self-effacing representation, however, he betrays something of the true nature of representation. Titus figures Lavinia's body as a "map of woe, that . . . talk[s] in signs" (3.2.12); her "martyr'd signs," he claims, speak (3.2.35–37). But maps, bodies, and silent signs do not, of course, "talk" or "say" anything for themselves; they must be given voice by others, and in the gap between a signifier and its enunciation there is a space for interpretation and misrepresentation. Moreover, although Titus suggests that he will match his words to Lavinia's signs, his own account of this process makes it quite clear that to represent Lavinia, he will first have to write her. Lavinia's expressions and gestures are not texts: Titus must transform her body—her nodding head, her winking eyes, her waving stumps—into language. This translation is remarkably violent: to make Lavinia into a text, Titus will "wrest"—that is, "wrench or twist"—an alphabet out of her; he will "force" letters out of her.[40]

All of Titus's representational wresting comes to naught: although act 3 is largely devoted to his attempts to interpret Lavinia's "martyr'd signs," he never gets any closer to knowing who has assaulted his daughter. Indeed, as he brings act 3 to its close, Titus seems to have given up both on speaking for Lavinia and on plotting a wondrous device: "Lavinia, go with me; / I'll to thy closet, and go read with thee / Sad stories chanced in times of old" (3.2.80–82). Titus repairs to this session of "sad stories" with Richard II's world-weary resignation, but perhaps his readings inspire Lavinia's unexpected reassertion of her capacity for self-expression at the beginning of act 4. It is an extraordinary scene: *"Enter Lucius' son, and Lavinia running after him, and the boy flies from her with his books under his arm. Enter Titus and Marcus."* Lavinia draws her family's attention to her nephew's copy of Ovid's *Metamorphoses* and manages to fumble through the leaves until she comes to the story of Philomela: crossing the sea to visit her sister Procne, Philomela is raped by her brother-in-law Tereus; Tereus cuts out Philomela's tongue and hides her in a prison; Philomela eventually discloses the identity of her assailant by weaving her tragic tale into a tapestry; Procne exacts revenge by murdering her own child and baking him in a pie she serves to his father. At first, Titus seems to accept Lavinia's literary identification: "Lavinia, wert thou thus surpris'd, sweet girl, / Ravish'd and wrong'd, as Philomela was, / Forc'd in the ruthless, vast, and gloomy woods" (4.1.51–53). But Titus begins almost immediately to assimilate Lavinia's rape to the historical precedent of Lucrece: "Give signs . . . What Roman lord it was durst do the deed: / Or slunk not Saturnine, as Tarquin erst, / That left the camp to sin in Lucrece' bed?" (60–63). Titus has missed his mark, and Lavinia must correct him; taking a staff in her mouth, she writes out the names of her assailants in a "sandy plot" (68): "*Stuprum—Chiron—Demetrius.*" (78). The parallel with Lucrece is even closer, apparently, than Titus imagined: just as Tarquin's son Sextus rapes Lucrece, so Saturninus's stepsons have raped Lavinia. Lavinia's spare text inspires Marcus to recast the entire family as the family of Lucrece:

> MARCUS. There is enough written upon this earth
> To stir a mutiny in the mildest thoughts,
> And arm the minds of infants to exclaims.
> My lord, kneel down with me; Lavinia, kneel;
> And kneel, sweet boy, the Roman Hector's hope,
> And swear with me, as with the woeful fere
> And father of that chaste dishonoured dame,
> Lord Junius Brutus sware for Lucrece' rape,
> That we will prosecute by good advice
> Mortal revenge upon these traitorous Goths,
> And see their blood, or die with this reproach.
> (4.1.83–93)

Marcus's analogy between Titus and Lucretius reveals some of the attraction of the Lucrece narrative: in Ovid's tale, Pandion plays no part in avenging his daughter Philomela's rape and maiming; undone, he immediately dies from grief. Assimilating Lavinia to Lucrece, then, gives Titus an active role to play. But if Marcus hopes to stir up more than a "mutiny in . . . thoughts," if he wants to arm more than "the minds of infants," he will need something more than Lavinia's sandy text and maimed body to do the stirring: galvanizing the people of Rome against the Tarquins required the spectacular display of Lucrece's *corpse.*

Titus has, in fact, already suggested that Lavinia emulate Lucrece:

> TITUS: . . . get some little knife between thy teeth,
> And just against thy heart make thou a hole,
> That all the tears that thy poor eyes let fall
> May run into that sink and, soaking in,
> Drown the lamenting fool in sea-salt tears.
> (3.2.16–20)

The means to death imagined here may seem absurdly fanciful, but Titus's language ominously echoes Lucrece's at the precise moment she determines to kill herself: "I . . . against my heart / Will fix a sharp knife" (*Rape of Lucrece* 1136–38; see Dover Wilson xix).[41] Marcus certainly takes Titus seriously: "Fie, brother, fie! Teach her not thus to lay / Such violent hands upon her tender life" (30–31). Moreover, as we are reminded at the end of the play, jumping from a precipice is an effective suicide and requires neither hands nor a tongue. Lavinia, however, gives no indication that she wishes to provide Titus and Marcus with the one indispensable prop of the republican rape topos: she never attempts to harm herself; she does not beg her own death when she writes in the sandy plot; and when Titus, after witnessing Lavinia's intense interest in her nephew's books, invites her to "[c]ome and take choice of all my library" (4.1.33), she sticks to Ovid's *Metamorphoses.* Surely, given his investment in Roman history and culture, Titus's library must include fine copies of Livy, Ovid's *Fasti,* and the many other works in which Lucrece's tragedy was recounted.

Titus and Marcus's attempt to translate Lavinia into Lucrece fails because it requires Lavinia's *consent.* Lavinia cannot be *compelled* to imitate Lucrece because Lucrece is defined precisely by willing and effecting her own death. But Lavinia's rejection of her family's effort to identify her with Lucrece is also deeply poignant, because Lucrece's suicide, as Shakespeare shaped it, so powerfully demonstrates the rule that one can never fashion one's historical identity. For Lucrece's decision to commit suicide in order to assert control over both her body and the interpretation of Sextus's assault ironically puts her corpse and the meaning of the rape into the hands of Brutus, who, as we shall see, cares nothing for her will. The complex relation between Lucrece's longing for death and her determination to *own* the outrage of Sextus's crime and to shape its consequence is resolved in her decision to summon her husband: "Yet die I will not, till my Collatine / Have heard the cause of my untimely death, / That he may vow, in that sad hour of mine, / Revenge on him that made me stop my breath" (1177–80). The speech Lucrece rehearses for this pitiable reunion is a cry for blood:

> "My resolution, love, shall be thy boast,
> By whose example thou revenged mayst be.
> How Tarquin must be used, read it in me:
>   Myself thy friend will kill myself thy foe,
>   And for my sake serve thou false Tarquin so.
>
> "This brief abridgment of my will I make:
> My soul and body to the skies and ground;
> My resolution, husband, do thou take;"
> . . . .
> "Thou, Collatine, shalt oversee this will."
> (1193–1200, 1205)

Lucrece, then, awaits not only her love but also the executor of her will and the inheritor of her vendetta.

In ancient and earlier English accounts of the fall of the Tarquins, Lucrece never enjoins her family to seek Sextus's death; Shakespeare's Lucrece is possessed by her desire for revenge. Before she will reveal the identity of her assailant, Lucrece exacts an oath from Collatine, her father, and their followers:

> "And for my sake, when I might charm thee so,
> For she that was thy Lucrece, now attend me:
> Be suddenly revenged on my foe,
> Thine, mine, his own; suppose thou dost defend me
> From what is past. The help that thou shalt lend me
>   Comes all too late, yet let the traitor die;
>   For sparing justice feeds iniquity.
>
> "But ere I name him, you fair lords," quoth shee,
> Speaking to those that came with Collatine,
> "Shall plight your honourable faiths to me,
> With swift pursuit to venge this wrong of mine;
> For 'tis a meritorious fair design
>   To chase injustice with revengeful arms:
>   Knights by their oaths should right poor ladies' harms."
> (1681–94)

Only after "each present lord began to promise aid . . . / Longing to hear the hateful foe bewrayed" (1696–98) does Lucrece, as she plunges a dagger into her breast, disclose the name of her rapist.[42]

Lucrece's suicide, as we have seen, at first produces self-indulgent tears rather than steely resolve, but Brutus rallies Collatine and Lucretius to their sworn oath:

> "Now by the Capitol that we adore,
> And by this chaste blood so unjustly stained,
> By heaven's fair sun that breeds the fat earth's store,
> By all our country rights in Rome maintained,
> And by chaste Lucrece' soul that late complained
>   Her wrongs to us, and by this bloody knife,
>   We will revenge the death of this true wife."
> (1835–41)

But after Collatine, Lucretius, and the other lords take up Brutus's cry for revenge, the poem abruptly ends without so much as a word about Sextus Tarquin:

When they had sworn to this advised doom,
They did conclude to bear dead Lucrece thence,
To show her bleeding body thorough Rome
And so to publish Tarquin's foul offense;
Which being done with speedy diligence,
The Romans plausibly did give consent
To Tarquin's everlasting banishment.

Rather than pursue the revenge Lucrece prescribes, Brutus and Lucrece's family transform her private tragedy into a political event: the public display of Lucrece's raped body "so moved" the people that "with one consent and a general acclamation the Tarquins were all exiled, and the state government changed from kings to consuls" (*Rape of Lucrece,* "The Argument," 33–36).

The founding of the Roman Republic was an astounding historical event, but Shakespeare makes "Tarquin's everlasting banishment" a bizarre anticlimax. Shakespeare's sources, to be sure, offered no foundation for revenge against Sextus: according to Livy, Sextus dies far from Rome at the hands of ancient enemies (1.60.2–3). But by inventing Lucrece's passion for revenge, Shakespeare figures Collatine and Lucretius as oath breakers, who, with their promises to kill Sextus still ringing in the air, swear a new oath to Brutus. Moreover, sacrificing the pursuit of Sextus in particular for the larger political purpose of expelling the Tarquins is a double betrayal: in her long speeches to her designated avengers (1613–59, 1676–1709), Lucrece mentions neither Lucius Tarquinius nor Rome's political plight; indeed, she seems anxious that "her loss" not occasion sweeping upheaval. After Sextus has left her, Lucrece seeks out a "well painted piece" of the siege of Troy (1443). As she contemplates the painter's feeling rendering of Hecuba "starring on Priam's wounds with her old eyes" (1448), Lucrece wonders that an epic catastrophe could issue from individual sin:

"Show me the strumpet that began this stir,
That with my nails her beauty I may tear.
Thy heat of lust, fond Paris, did incur
This load of wrath that burning Troy doth bear.
Thy eye kindled the fire that burneth here,
  And here in Troy for tresspass of thine eye,
  The sire, the sonne, the dame, and daughter die.

"Why should the private pleasure of some one
Become the public plague of many moe?
Let sin, alone committed, light alone
Upon his head that hath transgressed so;

> Let guiltless souls be freed from guilty woe.
>   For one's offense why should so many fall,
>   To plague a private sin in general?
> (1471–84)

Lucrece's demonization of Helen—Paris is merely "fond"?—raises complicated interpretive questions, to say the least, but my interest here is in Lucrece's construction of the Trojan War as a tragic lesson in politicizing the private.[43] This interpretation both assumes and produces a principle of just revenge: "Let sin alone committed, light alone / Upon his head that hath transgressed so." Sextus's sin, according to Lucrece's creed, justifies neither the overthrow of Lucius nor the risk of civil war.

Lucrece's revenge ethic is continuous with her profound emotional investment in privacy. Lucrece gives up her physical struggle against rape at precisely the moment Tarquin threatens to kill her and her servant, display their bodies in public, and proclaim them adulterers (1629–30). After Sextus leaves, Lucrece remains haunted by his threatening images of children singing of her "trespasses" (512–25):

> "O Night, thou furnace of foul reeking smoke,
> Let not the jealous Day behold that face
> Which underneath thy black all-hiding cloak,
> Immodesty lies martyred with disgrace.
> Keep still possession of they gloomy place,
>   That all the faults which in thy reign are made
>   May likewise be sepulch'red in thy shade.
>
> "Make me not object to the tell-tale Day,
> The light will show, charactered in my brow
> The story of sweet chastity's decay.
> The impious breach of holy wedlock vow.
> Yea, the illiterate, that know not how
>   To cipher what is writ in learned books,
>   Will quote my loathsome trespass in my look.
>
> "The nurse to still her child will tell my story,
> And fright her crying babe with Tarquin's name.
> The orator to deck his oratory
> Will couple my reproach to Tarquin's shame."
> (799–816)

The politically motivated display of Lucrece's "bleeding body" before crowds of people is a profound desecration. We cannot equate Brutus's exploitation of Lucrece's corpse with the violence of Sextus's rape, but it is striking that the tyrannical rapist's threat of public humiliation is morbidly fulfilled by his victim's family and the father of the republic.

Shakespeare figures the origin of Roman republicanism as an act of bad faith: the action that establishes Lucrece's rape as a public cause of freedom is itself a violation of her will. For the revenge Brutus, Lucretius, and Collatine fail to pursue is, we recall, a term of Lucrece's dying *testament:* she waits for Collatine that he might "oversee this will."[44] Collatine's betrayal of his duties as Lucrece's executor is, however, culturally sanctioned. Lucrece only imagines that she can bequeath her wrong—"This wrong of mine"—and the revenge it demands: the slave cannot own a wrong against her person, because she does not own her person; the slave has property in nothing, least of all herself, and thus has nothing to bequeath.

To be Lucrece is to lose control of one's legacy to the endless constructions and motivations of others. But the role of Lucrece, as I have suggested, can never be imposed on any subsequent woman. Put another way, Titus cannot unilaterally make himself into a type of Lucretius, and when Lavinia declines to play Lucrece, Titus seems to reembrace the tale of Philomela as the rough model for his revenge. Thus, for example, he slaughters Chiron and Demetrius and bakes them in a pie, which he will later serve to their mother and stepfather: "worse than Philomel you used my daughter," he charges the brothers before he cuts their throats, "And worse than Progne I will be revenged" (5.2.193–94). Here, then, Titus follows Lavinia's muse, and she willingly assists him by holding a basin to catch the blood—a "hateful liquor" to sauce the filial pie (see 5.2.164.sd; 5.2.180–83, 196–99). But at the infamous banquet where Tamora dines on her sons, Titus's plotting reverts to the republican rape topos: "Was it well done of rash Virginius," he asks Saturninus, "To slay his daughter with his own right hand, / Because she was enforc'd, stain'd, and deflow'r'd?" (5.3.36–38). When Saturninus casually assents, Titus constructs Virginius's slaying of Virginia as an authorization: "A pattern, precedent, and lively warrant / For me, most wretched, to perform the like" (5.3.43–44). Now Titus murders Lavinia. Virginius, unlike Lucretius, is a historical model Titus can imitate without the willing participation of his daughter. Indeed, it is precisely Virginius's disregard for his daughter's consent that defines the "pattern" he establishes; the type of Virginia, in turn, is defined by her absolute subjection to her father's will.[45]

Titus is, however, working from a somewhat defective "pattern": in Livy, Virginius murders his daughter *before* the despotic Appius Claudius can rape her. Some scholars have traced Shakespeare's error to Lodowick Lloyd's *The Marrow of History, or, The Pilgrimage of Kings and Princes* (1573): "How well was temperance regarded in Rome when Virginius slew his daughter Virginia, for that she *was deflouwered* of Appius" (107; emphasis added). Lloyd may have provided a slim literary basis for Titus's reference to a raped Virginia, but his very brief treatment of the story—there is nothing more of any substance than what I have quoted here—can hardly have motivated Shakespeare (or Titus) to invoke Virginius at the moment of Lavinia's murder. There is every reason to believe that Shakespeare was fully acquainted with the historical episode his hero appeals to at the moment of this astonishing infanticide: in republican historiography, the story of Virginia is explicitly linked with the story of Lucrece, for the rape of Virginia sparks the restoration of the republican freedoms that were first won in the wake of the rape of Lucrece.[46]

Among early English authors, the story of Appius and Virginia was almost as popular a subject as the rape of Lucrece. Shakespeare may well have read Livy's and Ovid's respective accounts of Virginia, but he could have encountered her in Chaucer, Gower, Lydgate, Pettie, Lloyd, and the interlude *Apius and Virginia.* Shakespeare's most likely English source, it seems to me, is William Painter's *The palace of pleasure* (1566). Certain details in *Lucrece* establish Shakespeare's familiarity with "The Storie of Lucrece" in Novel 2 of *The pallace of pleasure* (see Shakespeare, *Poems*, ed. Roe, 284n); just a few pages later, Shakespeare would have encountered in Novel 5 a near translation of Livy's republican attack on the *decemviri,* which Painter introduces by drawing a parallel between Appius's attempt to rape Virginia and the "no lesse filthie act, then was doen by Tarquinius, for the rape of Lucrece" (Di[r]). Painter begins with the largest political contexts of the origins of the *decemviri.* Rome has sent a delegation to Athens to study the laws of Solon and "to learne the Institucions, orders, and Lawes of other Greke citees" (Di[r]). When the delegates return, the tribunes are anxious to have their findings codified: "for that purpose, certaine officers were appoincted, called Decemviri: with soveraigne aucthoritie and power, to reduce the same into writyng" (Di[r]). This extraordinary, extraconstitutional power to legislate effectively obviates the role of both the Senate and the tribunate. The *decemviri* not surprisingly attempt to secure permanently their absolute power in Rome, but they are undone by their leader Appius Claudius's desire for Virginia, the daughter of Virginius, a republican-minded centurion. Appius induces Marcus Claudius to claim that Virginia is not the daughter of Virginius but was instead "borne in his house . . . the doughter of his owne bondwoman, who afterwardes beeyng stolen awaie, was caried to the house of Virginius, and supposed to be his childe" (Di[v]). Marcus accosts Virginia in the Forum and claims her, but her nurse's cries raise the people: Marcus, "seyng the maide was like to be rescued . . . by the multitude that was assembled," releases Virginia on condition that she will "accordyng to the lawe, make her apperance . . . before the consistorie, where Appius sat in judgement" (Di[v]). Appius rules that Virginia be delivered into Marcus's possession until her father, who is away from Rome preparing for a battle with the Sabines, returns to answer Marcus's suit: Appius plans to rape Virginia in the interval.

Icilius, Virginia's betrothed, senses the outrage of the assembled people and challenges Appius's judgment:

> I assure thee, the spouse of Icilius shall not remaine out of her fathers house. No although thou hast taken awaie from the Romane people, their Tribunes aide and appeales, whiche be twoo stronge fortes and holdes, of their common libertie. Is aucthoritie given thee, libidinously to abuse our wives and children?. . . . I will for myne owne part, and for the love of my beloved crie out for the aide of the Romanes that be present. . . . And for my parte, my life shall soner faile, in defending her libertie, then my faithe to her betrouthed. (Dii[r]–Dii[v])

For Icilius, an ex-tribune and "a manne of greate stoutness and tried valiance in the cause of the people," Marcus and Appius's attempt to seize Virginia is both a personal crisis and an object lesson in recent political history: before the people, he extols the tribunate as the fence that protected their "common libertie" from Tarquinian abuses.[47] The emboldened "multitude of their owne accords, helde up their hands promisyng to become suretie for Icilius," and Virginia is released into the custody of her family (Dii[v]).

Virginius returns the next day and appears in the Forum, where he and Icilius appeal to "the multitude" for their support (Diii[r]).[48] Although he sees how the wind is blowing, Appius renders a verdict for Marcus, "which sentence, semed so cruell, that it appalled the whole multitude" (Diii[r]) The people at first repulse Marcus's attempt to take possession of Virginia, but they give way when Appius, with "greate furie," accuses the people of sedition and sends a "Sergeant" to lay hold of Virginia. After this failure of the people's nerve, Virginius feigns resignation and begs leave to take his daughter and her nurse aside for a few moments; then, "pluckyng a sharpe knife from a Botcher that stoode by, he thruste the same to the hart of his doughter" (Diii[v]). Virginius figures his deed not as infanticide but as ritual sacrifice: "By this only meanes (doughter) I can make thee free. . . . This bloodde Appius I consecrate and bestowe upon thee" (Diii^v^). Virginia's bloody corpse works a distinctly Lucrecean magic: "Icilius and Numitorius took up the deade bodie, and shewed it to the people, who cried out upon the wickednesse of Appius" (Diii^v^). The people revolt and, with the encouragement of the defanged Senate, depose the *decemviri.* Appius commits suicide, and the tribunate is restored: the "Roman people made Aulus Virginius, Lucius Icilius, and Numitorius the[ir] Tribunes who with their assistants, first advanced and confirmed the libertie of the people" (Eii^v^–Eiii^r^).

Virginius's emancipation of Virginia—"By this only meanes (doughter) I can make thee free"—secures the "libertie of the people." But for all the talk of "defending [Virginia's] libertie," Virginius never even solicits his daughter's consent, and she dies without speaking a word. In Filippino Lippi's *Storia di Virginia* (1488–90?), Virginia is clearly shocked by her father's murderous blow, and, indeed, all of the onlookers, including Appius himself, recoil or flee from the *pollution* of infanticide (figs. 6–7). Many literary artists seem to have shared Lippi's horror: Chaucer apparently found Virginius's act so disturbing that he supplied Virginia with a meditation in which she reconciles herself to death and absolves her father (The Physician's Tale, 214–50); in Pettie's prose narrative, Virginia begs her father for death. But in Livy and Painter, Virginia is entirely mute. Virginius's infanticide, I believe, clarified and intensified for Shakespeare the paradox of the republican rape topos. Virginius and Icilius's rhetoric of freedom may suggest a quite broad challenge to Appius's tyranny, but it is also fashioned quite specifically in response to the false claim that Virginia is a *slave.* Virginius "frees" Virginia not only from Appius's sexual violence but also from Marcus's ownership. But Virginius's preemptive murder of Virginia in the absence of any encouragement from her suggests that, in his mind, she is *his* property. The father enacts the fundamental violation he seeks to prevent: he denies Virginia's capacity to consent.

The murder of Lavinia reveals and repeats the patriarchal tyranny lurking behind Virginius's republican revolt against political tyranny. We can see now that from the very beginning of the play—when Titus barters Lavinia to Saturninus and Bassianus claims her as his property—Shakespeare is fashioning a radical retelling not only of the rape of Lucrece but of the murder of Virginia as well.[49] When Titus takes his daughter's life, he fulfills the pattern established by Virginius, not because Lavinia is already a type of Virginia, but because he makes her a type of Virginia. Titus himself acknowledges that it is his own identification with Virginius—rather than any analogy between

Lavinia and Virginia—that motivates his act: "I am as woeful," he laments after he has imitated the terrible precedent, "as Virginius was" (5.3.50). It is a moment of rare, if incomplete, clarity for Titus: he half understands that Lavinia becomes a type of Virginia not because she's been raped but because he stabs her as she stands silently before him. We do not know what fate Virginia might have chosen for herself; Lavinia identifies herself with a raped and maimed maiden who was transformed into a bird. Unfortunately for Lavinia, Titus, rather than Apollo, is the god of her fate.

◇◇

Titus's murder of Lavinia ushers in the final resolution of the revenge plot: with the murders of Chiron and Demetrius already accomplished, Titus kills their mother Tamora; Saturninus kills Titus; Lucius kills Saturninus. The stage is now a tableau of slaughtered bodies, mute Romans, and the menacing Gothic army Lucius has mustered to overthrow Saturninus. Marcus, with Lucius in tow, mounts the upper stage to reassure the "sad-faced men, people and sons of Rome" (5.3.66) that he can "teach [them] how to knit again" Rome's "broken limbs . . . into one body" (5.3.69–71). But an anonymous Roman lord urges Lucius to explain Rome's plight: "Speak, Rome's dear friend, as erst our ancestor, / When with his solemn tongue he did discourse / To love-sick Dido's sad attending ear" (5.3.79–81). The suggestion that Lucius play Aeneas to the people's Dido is, to put it mildly, peculiar: Aeneas, of course, eventually deceives and abandons Dido. Whether the Roman lord is dropping Lucius a hint, anticipating what he expects will be a deceitful speech, or invoking, without irony, "*pius Aeneas*" is uncertain, but in Shakespeare's works, Aeneas is almost always a byword for betrayal.[50] Moreover, the particular Virgilian passage the Roman lord has in mind is itself a narrative of betrayal: "Tell us what Sinon hath bewitched our ears" (84). Sinon convinces the Trojans that he has deserted from the Greek forces because Ulysses and Calchas have marked him for sacrifice. The Trojans grant Sinon asylum, and he persuades them to bring the wooden horse into their city. Now we wait for a latter-day Aeneas to fill the "sad attending ears" of Rome's Didos with reports of a new Sinon who "hath bewitched [their] ears." Didos expecting Aeneas to deliver them from Sinon's lies are in very grave danger indeed, for Aeneas was to Carthage what Sinon was to Troy.[51]

When he addresses his "gracious auditory," Lucius takes the Virgilian cue to heart: instead of acknowledging his family's ruinous machinations, he blames all of Rome's troubles on the aliens Chiron and Demetrius (95–117).[52] Lucius's demonization of the Gothic brothers turns out to be a hustings speech. After he seconds Lucius by figuring Aaron, the "irreligious Moor," as the "[c]heif architect and plotter of these woes" (5.3.120–21), Marcus histrionically offers to submit himself and his nephew to Rome's judgment:

> MARCUS: Now have you heard the truth; what say you, Romans?
> Have we done aught amiss, show us wherein,
> And from the place where you behold us pleading
> The poor remainder of Andronici
> Will hand in hand all headlong hurl ourselves
> And on the ragged stones beat forth our souls
> And make a mutual closure of our house.
> Speak, Romans, speak, and if you say we shall,
> Lo, hand in hand Lucius and I will fall.
> (5.3.127–35)

Standing above the stage, Marcus imaginatively locates himself and his nephew on the Tarpeian rock from which Rome's internal enemies were traditionally thrown. No chorus of "Romans" begs them to save themselves, but Aemilius urges the Andronici not to do themselves in, and he recognizes Lucius as the new emperor:

> AEMILIUS: Come, come, thou reverend man of Rome,
> And bring our emperor gently in thy hand,
> Lucius, our emperor; for well I know
> The common voice do cry it shall be so.
> (5.3.136–39)

But just as Aemilius alone answered Marcus's appeal to the people's judgment, now the general acclamation Aemilius seems to anticipate is shouted not by "the common voice" but by Marcus alone: "Lucius, all hail, Rome's royal emperor!" (140).

This hailing of Lucius and Marcus's later acclamation—"Lucius, all hail, Rome's gracious governor" (145)—have a markedly supplemental quality. Aemilius twice calls Lucius "emperor" *before* Marcus, standing for the "common voice," hails his nephew as "Rome's royal emperor" (5.3.140). Perhaps Aemilius jumps the gun because he knows Marcus will acclaim Lucius—just as Lucius knew that Marcus would acclaim Saturninus—or perhaps he recognizes that Lucius, who has killed the previous emperor and has a formidable army at his back, is already the de facto ruler of Rome.[53] In this chaotic moment, Rome's patricians are somewhat less attentive to obscuring the fraud of political representation. If the silence of the people is palpable during the "election" of Saturninus, it should now, after so many scenes in which muteness is the sign of subjection and ruin, be all that we can hear. The play ends where it began: the very circularity of Shakespeare's plot is a rejection of the republican rape topos and a critique of representational politics.

Modern editors have insisted that both the First Quarto and Folio inappropriately attribute the two hailings of Lucius to Marcus and reassign them to "All" or "Romans."[54] Edward Capell, the first editor to emend "Marcus" to "Romans," argues that "the pretense that Marcus speaks for them is indeed foolish, and will never be set up by persons of understanding." I suppose Capell is, in a way, entirely right: the pretense that Marcus speaks for the people is "indeed foolish." But, of course, it is precisely that pretense that Shakespeare both represents and undermines in *Titus Andronicus.*

◇◇

I have been arguing that Shakespeare's critique of political representation in *Titus* turns on the shared muteness of Lavinia and the common people of Rome, but there is one articulate plebeian in the play. In act 4, scene 3 a "*Clown with a basket and two pigeons in it*" (4.3.76.1) wanders on stage while the now mad Titus is publicizing Saturninus's injustices: Titus has drawn up letters—addressed to the gods—proclaiming the infamy of the royal family and affixed these broadsides to arrows that he and his kinsmen are shooting in the general direction of the imperial palace.[55] The Clown is pursuing his own, more mundane business: "I am going," the rustic tells the old general, "with my pigeons to the tribunal plebs to take up a matter of brawl betwixt my uncle and one of the Emperal's men" (4.3.91–93).

Titus, prompted by Marcus, incorporates the Clown into his schemes against Saturninus, but he does so under the guise of putting himself at the Clown's service. When Titus discovers that the Clown is illiterate, he volunteers to write him "a supplication" (102) to present not to the tribunes of the people but to Saturninus himself. Titus thus proposes to represent the Clown: "*By me,*" he assures him, "thou shalt have justice at [Saturninus's] hands" (96; emphasis added). Titus composes the supplication, wraps it around a knife, and sends the Clown on his way. We never learn the contents of this letter, but it certainly is not intended to resolve the dispute between its bearer's uncle and the emperor's man:

Enter Clown
TAMORA: How now, good fellow, wouldst thou speak with us?
CLOWN: Yea, forsooth, an your mistress-ship be Emperial.
TAMORA: Empress I am, but yonder sits the Emperor.

> CLOWN: 'Tis he. God and Saint Stephen give you good-e'en. I have brought you a letter and a couple of pigeons here.
> *Saturninus reads the letter*
> SATURNINUS: Go, take him away, and hang him presently.
> CLOWN: How much money must I have?
> TAMORA: Come, sirrah, you must be hanged.
> CLOWN: Hang'd, by'Lady? Then I have brought up a neck to a fair end.
> (4.4.39–49)

After the Clown is taken off by the imperial guards, Saturninus rails against the "despiteful and intolerable wrongs" contained in the "supplication"—accusations, from what we can gather, that Titus's sons Quintus and Martius "have by [Saturninus's] means been butchered wrongfully" (53). Titus murders the Clown just as surely as Saturninus does.

The Clown's fate is predictable: anyone unfortunate enough to be represented by the brothers Andronici ends badly. The Clown is most obviously Lavinia's lowly double: both are pawns in Titus's political machinations, both die in the service of his schemes, both become mediums of his words even as he claims to speak for them.[56] The Clown, moreover, metonymically embodies the ghostly people of Rome: Titus delivers him into Saturninus's hands just as he delivered the people's votes and his own daughter into Saturninus's hands. The story of the Clown, then, is a little tragedy of representation within a fictive world in which all tragedies are tragedies of representation and all representation ends tragically. Tragedy may seem an impossibly grand claim for so humble a character and for so slight a scene, but the Clown's miserable fall is a distinctly English story that implicates Shakespeare's audience—at least the members of Shakespeare's audience, and they were many, who could not read supplications—in the larger tragedy of *Titus Andronicus*.

If the supplication is the instrumental cause of the Clown's death, his fate is sealed by his illiteracy. Writing here is both representation per se and a medium of representation: because written representation is opaque to the Clown, he has no access to the way Titus represents him. The whole of act 4—four scenes dominated by writing and reading—is designed to reproduce on stage the opacity of writing, the experience of illiteracy, representation as threshold. We recall that act 4 begins with a scene of reading and writing: Titus reads the passage in the *Metamorphoses* to which Lavinia has drawn his attention; Lavinia, in turn, writes the names of the rapists in the "sandy plot." Perhaps Lavinia's arduous inscription inspires the peculiarly literary campaign of intimidation Titus wages against the imperial family. In the next scene, Titus sends the two rapists "*a bundle of weapons*" with ominous "*verses writ upon them*" (4.2.1.sd); in scene 3, Titus shoots off his brace of letter arrows; and, finally, in scene 4, the Clown presents Titus's defiant supplication—wrapped around a weapon—to Saturninus.[57]

These scenes function as a series of literacy tests for the audience; they prepare the way, that is, for an identification between the illiterate audience and the Clown, and, thus, by extension, the people of Rome.[58] It is fitting that Lavinia, the aristocratic double of Rome's oppressed people, begins this process of identification. When Lavinia writes in the dust, she regains, for a brief moment, the capacity to represent herself, but the illiterate audience witness a staging of their own muteness, their own lack of writing. To be sure, when Titus reads out what Lavinia has written, he seems to enact the theater's refusal of textuality: on the stage, letters, even letters scrawled in sandy plots, are transformed into speech. But Lavinia's spare text is in Latin: "*Stuprum—Chiron—Demetrius.*"[59] I expect that some uneducated Elizabethans knew the meaning of *stuprum* (rape)—various cognates had passed into early modern English—and for all but the slowest spectators, Marcus's reaction to Lavinia's text would have served as a translation: "What, what! The lustful sons of Tamora / Performers of this heinous, bloody deed?" But Titus's response to Lavinia's revelation is another matter: "Magni dominator poli, / Tam lentus audis scelera, tam lentus vides?" (Great ruler of the heavens, are you so slow to hear of crimes and to observe them?). No one helpfully translates Titus's quotation from Seneca's *Hippolytus:* these lines would have remained entirely opaque to the illiterate—an oral representation of the textual, a moment of aural illiteracy. Having a character read Latin out loud is a marvelously efficient way to remind the illiterate members of the audience of their ignorance; one could hardly improve on the effect by displaying an inscription on a placard.

The scene in which Demetrius and Chiron puzzle over the strange package Titus has sent them *thematizes* the illiterate audience's experience of Titus's Senecan quotation:

> DEMETRIUS: What's here? A scroll, and written round about?
> Let's see. "*Integer vitae, scelerisque purus,*
> *Non eget Mauri iaculis, nec arcu.*" [The man of upright life and free
> from crime does not need the javelins or bow of the Moor.]
> CHIRON: O, 'tis a verse in Horace; I know it well.
> I read it in the grammar long ago.
> AARON: Ay, just; a verse in Horace—right, you have it.
> (*Aside*) Now what a thing it is to be an ass!

> Here's no sound jest. The old man hath found their guilt.
> (4.2.18–26)

The Horatian verse, like the quotation from Seneca, constitutes an aural blank spot for the illiterate audience, and their own incomprehension is theatricalized by Chiron. Chiron boastfully recalls his grammar but immediately demonstrates that the meaning of the lines, in fact, escapes him. Aaron's amusement is a lovely device: the illiterate audience understands the joke—the smug Chiron does not realize that Titus's choice of verse reveals that he knows the circumstances of his daughter's rape—at the same time they understand that, in virtue of their own incomprehension, it is also on them. Aaron never lets the brothers in on Titus's joke, and their ignorance lands them in the pie Titus cooks up for his revenge banquet. The Clown dies because he cannot read; Chiron and Demetrius are fatally obtuse readers.[60]

The relation between writing and violence and the politics of literacy were much on Shakespeare's mind in the early 1590s. In *Henry VI, Part 2* (1591), written just a year before Titus (Wells 111–13), Cade and his followers demonize writing as the instrument—perhaps even the positive condition—of their violent oppression at the hands of the lettered class. The rebellion briefly turns the world upside down when Cade makes literacy a capital offense: the rebels' first act is to hang the Clerk of Chatham "with his pen and inkhorn about his neck" (4.2.103–4) because he can "write and read" (4.2.86). Executing the literate because they are literate, Cade suggests in his indictment of Lord Say, is a very precise revenge: "Thou hast appointed justices of peace to call poor men before them about matters they were not able to answer. Moreover, thou hast put them in prison, and, because they could not read, thou hast hang'd them; when, indeed, only for that cause they have been most worthy to live" (4.7.38–43). Cade refers here to the so-called neck verse: in early modern England, one could escape the hangman by reading a few lines of Scripture in Latin. No Elizabethan, then, would miss the fine irony of Cade's response to Say's characterization of Kent as "*bona terra, mala gens*": "Away with him! away with him! he speaks Latin" (55). Sending a man to—rather than saving him from—the gallows because he speaks Latin merely turns the tables on the literate.[61]

Although the neck verse had originally been a benefit of clergy, by Shakespeare's time, laymen such as Ben Jonson could show off their Latin to save themselves from the rope. But the requirement of reading from Scripture in Latin—typically from the Fifty-first Psalm—to obtain grace and pardon preserved the religious resonance of the practice. With this context and his end on the gallows in mind, we can see that the Clown's fate is both sealed and foreshadowed in the way he first betrays his illiteracy:

> TITUS: Tell me, can you deliver an oration to the emperor with a grace?
> CLOWN: Nay, truly, sir, I could never say grace in all my life.
> TITUS: Sirrah, come hither: make no more ado,
> But give your pigeons to the emperor:
> By me thou shalt have justice at his hands.
> Hold, hold; meanwhile here's money for thy charges.
> Give me pen and ink.
> Sirrah, can you with a grace deliver up a supplication?
> CLOWN: Ay, Sir.
> (Bate, ed., *Titus* 4.3.97–105)

The Clown never explicitly states that he cannot read, but his admission that "he could never say grace in all [his] life" clearly suggests to Titus that he is illiterate. Titus firsts asks the Clown if he "can . . . deliver an oration to the emperor." After the Clown answers "Nay," Titus amends his question: "can you . . . deliver up a supplication?" J. Dover Wilson argues that the near identity of Titus's two questions indicates that Shakespeare revised this passage but forgot to strike the original from his manuscript.[62] Most editors have followed Wilson's lead; Wells and Taylor, for example, omit lines 97 and 98 from the Oxford edition. But the difference between *delivering an oration* and *delivering up a supplication* is a world of difference—it is, for the Clown, a fatal difference. Titus's second question is prompted by the discovery that the Clown is illiterate and thus incapable of delivering an oration. To deliver up a supplication to the emperor's hand, of course, requires neither literacy nor the grace of rhetorical performance Titus refers to in line 97. The grace Titus seeks in line 105 is now bodily grace: "Then here is a supplication for you. And when you come to him, at the first approach you must kneel; then kiss his foot; then deliver up your pigeons; then look for your reward" (108–15). Handing over a supplication or pigeons is one thing; performing a scripted oration is another.

How can Titus read the Clown's illiteracy from his inability to say grace? The logic here is somewhat obscure for us: surely these brief prayers could be transmitted orally. For Elizabethans, however, the link between literacy and saying grace was quite specific. Generations of English children first encountered the written word in *An A.B.C. wyth a Cathechisme,* one of the best-selling books in sixteenth- and seventeenth-century England. In its pages, thousands of Elizabethans, having first mastered the alphabet and the rudiments of grammar, tackled their first reading texts—the Ten Commandments, the Suffrages, and so on; at the end of *An A.B.C.,* they learned the graces said before and after meals (see fig. 8).[63] Saying grace, then, was a sign of literacy per se and of religious literacy in particular: the title pages of many editions of *An A.B.C.* identify the little book as "*an instruction to be learned of everye chylde before he be brought to be confyrmed of thee Byshoppe.*"[64] The Clown's inability to say grace not only establishes his illiteracy but invokes its fatal—perhaps its eternal—consequences: those who cannot say grace will find none on the gallows.[65] The Clown is not King Lear: he has not given away a kingdom; he has not been toppled from the summit of Fortune's wheel; he has not betrayed his daughter. Perhaps, however, it is not too much to say that Shakespeare was, even as he wrote his first tragedy, rethinking the genre when he fashioned a very humble character who dies because he never learned to read these words: "Good lord bless us and all thy gifts" (Civ^{v}); "The god of peace and love, vouchsafe always to dwell wythe us" (Cv^{r}); "Lord have mercy upon us. Christe have mercye upon us. Lorde have mercy upon us" (Cv^{v}).

My elaborate reconstruction of the cultural resonances of grace, hanging, illiteracy, and Latin gives, I fear, exactly the wrong impression of how this scene must have played in the Elizabethan theater. Everyone in Shakespeare's audience would have understood in a flash that the Roman Clown dies an English death. The Clown is kinsman to those "poor men" whose blood is on Lord Say's hands: "because they could not read," Cade charges Say, "thou hast hang'd them." The Englishness of the Clown's demise is reinforced by the odd emphasis on the mode of execution:

> SATURNINUS: Go, take him away, and hang him presently.
> CLOWN: How much money must I have?
> TAMORA: Come, sirrah, you must be hanged.
> CLOWN: Hang'd, by'Lady? Then I have brought up a neck to a fair end.
> (4.4.44–47)

Titus, famously, is a play of many executions: Titus orders Tamora's son Alarbus to be hacked to pieces ("with our swords, upon a pile of wood, / Let's hew his limbs till they be clean consum'd" [1.1.128–29]); Saturninus orders the beheading of Titus's sons Quintus and Martius; and Marcus, as the play ends, is preparing for Aaron "some direful slaught'ring death (5.3.143). Mixed in with these (more or less) juridical killings are more than half a dozen simple murders: Mutius, Chiron, Demetrius, Titus, Saturninus, Tamora, Lavinia, and Tamora's nurse all die by the sword. Amidst all these deaths by steel, the Clown alone is turned off on a gallows.

Shakespeare wants that English noose dangling in his audience's imagination the minute the Clown opens his mouth:

> *Enter the* Clown *with a basket and two pigeons in it.*
> TITUS: News, news from heaven! Marcus, the post is come.
> Sirrah, what tidings? Have you any letters?
> Shall I have justice? What says Jupiter?
> CLOWN: Ho, the gibbet-maker? He says that he hath taken them down again, for the man must not be hanged till the next week.
> TITUS: But what says Jupiter, I ask thee?
> CLOWN: Alas, sir, I know not Jubiter, I never drank with him in all my life.
> TITUS: Why, villain, art not thou the carrier?
> CLOWN: Ay, of my pigeons, sir—nothing else.
> TITUS: Why, didst thou not come from heaven?
> CLOWN: From heaven? Alas, sir, I never came from there.
> God forbid I should be so bold to press heaven in my
> young days.
> (Bate 4.3.77–91)

"Gibbet-maker" is the first substantive word that the Clown speaks and it signifies simultaneously "gallows maker" and, as a bungling of "Jupiter," fatal ignorance.[66] Characters who mistake the name of God for "gallows-maker" tend to be outside the decorous limits of tragic representation. The Clown is, after all, a clown, and all three of his malapropisms mark his estrangement from power and authority: "gibbet-maker" for Jupiter; "tribunal plebs" for *tribunus plebis;* "Emperal" for emperor. But the Clown is also the only entirely sympathetic character in the play, and his death by representation is especially resonant because Shakespeare has made him the play's only hope for benign representation: he is on his way to plead his uncle's case before one of the tribunes of the people. The Clown's efforts on his uncle's behalf conjure up the Edenic presence and orality Cade promises: he will offer the tribune pigeons instead of supplications, speak a few words, and settle the dispute. As the Clown rehearses his naive plan, we glimpse a kind of prehistoric world in which representation does not necessarily entail the representative's violence against the represented. But the Clown's vision of representation is erased by Titus's, and even the illiterate members of Shakespeare's audience who laugh at the rustic must sense that he figures them, that he brings home to them the larger tragedy of political representation his fate epitomizes: the Clown is representation's Fool, and he is their double.

4 *"Caesar is turn'd to hear"*

Theater, Popular Dictatorship, and the Conspiracy of Republicanism in *Julius Caesar*

Gnaeus Pompey's conquests in Asia were so vast that even "the stateliness and magnificence" of a Roman triumph proved to be an inadequate showcase for the spoils and prisoners he brought back to the city in 61 B.C.: "although he had two dayes space to shew [them]," Plutarch marvels, "yet he lacked tyme: for there were many things prepared for the shew that were not seen which would have served to have set out an other triumph" (trans. North 700).[1] Pompey had previously celebrated triumphs honoring his campaigns in Africa and Europe, and his sweeping victories on a third continent established him as a peerless general: "the greatest honor that ever he wanne, and which never other consull of the Romans but himself obtained, was this: that he made his third triumphe of the three partes of the world" (trans. North 701). This feat prompted comparisons with Alexander and made Pompey the darling of the Roman people. Pompey now turned his attention to domestic affairs, but within a few short years his autocratic management of Roman politics had cost him much of the popularity he had earned at the expense of Rome's enemies. Pompey apparently considered a return to the battlefield too arduous a path back to the people's hearts. Appian suggests that Pompey recovered the people's goodwill by supplying them with bread,[2] but Lucan gives equal credit to circuses:

Pompey (surpris'd with elder yeares)
His course in quiet glory steeres.
And (keeping state in peacefull gowne)
Followes not Mars for more renowne.

He dotes upon domesticke fame,
And so (to glorifie his name)
To State-affaires doth frame his bent.
And then (to give the world content)
With largesse plyes the common Rowt,
And, on the Theaters, sets out
His great exployts, and seruice done
Till through the peoples eares it runne,
Suffis'd when their applause is wonne.
No new imployments he requests;
But on his fore-past fortunes rests.[3]

The chief venue for this campaign of propaganda was the great theater built by Pompey himself in 55 B.C. The *theatrum Pompeii,* the first permanent theater in Rome, was a magnificent structure: the theater accommodated at least 17,500 spectators and perhaps as many as 40,000;[4] a temple dedicated to *Venus Victrix* rose from "the top of the central part of the *cavea* . . . so that the rows of seats might appear to be the steps leading up to the temple" (Nash 2:516);[5] the *porticus Pompeii* enclosed a vast rectangular court immediately behind the stage where spectators could seek shelter during rainstorms; and the *curia Pompeii,* an *excedra* within the *porticus,* provided the city with an assembly room near the theater (Platner 374–75). Constructing this enormously expensive complex of buildings was a winning investment: Plutarch says that the "many goodly plays" Pompey financed "to show the people pastime and pleasure made him againe to be very much esteemed of and beloved amongest the people" (704). By 52 B.C., Pompey was sole consul, master of the Senate, and the most powerful man in the world. Soon enough, however, an irresistible force, a new Alexander, who would prove fatal to Pompey, crossed the Rubicon.

It is one of the nice accidents of history that Julius Caesar was murdered in the *curia* built by the great rival he had defeated at the battle of Pharsalus in 48 B.C.[6] The Roman Senate had assembled for generations in the *curia Hostilia,* but in 44 B.C. that building was, by Caesar's own order, undergoing repairs, and the senators had to decamp to the *curia Pompeii.*[7] It is hard to imagine Caesar taking much pleasure in these ironies, but in his *Life of Brutus,* Plutarch remarks on the divine justice of the murder scene:

> Now a day being appointed for the meeting of the senate, at what time they hoped *Caesar* would not faile to come, the conspirators determined then to put their enterprise in execution, bicause they might meete safelie at that time without suspicion. . . . Furthermore, they thought also that the appointment of the place where the counceil shoulde be kept, was chosen of

purpose by divine providence, and made all for them. For it was one of the porches about the Theater, in the which there was a certaine place full of seates for men to sit in; where also was set up the image of *Pompey,* which the citie had made and consecrated in honor of him, when he did beawtifie that parte of the citie with the Theater he built, with divers porches about it. In this place was the assembly of the Senate appointed to be, just on the fifteenth day of the moneth of March . . . so that it seemed some god of purpose had brought *Caesar* thither to be slaine for revenge of *Pompeys* death. (1061)

Thomas North's translation flattens the detail of Jacques Amyot's "un conclave garni de sieges tout l'entour," but "a certain place full of seats" designates clearly enough the *curia.*[8] In his translation of the *Vie de Jules César,* however, North seriously and quite wonderfully bungles the topography of Caesar's death:

. . . le lieu auquel estoit lors assemblé le senat ayant une image de Pompeius, et estant l'un des edifices qu'il avoit donnez et dediez à la chose publique avec son theatre, monstroit bien evidemment, que c'estoit pour certain quelque divinité qui guidoit l'entreprise, et qui en conduisoit l'execution notamment en ceste place là. (Amyot 2:481)

. . . the place where the murther was prepared, and where the Senate were assembled, and where also there stoode up an image of *Pompey* dedicated by him selfe amongest other ornamentes which he gave unto the Theater: all these were manifest proofes that it was the ordinaunce of some god, that made this treason to be executed, specially in that verie place. (North 794)

Ignoring the modifier "et estant l'un des edifices [and being one of the edifices]," North collapses "le lieu" and "son theatre" and thus manages to enhance the high drama of Caesar's death by setting it not in Pompey's Court but in the Theater itself. Shakespeare had North at hand when he wrote *Julius Caesar* (1599), and North's carelessness would seem remarkably fortuitous, for it provided the dramatist with an irresistibly suggestive intersection between politics and theater. Shakespeare's handling of the theatrical setting of this most famous political murder has been crucial, not surprisingly, to several recent interpretations of the play.[9] But Shakespeare's Caesar, as it happens, does *not* die in Pompey's Theater.

Shakespeare departs—rather perversely it would seem—from North's *Life of Caesar,* his principal source, by relocating the murder scene to "the Senate House" and "the Capitol."[10] Pompey's Theater does figure importantly in Shakespeare's play: Cassius variously instructs Cinna to meet him at "Pompey's porch" (1.3.126, 147) and "Pompey's theatre" (1.3.152), where they will join "some certain of the noblest-minded Romans" (122) to plot the assassination of Caesar. Shakespeare, then, was certainly familiar with Pompey's Theater; why not stage the murder there?[11] Moreover, Brutus and Cassius repeatedly associate republican conspiracy and theater: "Let not our looks put on our purposes," Brutus encourages his co-conspirators, "But bear it as our Roman actors do, / With untired spirits and formal constancy" (2.1.226–27); and Brutus and Cassius, as soon as Caesar lies dead at their feet, begin to imagine theatrical reenactments of their liberation of Rome (3.1.111–19). Why pass up the chance to stage the fulfillment of this theatrical conspiracy as a scene in a theater?[12] Shakespeare, I suggest, quite deliberately detheatricalizes the assassination because the conspiracy is, in fact, antitheatrical. The republican appropriations of theatricality are always already undermined by the initial association of conspiracy with an *empty* theater: the conspirators meet at Pompey's Theater "after midnight" (1.3.163), when "there is no stir or walking in the streets" (1.3.127). In Elizabethan and Jacobean culture, the theater was a byword for publicness: alarmingly crowded, disturbingly open to anyone who could pay, theaters—especially amphitheaters like the Globe, where *Julius Caesar* was first performed in 1599—scandalously subjected the most private affairs and thoughts of both kings and clowns to the light of day and to the scrutiny of popular audiences.[13] The conspirators, then, transform Pompey's Theater into its own antithesis; the conspiracy is a betrayal of theater.

The aristocratic plot against Caesar must be hatched in private—must, that is, be conspiracy rather than theater—because the public, the common people in whose name Caesar is murdered, love Caesar. In a radical departure from his sources, Shakespeare figures the murder of Caesar as a betrayal of the people's will. Shakespeare establishes an *empty* theater as the symbolic locus of the conspiracy because a *full* theater was—in both Shakespeare's England and, as we shall see, the Rome of *Julius Caesar*—a place of popular judgment. The antitheatricality of the conspiracy, then, is an unmistakable sign of its antipopulism. Reshaping what had always been a narrative about aristocratic infighting into a play about popular politics, Shakespeare reconceives the conspirators' putative defense of the Roman Republic from Caesar's monarchism as a defense of the republic from popular dictatorship. But Brutus, though he knows the people love Caesar, constructs the conspiracy neither as a simple defiance of the people's will nor even as a paternalistic attempt to save the people from their own bad judgment. Indeed, Brutus commits himself to the plot against Caesar only after he has convinced himself that he embodies the general will; our interest here is in Brutus's delusion that he kills Caesar not in his own person but as the representative of all Rome. Shakespeare makes an empty theater the degree zero of this betrayal of the people's will and their right to judge their own enemies because he thinks of the theater as a model for genuinely democratic relations of power.[14]

◇◇

Elizabethan audiences at the Globe must have expected a play about the strivings of titans such as Caesar, Brutus, Cassius, and Antony—a play that captured something of the extravagant grandeur of Roman history.[15] Shakespeare, however, chose to begin his narrative of the fall of "the noblest man / That ever lived in the tide of times" (3.1.259–60) with a confrontation between a group of anonymous plebeians and two less than famous members of Rome's ruling class:

> FLAVIUS: Hence! home, you idle creatures, get you home:
> Is this a holiday? What, know you not,
> Being mechanical, you ought not walk
> Upon a labouring day without the sign
> Of your profession?—Speak, what trade are thou?
> CARPENTER: Why, sir, a carpenter.
> MARULLUS: Where is thy leather apron, and thy rule?
> What dost thou with thy best apparel on?
> You, sir, what trade are you?
> COBBLER: Truly, sir, in respect of a fine workman, I am but, as you would say, a cobbler.
> . . . .
> FLAVIUS: But wherefore art not in thy shop to-day?
> Why dost thou lead these men about the streets?
> COBBLER: Truly, sir, to wear out their shoes, to get myself into more work. But indeed, sir, we make holiday to see Caesar, and to rejoice in his triumph.
> (1.1.1–11, 27–31)

These exchanges haunt the confrontation between the senator Menenius and the nameless citizens during the first moments of *Coriolanus*, but Flavius and Marullus are not senators—they are the tribunes of the people. Caesar commands the affection of a cobbler; the plebeians' affection for Caesar puts them at odds with their own tribunes: these are the two things Shakespeare wants us to know at the beginning of *Julius Caesar*.[16]

Critics and editors often remark how closely Shakespeare's play follows Plutarch's *Lives*, but I cannot think of a Shakespearean work that more radically turns a source on its head: the politics of Plutarch's Rome—where Caesar is decidedly unpopular, the tribunes are the people's favorites, and the common citizens scarcely figure in the calculations of power—are completely unrecognizable by the end of the first scene.[17] Let me begin with the popular support Shakespeare's Caesar enjoys. In a passage North entitles "Why Caesar was hated," Plutarch suggests that the patrician conspirators and the common people were united by their loathing of the would-be king: "the chiefest cause that made him mortally hated, was the covetous desire he had to be called king: which first gave the people just cause, and next his secret enemies, honest colour to beare him ill will" (791). In Shakespeare's play, by contrast, Antony's fleeting attempt to crown Caesar—perhaps the outstanding evidence of "the covetous desire he had to be called king"—sparks a demonstration of Caesar's popularity. A little earlier in the *Life of Caesar,* Plutarch proposes another "chiefest cause" of the people's enmity: "the triumphe he made into Rome" to celebrate his victory over Pompey's sons "did as much offend the Romans, and more, than any thing that ever he had done before" (789).[18] Shakespeare not only makes Caesar the people's favorite, he transforms this famous affront into a popular celebration.

Recent critics have proposed various Elizabethan contexts for the tribunes' suppression of the people's holiday: for Mark Rose, Marullus and Flavius resemble "the Puritan preachers of [Shakespeare's] day" (292) who railed against traditional holidays and festive license (294); Richard Wilson sees the tribunes as spokesmen for an ambitious theater company newly sympathetic to secular authorities and anxious to distance itself from an older, carnivalesque brand of theater and the wrong sort of audience it attracted. That undesirable audience, Wilson argues, is figured by the Roman artificers of the first scene (46–51).[19] The cultural meanings of the tribunes' antifestive rhetoric may well be overdetermined, but these attempts to historicize the conflict between the tribunes and the people oddly abstract that conflict from its context in Shakespeare's play—a context that Shakespeare, as we have seen, has taken the trouble to invent. The Cobbler very precisely identifies the occasion for the people's festive mood: "we make holiday to see Caesar, and to rejoice in his triumph" (1.1.30–31). The tribunes, in turn, have very particular political motives for suppressing precisely this holiday, which they regard as a dangerous intersection of Caesar's ambition and the power of the people. As soon as he has dismissed the people from the stage (1.1.56–62), Flavius turns his attention to Caesar's designs on absolute power:

FLAVIUS: Go you down that way towards the Capitol;
This way will I. Disrobe the images,
If you do find them deck'd with ceremonies.
MARULLUS: May we do so?
You know it is the feast of Lupercal.
FLAVIUS: It is no matter; let no images
Be hung with Caesar's trophies. I'll about
And drive the vulgar from the streets;
So do you too, where you perceive them thick.
These growing feathers pluck'd from Caesar's wing
Will make him fly an ordinary pitch,
Who else would soar above the view of men
And keep us all in servile fearfulness.
(1.1.63–75)

In Plutarch's *Life of Caesar,* the tribunes remove "diadems" from the "images of *Caesar*" and thus become popular heroes: "the people followed them rejoycing at it, and called them *Brutes,* bicause of *Brutus,* who had in old time driven the kings out of Rome, and that brought the kingdom of one person, unto the government of the Senate and the people" (792; cf. *Life of Antony* 976). In Shakespeare's Rome, by contrast, removing "ceremonies" and "trophies" from statues of Caesar is an antipopulist action continuous with "driv[ing] the vulgar from the streets."

Ancient and earlier English writers assign the people—if they bother to mention them at all—a very modest role in the politics of Caesar's Rome. But Flavius figures popular support as the positive condition of Caesarism itself: the "growing feathers" that threaten to raise Caesar "above the view of men" are neither his patrician followers nor his army veterans but "the vulgar" of Rome.[20] From the tribunes' perspective, then, Caesarism is a double assault on republican order: Caesar's desire to usurp all political power and the people's unmediated participation in the empowerment of Caesar pose equally devastating threats to the function and authority of political representation.[21] As we shall see, Caesar hopes to transcend all other constituted authorities by appealing directly to the people's judgment, and the people, in turn, directly exercise power over Caesar. Caesarism, as Shakespeare elaborates it, is the collapse of the particular kind of mediation political representation institutes between the subject and the ruling class.[22]

The bitter dispute over Caesar's triumph unsettles the tribunes' claim to represent the people's will, but this particular rift between the people and their representatives also reveals the *fundamental* incompatibility between representational politics and the direct participation of the people in political life. The mere *presence* of a political public puts intolerable pressure on tribunal *representation:* when the people are present in their own persons, the tribunes' claim to represent them falters. Thus, Flavius and Marullus are obsessively concerned with the *publicness* of the people's holiday and are determined to send them home: "Hence! *home,* you idle creatures, get you *home*"; "you ought not *walk* / Upon a labouring day without the sign / Of your profession"; "wherefore are not in thy *shop* to-day? / Why dost thou lead these men about the *streets?* (1.1.1, 3–5, 27–8; emphasis added). Even after he has driven the people from the stage, Flavius fears a reassertion of their presence: "I'll about, / And drive away the vulgar from the streets," he tells Marullus as they part, "So do you too, where you perceive them thick" (1.1.69–71).[23] When the people leave their shops and homes and shed their identities as cobblers and carpenters, they become a public which seemingly has no need of representatives. Indeed, in the Cobbler's explanation of the people's presence in the streets we see a bold assertion of the people's power to function as a group: "we make holiday to see Caesar, and to rejoice in his triumph."[24] Here is the "we" of collective power in the absence of representation. The tribunes fear Caesarism because it makes the people themselves the vessels of their own power: Caesarism is an antirepresentational carnival of presentism.

◇◇

The first scene foregrounds the unfolding of the conspiracy in popular politics and forces the audience to consider any action against Caesar as an attack on the people. The second scene seems to restart the play in an aristocratic register: the tribunes, having displaced the people from the stage, are themselves displaced by Cassius, Brutus, and the patrician politics that overwhelmingly dominate ancient accounts of Caesar's fall. In his great attempt to recruit Brutus, Cassius never appeals to the general good of Rome; instead, he invokes Lucius Junius Brutus and the patrician origins of the republic, urges the affront Caesar's ascendance gives to his peers, and assures Brutus that "many of the best respect in Rome" (1.2.58) look to him for deliverance.[25] This elitist appeal seems oddly marginal to Brutus's warming to the plot: as his brother-in-law engages him in intimate conversation, Brutus is repeatedly distracted by the sound of the people shouting offstage. Those offstage shouts constitute the infiltration of the patrician by the popular. While Cassius and Brutus speak, we later discover, Antony and Caesar are staging a little drama before the crowds gathered to celebrate the Lupercalia and Caesar's triumph over Pompey:

Antony offers Caesar a crown three times, which Caesar rejects three times. Each time Caesar refuses the crown, the common people roar their approval. But Brutus, like the audience in Shakespeare's theater, cannot see this dumb show, and he radically misinterprets what he hears: "I do fear," he tells Cassius after the first shout, "the people / Choose Caesar for their king" (1.2.78–79). After the second shout, Brutus wonders, "[a]nother general shout? / I do believe that these applauses are / For some new honours that are heaped on Caesar" (130–32). "General" is an extraordinarily important word in Brutus's political vocabulary: he has just warned Cassius that he will entertain action against Caesar only if the cause is "the general good" (84); later, as he ponders joining the plot, Brutus muses "I know no personal cause to spurn at [Caesar], / But for the general" (2.1.11–12); and after the assassination, he assures Antony that he acted out of "pity to the general wrong of Rome" (3.1.170). Yet Brutus first begins to articulate this rhetoric of "the general good" at precisely the moment he believes the people are, by *general* acclamation, *choosing* Caesar for their king. Brutus, that is, begins to elaborate a populist justification for the assassination of Caesar (1.2.81–89) at the same instant he fears the people have willingly acclaimed Caesar their king (1.2.78–79).

Brutus quickly discovers that he has mistaken the meaning of the people's exclamations; a few moments after the shouting subsides, Casca, who will soon join the conspiracy, recounts the thwarted crowning:

> CASCA: . . . there was a crown offer'd him; and, being offer'd him, he put it by with the back of his hand, thus; and then the people fell a-shouting.
> BRUTUS: What was the second noise for?
> CASCA: Why, for that too.
> CASSIUS: They shouted thrice: what was the last cry for?
> CASCA: Why, for that too.
> BRUTUS: Was the crown offer'd him thrice?
> CASCA: Ay, marry, was't; and he put it by thrice, every time gentler than the other; and at every putting-by mine honest neighbors shouted. (1.2.222–32)

We might expect Brutus to seize happily upon this unexpected and reassuring evidence that the people do not, after all, want to make Caesar king, but instead he has some trouble digesting the information. His persistent questioning of Casca suggests, to be sure, that he is carefully verifying his mistake. But when Brutus asks "was the crown *offer'd* him thrice" immediately after Casca has indicated that Caesar "*put . . . by*" the crown a third time, his obsession with Antony's offering of the crown begins to sound like willful selectiveness or psycho-political denial. The point, Casca reiterates, is not simply that Caesar was *offered* the crown thrice; it is also that "he *put it by* thrice" in deference to the people's will.

This still won't do: Brutus asks Casca to "tell the manner of" the scene he has just finished describing in some detail ("he put it by thrice, every time gentler than the other"). An annoyed—or perhaps simply perplexed—Casca obliges:

> CASCA: . . . I saw Mark Antony offer him a crown . . . and, *as I told you,* he put it by once; but for all that, to my thinking he would fain have had it. Then he offered it to him again; then he put it by again—but to my thinking, he was very loath to lay his fingers off it. And then he offered it the third time; he put it the third time by and still as he refused it, the rabblement hooted, and clapped their chopt hands, and threw up their sweaty night-caps, and uttered such a deal of stinking breath because Caesar refused the crown, that it had, almost, chocked Caesar; for he swounded, and fell down at it. And for mine own part, I durst not laugh, for fear of opening my lips and receiving the bad air.
>
> . . . .
>
> He fell down in the market-place, and foam'd at the mouth, and was speechless.
>
> (1.2.236–53; emphasis added)

Brutus's reaction to this remarkable report is bizarrely casual: "'Tis very like," he says, "he hath the falling sickness" (251). Caesar did indeed suffer from the "falling sickness" (that is, epilepsy), but this particular episode is Shakespeare's invention and Brutus seems to have missed the import of its timing and circumstances. Shakespeare has made Caesar's falling sickness a political illness, for what Caesar chokes on is something like a reification of the people's political power: the crowd's rank breath is the sign, the palpable trace of their powerful voices.[26] But Brutus never even remarks Caesar's astonishing subjection to the common people, nor does he acknowledge that the people, by Casca's report, have not only the power but also, unlike the citizens in *Coriolanus,* the will to withhold their voices when Rome's first man solicits them.[27]

One of the shocking things about the play is how completely Shakespeare withholds from his audience the Caesar who was familiar to early modern readers and playgoers—the conqueror of the world and of Rome. In *A Discourse upon the Beginning of Tacitus* (1620), Hobbes reminds us of that other Caesar: "Pompey, though he affected the Monarchy, yet he took not the course that was fittest for it; for he then courted the State, when he knew that his

Rival had a purpose to use violence, and to ravish it. But Caesar knew the Republic to be feminine, and that it would yield sooner to violence, than flattery; and therefore with all his power assaulted and overcame it" (36). Here is Caesar as Tarquinian rapist; Shakespeare, by contrast, almost entirely omits Caesar's tyrannical dismantling of the republic and shows us a man who courts the people and desists when they say "no."[28]

Trailed by an entourage and a "throng" of people (1.2.21), Caesar first appears on stage immediately after the confrontation between the tribunes and the people. The dictator converses with his intimates, but as he is instructing Anthony to "touch Calphurnia" when he runs the Lupercalian circuit, the Soothsayer cries out "Caesar!"

> CAESAR: Ha! Who calls?
> CASCA: Bid every noise be still; peace yet again!
> CAESAR: Who is it in the press that calls on me?
> I hear a tongue shriller than all the music
> Cry "Caesar!" Speak. Caesar is turn'd to hear.
> SOOTH: Beware the ides of March.
> CAESAR: What man is that?
> BRUTUS: A soothsayer bids you beware the ides of March.
> (1.2.13–19)

Someone from the crowd calls out Caesar's name and the master of the world *turns around* to answer.[29] This strikes me as an uncanny early modern instance of "that very precise operation" Louis Althusser "call[s] *interpellation* or hailing, . . . which can be imagined along the lines of the most commonplace everyday police (or other) hailing: 'Hey, you there!'"

> Assuming that the theoretical scene I have imagined takes place in the street, the hailed individual will turn round. By this mere one-hundred-and-eighty-degree physical conversion, he becomes a *subject.* Why? Because he has recognized that the hail was "really" addressed to him, and that "it was *really him* who was hailed" (and not someone else). . . . Naturally, for the convenience and clarity of my little theoretical theatre I have had to present things in the form of a sequence, with a before and after, and thus in the form of a temporal succession. There are individuals walking along. Somewhere (usually behind them) the hail rings out: "Hey, you there!" One individual (nine times out of ten it is the right one) turns around, believing/suspecting/knowing that it is for him, i.e., recognizing that "it is really he" who is meant by the hailing. But in reality these things happen without any succession. The existence of ideology and the hailing or interpellation of individuals as subjects are one and the same thing. (130–31)

The Soothsayer, of course, does not cry out "Hey, you there"; rather, he calls out Caesar's proper name. But the specificity of this hailing *intensifies* our sense that Caesar is Caesar precisely because he turns. What is striking here is the anonymity of the hailer and the fame of the hailed. Both before and after he turns, Caesar does not know who has hailed him: "Who is it in the press that calls on me?"; "What man is that?" Caesar *recognizes* the authority of the hailer without *knowing* him: to be Caesar, then, is to be the subject who is subject to everyone and *anyone.* We can now begin to see the complexity of Caesar's seemingly monomaniacal tendency to refer to himself in the third person: Caesar first speaks his own name ("Caesar is turned to hear") only *after* he is named by an unfamiliar voice calling out from "the press." "Every individual is called by his name," Althusser argues, "in the passive sense, it is never he who provides his own name" (133), and this holds true even for, especially for, Caesar, who belongs so little to himself that his *proper* name seems the possession of anyone who speaks it. Caesar exists only in the third person.

Caesar is so wholly the people's creature that he cannot, at least in public, even acknowledge that there is anything left of the private man. Thus, Artemidorus's attempt to inform Caesar of the plot, even as he walks to his doom, fails because he appeals to Caesar's personal interests:

> ART: Hail, Caesar! Read this schedule.
> DECIUS: Trebonious doth desire you to o'er-read,
> At your best leisure, this his humble suit.
> ART: O Caesar, read mine first; for mine's a suit
> That touches Caesar nearer. Read it, great Caesar.
> CAESAR: What touches ourself shall be last served.
> ART: Delay not, Caesar. Read it instantly.
> CAESAR: What, is the fellow mad?
> (3.1.3–9)

Artemidorus hails the wrong Caesar. Caesar cannot act for himself because his identity as "Caesar" requires that he always turn away from himself to hear the other; he becomes himself, assumes his subjecthood, as he turns toward the public, which, in turn, is constituted as authority—as what Althusser calls "the Other Subject"[30]—in virtue of his turning.[31] In North's Plutarch, by contrast, Caesar is intensely interested in Artemidorus's letter about "matters of great weight" that "touche [him] nearly": "*Caesar* tooke it of him, but coulde never read it, though he many times attempted it, for the number of people that did salute him" (794).[32] Even in Plutarch, then, Caesar's fate is simply his position as the object of everyone's salute; in Shakespeare's play, however, that is a fate Caesar makes for himself.

◇◇

Brutus's characteristic subordination of his personal interests to the general interest would seem to make him a slightly distorted double of Caesar: after all, Caesar's fatal response to Artemidorus—"What touches us ourself shall be last serv'd"—reconciles Brutus's rhetoric of "the general good" and the royal plural. But Brutus's relation to "the general" is not at all like Caesar's: before the Forum scene, we never witness or even hear reports of any direct intercourse between Brutus and the Roman people. Instead, Cassius supplies Brutus with *reports* of his standing among his fellow Romans. Cassius figures Brutus's defective relation to Roman opinion as a failure to attain what we might call third-personhood:

> CASSIUS: Tell me, good Brutus, can you see your face?
> BRUTUS: No, Cassius, for the eye sees not itself
> But by reflection, by some other things.
> CASSIUS: 'Tis just;
> And it is very much lamented, Brutus,
> That you have no such mirrors as will turn
> Your hidden worthiness into your eye,
> That you might see your shadow. I have heard
> Where many of the best respect in Rome—
> Except immortal Caesar—speaking of Brutus,
> And groaning underneath this age's yoke,
> Have wish'd that noble Brutus had his eyes.
> (1.2.50–61)

Cassius does not dispute Brutus's claim that he cannot see his own face because the "eye sees not itself." Rather, he suggests that Brutus look at himself with someone else's eyes, that he see by reflection the "hidden worthiness" so transparent to his noble peers. If Brutus could only see himself as a shadow, perhaps as a reflection in an eye, he could see himself in the third person.

Cassius's first gambit to enlist Brutus fails: "you would have me seek into myself," Brutus warns him, "For that which is not in me" (1.2.63–64). Cassius's mistake is to offer Brutus a mirror composed of the elite opinion of "many of the best respect in Rome." At the end of the scene, *after* he has registered Brutus's response to the people's shouts and his protestations about "the general good," Cassius will rework the mirror device to accommodate his friend's odd populism. Thus, after Brutus leaves the stage, Cassius plots to convince him that "Rome" expects him to liberate the republic from Caesarism:

I will this night,
In several hands, in at his window throw—
As if they came from several citizens—
Writings, all tending to the great opinion,
That Rome holds of his name; wherein obscurely
Caesar's ambitions shall be glanced at.
(1.2.315–20)

The movement from "many of the best respect in Rome" to "several citizens" may seem rather modest: in Elizabethan taxonomies of social order, "citizens and burgesses" immediately follow the nobility.[33] But many Elizabethan writers understood that "citizen" designated a much larger class of persons in old Rome; and in *Titus, Caesar,* and *Coriolanus,* Shakespeare explicitly figures "plebeians" as "citizens."[34]

Cassius's conspiracy to win Brutus over to the conspiracy seems to establish Brutus's integrity as a public man: the plan to write a series of notes in "several" hands suggests that Brutus will act only if he believes that Rome wants him to act.[35] But, of course, Cassius simultaneously assumes—justly, as we shall see—that Brutus may well conclude from a mere handful of notes that Rome wills Caesar's death.[36] This is an especially telling assumption given the ample evidence the day's events have afforded of the people's attitude toward Caesar. The people do not wish to make Caesar king, but neither do they wish his death: immediately before the bout of "falling-sickness," Casca tells Brutus and Cassius, Caesar "perceiv'd the common herd was glad he refus'd the crown . . . [and] pluck'd me ope his doublet, and offer'd them his throat to cut" (1.2.261–63). There are no takers. Indeed, when Caesar recovers his senses and begs the people's indulgence, "[t]hree or four wenches, where I stood," Casca reports, "cried, 'Alas, good soul,' and forgave him with all their hearts; but there's no heed to be taken of them; if Caesar had stabb'd their mothers, they would have done no less" (1.2.268–72).

The image of Caesar's radical, visceral, messy, noisy subjection to the fleshly people in a public place haunts the moment when Brutus, alone at night in his orchard, channels Rome's will out of a seventeen-word note Cassius—a very economical Cyrano—has forged. Brutus's servant Lucius finds the paper while "searching the window for a flint" (2.1.35), and reading the letter out loud to himself fires Brutus's growing inclination to the plot:

Brutus, thou sleep'st; awake, and see thyself.
Shall Rome, etc.? Speak, strike, redress.
"Brutus, thou sleep'st; awake!"

> Such instigations have been often dropp'd
> Where I have took them up.
> "Shall Rome, etc.?" Thus must I piece it out:
> Shall Rome stand under one man's awe? What, Rome?
> My ancestors did from the streets of Rome
> The Tarquin drive when he was call'd a king.
> "Speak, strike, redress." Am I entreated
> To speak, and strike? O Rome, I make thee promise,
> If the redress will follow, thou receivest
> Thy full petition at the hand of Brutus.
> (2.1.46–58)

The letter, echoing Cassius, asks Brutus to "see" himself, but Brutus does not so much see himself as hail himself in something like the Althusserian sense of the word. The unlikely operation of interpellating oneself, I want to argue, is the genesis of political representation. How does one hail oneself? To read the letter aloud is necessarily to articulate the words of the other, but by the time Brutus repeats the letter's initial command ("Brutus. . . . awake"), he is performing rather than quoting the hailing. "Brutus, thou sleep'st; awake!": thus, Brutus addresses himself in Rome's voice and becomes the Other Subject. And performing the other—playing Rome—is the positive condition for becoming himself. As he reaches the end of his soliloquy, Brutus brings, in a wonderfully balanced sentence, both Rome and himself into being: "O Rome, I make thee promise, / If the redress will follow, thou receivest / Thy full petition at the hand of Brutus." Brutus hails Rome—"O Rome"—precisely as the Brutus whom Rome has hailed ("Brutus, thou sleep'st"). Put another way (another way that is the same way), Brutus hails precisely the Rome that hails precisely this Brutus. It is at this moment that Brutus, for the first time in the play, refers to himself in the third person.

The circularity of this remarkable interpellation is peculiar to representational politics. Pierre Bourdieu figures the generation of the representative and the group he represents as perfectly recursive: "*in appearance* the group creates the man who speaks in its place and in its name . . . whereas *in reality* it is more or less just as true to say that it is the spokesperson who creates the group" (*Language,* 204).[37] In the orchard scene, we see the grand alchemy of political representation played out in a small whirl of fantastical subject formation. Brutus identifies himself as the object of Rome's demand for action at the exact moment he constructs his own voice as the voice of Rome. Brutus interpellates himself as representative through representation.

Brutus's ventriloquizing of Rome is an act of bad faith, but it is not merely bad faith.[38] Immediately before he reads the letter, Brutus is mulling over the bloody course of action he expects Cassius to propose: "It must be by [Caesar's] death. And for my part, / I know no personal cause to spurn at him, / But for the general" (2.1.10–12). Taken individually, Brutus's articulations of selflessness can look like exercises in spin control: "I slew my best lover for the good of Rome" (3.2.46) Brutus tells the crowd in the Forum; "pity to the general wrong of Rome" forced his hand, he assures Antony (3.1.171); only "the general good" is a sufficient cause for action, he warns Cassius (1.2.84). But in the orchard scene, Brutus's only audience is himself; this is a story he tells himself and tells himself in private too. But why should we think of this story as the Representative's Tale? Claiming to act for the general *good* does not, after all, necessarily entail claiming to articulate the general *will:* in *Coriolanus,* for example, the paternalistic Menenius tries to convince the plebeians that the oligarchic system of government they are seeking to destroy is, in fact, a splendid arrangement for them and a self-sacrificing hardship for the oligarchs who must "care for" them "like fathers" (1.1.75). But Brutus is no paternalist, and the distinctions he draws between personal and public interest are continuous with displacing, usurping, becoming—that is to say, representing—the people.

The Brutuses we meet in Plutarch, Appian, and earlier English writers never express any interest at all in the general good, much less in the relation between their personal interests and the interests of the Roman people. Shakespeare's inspiration here is the novel political rhetoric of his own time. Before Elizabeth I's reign, the sorts of distinctions Brutus makes are almost entirely alien to parliamentary discourse, but they become commonplace in the 1580s and 1590s. Indeed, some MPs believed that subordinating their particular interests to the general interest was the positive condition of effective legislation: "A lawe framed out of the *private* affecions of men," argued an anonymous MP in 1597, "wil never tend to the *generall* good of all; and if every one may putt in a caution to save his owne *particuler* it will never prove a lawe of restraint, but rather of loosenes and libertie" (*PPE* 3:220). The distinction drawn between the particular and the general—these are precisely Brutus's terms: "for my *part,* / I know no personal cause to spurn at him / But for the *general*"—opens up a gap that seemingly only representation can bridge.[39] Consider Francis Alford's attack on a bill offered in 1585 to restrict the hunting rights of all but the Elizabethan elite: "we must not considder our owne selves in this bill and our owne *privat* plesure because fewe of us conteyned in it, but our poor neighbors in the country" (*PPE* 2:122).[40] It is precisely Alford's difference from those who would be adversely affected by the proposed bill that requires him to speak for them: "I am not so meane but I have x^{li} by yeare and therfore without the compass, but I speak for the common subiectes" (*PPE* 2:122). We might want to allow that Alford maintains a distinction between himself ("I am not so meane") and those for whom he speaks ("I speak for the common subiectes"), but ventriloquizing the desires of those common subjects *is* speaking for and as those common subjects. This odd movement from distinguishing oneself from the other to speaking for the other—the movement of representation—is clearer still in Richard Martin's speech in 1601 against monopolies and their impact on the poor:

> I doe speake *ffor* a towne that greyves and pynes, *ffor* a countrye that groneth and languisheth under the burthen of monstrous and unconscionable [monopolies] . . . of starche, tynne, ffyshe, clothe, oyle, vinegar, salte and I know not what. . . . Yf these blood-suckers be still lette alone to sucke up the best and principallest commodities, which the earth there hath given us; what shall become of *us,* whom the fruits upon *our* own soil, and the commodities of *our* own labor, which with the sweat of *our* brows (even up to the knees in mire and dirt) *we* have labored for, shall be taken by warrant of supreame authority, which the poor subject dares not gainsay. (*PPE* 3:375; emphasis added)

Martin begins by speaking *for* his less fortunate constituents, but by the end of his speech this well-to-do Middle Temple lawyer includes himself in the impoverished plural and speaks *as* a manual laborer.[41]

Cassius's letter, then, brilliantly seizes on Brutus's rhetoric of the general good and urges him toward the moment of representation: the crucial lacuna in "*Shall Rome, etc.*" invites Brutus not to mouth Rome's words but to put words in Rome's mouth.[42] "Shall Rome, etc. Thus must I piece it out": to piece out that "etc." Brutus must speak not in his own person but as Rome. Thus, Brutus's anxiety about Caesar's ambition—"He would be crown'd" (2.1.12)—fills up the empty propositional content of Rome's rhetorical question to Brutus: "Shall Rome, etc.?" becomes "Shall Rome stand under one man's awe?" When Brutus supplies "Rome" with those words, he fulfills the letter's second command ("Speak"); and once he has spoken as a Rome that rejects Caesar, the striking and redressing follow inevitably.

That Brutus must "piece . . . out" the letter, must supplement its fragmentary signs, draws our attention to the way in which the voice of the people is always, in the culture of representational politics, a fiction, a fabrication. The imaginative and the ideological, as Althusser suggests, are continuous rather than divergent, and as we watch Brutus transforming Cassius's pitifully spare script into "Rome," we should recall that the phrase "piece out," which appears only a handful of times in Shakespeare's works, is the linchpin of perhaps the most famous account of the theatrical imaginary in all of dramatic literature.[43] Speaking as a representative of the acting company, the Prologue in *Henry V*—first performed, like *Caesar,* in 1599[44]—asks the audience to

> Piece out our imperfections with your thoughts:
> Into a thousand parts divide one man,
> And make imaginary puissance,
> Think, when we talk of horses, that you see them
> Printing their proud hoofs i'th' receiving earth;
> For 'tis your thoughts that now must deck our kings.
> (23–28)

The imaginative economy of political representation, then, is very like the imaginative economy of theatrical representation: one actor stands for a thousand in the theater, and every MP in the House of Commons, according to Coke, "represent[s] a thousand of men" (D'Ewes 515); and whereas the humbly born play kings on the stage, important country gentleman and Middle Temple lawyers in St. Stephen's Chapel speak in the voices of the Elizabethan underclass.

The enabling premise of political representation is, as the MP Arthur Hall scandalously claimed in 1576, irrational: "your number of Parliament men you see in your house are fewe to the huge multitude of them whose consents are bounde by your agreemente" (Eii). One *sees* only a few hundred men in the Parliament House, but one must believe that millions of men and women are present: to credit representation, then, is an act of faith, a belief in things unseen.[45] The Prologue of *Henry V* puts the imaginative burden of theatrical representation on the *audience,* on those who must empower the fiction that one man stands for a thousand or that a glovemaker's son is a king; in *Caesar,* by contrast, the imaginative burden of political representation falls equally to the *representative.* For Brutus's ideological act of bad faith—his construction of Rome out of a few letters—is also an act of imagination: to piece out Rome's voice is to piece out himself as Rome. The representative must fashion for himself an artificial identity. The MP William Hakewill claimed that his representational impersonations, which we encountered in Chapter 2, were an imaginative necessity. Speaking in 1601 against a bill to restrict debt and credit, Hakewill suggested to his fellow MPs that they could think themselves through the gulf between personal interest and the interests of others neither by reasoning with themselves that the good of the many outweighs the desires of the few nor by reinterpreting true "personal" interest *as* communal interest. One transcends the narrowly personal, Hakewill argued, by playing the other:

> I ame a man of that rancke and condicion, that I never sell, I seldome buye, and paye reddie monye; and the safest course this bill offers to me *ffor my perticuler.* But the greate mischeife that will redound by it to the commons is that which makes me speak. . . . We must laye downe the respectes of our owne persons, and put on others' and their affections ffor whome wee speake, ffor they speake by us. If the matter which is spoken of touche the poore, then *thincke me* a poore man. He that speakes, sometymes, he must be a lawyer, sometymes a paynter, sometymes a marchante, some tymes a meane artifycer. (*PPE* 3:432–33; emphasis added)

Supporting the bill would be "the safest course" for William Hakewill in his particular, but the bill would cause "great mischief" to the commons. Hakewill, then, cannot speak against the bill in his own person: the representative can only articulate the general good by abandoning his own person to an artificial person.

Hakewill imports into St. Stephen's Chapel the imaginative process elaborated at the Globe by the Prologue of *Henry V:* the lowly player depends on the audience's thoughts to deck him a king; the privileged MP must sometimes *be* a poor man, a mean artificer, and his audience must *think* him a poor man, a mean artificer.[46] But Hakewill's "audience" is, of course, composed entirely of his fellow performers: the mean artificer had no access at all to, and no way to judge, Hakewill's impersonation.[47] The early modern House of Commons was perhaps not quite as private as Brutus's orchard, but when MPs ventriloquized England's desires, the people for whom they spoke had no opportunity to contradict them. When, for example, the anonymous opponent of the Enclosure Bill of 1597 warns that "the eyes of the poor are upon this parliament," he speaks *of* a virtual audience rather than *to* a real audience. For this MP, the House of Commons becomes "an epitome of the whole realm" by absorbing and replacing its potential audience and the rest of the "real world" beyond St. Stephen's. On this account, political representation can do what theatrical representation cannot: St. Stephen's Chapel and the MPs actually are the realm and its subjects rather than mere "ciphers to this great accompt" (*Henry V,* Prologue, 15). This construction of representation could hardly be more alien to Shakespeare's theater. For if the MPs claimed to be the representational mediums through which St. Stephen's became the realm, Shakespeare's "wooden O"

(Prologue, 13), conversely, became the Globe, because it was full of people who represented the world. Theatrical representation, Harry Berger has argued, "constructs the audience metonymically as a representative standing for the 'world'" (152).[48] Because the members of the audience are themselves tokens of places, classes, occupations, genders, they, as much as the players and the playwright, are the vehicles by which the World is imported into the Globe. Early modern political representation and theatrical representation, then, institute different relations to the worlds they claim to represent: whereas Shakespeare's company must ask the audience "gently to hear, kindly to judge, our play" (*Henry V*, Prologue, 34), our anonymous defender of poor farmers, having absorbed his audience into the Commons, comfortably reassures his colleagues "we now sit in judgment over ourselves."

◇◇

Brutus does not, in the end, have the luxury of judging himself. When they learn of Caesar's death, the people demand an accounting: the famous Forum scene begins with the plebeians shouting "we will be satisfied" (3.2.1). The conspiracy is no longer sheltered in an empty theater or an orchard. Brutus promises that "public reasons shall be rendered, / Of Caesar's death" (3.2.7–8): public because they will be articulated before the people and because they explain why the general good demanded the murder. In the prologue to his oration, Brutus subjects himself to his audience: "Censure me in your wisdom, and awake your senses, that you may the better judge" (16–17). Brutus has throughout the play displayed a tin ear where popular politics is concerned, but perhaps the sheer force of the people's presence helps him rise to the occasion. For Brutus ends his speech by providing the people with a first-rate imitation of Caesar: "With this I depart: that as I slew my best lover for the good of Rome, I have the same dagger for myself when it shall please my country to need my death" (3.2.44–47). This ritual subjection to the people's will repeats Caesar's sacrificial gesture after the thwarted crowning: "he plucked me ope his doublet and offered them his throat to cut" (1.2.264–66). And what worked for Caesar works for Brutus: until this moment, his plebeian audience has given him a supportive but decidedly quiet hearing; now, rejecting his offer to sacrifice himself, they erupt in raucous celebration.

> ALL THE PLEBEIANS: Live, Brutus! live, live!
> FIRST PLEBEIAN: Bring him with triumph home unto his house.
> SECOND PLEBEIAN: Give him a statue with his ancestors.
> THIRD PLEBEIAN: Let him be Caesar.

FOURTH PLEBEIAN: Caesar's better parts
Shall be crown'd in Brutus.
(3.2.49–53)

When the Third Plebeian proposes that Brutus "be Caesar," he in no way suggests that Brutus become king; similarly, the Fourth Plebeian wants to crown in Brutus not Caesar's monarchic ambitions but instead his willingness to bow to the people's desire that he *refuse* the crown. Brutus becomes Caesar at precisely the moment he finally subjects himself not to a mediated Rome, not to a Rome of his own representational fabrications, but to the Roman people in their own persons. When he is theirs, he becomes Caesar.

Brutus's fleeting success in the Forum scene reveals that "Caesar," a signifier that seemed so uniquely attached to a particular person, designates instead a role that others may play. "Caesar" will, of course, become the featured part in imperial history, but here, by contrast, "Caesar" designates the subjected sovereign, or, rather, the sovereign people's subject.[49] For Caesar's own career and the Forum scene establish "Caesar" as a role that cannot be self-fashioned: only the people can name and thus create a Caesar. "Let him be Caesar" is the populist speech act that, for a moment, makes Brutus the most powerful man in Rome.

"Caesar" is one of Shakespeare's names for the people's subject; the other is "actor." In Casca's summing up of the thwarted coronation, the actor is the explicit figure for Caesarism: "If the tag-rag people did not clap him and hiss him, according as he pleas'd and displeas'd them, as they use to do the players in the theater, I am no true man" (1.2.255–58). When Brutus hears the "applauses" (1.2.131) ringing out offstage, he hears the people expressing their approval *as an audience* of Caesar's refusal of the crown; their theatrical authorization of this particular ending to the play Antony and Caesar enact is identical to their unwillingness to make Caesar king.[50] In *Caesar,* the people of Rome are like a theatrical audience when—and only when—they retain their power rather than delegate their authority to others.[51] Theatrical relations of power, then, are democratic, and theatrical representation, as Shakespeare figures it in *Julius Caesar,* is far more radical than the political representation of tribunes, senators, or conspirators.[52]

The audience that celebrates Caesar but refuses to crown him is, from Casca's description, a distinctly Elizabethan audience:

> He put it the third time by. And still as he refus'd it, the rabblement hooted, and clapp'd their chopt hands, and threw up their sweaty night-caps, and uttered such a deal of stinking breath because Caesar refused the crown, that

> it had, almost, chocked Caesar; for he swoonded, and fell down at it. And for mine own part, I durst not laugh for fear of opening my lips and receiving the bad air. (1.2.239–47)

The politics of halitosis in Caesar's epileptic episode is borrowed from theatrical politics: antitheatricalists and playwrights alike figured bad breath as one of the defining attributes of the lowliest theatergoers. At the amphitheaters, Thomas Middleton lamented, the playwright had to please not only the perfumed gallants in the expensive galleries nearest the stage but also the "dull Audience of Stinkards sitting in the Penny Galleries of a Theater" (Gurr 91). By contrast, in a pricey private theater such as Paul's, Marston's Ned Planet gratefully reflects, "a man shall not be choacked / With stench of Garlicke."[53]

"Choacked / With stench of Garlicke": the etiology of Caesar's marketplace swoon is theatrical. The people roar "a deal of stinking breath because Caesar refus'd the crown," and that breath causes Caesar to choke and fall to the ground. We see here a parody of divine inspiration: the tribunes fear that the people feather the wings on which Caesar will ascend to superhuman heights, but the crowd's breath instead fills Caesar's lungs and tumbles him to the earth. This moment, with its grotesque physicality, seems to me the culmination of the carnivalesque holiday the cobbler and his fellows try to make for themselves in the first scene. The people's holiday finds its fulfillment not in the creation of a Boy Bishop or a Lord of Misrule but in the experience of withholding and denying power. The people's celebration of Caesar is a little more—or perhaps a little less—than Caesar himself expects.[54] Carnivalesque reversals of order in a republican culture might take the form of creating a king—this is certainly Caesar's hope; but the people's release from republicanism takes a radical rather than a conservative turn.[55] The carnivalesque fantasy representationalism engenders here is the withholding of authorization.[56] Theater is Shakespeare's model for this economy of power: at the moment the people refuse to empower Caesar, Shakespeare figures them as Elizabethan groundlings.

The most influential new historicist argument about early modern drama posits a homology between theater and Elizabethan monarchy, but Shakespeare and many other early modern observers elaborate an *opposition* between theatrical relations of power and monarchy.[57] Indeed, the public theater's apparent service to the crown, the antitheatricalist John Cocke warned his readers in 1615, was itself simply one more theatrical deception:[58] "the player . . . pretends to have a royall Master or Mistresse, [but] his wages and dependence prove him to be the servant of the people."[59] For Cocke, then, the liveries worn by the King's Men are costumes. New historicist determinists and oppositionalists are equally confounded by Cocke's critique of theater, which figures the player neither as royal dependent nor as masterless rebel. The theater, in Cocke's view, undermines the traditional sociology of patronage by replacing "the royall Master or Mistresse" with a rival master—the common people.[60]

Cocke's materialist critique is typical of early modern attacks—leveled by playwrights and antitheatricalists alike—on the democratizing effect of a market-based theater that admitted anyone who could pay and, moreover, allocated different grades of seats according to progressive admission prices rather than social status. "Sithence then the place is so free in entertainment," Thomas Dekker complained in 1609, "allowing a stoole as well to the Farmers sonne as to your Templer . . . your Stinkard has the selfe-same libertie to be there in his Tobacco-Fumes, which your sweet Courtier hath. . . . your Carman and Tinker claime as strong a voice in their suffrage and sit to give judgment on the plaies life and death, as well as the prowdest *Momus* among the tribe of *Critick.*"[61]

The price of admission, then, secures the tinker not only a place in the theater but the right to judge the play. Figuring the theater audience as a jury rendering judgment on a "plaies life or death" was a very well-worn gesture in early modern prologues and epilogues,[62] but Dekker weds this commonplace juridical metaphor to a relatively novel political metaphor: figuring the audience's judgment as "their suffrage" suggests that theater models elective politics.

In the Induction to *Cynthia's Revels* (1600), Ben Jonson stages the first theatrical appeal for an audience's suffrage. Three members of the Children of the Chapel Royal, the company that performed the play at the Blackfriars theater, are vying for the honor of performing the Prologue when one boy suddenly appeals directly to the audience: "I plead possession of the cloak: Gentles, your suffrages I pray you." When the other boys protest this maneuver, our hero proposes an election: "Why, will you stand to most voices of the gentlemen? Let that decide it." Jonson, then, subjects not the play itself but rather a casting decision to the elective power of the audience, but at the moment that single boy actor appeals to the audience, the play itself is, at least within the fiction Jonson has created, subject to their consent. Jonson predictably has the other two boys thwart this exercise in theatrical democracy, but the first boy's fleeting transformation of the stage into the hustings acknowledges the theater's potential as a model for popular empowerment.[63] The Prologue to John Fletcher's *The Humorous Lieutenant* (1619) elaborates in greater detail the subjection of the playwright and the entire company to a regime of suffrage:

Would some man would instruct me what to say:
For this same Prologue, usuall to a play,
Is tied to such an old forme of Petition,
Men must say nothing now beyond commission:
. . . .
We have a Play, a new play to play now,
And thus low in our Plaies behalfe we bow;
We bow to beg your suffrage, and kind eare . . .
(Prologue.1–4; 8–10)

Bowing and begging a popular audience for suffrages did not sit well with some Renaissance playwrights.[64] In the Prologue to *The Emperor of the East* (1631), Philip Massinger assures his well-to-do Blackfriars audience that he prefers not to "sue, / Or basely beg . . . suffrages" from amphitheater groundlings but would rather trust his work to the "faire censures" of the "free, and ingenious spirits" at the indoor theaters (10–11).[65]

The rhetoric of suffrage is the superstructural translation of what Cocke and others identify as the conditions of theatrical production. Jonson, with typical penetration, sees admission fees and suffrage as continuous. Thus, as the Scrivener brings the "Articles of Agreement" between "the Author of *Bartholomew Fair* [1614]" and the "Spectators or Hearers at the Hope" theater to a conclusion, he figures their suffrage as a supplement to their admission fees: "In witness whereof, as you have preposterously put to your seals already (which is your money) you will now add the other part of suffrage, your hands."[66] Fletcher's Epilogue to *The Loyal Subject* (1618?) similarly figures the audience's applause as a sign of consent that supplements the money they have already paid:

Though something well-assur'd, few here repent
Three houres of pretious time, or money spent
On our endeavours, Yet not to relye
Too much upon our care, and industrie,
'Tis fit we should aske, but a modest way
How you approve our action in the play.
If you vouchsafe to crowne it with applause,
It is your bountie, and you give us cause
Hereafter with a generall consent
To study, as becomes us, your content.
(1–10)

The time and money the audience have spent can only be repented, not reclaimed; thus, Fletcher's Epilogue seems to sidestep reluctantly into his appeal for a sign of judgment. Indeed, there is a hint of extortion in the Epilogue's suggestion that a sign of general consent to the performance just concluded will encourage the author and the company to do their best to please in the future.[67] Of course, the author and the company, possessed though they may be of the audience's money, remain very much dependent on their approval: the potential patrons of future performances will not materialize if the play is hissed.

The Epilogue to *The Loyal Subject* seems to mix its political metaphors: the audience's "general consent," signified by their applause, will "crowne" Fletcher's play. In the Prologue he wrote for Fletcher's *The Elder Brother, A Comedy* (1635), Massinger plays with the same tension between the image of crowning and the rhetoric of election: "But that it would take from our modesty / To praise the Writer, or the Comedy, / Till your fair suffrage crown it, I should say, / Y'are all most welcome to no vulgar Play." In the Prologue to *The Coronation* (1634), James Shirley takes Fletcher's and Massinger's device a step further: "There is no Coronation to day, / Unlesse your gentle votes doe crowne our Play." Shirley makes the coronation of his fictive queen subject to the "votes" that must crown the play.[68] Asking the audience to crown a play with applause, suffrage, and consent subjects monarchism to the popular politics of theater.

Elizabethan, Jacobean, and Caroline playwrights were familiar enough with historical and contemporary examples of elective monarchy, but the institution was entirely foreign to the ideology of English monarchism. The Tudor and Stuart monarchs vehemently opposed even the notion that entrenched hereditary kingship originated in a prehistoric act of popular empowerment. For example, the Canons of 1606 warn that

> if any man shall affirm that men at first . . . chose some among themselves to order and rule the rest, giving them power and authority to do so and that consequently all civil power, jurisdiction and authority was first derived from the people, and disordered multitude; or either is originally still in them, or else is deduced by their consents naturally from them, and is not God's ordinance originally descending from him and depending upon him, he doth greatly err. (qtd. in Kenyon 11–12)[69]

James I, in particular, defined English monarchy in opposition to elective monarchy: "the King," the earl of Salisbury admonished the Commons in 1610, "takes himself to be beholding to no elective power, depends upon no popular applause . . . he derives the lines of his fortunes and greatness from the loins of his ancestors" (*PP 1610* 2:49).[70]

It should not surprise us, then, that theatrical relations of power, in James's view, were a model not of monarchy but of popular rebellion: the "chief failing" of his Scottish subjects, James wrote in *Basilicon Doron,* was manifest in their tendency to constitute themselves as an *audience* rather than as *subjects:* "all the common people of this kingdom . . . are subject to one fault. . . . which is to judge and speak rashlie of their Prince: setting the commonweale upon four proppes as we call it; ever wearying of the present estate, and desirous of novelties" (1:93). James conflates the theatrical power of the people—their capacity to set the entire commonwealth on a stage ("four proppes")—and their political power. For the "present estate" the king's subjects tire of is at once the "estate"—the show, the symbolic display—of monarchic political culture and the actual political "estate," the state of governance, itself. James clearly figures his audience's theatrical restlessness as potentially revolutionary. The king's own marginal notes to the *Basilicon Doron* trace the phrase "desirous of novelties" to Sallust's characterization of rebellious commoners as "cupidae rerum novarum." *Res novae* is a Latin idiom for revolution.[71] Thus, James imagines that if the people are not satisfied with the monarch's estate—his show and his governance—they will close out his run on the boards of state.

Casca's description of Caesar as subjected player fully encompasses and, indeed, trumps the conflation of applause and suffrage we have been tracing in seventeenth-century prologues, epilogues, and political discourse. When he submits his monarchic ambition to the people's judgment, Caesar is like the Prologue to *The Coronation:* Caesar the would-be player-king hopes to be crowned by the votes of the "tag-rag people." But Caesar's theatrical solicitation of the people's suffrages is like an election without election because the people refuse to invest him with their power.[72] In early modern parliamentary elections, voters typically voted by voice and celebrated the moment of election with shouts and the "throwing up of cloaks, hats and caps."[73] In the crowning scene, these traditional signs of empowerment signal instead the withholding of the suffrage Caesar seeks: "he put it the third time by. And still *as he refus'd it,* the rabblement hooted, and clapp'd their chopt hands, and threw up their sweaty night-caps, and uttered such a deal of stinking breath because Caesar refus'd the crown, that it had, almost, chocked Caesar" (1.2.243–48). In theaters and popular dictatorships, the people never fully and irrevocably yield their power to judge.[74]

◇◇

I have been arguing, along the lines suggested by Cocke, that the economic basis of the professional theater made it a model of popular—even democratic—politics rather than monarchic politics. Cocke's analysis also suggests that the structure of theatrical patronage shaped the theater's most fundamental representational aesthetic: "the player . . . pretends to have a royall Master or Mistresse, [but] his wages and dependence prove him to be the servant of the people. When he doth hold conference upon the stage; and should looke directly in his fellows faces; hee turnes about his voice into the assembly for applause-sake, like a Trumpeter in the fields, that shifts places to get an eccho" (qtd. in Chambers 2:256). This vulgarity, this publicness is not a function of the theater's artistic limitations but a secondary superstructural effect of its political economy: the actor who extravagantly plays to the popular "assembly"—a term that almost always designates a deliberative or legislative body in early modern English— plays to his base.

The political aesthetic of theatrical representation, as Cocke describes it, is fundamentally opposed to conspiracy. To hold a *private* conference on stage—to fail to acknowledge the popular audience—would be the opposite of the "theatrical" in both Cocke's and Michael Fried's sense of the term. Cocke instead imagines the actor as effectively always already silently hailed by a popular assembly: "hee turnes" toward them, turns away from his fellow actors, in anticipation of, and to solicit, their applause and approval. He is their subject. Caesar, then, is the embodiment of Cocke's actor, and Shakespeare starkly juxtaposes his theatricality with the antitheatrical conspiracy. Thus, for example, at precisely the moment when Caesar is subjecting himself as an actor to the applause and roars of the "tag-rag people" of Rome, Brutus is holding a conference on stage with Cassius. While Caesar offers his throat for Rome to cut, Brutus and Cassius have literally turned their backs on the popular audience Caesar is facing.

Brutus and Cassius's private conference is, of course, conducted in full view and hearing of Shakespeare's audience: as Brutus and Cassius turn from the Roman people, they turn toward us. Throughout the play, Shakespeare relentlessly theatricalizes the antitheatrical conspiring of the plotters. Cassius, Brutus, and the other conspirators, turning their voices into the assembly when they should instead whisper inaudibly, make us the privileged witnesses of everything they seek to conceal from their fellow Romans: their decisions to spare Antony, exclude Cicero from the plan, entice Caesar with the promise of a crown, package the assassination for popular consumption, and so on. There is one moment when Shakespeare does not theatricalize conspiracy but instead theatrically represents the antitheatrical opacity of conspiracy. After the conspirators meet at Pompey's Theater, they call on Brutus at his home. Brutus shakes hands all around and asks them their business:

BRUTUS: What watchful cares do interpose themselves
  Betwixt your eyes and night?
CASSIUS: Shall I entreat a word?
  They whisper.
  (2.1.98–100)

In the orchard of a private home, just before daybreak, surrounded by, of all things, conspirators, Cassius and Brutus exchange secret words that are never revealed to us. They whisper. They breathe together. *Conspirant.* While the other conspirators speak audibly among themselves for some dozen lines, Cassius, we assume, is telling Brutus what was said at Pompey's Theater. When Brutus next speaks audibly, he for the first time identifies himself as a member of the plot: "Give me your hands all over, one by one" (112). Brutus has already taken his guests' hands; he takes their hands a second time, because he is now one of their number in the plot to murder Caesar. But the moment of conspiracy—the moment when Cassius speaks the "word" he entreats, when he articulates the "watchful cares" that have occupied him in Pompey's Theater—is withheld from us and remains private. The empty theater and this whispering, then, are doubles for one another, repositories of speech we never hear. Shakespeare withholds from representation the meeting at Pompey's Theatre and preserves the opacity of this moment to mark out conspiracy as antitheater.

The conspirators themselves, of course, think of theatricality as a mode of conspiracy. When Cassius, Casca, Decius, Cinna, Metellus Cimber, and Trebonius arrive at Brutus's door, Lucius reports to his master that he is unable to discern the identities of the visitors: "their hats are plucked about their ears, / And half their faces buried in their cloaks, / That by no means I may discover them" (2.1.73–5). But the very opacity that Lucius describes is immediately transparent to Brutus:

> They are the faction. O conspiracy,
> Sham'st thou to show thy dangerous brow by night,
> When evils are most free? O, then by day
> Where wilt thou find a cavern dark enough
> To mask thy monstrous visage?
> (77–81).

Where will conspiracy hide its monstrous visage? Not in a cavern, Brutus concludes, but in playing: "Seek none, conspiracy; / Hide it in smiles and affability" (81–82). At the end of his meeting with the faction, Brutus explicitly identifies theater as a model for conspiratorial dissimulation: "Let not our looks put on our purposes, / But bear it as our Roman actors do, / With untired spirits and formal constancy" (225–27).

Cassius hides conspiracy in an empty theater; Brutus cloaks it in a perversion of acting (acting is an open secret). And yet Brutus later proposes theater as a mode of *publicizing* and securing popular support for the assassination:

BRUTUS: Stoop, Romans, stoop,
And let us bathe our hands in Caesar's blood
Up to the elbows, and besmear our swords:
Then walk we forth, even to the market-place,
And waving our red weapons o'er our heads,
Let's all cry, "Peace, freedom, and liberty!"
CASSIUS: Stoop then, and wash. How many ages hence
Shall this our lofty scene be acted over,
In states unborn, and accents yet unknown!
BRUTUS: How many times shall Caesar bleed in sport
That now on Pompey's basis lies along
No worthier than the dust!
CASSIUS: So oft as that shall be,
So often shall the knot of us be call'd
The men that gave their country liberty.
(3.1.105–18).

I will return to the stage history Brutus and Cassius anticipate, but I want to attend first to the scene Brutus plans for the marketplace. We might consider this proposed demonstration theater rather than mere display, because Brutus supplies his troop with an action to play and a line to speak, but I am more interested in the particular notion of theatricality implied by Brutus's use of Caesar's blood as makeup and the conspirators' swords as props.

It is as if Shakespeare is restaging as tragedy the comic aftermath of the Gad's Hill caper in *Henry IV, Part I* (1598), written just a year before *Caesar*. Under Hal's fierce interrogation, Peto and Bardolph confess that they, along with Falstaff and Gadshill, fled a "band of robbers"—in fact, Hal and Poins in disguise—and then, at Falstaff's direction, fabricated the signs of a terrible and brave fight:

PRINCE: Faith, tell me now in earnest, how came Falstaff's sword so hacked?
PETO: Why, he hacked it with his dagger, and said he would swear truth out of England but he would make sure you believe it was done in fight, and persuaded us to do the like.
BARDOLPH: Yea, and to tickle our noses with spear-grass, to make them

> bleed, and then to beslubber our garments with it and swear it was the blood of true men. I did that I did not this seven year before, I blushed to hear his monstrous devices.
> (2.5.306–9)[75]

Falstaff's "devices"—a term with specifically theatrical resonances in early modern England—seem worlds away from Brutus's. Falstaff uses props and makeup to create the false appearance of having spilt the blood of his assailants, to produce belief in the absence of truth ("he would swear truth out of England but he would make you believe it was done in fight"). Brutus and the other conspirators, by contrast, have indeed murdered Caesar; the blood they smear on their hands and swords is, in fact, blood they have spilt. But this is very odd: their swords and hands are *already* bloodied.

Why does Brutus supplement real blood with real blood? One might argue that Brutus seeks only to make the evidence of the assassination more visible to the crowd, but Brutus's devices are much closer to Falstaff's than we might at first suspect. The deceptiveness of Falstaff's chief device is not internal to the prop itself: the blood is, after all, real blood. Falstaff turns his own real blood into stage ketchup by falsifying the relation between signifier and signified. We can begin to see the conspirators' "red weapons" and blood-bathed arms as cousins to Falstaff's hacked sword and beslubbered garments, once we recognize that the marketplace scene Brutus envisions is part of a larger plan to *falsify* the nature of Caesar's death.[76] Brutus has all along anxiously anticipated how the assassination will appear to the people.[77] He rejects Cassius's suggestion that Antony die with Caesar, for example, because a double murder will not play well: "Our course will *seem* too bloody" (2.1.162; emphasis added). Pondering the case of Antony leads Brutus to a consideration of how to spin the murder of Caesar:

> Let's be sacrificers, but not butchers, Caius.
> We all stand up against the spirit of Caesar,
> And in the spirit of men there is no blood.
> O, that we then could come by Caesar's spirit,
> And not dismember Caesar! But, alas,
> Caesar must bleed for it. And, gentle friends,
> Let's kill him boldly, but not wrathfully.
> Let's carve him as a dish fit for the gods,
> Not hew him as a carcass fit for hounds.
> And let our hearts, as subtle masters do,
> Stir up their servants to an act of rage,
> And after *seem* to chide 'em. This shall make

> Our purpose necessary, and not envious;
> Which so appearing to the common eyes,
> We shall be call'd purgers, not murderers.
> (2.1.166–80; emphasis added)

Brutus's Falstaffian manipulation of Caesar's blood is designed to convince "the common eyes" that Caesar has been sacrificed rather than butchered.[78] The blood that splatters on the conspirators' swords and arms as they stab Caesar and the blood Brutus smears on his sword and arms signify two quite different things. The former is the blood of an especially messy and violent murder; the latter, Brutus hopes, in both its excess and its odd precision ("up to the elbows"), will give the appearance of orderly sacrifice, of carving rather than hewing.[79]

When Brutus appears in the Forum, bloody to the elbows, his first theme is sacrifice: "If there be any in this assembly, any dear friend of Caesar's, to him I say that Brutus's love to Caesar was no less than his. If then that friend demand why Brutus rose against Caesar, this is my answer: Not that I loved Caesar less, but that I loved Rome more" (3.2.18–23). Loving Rome more than Caesar, Brutus suggests, entails loving the general good more than personal good, for making Caesar a public sacrifice required a personal sacrifice: "With this I depart, that, as I slew my best lover for the good of Rome, I have the same dagger for myself, when it shall please my country to need my death" (3.2.45–48).[80] No friend of Caesar's in the assembly calls out for Brutus's death; indeed, all of the plebeians cry out "Live, Brutus! live! live!" (49). By granting Brutus life, the people simultaneously reciprocate his sacrificial gesture—Brutus kills *his* "best lover" that *they* might "live all free men"—and thereby establish (however briefly) the killing of Caesar as a communal sacrifice that arrests violence and secures "[p]eace, freedom, and liberty!" (3.1.110).

Brutus's performance in the Forum has a Falstaffian audacity to it: in Shakespeare's play, Caesar is stabbed by seven men in front of an audience of six, but Brutus's bloody display and sacrificial rhetoric refigure this murder as a communal act. By contrast, ancient historians tell us that the conspirators planned to kill Caesar in the Senate before a large assembly in part because they believed the spectators would become actors. In Plutarch, "the conspirators determined then to put their enterprise in execution, bicause they might meete safelie at that time without suspicion, and the rather, for that all the noblest and chiefest men of the citie would be there. Who, when they should see such a great matter executed, would every man then set to their handes for the defense of their libertie" (trans. North, 1061). According to the Tudor translation of

Appian, the conspirators hoped that "though the Senatoures were not privie, yet when they sawe the deede, they woulde helpe to it, as they saye happened to *Romulus* . . . thys acte . . . beeyng doone in the place of Counsel, shoulde not be thoughte a treason, but a deede of the Citie, voyde of dreade of *Caesars* army, bycause it was a common consent" (18). The historical conspirators hope that being present at the deed will recruit nonconspirators to lend their hands to the deed itself; Shakespeare's Brutus, by contrast, seeks to create an illusion of communal participation *after* Caesar has already been killed. Brutus implicates the people in Caesar's death by constructing them as the sacrificial beneficiaries of his spilt blood: "Had you rather Caesar were living, and die all slaves," Brutus asks the crowd, "than that Caesar were dead, to live all free men?" (3.2.23–25). But Brutus's question aims at something more than securing the people's approval of a done deed. The first part of Brutus's question is straightforward enough: would you prefer that Caesar were now alive even though he would enslave you and thus make your lives living death? Caesar is dead; thus, the propositional content of Brutus's question is expressed as counterfactual. The second part of Brutus's question—"[Or] had you rather . . . that Caesar were dead, to live all free men?"—is less transparent. Caesar *is* dead at the time of Brutus's utterance, but Brutus renders the proposition "Caesar is dead" counterfactual. It is impossible to yoke the two parts of Brutus's question into a coherent whole, but the (irrational) perlocutionary effect of Brutus's utterance is to suggest that Caesar's life is in the people's hands; Brutus is asking his audience to turn their thumbs up or down over a corpse. He does not want to establish the people as accessories after the fact; he wants to figure them as accomplices in the doing of the deed. Brutus's motivation for seeking this retrospective authorization collapses his cherished distinction between the personal and the general: if the entire community shares the guilt for Caesar's death, seeking revenge against Brutus would violate the very sacrificial logic that makes Caesar's death meaningful and beneficial to them (they will "*live* all free men" rather than "die all slaves" only if Caesar's death is sacrificial).[81]

In Brutus and Cassius's vision of the theatrical history of their liberation of Rome, we can see both the eternal republic the illusory sacrifice promises and an endless repetition of the secondhandedness of the people's relation to the violent refounding of that republic:

CASSIUS: How many ages hence
Shall this our lofty scene be acted over,
In states unborn, and accents yet unknown!
BRUTUS: How many times shall Caesar bleed in sport

> That now on Pompey's basis lies along
> No worthier than the dust!
>
> CASSIUS: So oft as that shall be,
> So often shall the knot of us be call'd
> The men that gave their country liberty.
> (3.1.111–16)[82]

Cassius is not concerned with aesthetic judgments; he anticipates instead that theatergoers will perpetually ratify the conspirators' actions by constructing those actions on the conspirators' terms: to accept them as "the men that gave their country liberty" is to accept their killing of Caesar as a sacrifice.[83]

But why do Brutus and Cassius anticipate only approving audiences? Theatergoers, as Casca reminds us, both clap and hiss. Cassius's anticipation of universal and eternal approval depends on a vision of history and a theory of theater. Brutus and Cassius expect that the death of Caesar and the restoration of the republic will bring political history to an end: reenactments of their restoration of the republic will never be hissed because they will always be staged in republican states before audiences of confirmed republicans. In this republican future, Cassius assumes, dramatizations of the conspiracy will never contest its motives or results because history totalizes theater.[84] Thus, republicanism models both Brutus's ersatz sacrifice and Cassius's defanged theater. Brutus's performance in the Forum creates the illusion of communal judgment even as it makes the people's authority and power to judge secondhand, marginal, belated. We need only recall the moment when Caesar bares his throat to the people's knives to see that the scene of popular judgment Brutus stages in the Forum is an empty illusion. Similarly, in Cassius's theater, the audience, far from exercising the power to decide a "plaies life or death," acts out an empty exercise in affirmation. The function of theater in the static republican future will be to bear witness to and celebrate history rather than to act in history. Theater here is not a place of presence and action; the theatrical is merely a sign of things already done.[85] Cassius's theater, then, will endlessly repeat, affirm, and contain the great subversion of Caesarism. The theatrical audiences Brutus and Cassius anticipate might well say to themselves, "there is subversion, no end of subversion, only not for us."

◇◇

The mere presence of Shakespeare's audience subverts Brutus and Cassius's dream of an eternal and universal republic even as they dream it: Elizabeth I's subjects at the Globe did not need to wait for act 5 and Antony and Octavian's triumph at Philippi to know that the conspirators lose the battle for history. Losing in history need not, of course, entail losing on the stage: though Brutus and Cassius cannot imagine a negative representation of the republican conspiracy being staged in a republic, anyone not committed to their totalizing account of the relation between politics and culture can imagine a dramatic valorization of republicanism in a monarchic state. Indeed, Brutus loses on Shakespeare's stage not because Shakespeare must, as a good Elizabethan subject, endorse Caesar's monarchism; Shakespeare's critique of Brutus's republicanism, I have been arguing, is radical rather than conservative. In the name of republicanism, Brutus kills Caesar at the height of his popularity and then tries to convince the people that this murderous usurpation of their power was a life-giving sacrifice that enacted rather than subverted the general will. Brutus loses at the Globe not because his republicanism is antipopulist but because his Falstaffian fabrication of sacrifice—his attempt to obscure his antipopulism—has been undermined by Shakespeare's lifting of the veil.

Before we see Brutus's triumph in the Forum, we see an impromptu trial run of his performance fail miserably. The first audience to Brutus's play of bloody swords and hands is Antony, who returns to the Senate House just as the conspirators, newly made up in Caesar's blood, are leaving for the marketplace. Antony immediately remarks the conspirators' "swords . . . rich / With the most noble blood of all this world" (3.1.155–56) and their "purpled hands" (158). When Brutus realizes how moved Caesar's friend is, he tries to contextualize the bloody spectacle by giving Antony a preview of the sacrificial rhetoric he will later deploy in the Forum: "pity to the general wrong of Rome, . . . / Hath done this deed on Caesar" (170–72); "I, that did love Caesar when I struck him, / Have thus proceeded" (182–83). Brutus's words fall flat. Even in the presence of the men he fears may kill him, Antony cannot fully suppress his revulsion: "Shall it not grieve thee," Antony says to the dead Caesar, "To see thy Antony making his peace, / Shaking the bloody fingers of thy foes. . . . here thy hunters stand, / Sign'd in thy spoil, and crimsoned in thy lethe" (196–98, 205–6). The effect of the very display Brutus has designed to pass the conspirators off as "sacrificers . . . not butchers" is almost comically disastrous: "O pardon me, thou bleeding piece of earth," Antony begs his dead friend as soon as the conspirators have departed, "That I am meek and gentle with these butchers" (256–57).

Antony is, to be sure, a biased audience, but his devastating deflation of Brutus's spectacular and rhetorical "devices" nonetheless makes it extraordinarily difficult for any member of Shakespeare's audience—wherever his or her emotional and political sympathies may lie—to accept the spin Brutus puts on Caesar's death. When Antony calls the conspirators "butchers," we are reminded—even if we approve of the assassination—that Brutus is, at that very moment, trying to create an *appearance* of sacrifice that will obscure butchery. When Brutus speaks to the people in the Forum, his sacrificial gambit has already been emptied out for Shakespeare's audience. The undoing of Brutus's attempt to stage sacrifice, then, begins in Shakespeare's theatricalizing of conspiracy: seeing the bloody swords and arms is not quite the same when one has first witnessed Brutus calculating their effect.[86]

The plebeians in the Forum do not, of course, have the advantage of the backstage glimpses Shakespeare allows his audience, and Brutus's performance works a magical effect on them.[87] Indeed, when Antony follows Brutus in the rostrum, the crowd seems hopelessly against him: "'Twere best," the Fourth Plebeian says ominously, "he speak no harm of Brutus here" (3.2.68). How does Antony turn the tide against Brutus? We have come back round to a question of historical representation: how, on Shakespeare's account, do the conspirators lose the battle for Rome? Antony reminds the people of Caesar's selflessness, hints that Caesar's will includes generous bequests to the plebeians, and challenges Brutus's claim that Caesar aimed at kingship.[88] Antony's vision of a Caesar who sacrifices all and asks for nothing in return begins to turn the crowd against Brutus and the conspirators,[89] but Antony fully achieves his purpose only when he conducts a clinical yet emotional reconstruction of Caesar's death:

> If you have tears, prepare to shed them now.
> You all do know this mantle: I remember
> The first time ever Caesar put it on:
> 'Twas on a summer's evening, in his tent,
> That day he overcame the Nervii.
> Look, in this place ran Cassius' dagger through;
> See what a rent the envious Casca made;
> Through this the well-beloved Brutus stabbed,
> And as he plucked his cursed steel away,
> Mark how the blood of Caesar followed it . . .
> . . . .
> O, now you weep, and I perceive you feel
> The dint of pity; these are gracious drops.
> Kind souls, what weep you when you but behold
> Our Caesar's vesture wounded? Look you here!
> Here is himself, marr'd, as you see, with traitors.
> (3.2.171–80; 195–99)

Brutus's decision to let Antony bring the body to the Forum is an astonishing miscalculation: the meager props Brutus hopes will signify sacrificial carving are trumped, to say the least, by the butchered corpse Antony unveils. Antony's postmortem is spectacularly affective and effective:

> FIRST PLEBEIAN: O piteous spectacle!
> SECOND PLEBEIAN: O noble Caesar!
> THIRD PLEBEIAN: O woeful day!
> FOURTH PLEBEIAN: O traitors, villains!
> FIRST PLEBEIAN: O most bloody sight!
> SECOND PLEBEIAN: We will be revenged.
> ALL THE PLEBEIANS: Revenge! About! Seek! Burn! Fire! Kill! Slay!
> Let not a traitor live!
> (3.2.200–207)

The unanimous cry for "Revenge!" is the unmistakable sign that the illusion of sacrifice has been shattered. Brutus sought to implicate the people in Caesar's death precisely because the universally shared guilt of a communal sacrifice makes revenge impossible and unnecessary. Now Antony has set in motion the cycle of reciprocal violence that will consume Rome in civil war.

Antony undoes the putative sacrifice by reversing Brutus's Falstaffian falsification of Caesar's blood: Brutus separates Caesar's blood from his body and transforms it into a symbol, a sign of freedom and liberating sacrifice; Antony's autopsy reconnects the blood on Brutus's "cursed steel" to the wounds in Caesar's "vesture" and his body.[90] The "piteous spectacle" of Caesar's body reveals that he has died of particular but random wounds inflicted haphazardly by a handful of men; it is impossible to read sacrifice—at least of the sort Brutus aims at—from this corpse. But the effect of Antony's postmortem on the people exceeds the effect of forensic evidence on a jury. The simple presence and familiarity of the corpse must recall to the people their affection for the man. We must remember that the popular enmity toward Caesar Brutus very briefly produces is a radical aberration in Shakespeare's Rome: Antony triumphs over Brutus simply by reviving the feelings the people have expressed throughout the play.[91] But Caesar's fragile, mortal, vulnerable body also reminds the people of the power they once enjoyed in relation to Caesar: the body they see before them is the body that Caesar offered to them after the thwarted crowning. The "piteous spectacle," in other words, is, in part, the spectacle of the violence that was properly theirs usurped. Caesar was once theirs to kill. The sight of the body, then, opens the people's ears to Antony's suggestion that they held a kind of communal property in Caesar: the body before them, Antony tells the people, was "our Caesar." And the outrage against "our Caesar" is an outrage against the people and all of Rome:

> Even at the base of Pompey's statue
> (Which all the while ran blood) great Caesar fell.
> O, what a fall was there, my countrymen!
> Then I, and you, and all of us fell down,
> Whilst bloody treason flourish'd over us.
> (3.2.190–94)

The death of Caesar is not a universal blessing but a universal loss.

I have been arguing that Antony must unravel Brutus's construction of Caesar as communal sacrifice before he can move the people to reclaim Caesar as their Caesar. But creating a sense of community in Caesar does not desacralize Caesar himself. Antony begins his work by having the people "make a ring about the corpse" (3.2.159) and in the center of this ritual circle he resacralizes Caesar's blood even as he insists that the blood on Brutus's sword and hands is *merely* the blood of murder: "Let but the commons hear [Caesar's] testament," he predicts, "And they would go and kiss dead Caesar's wounds, / And dip their napkins in his sacred blood, / Yea, beg a hair of him for memory" (3.2.134–38).[92] The exact nature of the sacredness Antony attributes to Caesar is somewhat confused or perhaps simply overdetermined: does the memorial hair suggest sainthood to a Christian audience, or perhaps even Christ's martyrdom? Or do the dipping of the napkin and Antony's later image of "put[ting] a tongue / In every wound of Caesar" (230–31) also suggest the totem meal of primal pagan sacrifice? For our purposes here, it is enough to recognize that the invitation to share out Caesar's blood and hair among the people is part of Antony's attempt to create a ritual experience of community in Caesar. Antony, then, does not simply erase communal sacrifice; the "*gracious* drops" he wins from the people reconsecrate Caesar's bloody corpse as sacred victim.[93] Perhaps, then, Antony rewrites Caesar's death as a very particular kind of failed sacrifice—a sacrifice that creates community but also produces a Judas. Thus, the sacredness of Caesar and the necessity of revenge are continuous rather than opposed: "We'll burn his body in the holy place, / And with the brands fire the traitors' houses" (3.2.247–48). The first step in Caesar's deification is continuous with the destruction of his killers.

◇◇

I want to return briefly to the central concerns of this chapter—Brutus's construction of himself as representative, Caesarism, and theater—by revisiting the moment when Brutus offers himself as a sacrifice to the Roman people: "With this I depart, that, as I slew my best lover for the good of Rome I have the same dagger for myself, when it shall please my country to need my death" (3.2.45–48). Brutus has conned this grand gesture from Casca's report of Caesar's performance in the marketplace: "he pluck'd me ope his doublet and offer'd them his throat to cut" (1.2.261–63). But Brutus does not get Caesar's sacrificial submission quite right: Caesar offers his throat to the people's knives; Brutus offers to kill himself with his own dagger if the people will it. Caesar submits himself to a mass communal bloodletting; Brutus proposes that he will sacrifice himself. This conflation of suicide and sacrifice suggests that Brutus cannot properly conceive sacrifice because he cannot imagine the people acting out their own will in their own persons. The defect in Brutus's sacrificial thinking, that is, is simply the representationalism that governs all of Brutus's thinking: Brutus imagines that he will function as the instrumental agent of the general will at the moment he kills himself. Brutus the artificial person—the man who hails himself in Rome's voice—will kill Brutus the natural person. Brutus's construction of suicide as sacrifice is, moreover, entirely consistent with his habitual rhetoric: killing himself would simply be an extreme case of subordinating the personal to the general. The rhetoric of representation is always a sacrificial rhetoric. In the event, when Brutus learns how Antony has "moved" the people in the Forum, he does not cut his own throat; instead, he and Cassius "rid[e] like madmen through the gates of Rome" (3.2.271). Brutus has always counted on speaking the general will in the absence of the people themselves; he has always been able to count, that is, on the not entirely surprising coincidence between his personal will and the general will as he articulates it. Once the people speak their own will ("Revenge!"), Brutus decides he would prefer not to enact it.

Brutus's representationalism does not give the people much to do. Their role in the self-sacrifice he proposes would be identical to the role he gave them in Caesar's death: they will be the agents of his death; his death will fulfill their will; but they will have no hand in his slaughter. They will be alienated from their own agency. This is the essence of political representation and the antithesis of both Caesar's popular dictatorship and theatrical relations of power. Caesar never proposes to speak for the people nor to determine the common good; rather, he submits himself directly to the people's judgment and to their knives. Brutus's representationalism is a facsimile of acting: like the MP William Hakewill, who is prepared to "be [sometimes] a lawyer, sometymes a paynter, sometymes a marchante, some tymes a meane artifycer," Brutus is a one-man Globe. But playing the role of one's own audience is the antithesis of theater. Caesar, for all his absorption in his singular role of "Caesar," is, in his utter subjection to the audience, the political translation of the actor.

Brutus's odd notion that he could end his life by playing the roles of both sacrificial victim and sacrificial agent deepens the pathos of his death. In the Forum, Brutus cannot quite conceive of putting the dagger in the hands of the people, but when he gives up the ghost at Philippi, he wants someone else to hold the fatal sword:

> BRUTUS: Sit thee down, Clitus. Slaying is the word.
> It is a deed in fashion. Hark thee, Clitus.
> *He whispers.*
> CLITUS: What, I, my lord? No, not for all the world.
> BRUTUS: Peace then. No words.
> CLITUS: I'll rather kill myself.
> BRUTUS: Hark thee, Dardanius.
> *He whispers.*
> DARDANIUS: Shall I do such a deed?
> CLITUS: O Dardanius!
> DARDANIUS: O Clitus!
> CLITUS: What ill request did Brutus make to thee?
> DARDANIUS: To kill him, Clitus. (5.5.4–12)

Brutus next appeals to Volumnius: "I prithee / Hold thou my sword-hilts, whilst I run on it" (27–28). Volumnius refuses, and, finally, Brutus turns to Strato:

> BRUTUS: Hold then my sword, and turn away thy face,
> While I do run upon it. Wilt thou, Strato?
> STRATO: Give me your hand first. Fare you well, my lord.
> BRUTUS: Farewell, good Strato.
> *Strato holds the sword, while Brutus runs on it.* (5.5.47–50)

In the Forum, Brutus imagines that he can play two roles at once, but his end at Philippi seems a cruel reversal of this fantasy: now Brutus discovers that he cannot commit suicide without the help of another set of hands. Later, while Antony and Octavian gaze at Brutus's corpse, Strato manages both to tell a sweet lie about his master's end and to report it truly: "Brutus only overcame himself, / And no man else hath honour by his death" (5.5.56–57).

Figure 1. *The House of Commons in St. Stephen's Chapel.* Engraving, 1624. Harley MS, fol. 4. Reproduced by permission of the British Library.

Figure 2. *The Names of the knights, citizens and burgesses of the counties, cities and burrough-townes of England and Wales and the Baronie of the Ports now sitting in Parliament, holden at Westminster the 17 of March 1627.* Woodcut, 1628. © The Society of Antiquaries, London. Reproduced by permission.

Figure 3. *Platform of the lower house of this present Parliament, assembled the thirteenth day of April, 1640.* Engraving, 1640. British Museum Print Room. Reproduced by permission of the British Museum.

Figure 4. *James I in the House of Lords.* Engraving by Ronald Elstrack, 1604. Reproduced by permission of the British Museum.

Figure 5. *The Manner of the sitting of the Lords spirituall and temporall, as peeres of the realme in the higher house of Parliament, according to their dignities, offices, and degrees, with other officers of their attendance.* Woodcut, 1628. © The Society of Antiquaries, London. Reproduced by permission.

Figure 6. Filippino Lippi, *Storia di Virginia* (1470–80?). Louvre, Paris. Photo: Erich Lessing / Art Resource, N.Y. Reproduced by permission.

Figure 7. Detail of Filippino Lippi, *Storia di Virginia.* Photo: Réunion des Musées Nationaux / Art Resource, N.Y. Reproduced by permission.

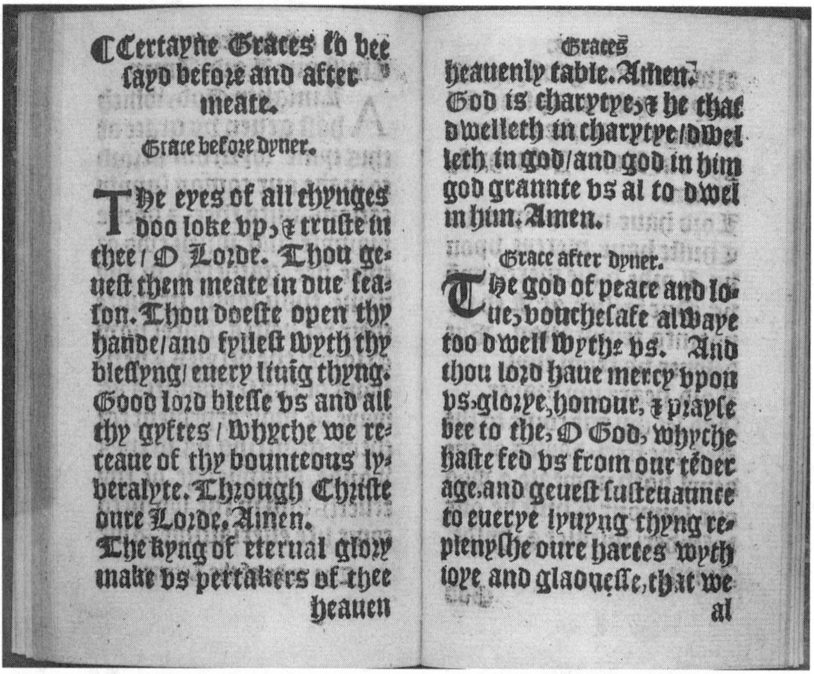

Certayne Graces to bee sayd before and after meate.

Grace before dyner.

The eyes of all thynges doo loke vp, & truste in thee / O Lorde. Thou geuest them meate in due season. Thou doeste open thy hande / and fyllest wyth thy blessyng / euery liuig thyng. Good lord blesse vs and all thy gyftes / whyche we receaue of thy bounteous lyberalyte. Through Christe oure Lorde. Amen.

The kyng of eternal glory make vs partakers of thee heauen

Graces

heauenly table. Amen.

God is charytye, & he that dwelleth in charytye / dwelleth in god / and god in him god graunte vs al to dwel in him. Amen.

Grace after dyner.

The god of peace and loue, vouchesafe alwaye too dwell wyth vs. And thou lord haue mercy vpon vs, glorye, honour, & prayse bee to the, O God, whyche haste fed vs from our tēder age, and geuest sustenaunce to euerye lyuyng thyng replenyshe oure hartes wyth ioye and gladnesse, that we al

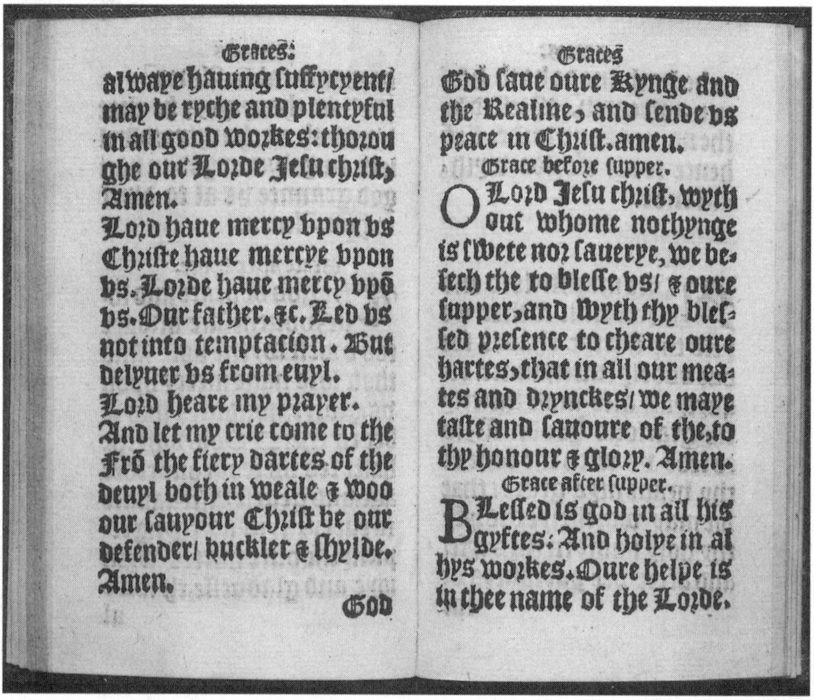

Graces.

alwaye hauing suffycyent / may be ryche and plentyful in all good workes: thorou ghe our Lorde Jesu christ, Amen.

Lord haue mercy vpon vs Christe haue mercye vpon vs. Lorde haue mercy vpō vs. Our father. &c. Led vs not into temptacion. But delyuer vs from euyl.

Lord heare my prayer.

And let my crie come to the

Frō the fiery dartes of the deuyl both in weale & woo our sauyour Christ be our defender / buckler & shylde. Amen.

God

Graces

God saue oure Kynge and the Realme, and sende vs peace in Christ. amen.

Grace before supper.

O Lord Jesu christ, wyth out whome nothynge is swete nor sauerye, we besech the to blesse vs / & oure supper, and wyth thy blessed presence to cheare oure hartes, that in all our meates and drynckes / we maye taste and sauoure of the, to thy honour & glory. Amen.

Grace after supper.

Blessed is god in all his gyftes: And holye in al hys workes. Oure helpe is in thee name of the Lorde.

Figure 8. *An A.B.C. with a Catechisme.* London, 1551. Civ^{v}–Cvi^{r}. Reproduced by permission of the John Rylands University Library of Manchester.

5 “*Worshipful mutineers*”

From *Demos* to Electorate in *Coriolanus*

In the corporation records of Elizabethan Warwick, the big town just eight miles up the road from Stratford-upon-Avon, the name Richard Brookes is a talismanic sign of subversion and disorder. Brookes's early career in Warwick did not promise Marlovian rebellion: a well-connected man of some substance, he became a principal burgess in 1565 (*BB* 7).[1] But in 1582, Brookes's fellow civic leaders expelled him from the borough corporation (*BB* 367). In a lengthy account of the “speciall causes” for this unusual action, John Fisher, the town clerk, reported that Brookes “spareth no labor nor cost to send for divers unworthy Inhabitants of the said borough perswading alluring & procuring them with swete woordes & dissembling dayntys to put their hands to his develisshe devices . . . [and] to stirre up light & lewde heades to mutynye & uproure against the officers of this borough” (*BB* 377–78).

In early modern England, this sort of rhetoric was typically reserved for witches, Jesuit agents provocateurs, leaders of agrarian riots, and, of course, actors. Brookes, however, wanted the people of Warwick to join him in neither Satanism, popish plots, anti-enclosure risings, nor playing. Brookes's sins, to be sure, stain dozens of pages in *The Black Book of Warwick:* he wore “undecent apparell . . . betokening him rather to be a miller then a magistrate” (*BB* 371); he violated prohibitions on publicizing the secret transactions and proceedings of corporation meetings (373);[2] in 1576, he engaged in a mock epic legal dispute that ended in his violent defense—bows and arrows are mentioned—of a barnful of hay (289–96); and so on and so on for decades. The Battle of the Barn undoubtedly established Brookes as Warwick's most colorful citizen, but he remained a principal burgess—one of the thirteen men who governed the town—for another six eventful years.[3] Brookes became "an open Enemye" of the corporation and the object of Fisher's nearly hysterical wrath only after he began to encourage the lesser freemen of Warwick to demand increased access to the burgesses' handling of corporation finances and a greater voice in municipal and parliamentary elections (313).[4]

The evolution of Warwick's civic government reveals the complex layering and diffusion of power in early modern England and the role political representation played in containing popular unrest. A dozen Elizabethan and Jacobean town histories tell much the same story, but Warwick commands our special attention because the "mutynye & uproure" Brookes allegedly promoted would have been very, very local history for a Stratford resident, and I believe that Shakespeare knew it well. Henry VIII granted Warwick's original Charter of Incorporation in 1546 (*BB* 227), but town government took shape under the provisions of letters patent issued by Philip and Mary in 1554: municipal authority was invested in a bailiff and twelve principal burgesses (89); in the annual election of the bailiff, the inhabitants of the town were granted the right to choose between two candidates nominated by the burgesses; the burgesses alone held the power to create new burgesses to fill vacancies in their own body; and the corporation council was empowered, but not required, to appoint a secondary council of assistants (341). In 1564, the corporation oligarchy decided to create a "common council" of twenty-four assistants (10)—a response, it seems, to the commoners' complaints that the town's financial affairs were conducted secretly and, perhaps, not very ethically (12). Creating the common council, however, was clearly an attempt to contain dissent rather than a program of democratization. The burgesses, rather than the commoners, chose the assistants, and the new common council enjoyed only a very limited role in town governance. What little the assistants were to learn of corporation affairs, moreover, was not to be disseminated to their fellow townsmen and women: "such thynges as ye are or shallbe callid to counsell of within the same borough ye shall kepe secret and not reveale the same unto any person out of the counsell house" (11). The secrecy oath reproduced locally one of the great contradictions of national political representation: the same corporation orders that enjoined the assistants never to disclose corporation proceedings to mere commoners also mandated that they "should be as it were the mowth of all the commoners. And what they agree unto shalbe taken as the consent of all the commoners in any election" (16). In Warwick, the containment of dissent took the form of political representation: by creating a nearly powerless common council, the principal burgesses could now simultaneously construct their decisions as the embodiment of the general will and exclude all but twenty-four of the town's commoners from political life.

In Elizabethan and Jacobean towns, common councils and similar ancillary bodies generally succeeded in satisfying the ambitions of lesser freemen: election to the council was a first step toward becoming a principal burgess. The new council in Warwick would seem a model of this system: many of the agitators for the reform of borough finances were made assistants and later became principal burgesses; four served terms as bailiff. Thus, the corporation government slowly co-opted the rebels into the ruling elite. As we shall see, the senators in *Coriolanus* similarly hope to contain a massive rebellion by admitting a mere five tribunes into the ranks of the governing class. But the creation of the Warwick common council—despite the opportunities for new dignities and advancement it provided—failed to defuse popular challenges to the authority of the burgesses. The junior members of Warwick's governing class soon grew restive: in 1571, John Green complained that in the election of the official who received borough rents "he & his company thought themselves . . . greatly restrained" because they had to choose one of the principal burgesses (*BB* 57). "If they might not choose where they woold," Green argued, "either of the principall burgesses or comoners it was no free choice" (59). Green's *political* campaign for an open election is continuous with the assistants' persistent frustration over *fiduciary* matters: "What came of the monye neither in whose keaping it was nor howe it was bestowed neither were they made privie of the graunting of any thing by the said borough but were used as ciphers not to be reconid of" (57).[5] In 1573, Green put the issue in a wider constitutional context: "The burges acompt" should be open to any free man of the town, for they were all materially affected by the burgesses' financial decisions. "All matters & causes that may *towch* & concerne the comon state & welth of" the town, Green argued, "should have their voices & consents as well as any other had" (108; emphasis added). Green thus adopts for borough government one of the great maxims of the nation's government: for centuries, English political theorists had argued the necessity of Parliament from the principle that *quod omnes tangit ab omnibus approbari debet* (what touches all must be approved by all).[6]

The burgesses were not receptive to the proposals of Green's faction: John Fisher quickly persuaded his colleagues to dismiss the sitting common councilors and to reduce the body's number from twenty-four to twelve.[7] The reconstituted council would consist of

> Assistants to the said Balief & principall burgesses to do those things that the comon multytude should ells doo. That is to say to choose the bailief electid out of two psons to be named by the bailief & principall burgesses and to assist the bailief & principal burgesses in the eleccion of Burgesses for the p[ar]liament. But in all other matters or causes whatsoever they should have no voices neither affirmative or negative. (*BB* 106)

There had been a flaw, Fisher realized, in the burgesses' thinking in 1564: the new councilors had a voice in few matters, but on those rare occasions they could outvote their betters. The imbalance might not have serious consequences at first, but an unreformed council, Fisher feared, would eventually "take the ordering of things into their owne hands" (*BB* 104). If "your nomber is greater," he helpfully explained to the twenty-four assistants he wanted to sack, "it folowth that yor auctoryty in evry singler p[er]son being asmuch as any of us, your nomber being greater than ours must allure us to consent will we nil we & so should it come to passe that the foot should govern the hed & the meanest him of best calling" (112).[8] The reconstituted common council would, like its predecessor, displace "the comon multytude," but the new representative body would not reproduce the multitude's power of numbers. In 1564, the Warwick oligarchy had contained popular protest by reducing the multitude to representatives; in the early 1570s, it sought better control and management of the representatives.[9]

For six years, we hear little of the now even more toothless common council, but in 1579 the assistants got an unexpected boost. Richard Brookes, still a burgess, took up the good old cause with a vengeance: in a letter to the earl of Warwick, Brookes, Robert Philips, Thomas Olney, and John Yardley charged that unnamed burgesses had used for "their owne gayne" and "private advantage" the profits from charitable trusts Thomas Oken had established for the benefit of ministers, the poor, and young artificers (*BB* 314). To this familiar charge of fiduciary impropriety, Brookes and his colleagues added a strictly political complaint: "the Bailiffes are and have been unduly & not lawfully chosen" (314). In his capacity as lord of the manor, Warwick promptly wrote the bailiff and burgesses to express his deep concern (316–17). In Fisher's eyes, Brookes's suit to the earl was a declaration of war: Brookes had been a nuisance; now he "becometh an open Enemye and voweth the overthrow and breking the neck of the corporation which he puttith in ure to the uttermost of his power" (313–14). Fisher's mood surely did not improve when he discovered that Brookes's confederates John Green, William Ffrekulton, and

Thomas Powell had already opened a second front in the Court of Requests: Fisher, Richard Fisher, Richard Townsend, and Richard Roo, they charged, had betrayed Oken's trust (319; see also 320, 323, and 329). The Court of Requests dismissed the charges, but Brookes immediately began to pursue yet another avenue of attack: "After thes things so handled," Fisher reports, "Brookes and some of the forenamed compleyners finding no ways to woork their willes devised or caused to be devised . . . matter to sett the worst sort on woork either to make some notable ryott styrre or mischief not only against the said Jo. ffisher but also rebellion against the Balief & his Assistants and that under the pretence of pittifull peticion" (*BB* 323).

In "divers libelles" left in public places (*BB* 323), the Cassius of Warwick addressed the burgesses in the voice of "your poore and needye neighbours . . . who most humbly beseche you to have regard to the voyce & groning lamentacion of such as bee poore & nedely distressed" (324). The loudest groans accused Fisher and Richard Townsend of misusing three trusts meant to benefit "young begynners" (324).[10] Finally, Brookes concocted a zany scheme to get himself a hearing in the Court of Chancery: Brookes's comrade Thomas Olney brought a case in Chancery charging *Brookes* with using the trusts for private gain; Brookes planned to defend himself by pointing the finger at Fisher. Once he had the great court's attention, he would for good measure claim that the town corporation chose bailiffs and new burgesses who enjoyed no popular support (325–27). The judges dismissed the case (328–29).

Brookes's four-pronged assault on the prerogatives and financial propriety of the principal burgesses earned him his expulsion in 1582: their fellow governor, the burgesses found, had "most unnaturally practised to perturbe the quyet peace & humanytye of the weale publique, wherof he was a member and ought to have beene a father & defender" (*BB* 369). Brookes, however, was hardly the only class traitor in Warwick: for if he had recruited "divers unworthy Inhabitants"; his party also included the former bailiffs William Ffrekulton (1568), Thomas Powell (1569), Robert Phillips (1571), and John Green (1576). Why did these four men of high standing "put their hands to [Brookes's] develisshe devices" (377)? Perhaps these wayward town fathers felt they were losing a battle for supremacy with the particular burgesses they repeatedly accused: in the period stretching from the institution of the first common council to Brookes's "open" rebellion, John Fisher, Richard Fisher, Richard Roo, and Richard Townsend collectively won the bailiff's office in 1563, 1564, 1566, 1574, 1577, 1578, and 1579. John Green's term in 1576 ended a five-year drought for the Brookes faction but gave way to three consecutive Fisherite bailiffs.[11] John Fisher himself believed that Brookes had made himself the champion of the assistants' cause in order to recover power within the corporation of principal burgesses. Fisher's deepest fear was not that Brookes would install a popular dictatorship but that he would use the people to install himself as bailiff, "which office hee so affectith that he hath not lett to saye he will Rule the next yere as pleaseth him, which (if should bee suffred) woolde bee most tyranycally and uncharitably no doubt, if he might aspire unto that place wherin he might under colo^r^ of regiment rule by will" (378).

Brookes's expulsion from the corporation did not diminish his ambitions. One by one, the attacks he had launched in 1579 came to naught, but in 1583 Brookes persuaded the earl of Leicester, the earl of Warwick's brother, to look into the matter of Thomas Oken's trusts (*BB* 328). On Leicester's instructions, Sir Thomas Lucy (*that* Sir Thomas Lucy), Thomas Leigh, and Edward Broughton traveled to Warwick for a public airing of the charges—too public an airing for John Fisher, who objected to answering questions before a "multitude" (340).[12] Fisher and several others named by Brookes managed, despite some very sticky moments, to exonerate themselves of the most serious charges, but Brookes immediately shifted his ground to political matters (341).[13] Borough elections, the Brookesites claimed, were a sham: in the election of bailiffs "a fewe sometymes not past six or seven clamyng the whole power to themselves have made eleccions" (342); and new burgesses were created without any participation by the assistants or the people themselves. The renegades proposed that "the whole multytude" should choose both the bailiff and new burgesses (342). Brookes, perhaps, was looking for a way to return from political exile. In any event, "the mocyon broching the generallytie in eleccion was thought to be very dangerous" (344), and Fisher rightly claimed that such a proposal was a direct violation of the charter of 1554. Nonetheless, first Broughton and later the earls of Warwick and Leicester advocated enfranchising the entire town (342, 351–52). For several years, the two factions waited for various courts to rule on the political rights of Warwick's lesser townsmen, but on the strength of Warwick and Leicester's support, Brookes called on the burgesses to disband themselves in order that the whole town might elect a new body of principal burgesses (353). Brookes, much to Fisher's alarm, had already recruited forty followers for the proposed election. Fisher and his colleagues countered by hand-picking "a nombr of the most honest & best sort of thinhabitants," who assembled to declare their loyalty to the status quo (354).

Fisher, adopting Brookes's strategy, deployed "the people"—his very selective construction of the people—against his patrician foe. Between 1579 and 1585, "popular politics" in Warwick was almost always manipulated by rival factions within the town's ruling elite.

Although Brookes seems rather to have enjoyed these years of battling, he always came out the loser: despite support from the great earls, Sir Fulke Greville (the poet's father), and other important Warwickshire residents, his attempts between 1583 and 1585 to remake the council of principal burgesses never succeeded. But then, long after he had been barred from the corporation, the indomitable Brookes finally won a spectacular victory over his enemies: he seized on the parliamentary elections of 1586 to rekindle the "dissencion amongs the townesmen namely betwene the Balif & Burgesses on the one side & other Comoners on the other side" (*BB* 390). Before the election writs arrived, the earl of Warwick wrote to the principal burgesses to designate his choice for one of the borough's two seats: "I have thought good to recomend unto youe my coosen *M*r Thomas dudley whom I wold not in any sorte to be disapoyntid of the one place and the other I doo very willingly & freely leave to your owne libertye to choose" (389). In a routine election, the burgesses chose one of their own number to join the earl's candidate; the borough's several hundred enfranchised freemen then assembled to "vote."[14] In 1586, the burgesses decided on John Rigley but soon learned that Job Throckmorton—whose father Clement had sat for Warwick, but who was himself neither a burgess nor a resident of the town—had already persuaded many of the town's commoners to give their voices to him. The burgesses clucked about carpetbagging (386–87),[15] but they were alarmed not by Throckmorton's address but by his direct appeals to an electorate that had hitherto come to the hustings merely to nod their heads, as well as by the very bad company he kept:

> Mr Job Throckmorton made very great labour to many of the Inhabitants of this borough for their voyces to choose him for one of the burgesses of the parliament wherin being much assistid by the Busie Richard Brook and his complices . . . & others of the meaner sort. They prevalid so much with the husbandmen in the brige end & west strete & others that had litle to do in that matter as Mr Throckmorton was put in good hope to have the voyce of the multitude to choose him . . . Mr Throckmorton encouraged in his enterprise came to Warwick to gratulate his welwillers and at the swanne made a solemne dynner wither were brought unto him by Brooks & the other factors p[ro]curement Lx or nere Lxxx of the meanest inhabitants of this borough. (*BB* 389–90)

Throckmorton may have treated "the meaner sort," but he also enjoyed the support of Fulke Greville and Sir John Harrington.[16] Throckmorton's powerful sponsors warned the town corporation not to pull any tricks—Elizabethan sheriffs were not above holding elections without advance warning (or on the wrong day, or in the wrong place, and so on)—and the burgesses, realizing they could not deal cavalierly with such men, invited Throckmorton to a parley (391).[17]

Fisher and his fellow burgesses were principally concerned with the implications of Throckmorton's candidacy for town politics: "he had greatly sought by undue meanes to be placed [as] one of their Burgesses for the parliament wherby was like to happen very perillous division & disencion emongs the townes men" (*BB* 392). Throckmorton would not budge: he already had a hundred supporters and "he myndeth to put it to the Jurye by election trusting that Mr. Balief will doo as before he had p[ro]mised to make publik proclamacion of the place & tyme . . . he woold not have this matter huddled upp in a corner as the most your matters bee amongs your selfs and not in publik" (393). Throckmorton's jibe at the burgesses' secretive handling of town government—the grievance that first sparked popular agitation against the oligarchy—must have made it all too clear that he was prepared to exploit the long-standing "division & disencion emongs the townes men." Perhaps Throckmorton's readiness to put the choice between himself and Rigley "to the Jurye by election" was even more chilling: if "the worst sort of the Inhabitants, who in deed have no Interest in this matter" (393), played a decisive role in a parliamentary election, they might well be emboldened to renew their claims for a greater role in municipal affairs.

Fisher and the corporation folded: they made Throckmorton a burgess of the town and put him forward with Dudley (397). Fisher, however, closed the negotiations with a bitter reprimand:

> But I must let you knowe, that your so seking the place without or as I may saye against our good willes, I meane M[r] Balief & principall Burgesses & other burgesses who justly have most Interest in thies accions, did not a litle trowble us . . . and so much the more that wee p[er]ceivd your famyliarity with Richard Brooke, and his diligent laboring of those that be redy to ronne headlong into any looseness. (*BB* 397)

To appeal directly to an electorate was, in the eyes of many Elizabethans of substance, a form of "looseness." Warwick's corporation had created a putatively representative body of assistants in order to *contain* "looseness" and to disempower the common inhabitants of the town. If the town's commoners were allowed to choose among candidates rather than assembled to nod their assent to the corporation's chosen candidates, the whole scheme of political representation-as-containment—a strategy practiced by dozens of borough oligarchies all over England—would collapse. Or would it? I will soon return to this question by way of a genuine election contest.

Whig and revisionist historians of early modern parliamentary elections agree on at least one thing: as the number of election contests for seats increased, voters gained power. Mark Kishlansky's seminal revisionist study of parliamentary elections—a study that begins with a reading of *Coriolanus*—demonstrates that Whig historians who focused on the *politics* of "contested" elections neglected the *social* process by which almost all knights and most burgesses attained their seats in St. Stephen's and thus distorted early modern parliamentary politics generally.[18] In nine out of ten Elizabethan and Jacobean elections, potential competition—if there was any—for a shire's or borough's seats in the House of Commons was managed by behind-the-scenes power brokers.[19] In a typical election, Kishlansky demonstrates, two candidates were selected by and from within social elites and then presented to enfranchised shire freeholders and borough freemen, who merely "appear[ed] at the place of election to shout or say aye to the proposal of the nominee's name" (10). Prior to 1586, for example, Elizabethan Warwick's parliamentary elections had been uncontested: the lord of the manor picked one "candidate," and the bailiff and twelve principal burgesses picked the other. Because early modern elections so seldom involved *choice,* Kishlansky terms the process by which MPs typically attained their seats "selection." Coriolanus's candidacy for consul, Kishlansky suggests, is a textbook early modern selection: the ruling elite (Rome's senators) unanimously nominate Coriolanus for an "elective" office; the electorate (Rome's plebeians) play "no part in generating candidates" and have "no candidates from which to choose" (6). Instead, they merely affirm the senate's choice. *Coriolanus* "so accurately portray[s] the process by which officeholders were selected in the early seventeenth century that one must conclude that Shakespeare had first-hand experience, either of wardmote selections to the London Common Council or of parliamentary selections themselves" (5).

During Shakespeare's lifetime, the value of possessing the franchise—of having a "voice," to use the term for vote that resonates throughout *Coriolanus*—was dubious at best: simple voters were at the bottom of a highly vertical structure of power. On the eve of the 1604 elections, Lord Sheffield, lord president of the Council of the North, wrote to Sir William Wentworth to recommend Francis Clifford and Sir John Savile for the shire's two seats. Sheffield's expectations were clear: "yow will give your voyces of your selves and your tenants . . . with these two gentlemen onelie" (*Wentworth Papers* 47–48). The earl of Suffolk's warning in 1604 to "all his servants, tenents, and townsmen" in Saffron Walden was blunter still: "in the election of the knights of the shire [Suffolk] . . . I do expect . . . as I am lord of the town and most of you my tenants . . . that you give your *free consents* and voices to my good friend Sir Edward Denny, knight; which if you do not . . . I will make the proudest of you all repent it, be you well assured" (qtd. in *HC* 70; emphasis added). In the case of borough elections, many magnates and lords of the manor did not bother with the nicety of strong persuasion: in 1601, for example, Sir George Carey, governor of the Isle of Wight, commanded three boroughs to send him their election writs along "with a blank, wherein I may insert the names of such persons as I shall think fittest to discharge that duty for your behalf" (qtd. in Loach 148).[20] Finally, if local social networks dominated parliamentary elections, the organs of the national government occasionally weighed in as well. In 1601, the Privy Council was concerned that Sir Thomas Leighton, a candidate much to Elizabeth's liking, was meeting with various obstacles in his effort to become a knight for Worcestershire: "[I]t is not our meaning in any sorte to restrayne or hinder the *liberty of a free election,*" they informed Worcester's town officers, but "because it is suspected that some undue proceeding may be used against [Leighton] . . . wee thought good to admonishe you . . . that . . . her Majesty . . . would be very sensible of any evil measure which by undue practises should be offred him" (*APC* 32:251; emphasis added).[21]

"Free consents"; "free election": these were seemingly meaningless phrases in almost all Elizabethan and Jacobean parliamentary elections. Indeed, the pressure the great brought to bear on "free elections" occasionally made the Commons resemble the upper house: "In Herefordshire, a Croft had sat for one county seat in every parliament but one between 1563 and 1621" (Kishlansky 26); in Warwickshire, where Shakespeare would have been entitled to vote in 1597, 1601, 1604 and 1614, the poet and courtier Fulke Greville served first as the junior knight in 1586 and then as the senior knight in 1588, 1593, 1597, 1601, and 1621 (*HC* 49). With some justice, then, Arthur Hall characterized the Commons as a minor league for the nobility: "The third of the Commons, wherein is comprised the younger sonnes of the nobility, and in a manner all the heirs apparente, very few except, the fathers living, al the gentry & the whole rest" (Hall Ei^{v}). In Hall's little fiction, we recall, this advice is part of a book a father has written for his son on the occasion of his "election" to the

Commons: "Sonne," the father begins, "for as much as I now have obtayned for you my place in the common house of Parliament" (A^r). Perhaps an Elizabethan audience would not have been entirely surprised when Titus Andronicus and his brother Marcus manage an imperial election so as to secure the succession of the dead emperor's eldest son.

Kishlansky, then, seems fully justified when he warns Whig historians to stop seeking the roots of representative democracy in Elizabethan and Jacobean England: "it is to the mid-seventeenth century that we must look to understand the origins of participatory democracy" (230). Only genuine electoral contests, substantive campaigns, and, eventually, a party system can give voters choice and thus power: "All the ills of democracy," Al Smith said, "can be cured by more democracy." But "curing" the defects of primitive political representation—widening the franchise, increasing the number of electoral contests, and so on—does not, in fact, transform political representation into "participatory democracy": political representation perfected is not democracy. Rather, Rousseau would no doubt argue, a wider franchise swells the legions of the deluded and election contests—as opposed to selections—merely intensify the delusion that enfranchisement is empowerment. I want now to turn to *Coriolanus* by way of one last chapter from the annals of early modern electoral politics—a genuine contest that will suggest why Kishlansky's absolute distinction between "contests" and "selections" is misguided and why Elizabethan and Jacobean elections may have made a radical rather than a reformer out of Shakespeare.

When Gloucester's corporation officers—the mayor and twelve aldermen—received the election writs for James I's first Parliament, they proceeded, in time-honored borough fashion, to select two "official" candidates to present to the roughly 400–500 qualified voters of the town for ritual affirmation. But John Jones, an alderman, decided to stand against the official candidates—Nicholas Overbury, the town recorder, and Thomas Machen, another alderman. Gloucester's corporation, unlike Warwick's in 1586, could not resolve the competition before the election. The mayor and the other aldermen repeatedly admonished the rebel to give up his ambition, but Jones proceeded to "solicite and stir up many of the basest & meanest burgesses" whom he "seduced against the corporation's decision."[22] Jones's seductiveness is a match for Brookes's "devilish devices" for mutiny and uproar: in the Renaissance, "seduction" routinely designated the undermining of hierarchical relationships and often carried demonic overtones.[23] Jones did indeed articulate a popular—and thus virtually demonic—campaign theme: he pledged to protect the economic interests of the commoners rather than of the wealthy burgesses, and he promised more fairs. These promises persuaded "many of the meaner sort of Burgesses to promise to give their voices with him" (55).

The borough's official report suggests that Jones's election entertainments were just as seductive as his policy proposals. Jones marshaled his supporters into the town and saw to it that they were "kept together in several Inns, Taverns & Alehouses there drinking and carousing in very disorderly manner" (55). The disorderliness Jones encouraged was much in evidence during the election the next day. Jones's party entered the town hall repeatedly shouting "john jones for burgess," and the more the mayor, aldermen, and sheriff "laboured to stay the unruly clamour, the more they still cried and shouted out Jones, Jones for A Burgess!" (55). Despite, or perhaps because of, the mayor's and aldermen's obvious disapproval, Jones was "by the meaner sort of Burgess & by the multitude of voices" elected, along with Overbury, to represent the borough in Commons. The subsequent victory celebration was remarkable: for fifteen minutes, the electorate remained in the hall to "cry out & shout in most outrageous manner with throwing up of cloaks, hats and caps"; after leaving the hall, the crowd appropriated one of the town's churches, St. Mary de Rapt, and rang the tower bells; finally, fortified with much beer—provided of course by the new MP—the voters surrounded the town hall and greeted the departing mayor, aldermen, and common councilors with cries of "Jones, Jones for A Burgess."

The behavior of the Gloucester electorate—especially as seen through the eyes of town officials—looks very much like carnivalesque misrule.[24] Jones's electioneering promoted Rabelaisian drinking, eating, and carousing, but the voters' postelection festivities were far more explicitly political: the usurpation of the church and the unsanctioned ringing of its bells certainly constituted misrule, and the crowd seems even more boisterously subversive when they surround the town hall to remind the municipal governors of the primacy and efficacy of popular empowerment: serenading the departing mayor and councilors with choruses of "Jones, Jones for A Burgess," the commoners celebrate their decisive role in the election.[25] The governors of Gloucester may have regarded this affront as "mutynye & uproure," but early modern election contests were carnivalesque: that is, they *institutionalized* misrule by making the momentary subjection of the ruling (the MPs) to the ruled (the electorate) the positive condition for reproducing the House of Commons and, therefore, the entire political culture. The election of Jones did not constitute a moment of systemic breakdown: the Gloucester election reproduced England's settled political culture no less effectively than the many dozens of quiet "selections" that took place simultaneously all over England. Nor did the contest give Gloucester's voters any more influence over parliamentary politics than the tamest of tame selections would have. After all, the misrule of Gloucester's freemen, like that of a carnival king or boy bishop, was fleeting. While Jones attended parliamentary sessions for six years—sessions to which the men who empowered him had no access at all—his supporters exhausted their political power, energy, and capital in one day and went home. At the moment they yielded their voices, I suggest, the people of Gloucester were, to quote Rousseau, "nothing": "Le peuple anglais pense être libre, il se trompe fort: il ne l'est que durant l'élection des membres du parlement; sitôt qu'ils sont élus, il est esclave, il n'est rien. Dans les courts moments de sa liberté, l'usage qu'il en fait mérite bien qu'il la perde" (190).[26]

The contested election—with its spectacle of the (relatively) high asking the humble for their empowering voices—created, in a way selections obviously did not, the illusion that political representation empowers the people. The contested election also potentially revealed, in a way selections obviously did not, that political representation per se disempowers the people. It is precisely because the voters seem to be in a state of rebellion before and at the moment they indicate their choices that the aftermath of the election so powerfully suggests that voting itself—even when there is choice and contest—is the end rather than the beginning of power: the closer an election came to spinning out of control, the more profoundly it institutionalized misrule. Shakespeare develops just such an ideological critique of political representation not by writing a play about a particular election contest but by imagining in *Coriolanus* the mythic origins of political representation itself. In fact, the founding of the Roman tribunate did not mark the beginning of political representation in the West. The Roman tribunes were not, Rousseau rightly and passionately insists, "représentants":

> L'idée des représentants est moderne. . . . Dans les anciennes Républiques, et même dans les monarchies, jamais le peuple n'eut de représentants: on ne connaissait pas ce mot-là. Ils est très singulier qu'à Rome, où les tribuns étaient si sacrés, on nait pas même imaginé qu'ils pussent usurper les fonctions du peuple, et qu'au milieu d'une si grande multitude ils n'aient jamais tenté de passer de leur chef un seul plébiscite. (190)

Shakespeare's tribunes, who claim to stand, speak, and act for the people, are decidedly modern representatives. Shakespeare transforms the rebellion that secured the perfecting of the Roman Republic into a rebellion that ends in the establishment of political representation. He figures this primal bargain (peace in exchange for representation) as a disaster for the people—a bargain in which they lose all of their power and gain only a spectral role in Roman political life. In *Coriolanus,* the election of the tribunes constitutes not mutiny but the containment of mutiny, the transformation of mutiny into an empty ritual.

At the end of his reading of *Coriolanus,* Kishlansky argues that the disintegration of Coriolanus's bid for the consulship—the people revoke their voices almost as soon as they have given them to the great general—is "Shakespeare's recreation of [a] selection process failure" (7): that failure "equals catastrophe. Riot, near rebellion, death and destruction all flow from this one event" (7). Kishlansky assumes that riot and rebellion are bad, but we must remember that riot and rebellion are the positive condition for the creation of the tribunate. In *Coriolanus,* Shakespeare is not concerned to show that the failure of the selection process produces "near rebellion . . . and destruction"; he wants, rather, to suggest that Rome's plebeians should never have traded in their rebellion for representation in the first place.[27]

◇◇

Coriolanus (c. 1608) begins with a popular uprising: Rome's starving plebeians, convinced that the patricians are hoarding corn, have armed themselves and are marching on the Capitol. The revolt ends when the Senate grants the plebeians the right to elect five tribunes to represent them in Rome's government. The club-wielding commoners confirmed for generations of critics Shakespeare's horror of the lower orders.[28] In recent years, by contrast, Annabel Patterson, Anne Barton, Leah Marcus, Vivian Thomas, Shannon Miller, R. B. Parker, Thomas Sorge, Michael Bristol, Lars Engle, and other scholars have figured *Coriolanus* as the work of a prescient liberal who championed "the people" and "belie[ved] that Jacobean England desperately needed to borrow from the strengths, as well as learn from the difficulties, of republican political theory" (*SPV* 122).[29] The recovery of an oppositional *Coriolanus* has depended, for the most part, not on demonizing Coriolanus but on valorizing the plebeians, who are strikingly different, Sorge argues, from the "mindless, demoralized rabble" (233) we encounter in the work of Shakespeare's contemporaries. Patterson similarly claims that *Coriolanus* marks a revolution in the dramatic representation of common people: "The play's second line . . . 'Speak, speak,' for the first time allows the people to speak *for themselves* as a political entity, with legitimate grievances, and with a considerable degree of political self-consciousness" (*SPV* 127). Given this opportunity "to speak *for themselves,*" the articulate plebeians discredit entrenched aristocratic ideologies and persuasively justify their rebellion.[30]

For Whig Shakespeareans, the key target of plebeian "political self-consciousness" is Menenius's Fable of the Belly.[31] Soon after the play begins, the "*mutinous Citizens*" (1.1.0) making their way to the Capitol are confronted by the patrician Menenius, who at first seems to imagine that he can quell the uprising simply by reminding the plebeians of the ideology of oligarchic republicanism: "I tell you, friends, most charitable care / Have the patricians of you. . . . you slander / The helms o'th' state, who care for you like fathers" (1.1.63–75). When the First Citizen reacts with derision, Menenius repackages his naked paternalism as "a pretty tale" of "a time when all the body's members / Rebell'd against the belly" (88, 94–95): the Members claim that the idle Belly feeds himself on their labor and hoards from them the food they have harvested; the Belly replies that, on the contrary, he altruistically distributes the choicest "flour" to the whole body, reserving for himself "but the bran" (143–44). The "senators of Rome," Menenius tells his audience of plebeian members, "are this good belly," and all "public benefit . . . proceeds or comes from them to you, / And no way from yourselves" (146–52).

The First Citizen, as the Whigs powerfully demonstrate, dismisses Menenius's application of the fable to their Rome and offers a convincing critique of the gross inequalities and injustices it is designed to mystify: "Shakespeare had not only pierced the fable's hide, he permitted his plebeians to do so as well" (*SPV* 135).[32] This plebeian triumph over aristocratic ideology, the Whigs argue, reveals Shakespeare's view of his own political culture, for Menenius's paternalistic fable mirrors the ideology of the Jacobean ruling elite, and the plebeians' complaints echo the grievances of the Midland peasants who, in 1607, rioted over enclosures and inflationary grain prices.[33] Thus, the plebeians' encounter with Menenius, Sorge claims, encourages the lowlier members of Shakespeare's audience to recognize and reject the orthodoxy of their own governors: "the . . . audience become[s] aware of how the Roman citizens see through the representations of their superiors, of how the rhetorical arsenal of the rulers is no longer effective in manipulating the subordinate classes . . . [the people] free themselves from the representations of the rulers by testing the validity of these representations (233)."

The Whigs, however, do not see in the First Citizen's deflation of Menenius's Belly a call for the violent overthrow of either the oligarchic Roman Senate or the English monarchy and House of Lords. Rather, the popular protest against the evils of grain hoarding and rampant usury demonstrates "that the people are in desperate need of representation" (Thomas 180). The Whig *Coriolanus* promotes the establishment of a "constitution that provided, through the tribunate, for popular representation" as a triumph for *all* Rome and as an historical model for Jacobean England (*SPV* 123).

If *Coriolanus* merely gives a positive account of "popular representation," what lesson could it have held for Shakespeare's audience? After all, English political thinkers and politicians had for generations compared England's *settled* "mixed estate" to precisely the perfected Roman Republic—that is, the addition of the plebeian tribunate to the patrician consulate and senate—that emerges in *Coriolanus:* thus, the knights and burgesses of the House of Commons were often styled—sometimes admiringly, sometimes venomously—the "tribunes of the people."[34] In the House of Commons, England already had an elected legislative and juridical body charged with the representation of the people. But the tribunate, Patterson argues, was *more* representative than the early modern Commons: *Coriolanus,* then, had a radical import for Shakespeare's England because it championed a representational system that "admitted that huge group of persons that English electoral law excluded" (129). In *Coriolanus,* the citizens who secure the franchise are reviled by Menenius as "apron-men . . . garlic-eaters. . . . [and] crafts" (4.6.100, 102, 124). The unenfranchised Jacobean garlic-eaters in Shakespeare's audience would have seen in their fictional Roman counterparts a brief for their own participation in parliamentary elections.[35] "Allow[ing]" Rome's mechanicals to "*speak for themselves*" with wit and political savvy, Shakespeare makes his case, to Jacobean mechanicals and governors alike, for a government in which all the people of the realm have a voice.

It seems odd to put so much stock in the capacity of the "hungry commoners . . . [to] speak for themselves" (Patterson, *Fables* 121) and then to argue that Shakespeare advocated representational politics—that is, a system in which representatives speak for the people. If the people can "speak for themselves," why should they elect tribunes to speak for them? Patterson herself claims that Shakespeare's plebeians "require no ventriloquizers because they are not dummies" (*SPV* 131). Political representation, according to Patterson's version of Madisonian thinking, is a practical necessity: "the point that Shakespeare apparently wished to make was that Rome's plebeians, though they needed the tribunes as a structural device, were not the pathetic nonentities, aimless and inarticulate . . . that readers from Gildon to Grass have thought they saw" (132). If the tribunes are nothing more than a "structural device" through which the people speak and exercise their will, then the difference between the people and their tribunes is merely technical. Other Whig critics similarly conflate the people and the tribunes: Bristol divides the new Rome into "three sociohistorical categories—Coriolanus, patricians, and the plebeians and the tribunes" (207); Miller argues that "Coriolanus tries to negate the people's power, embodied in the tribunes" (305); and Sorge sees the creation of *tribunes* as "the emergence of a new, fairly self-contained social body that finds its center in the *citizens*" (236; emphasis added).[36]

To argue that political representatives are merely a "structural device" or to conflate the people and their representatives is to confuse democracy with what is now generously called representative democracy. Put another way, Patterson and the Whigs, for all the importance they attach to plebeian speech, do not distinguish between speaking for oneself and being spoken for by representatives, and they thus construct political representation *precisely as the ideology of early modern political representation constructs political representation.* Let me clarify and complicate the peculiar confusion I have been describing by turning to a closely related problem in Whig thinking. Whig critics adduce Shakespeare's endorsement of popular *political* representation from his positive *theatrical* representation of the people:

> By returning to Roman history, more specifically to a founding moment in the Roman republic, Shakespeare countered his skeptical analysis, in *Julius Caesar,* of republicanism in decay with a study of its beginning. In this play [*Coriolanus*] the plebeians themselves (as distinct from their tribunes) are generously represented, and the popular voice, *as they themselves speak it,* has genuine grievances to express. (*SPV* 11; emphasis added)

Patterson, then, derives Shakespeare's support for political representation from his positive theatrical representation of the people. On the one hand, bypassing the tribunes themselves—one would have expected an endorsement of political representation to include a generous representation of political representatives—is very nearly an interpretive necessity for Patterson: Shakespeare transforms Plutarch's "seditious" tribunes, who "cried out upon the noble men," into the thoroughly miserable Brutus and Sicinius, who revile the people as "beasts" and are motivated entirely by self-interest.[37] On the other hand, Patterson's conflation of theatrical and political representation is ideologically consistent as well as interpretively convenient, for she assimilates theatrical representation to the model of (the mystified form of) political representation: even as she distinguishes between the plebeian voice and the tribunal voice within Shakespeare's fictive Rome, Patterson collapses speaking for oneself and being "generously represented." Now Shakespeare, generously representing Rome's commoners even as they speak for themselves, is the people's tribune.

Shakespeare's entire political meditation in *Coriolanus* turns on dramatic juxtapositions between the people and their representatives, speaking for oneself and being spoken for, political representation and theatrical representation. Indeed, for the first 215 lines of the play, Shakespeare gives us a glimpse of the people *before* the advent of the tribunate precisely so that we may see that representation, far from being a "structural device," changes *everything.* The founding of the tribunate marks a radical transformation—and not for the better—in the people's comportment, manner of speech, and self-conception and in their role in Roman political culture. The institutionalization of popular power transforms the citizens, who before they attain representation are just as smart and confident as the Whigs claim, into the fickle and confused rabble Coriolanus scorns.

In Shakespeare's radical rewriting of Plutarch, Livy, and other sources, the election of the tribunes instantaneously disempowers the people and usurps their voices. The tribunate is born offstage on "the other side o'th' city" at precisely the same time the First Citizen's savage contempt for the Fable of the Belly is absorbing the attention of Menenius, the other plebeians, and the audience. Just as the plebeians, having rejected Menenius's tale, are preparing to proceed to the Capitol, Caius Martius, who will soon give himself the name Coriolanus, arrives to report the great constitutional innovation:

> MENENIUS: What says the other troop?
> MARTIUS: They are dissolved. Hang 'em.
> They said they were an-hungry, sighed forth proverbs—
> That hunger broke stone walls, that dogs must eat,
> That meat was made for mouths, that the gods sent not
> Corn for rich men only. With these shreds
> They vented their complainings, which being answered,
> And a petition granted them—a strange one,
> To break the heart of generosity
> And make bold power look pale—they threw their caps
> As they would hang them on the horns o'th' moon,
> Shouting their emulation.
> MENENIUS: What is granted them?
> MARTIUS: Five tribunes to defend their vulgar wisdoms,
> Of their own choice. One's Junius Brutus,
> Sicinius Velutus, and I know not . . .
> (1.1.202–15)

Why would Shakespeare deny his audience the founding scene of political representation? Why limit the theatrical representation of the birth of the tribunate and the first tribunal election to the offstage shouts our band of citizens hear at 1.1.45?

Because we do not see the scene Martius describes, certain aspects of the constitutional resolution of the revolt remain murky, even mysterious: who wrote and presented the petition? Who spoke for the patricians? If the offstage shouting we hear at 1.1.44.sd is the same shouting Martius refers to at 1.1.212, what does it signify? The people's approval of the constitutional alteration? Or are we hearing the people shouting for candidates in the tribunal elections? How was the first election conducted? It is, however, what we do know rather than what we do not know that most profoundly troubles the legitimacy of representation. When Brutus later claims that he and Sicinius "by the consent of all . . . were established the people's magistrates" (3.1.200–201), we know he is indulging in politically motivated exaggeration: the citizens we see on stage in act 1 were present neither when the constitution was amended nor when Sicinius and Brutus were elected.[38] One might develop a Whiggish contextualization of Brutus's boast: Shakespeare here exposes the gap between the early modern MPs' habitual claim that they were empowered by universal consent—"the whole realm hath chosen us to sitt here diligently to enquire what is beneficiall or hurtfull for the same" (*PPE* 1:130)—and the reality of a limited franchise. *Coriolanus* is, to be sure, an indictment of Brutus's and Sicinius's performances as representatives and a critique of particular aspects of early modern parliamentary politics. But Shakespeare reimagines the advent of the tribunate as the birth of political representation in the West in order to develop a critique of political representation per se: widening the franchise will not redeem political representation because enfranchisement is an illusion of power; under a regime of representation, widening the franchise would, *Coriolanus* suggests, merely swell the ranks of the deluded.[39]

Political representation, we must remind ourselves, is not among the aims of the citizens we see in act 1: indeed, they seem to have had no inkling of such a demand. The citizens' general objective of storming the Capitol subsumes very clear, very particular goals: corn at fair rates, restrictions on usury, and the elimination of Caius Martius. The people, the First Citizen reminds Menenius, have repeatedly aired these grievances: "Our business is not unknown to th' senate. They have had an inkling this fortnight what we intend to do, which now we'll show 'em in deeds. They say poor suitors have strong breaths; they shall know we have strong arms, too" (1.1.55–59).

The senate's concession to the people on "the other side o'th' city" seems to confirm the efficacy of transforming "strong breaths" into "strong arms." Perhaps, then, our citizens greet Martius's report with silence rather than "shouts"—one of the traditional signs of approbation at early modern elections—because they sense that the new order has betrayed their cause. For the rebellion seems oddly to empty itself out at the moment of its triumph: the plebeians have taken up arms precisely because words failed to move their governors; now they agree to lay down their "strong arms" in exchange for *voices* in the political system. Shakespeare departed sharply from his source here in order to intensify our sense that the people are giving up power. The violent origin of political representation in *Coriolanus* is not modeled on Plutarch's account of the origins of republicanism. According to Plutarch, the citizens, far from violently assaulting the Capitol, peacefully "forsooke the cittie, and encamped them selves upon a hill, called at this daye the holy hill, alongest the river Tyber, offering no creature any hurte or violence" (trans. North 512). The senate, no doubt wondering who would feed the patrician belly, induced the people to return by promising them tribunes and new measures against usury.

In *Coriolanus,* the tribunate institutionalizes the people's power by converting the power of their violent bodies into putatively powerful voices. This is reverse alchemy, for the "voices"—the franchises—the people gain are the means by which they enslave themselves to representatives, and to acquire them they give up not only their physical power but, ironically, their voices as well. With the election of the tribunes, Coriolanus reports, the people "are dissolv'd." Coriolanus never quite appreciates the felicity of his own choice of words, for the tribunate does not simply put an end to the rebellion; its routine effect—indeed, its institutional mission—is to "dissolve" the people. From the moment the tribunes arrive on our side of the city, the people virtually disappear from the stage: before Brutus and Sicinius first appear at 1.1.226, the plebeians have 85 lines; in the remainder of a very long play, the people speak fewer than 100 lines, while their tribunes have nearly 500. The relation between the plenitude of tribunal speech and the people's loss of voice is fully felt, of course, only as the play unfolds. By the end of the first scene, however, we can already begin to see why Shakespeare has juxtaposed the offstage and onstage rebellions: the now silent people "*steal away*" (1.1.250.sd), while the tribunes, senators, and patricians depart for the Capitol. The new order created offstage accomplishes precisely what Menenius seeks to achieve through the Fable of the Belly: while the old patrician bamboozlement is failing to pacify the citizens onstage, the new bamboozlement of political representation is containing the revolt on "th'other side o'th' city."[40] Here, then, is the truly radical message *Coriolanus* held for Shakespeare's audience: political representation dissolves the people, makes them nothing.[41]

When the play begins—when the people are politically unrepresented yet already constitute a coherent political force of their own—the plebeians articulate two motives for the rising: they want corn (1.1.4–5), and they want restrictions on usury (79–80). Coriolanus is an obstacle to achieving these ends, and the citizens thus resolve to kill him (7–12). The Capitol is both the literal and symbolic positive objective of the people's rebellion. Indeed, the plebeian political struggle is expressed as a kind of topographical pun, a desire to subject the patrician Capitol, with its Senate House full of hoarded political power and its symbolic association with "storehouses crammed with grain" (1.1.78–79), to the competition, liquidity, and openness of the plebeian marketplace. According to Coriolanus, the people will gain political power simply by subjecting the Capitol to publicity and speculation:

> They'll sit by th'fire and presume to know
> What's done i'th'Capitol, who's like to rise,
> Who thrives and who declines; side factions and give out
> Conjectural marriages, making parties strong,
> And feebling such as stand not in their liking
> Below their cobbled shoes.
> (1.1.189–94)

Coriolanus's horror of public politics is not unlike Robert Cecil's anxiety about leaks during the monopoly debates of 1601: "I needes [must] give yow this ffuture caution, that whatsoever is subjecte to a publique expectacion cannot be good. . . . I have hearde my selfe, beinge in my coache, these wordes spoaken alowde: 'God prosper those that further the overthrowe of these monopolies'" (*PPE* 3:398). Coriolanus similarly fears that once the people have gained access to the business of the Capitol, they will exercise power to "prosper those" whom they favor.[42] The plebeians, to be sure, get some corn "gratis" (3.1.45) and help to banish Coriolanus from Rome, but they never gain significant influence in the Capitol.[43] Although the creation of the tribunate seems to relocate some political power from the Capitol to the marketplace, the Capitol remains the place where wars are planned (1.1.244–45), great victories celebrated (2.1.202), material resources allocated (3.1.44–45), and consuls selected (2.2.133–34). The real capital that enables one to produce and control new political and economic wealth remains locked up in the Capitol, safe from the people, who, in Coriolanus's words, want to "break ope the locks o'th' senate" (3.1.141).[44] Coriolanus's fears are profoundly misplaced: the people never get to the Capitol, and it is precisely the tribunate that secures the aristocracy's hold over the seat of power.

◇◇

The people do not steal their way back into the political arena until Coriolanus stands for consul: having led the Romans to a great victory over the Volscians, Coriolanus is "selected" by the Senate, but he must still humble himself in the marketplace and solicit the people's voices for the consulship. The tribunes have "lessoned" (2.3.177) and "fore-advised" (191) the people to provoke Coriolanus into a disastrous outburst; instead, they bestow on him Rome's most powerful office. Sicinius is understandably amazed: "putting him to rage," he scolds his bad pupils, "You should have ta'en th'advantage of his choler / And passed him unelected" (2.3.197–98). At the end of this book, I will return to the people's tragic confusion as they give their voices to their ancient enemy, but I want here to consider the aftermath of Coriolanus's improbable, if fleeting, electoral triumph. After Coriolanus abandons the marketplace for the Senate House, the people themselves cannot quite believe what they have done (155–73), and they eagerly approve the tribunes' proposal to revoke the consulship and put Coriolanus to a second test (205–12).

Goading Coriolanus into a rage turns out to be child's play: the tribunes intercept him as he leaves the Capitol, and he reviles them before they can even open their mouths (3.1.22–25). After Coriolanus has indulged himself in several extravagant rants against the "rank-scented meinie" (70), Sicinius arrests him: "He's spoken like a traitor, and shall answer / As traitors do" (165–66). Or, rather, Sicinius tries to arrest him:

SICINIUS: Go call the people, [*Exit Aedile*]
[*To Coriolanus*] in whose name myself
A foe to th' public weal. Obey, I charge thee,
And follow to thine answer.
CORIOLANUS: Hence, old goat!
. . . .
COMINIUS: [*to Sicinius*] Agèd sir, hands off.
CORIOLANUS: Hence, rotten thing, or I shall shake thy bones,
Out of thy garments.
SICINIUS: Help, ye citizens!
Enter a rabble of Plebeians, with the Aediles
(3.1.176–79, 180–82)

Sicinius's hope that Coriolanus will simply submit to the new economy of power is as fond as Menenius's fantasy that he need only tell the plebeians his "pretty tale" (1.1.88) to put down the revolt. The declarations Marcus Andronicus articulates in the representative "we" command his Rome, but when Sicinius issues orders in what we might call the representative imperative—"the popular shall," to borrow Coriolanus's contemptuous term—Coriolanus calls his bluff. Even after Sicinius musters the people, Coriolanus refuses to obey:

> BRUTUS: By the consent of all
> We were established the people's magistrates.
> . . . .
> BRUTUS: Or let us stand to our authority,
> Or let us lose it. We do here pronounce,
> Upon the part'o'th' people in whose power
> We were elected theirs, Martius is worthy
> Of present death.
> SICINIUS: Therefore lay hold of him,
> Bear him to th' rock Tarpeian; and from thence
> Into destruction cast him.
> BRUTUS: Aediles, seize him.
> ALL THE CITIZENS: Yield, Martius, yield.
> (3.1.200–201; 207–14)

Coriolanus responds to this outpouring of "strong breath" by drawing his sword and beating the tribunes, their aediles, and the people from the stage.[45]

Sicinius and Brutus's *personal* helplessness in the face of Coriolanus's refusal to recognize their authority reminds us that tribunal power originates in the people's potential for violence. And even as the tribunes lose this initial battle, they begin to win the war: the failure of the representative imperative does not, as we might expect, embolden the patricians; on the contrary, the sight of the people en masse confirms their determination not to fight a civil war against "the numbers" (3.1.230–34; 328–38). Coriolanus—his sword still out, his blood up—calls the patricians to battle, but they instead insist that he appease the people and their tribunes.[46] Coriolanus reluctantly returns to the marketplace but fails miserably, and the people and the tribunes banish him from Rome: "our dastard nobles," Coriolanus later fumes to Aufidius, "Have all forsook me . . . And suffered me by th' voice of slaves to be / Whooped out of Rome" (4.5.76–79).

Coriolanus's banishment would seem to vindicate representational politics: if the *voices* of the people drive Coriolanus from Rome, if the "clusters . . .

hoot him out o'th'city" (4.6.130–31), then the foundational exchange of "strong arms" for voices might be sound enough after all. But the triumph of representational politics is not, in the end, a triumph for the people themselves. For even as the people provide the physical threat necessary to accomplish the banishment, their own sense of their role in the great victory reveals how profoundly political representation has tamed them. The people are not unaware, to be sure, that their presence empowers the tribunal "shall": as he girds himself for Coriolanus's second appearance in the marketplace, the First Citizen braves, "He shall well know / The noble tribunes are the people's mouths, / And we their hands" (3.1.270–72). In the play's first scene, the First Citizen's witty and penetrating critique of the Fable of the Belly reduces Menenius to sputtering and name-calling; now the First Citizen figures himself as an inarticulate hand ready to strike blows for those who have usurped his tongue. Before representation, the First Citizen is both the rebellion's brains and part of its brawn; after representation, the First Citizen is merely muscle—he has assumed, in other words, the role of "member" Menenius so unconvincingly tries to cast him in at the beginning of the play.

"The noble tribunes are the people's mouths, / And we their hands": even as he speaks, the First Citizen imagines himself alienated from his own voice. But the First Citizen's self-effacement, depressing as it is, turns out to be a rosy delusion: as the banishment scene develops, we discover that he and his fellow citizens are the mouths of the tribunes. As they prepare for Coriolanus's return to the marketplace, Brutus and Sicinius instruct their aedile to orchestrate the plebeians' response:

> SICINIUS: Assemble presently the people hither,
> And when they hear me say "It shall be so
> I'th' right and strength o'th' commons," be it either
> For death, for fine, or banishment, then let them,
> If I say "Fine," cry "Fine!", if "Death," cry "Death!",
> Insisting on the old prerogative
> And power i'th' truth o'th' cause.
>
> . . . .
>
> BRUTUS: And when such time they have begun to cry,
> Let them not cease, but with a din confused
> Enforce the present execution
> Of what we chance to sentence.
> (3.3.12–22)

The play begins with the First Citizen and the Second Citizen debating the wisdom of killing Coriolanus; now Sicinius and Brutus, in the absence of any consultation with the people, have usurped that decision. The tribunes will pronounce a sentence; the people will simply give their assent. The people's tongues no longer express rational thought but produce instead "a din confused" to enforce the decisions of others.

The people, then, are the "structural device" by which the tribunes rule. After Coriolanus has returned to the marketplace to take his medicine, the aedile gives the people their final instructions as he ushers them like children from the wings to the stage: "List to your tribunes. Audience! / Peace, I say" (3.3.42–43). The tribunes' claim that Coriolanus is "a traitor to the people" provokes the desired response—"The fires i'th' lowest hell fold in the people!" (3.3.71)—but the excited citizens render their verdict before they have been fed their line: "To th' rock," they all cry, "to th' rock with him!" (79). For one moment, the people recover their voices and pronounce the same judgment they rendered in the play's first scene: they resolve that Coriolanus should die. But the tribunes, though they themselves once sought Coriolanus's death, have decided on banishment—a punishment that might simultaneously satisfy the people, mollify the patricians, and, of course, remove Coriolanus from Rome's political equation. Sicinius now must hush the very people whose mouth he claims to be: "Peace!" (80). Sicinius's terse command marks the difference between democracy and representation: the people render their judgment, but they are the electorate now, not the *demos.*[47] Put another way, the will of the people does not *necessarily* correspond to the will of "the people" as the tribunes define it. Thus, as he banishes Coriolanus, Sicinius invokes the very people who have just called for Coriolanus's death:

SICINIUS: . . . in the name o'th' people,
And in the power of us the tribunes, we
E'en from this instant banish him our city
In peril of precipitation
From off the rock Tarpeian, never more
To enter our Rome gates. I'th' people's name
I say it shall be so.
ALL THE CITIZENS: It shall be so,
It shall be so. Let him away. He is banished,
And it shall be so.
(3.3.103–11)

The people, though they have just seconds earlier indicated a different judgment, now mechanically act out the role the tribunes have scripted for them: "It shall be so, / It shall be so. Let him away. He is banished, / And it shall be so."

(3.3.109–11). This little moment demonstrates Sicinius's economy of representational power: the people's power is not in the people themselves but in those who speak in their name.

In the rest of the glorious populist drama of Coriolanus's banishment, the people are mere puppets:

> BRUTUS: There's no more to be said, but he is banished,
> As enemy to the people and his country.
> It shall be so.
> ALL THE CITIZENS: It shall be so, it shall be so.
> . . . .
> AEDILE: The people's enemy is gone, is gone.
> ALL THE CITIZENS: Our enemy is banished, he is gone. Hoo-oo!
> SICINIUS: Go see him out at gates, and follow him,
> As he hath followed you, with all despite.
> Give him deserved vexation. Let a guard
> Attend us through the city.
> ALL THE CITIZENS: Come, come, let's see him out at gates. Come.
> The gods preserve our noble tribunes! Come.
> (3.3.121–24, 140–47)

"Hoo-oo!" We are worlds away from the moment when Menenius, astonished by the bold First Citizen, who impatiently (and unerringly) finishes his sentences for him, exclaims, "'Fore me this fellow speaks! What, then, what then?" (1.1.118). The Whigs rightly claim that the people who match wits with Menenius and who debate amongst themselves how best to conduct the rebellion are not, as so many critics have claimed, a rash mob but rather an articulate, deliberative, and purposeful group of distinct individuals. Political representation turns the citizens into a mindless, undifferentiated chorus; political representation turns the citizens into a mob.

◇◇

The scene of the tribunes and their aedile plotting to manage the people's participation in the judgment of Coriolanus immediately follows a scene in which Coriolanus's mother and friends teach him how to dupe the people into forgiving him and reaffirming his election to the consulship (3.2). Although the scenes unfold sequentially, they are superimposed in the political imagination of the play: while the people wait in the public marketplace, the patricians and the tribunes privately scheme to master them.

Volumnia tells her son that the task facing him is simple enough: feign humility; pretend that you will serve the people; "frame / Thyself, forsooth, hereafter theirs . . . go, and be ruled" (3.2.84–90). Two notorious characters provide Coriolanus and his handlers with models for framing an artificial self to conceal one's true self. One is the sharp dealer: "Mother," Coriolanus promises, "I am going to the market-place: / Chide me no more. I'll mountebank their loves, / Cog their hearts from them, and come home beloved / Of all the trades in Rome" (131–34). The other is the actor. Indeed, the mountebanking politician is not merely analogous to the actor; he is a subspecies of actor. When Volumnia warns Coriolanus that regaining the people's voices will require that he "perform a part / Thou hast not done before" (108–9), she means the part of "player" as much as the part of "public servant." Coriolanus's commitment to an absolute, essential self has so estranged him from being "false to [his] nature" (14) that deception seems to him a trade rather than a practice. He is, he reminds his mother, the antithesis of the actor: "I play / The man I am" (14–15). To play the politician, Coriolanus must first transform himself into an actor:

> Away, my disposition; and possess me
> Some harlot's spirit! My throat of war be turned,
> Which choired with my drum, into a pipe
> Small as an eunuch or the virgin voice
> That babies lull asleep! The smiles of knaves
> Tent in my cheeks, and schoolboys' tears take up
> The glasses of my sight! A beggar's tongue
> Make motion through my lips, and my armed knees,
> Who bowed but in my stirrup, bend like his
> That hath received an alms!
> (111–20)

Rather than invoking a muse, Coriolanus summons the demon of theatricality: only the spirit of a "harlotry player"—a familiar figure in the rhetoric of Elizabethan and Jacobean antitheatricalism—could teach him to speak another's words, imitate another's actions, and play a woman's part.

Volumnia coaches Coriolanus to demonstrate his submission in the most vulgar form of theater—spectacle and dumb show:

> Go to them, with this bonnet in thy hand,
> And thus far having stretched it—here be with them—
> Thy knee bussing the stones—for in such business
> Action is eloquence, and the eyes of th'ignorant
> More learned than the ears.
> (3.2.73–77)

The "business" Volumnia has in mind here is equally acting and politics.

Her theory of effective spectacle—a theory shared by the tribunes (2.1.204–9)—unmistakably echoes one of the most familiar strains of Jacobean antitheatricalism: the lower orders went to see rather than hear a play. According to Andrew Gurr, when a playwright such as "Jonson called his audiences 'spectators,' as he almost invariably did, he was covertly sneering at the debased preference for stage spectacle rather than the poetic 'soul' of the play" (85). Thomas Heywood similarly disparaged common theatergoers as "the throng, who come rather to see than to heare" (qtd. in Gurr 96).

Like most antitheatricalists, Volumnia believes in the efficacy of theater because she believes in the vulgarity and malleability of the audience. Coriolanus has far deeper fears about theater: he breaks off his incantation to the theatrical spirit precisely as he acknowledges theatricality's power to transform players rather than spectators: "I will not do't, / Lest I surcease to honour mine own truth / And by my body's action teach my mind / A most inherent baseness" (3.2.120–23). Coriolanus, of all people, here echoes the anxiety that playing eventually transforms the player into what he plays. To translate Coriolanus's fear of playing back into political language, we might say that he is constitutionally ill-suited to artificial personhood: the tribunes Sicinius and Brutus never worry that a "beggar's tongue" will "make motion" through their lips; the savviest representatives know that artificial personhood is an ideological construct.

Coriolanus preparing to mountebank the people; the tribunes and their aedile preparing to orchestrate the people's response to Coriolanus's performance: Shakespeare publicizes on his stage precisely what Rome's patricians and tribunes alike would use theatricality to obscure—the abject position of the people (either yielding their voices in exchange for a show of groveling or parroting the lines supplied to them by the men who claim to speak for them). Shakespeare's mode of critique in *Coriolanus,* as in *Caesar,* is publicity. Scandalous revelation about political representation follows scandalous revelation: in seven different scenes, Shakespeare's audience watches the tribunes plot self-serving manipulations of the people (see, e.g., 1.1.251–78; 2.1.203–57; 2.3.253–61; and 3.3.1–30); and whenever we listen in on the proceedings at the Senate House, we discover that the tribunes achieve power not as the people's servants but as their masters. Shakespeare's demystification of representational politics shows off and depends on the very publicness—on the presence of the public itself and on openness—that distinguishes theatrical and political representation.

◇◇

The banishment scene ironically reveals how little the patricians have to fear from the pathetic "dummies" who hoot Coriolanus out of Rome on the cues of their tribune masters. Indeed, Coriolanus must be banished precisely because he is the only patrician who actually believes that the tribunate empowers the masses rather than a handful of representatives. Coriolanus, it must be said, considers the tribunes themselves to be a gross affront to Roman nobility—"they do prank them in authority / Against all noble sufferance" (3.1.24–25)—but it is his anticipation of a popular dictatorship that moves him to advocate civil war:

> . . . why,
> You grave but reckless senators, have you thus
> Given Hydra here to choose an officer?
> That, with his peremptory "shall," being but
> The horn and noise o'th' monster's, wants not spirit
> To say he'll turn your current in a ditch
> And make your channel his? If he have power,
> Then vail your impotence;
> . . . .
> . . . You are plebeians
> If they be senators, and they are no less
> When, both your voices blended, the great'st taste
> Most palates theirs. They choose their magistrate,
> And such a one as he, who puts his "shall,"
> His popular "shall," against a graver bench
> Than ever frowned in Greece.
> . . . .
> . . . Thus we debase
> The nature of our seats, and make the rabble
> Call our cares fears, which will in time
> Break ope the locks o'th' senate and bring in
> The crows to peck the eagles.
> (3.1.94–101, 104–10, 138–42)

The tribunate—like the common council in Warwick—is undoubtedly a concession on the part of the oligarchs. We have no reason to believe that, in the absence of popular revolt, the senators would part with even the "superfluity" of aristocratic wealth the people demand (1.1.14–16). With the exception of Coriolanus, however, the patricians understand that the tribunes themselves will actively shoo plebeian birds away from the senate: two arriviste crows seeking distinction on the great ornithological chain of being are going to close the door of their new coop behind them as quickly as they can.

The tribunes recognize that the patricians will support the tribunate only if it masters the people themselves: here, personal desire and political necessity are in happy sympathy, for the tribunes want to be the people's masters not their fellows. After the heady victory over Coriolanus, the tribunes do not seek further concessions from the senate nor do they invite the crows to flood the seemingly weakened Capitol. On the contrary, the tribunes' first concern is to restore order, to smooth any ruffled patrician feathers, and to contain the popular passions that were necessary to expel the great general from Rome. Thus, Sicinius and Brutus anxiously instruct their aedile to clear the people from the streets:

> SICINIUS: Bid them all home. He's gone, and we'll no further.
> The nobility are vex'd, whom we have sided
> In his behalf.
> BRUTUS: Now we have shown our power,
> Let us seem humbler after it is done
> Than when it was a-doing.
> SICINIUS: Bid them home.
> Say their great enemy is gone, and they
> Stand in their ancient strength.
> BRUTUS: Dismiss them home.
> (4.2.1–7)

We should recall here Flavius and Marullus's obsessive determination to "drive away the vulgar from the streets" and back to their homes and shops (*Julius Caesar* 1.1.1–71). In *Coriolanus,* as in *Julius Caesar,* domesticating the people is the institutional mission of political representation and the condition of its creation and survival: if the people constitute themselves as a political force—if they simply stay in the streets—neither the patricians nor, for that matter, the people will have any use for tribunes.

Sicinius and Brutus, then, achieve a double triumph: the banishment of Coriolanus satisfies their plebeian constituency, and the immediate containment of the people after the banishment satisfies their patrician partners.[48] At the end of act 1, scene 1, the arrival of the newly minted tribunes silences the people, but the First Senator must scold the people from the stage: "Hence to your homes, be gone" (248). After the people "*steal away*" (1.1.250.sd), first the senators and then the tribunes make their way up to the Capitol. The end of the first scene, then, dramatically groups the tribunes not with the people but with the patrician class. This earlier, perhaps still tentative, separation of the people from a ruling elite that now includes the tribunes is perfected when

Brutus and Sicinius order the people back to their homes and shops and thus replace the senators as the proximate rulers of Rome's citizens. Thus, when we first see the tribunes in the post-Coriolanian Rome, Sicinius is congratulating himself and Brutus for pacifying the plebeians:

> Here we do make his friends
> Blush that the world goes well, who rather had,
> Though they themselves did suffer by't, behold
> Dissentious numbers pest'ring streets than see
> Our tradesmen singing in their shops and going
> About their functions friendly.
> (4.6.4–9)

Menenius, of course, is chief among Coriolanus's friends, but one would not figure him for a blusher. Even Menenius, however, concedes Sicinius's claim that "Coriolanus is not much missed / But with his friends" (4.6.14–15): "All's well," the old patrician allows, "and might have been much better if / He could have temporized" (17–18).

Menenius himself "temporizes" because he has always recognized—with disgust—that Sicinius and Brutus are motivated not by political radicalism but, on the contrary, by personal ambition. Here, again, at least according to Menenius, there is a coincidence between the particular character of the tribunes' ambition and the patricians' expectation that they will "master" the people:

> You are ambitious for poor knaves' caps and legs. You wear out a good wholesome forenoon in hearing a cause between an orange-wife and a faucet-seller, and then rejourn the controversy of threepence to a second day of audience. When you are hearing a matter between party and party, if you chance to be pinched with the colic, you make faces like mummers, set up the bloody flag against all patience, and in roaring for a chamber-pot, dismiss the controversy bleeding, the more entangled by your hearing. (2.1.67–76)

Menenius's unflattering account of the tribunes' juridical temperament may owe something to early modern characterizations of MPs: recall, for example, the unfortunate Thrower, who was arrested by the Commons for joking that the MPs were entirely capable of squandering hours debating a bill to regulate the wires women used to support elaborate hair styles (D'Ewes 54). Arthur Hall certainly shared Thrower's (and Menenius's) opinion: imaginatively addressing his old enemies in the Commons, F.A.'s father rails against the "furious and chollericke words" of the "fether headed fellow[s] . . . [who] seke vaine glorye by far fetched eloquence and nedelesse phrases, delating the matter to shew the ripeness of your judgement more than directly to go to the cause and make it understood" (Hiii^{v}).

Hall, as we saw in Chapters 1 and 3, made far more damning charges: the people of England, according to F.A.'s father, can expect little from the many MPs who "gape for ambition" (Fi^{r}).[49] In Shakespeare's England and in Menenius's Rome, it is the charge of ambition that cuts to the quick: according to Menenius, the tribunes, still so new to their offices, have already set themselves up as rulers over orange-wives, faucet-sellers, and the rest of Rome's common citizens. It is, however, precisely this vertical separation of the tribunes from the people that the patricians seek: in the first scene in the Senate House, the senators ask the tribunes—the "masters o'th' people" (2.2.51, 77), as the patricians call them—to reconcile the people to the Senate's decisions (2.2.51–58). The very absence of the people from the Senate House is itself a sign of the tribunate's usefulness to the patricians: instead of confronting the *demos,* the patricians hope to manage the people through mediating governors. The tribunes, in turn, have already begun to set up a level of mediation between themselves and the people: the Aedile communicates their instructions to the people before Coriolanus's return to the marketplace, executes their order to clear the streets after the banishment, and, as we shall see, metes out the tyrannical punishments they devise.

We never quite see the people doff their caps or bend their knees to the tribunes, but Brutus and Sicinius certainly enjoy the adulation of their subjects after Coriolanus's defeat:

> *Enter three or four Citizens*
> ALL THE CITIZENS: The gods preserve you both.
> SICINIUS: Good e'en, our neighbors.
> BRUTUS: Good e'en to you all, good e'en to you all.
> FIRST CITIZEN: Ourselves, our wives and children, on our knees
> Are bound to pray for you both.
> SICINIUS: Live and thrive.
> BRUTUS: Farewell, kind neighbors.
> We wished Coriolanus had loved you as we did.
> ALL THE CITIZENS: Now the gods keep you!
> (4.6.22–27)

In public, the tribunes carefully deploy a rhetoric of equality: the citizens are their "neighbors." Once the grateful citizens are out of earshot, Sicinius breathes a sigh of relief: "this is a happier and more comely time / Than when these fellows ran about the streets / Crying confusion" (4.6.29–31). "These fellows": the tribunes no longer think of themselves as part of the plebeian class, and the people, in their turn, now exalt their representatives as demigods.

"Live and thrive" the gracious tribune-kings tell their subjects, but their benevolent reign degenerates with shocking rapidity into tyranny. As Brutus and Sicinius are savoring the vision of the citizens kneeling in prayer, their Aedile bursts in with dreadful news: "Worthy tribunes, / There is a slave whom we have put in prison / Reports the Volsces, with two several powers, / Are entered in the Roman territories" (4.6.39–42). Brutus's regal reaction to this report is worthy of Cleopatra: "Go see this rumorer whipped. It cannot be / The Volsces dare break with us" (49–50). Menenius counsels the tribunes to "reason with the fellow, / Before you punish him, where he heard this, / Lest you shall chance to whip your information / And beat the messenger who bids beware / Of what is to be dreaded" (53–57). Sicinius, however, has already developed the tyrant's capacity to refuse unwelcome news: "Tell not me. / I know this cannot be" (57–58). When a messenger arrives to report that the senators are alarmed, Sicinius roars, "'Tis this slave" and orders the Aedile "Go whip him fore the people's eyes" (61–62).

Sicinius's lightning instinct for staging an exemplary scene of discipline and punishment suggests that the new order will not abandon the cruel methods of the old: surely the public whipping is intended to warn the audience of citizens that, though they themselves are not slaves, they too may feel the Aedile's lash. Why has Shakespeare made the unfortunate bearer of bad news a slave? Shakespeare had no source for this episode, and, on at least two counts, it seems an odd invention.[50] There were slaves in republican Rome, but, before this moment, we hear nothing of them in *Coriolanus.* And why would a slave possess intelligence about Volscian troop movements? Perhaps the "slave" is not a slave at all. Coriolanus, for one, routinely refers to Rome's *citizens* as "slaves" (1.1.197, 1.5.7, 1.6.7, 4.5.78). With two exceptions (1.9.5, 5.6.105), the tribunes and their Aedile are the only other characters in the play who use the word "slave."[51] Perhaps "slave," in a language shared by Coriolanus and the tribunes, simply designates an unruly subject. That language is, of course, the language of tyranny.[52] The man the tribunes order to be whipped may well be a citizen who is about to discover that he is now a "slave": to be subjected to an arbitrary whipping is to be a slave indeed. The audience to this spectacle will experience the tribunes' discipline as well: to be subjected to a display of arbitrary, coercive power—whether its victim is a slave or citizen—is to be enslaved.

"Slave" was a remarkably resonant word in Elizabethan and Jacobean political discourse. Near the end of his chapter "Of Degrees of People in the Commonwealth of England," William Harrison is proud that his taxonomy can reach no lower than "day labourers, poor husbandmen, and some retailers (which have no free land), copyholders, and artificers, as tailors, shoemakers, carpenters, bricklayers, masons, etc.":

> As for slaves and bondmen, we have none; nay, such is the privilege of our country by the especial grace of God and bounty of our princes that if any come hither from other realms, so soon as they set foot on land they become so free of condition as their masters, whereby all note of servile bondage is utterly removed from them, wherein we resemble . . . the old Indians and the Taprobanes, who supposed it a great injury to Nature to make or suffer them to be bond whom she in her wanted course doth product and bring forth free. (Harrison 118)

Slavery is so alien to England that slaves "from other realms," at the first touch of English soil, become free not only in legal fact but in spirit: "all note of servile bondage is utterly removed from them." God and Nature endow all human beings with freedom, but only godly English princes preserve that freedom.

Harrison's brand of exceptionalism—England's rejection of slavery, its devotion to freedom distinguishes it from other modern polities—was haunted and shaped by the specter of bondage: after all, the island had, as Ben Jonson would remind James I at his coronation, suffered under "the Roman, Saxon, Dane, and Norman yoke" ("Speeches of Gratulation," 6). If those yokes seemed safely dusty, the bondage of Catholicism was still fresh in many minds: when he introduced the subsidy bill in the House of Commons in 1576, Sir Walter Mildmay suggested that Elizabeth's subjects would happily supply the queen who "even at her first entry, did loosen us from the yoke of Rome" (*PPE* 1:502). The MPs and the nation looked, above all, to the monarch to protect them from foreign oppressors: the petition for the execution of Mary that the Lords and Commons presented to Elizabeth on November 12, 1586, said that only "the great mercye and providence of God and your Hignes' singular wisdome" had prevented Mary from "bringinge us and this noble crown back agayne into the thraldome of the Romishe tyrranye" (*PPE* 2:244). In 1593, Sir Henry Unton urged his fellow MPs to grant a subsidy quickly, for England had many Catholic enemies: "They prepare mighty forces in many places. . . . Their ende is to imprinte a depe marke of the yoke of bondage into our neckes and into our hartes that we shall see nothinge but the markes of bondage, feele nothinge but the printes and [blank] of bondage, and suffer nothinge but never-endinge miseries and calamities" (*PPE* 3:55).

The knights and burgesses did their part to protect the realm from foreign tyrants by supplying the monarch, but they also claimed for themselves the responsibility of protecting the English people from domestic tyranny. Calling Elizabeth or James a tyrant would have been fatally direct, but MPs, political philosophers, and other observers did sometimes claim that a royal attempt to undermine the freedoms of the House of Commons or to alienate the subject's property in the absence of consent threatened to turn the free English into slaves. In 1585, Elizabeth instructed Sir John Puckering, the speaker of the House, to tell the MPs that their discussions of religion—several MPs had been pressing for reforms that Archbishop Whitgift considered radical and populist—were at an end: she "condemned the whole House that would enter into the discourse of anie matter which she had expresslie forbidden" (*PPE* 2: 182). In his parliamentary diary, Sir William Fitzwilliam recorded the MPs' reaction:

> With this message the House found them selves so greatlie moved and so deeplye wounded as they could not devise which waye to cure themselves agayne, for so theire case stoode, as either theie must offende their gracious soveraigne . . . or els to suffer the liberties of their House to be infringed, wherby theie shoulde leave their children and posteritie in thraldome and bondage they themselves by their forefathers beinge delivered into freedom and libertie. (*PPE* 2:183)

Like Fitzwilliam, most MPs were loath to offend Elizabeth, but they continued to debate religion and to seek an "underhande" way "that shoulde as forceibli restore the libertie of the House as anie violent action openlie used" (*PPE* 2:184).

In 1610, the MPs worried that a different species of royal oppression would enslave them: during the debates over James I's attempt to levy impositions without parliament's consent, Heanage Finch reported that the people of the realm "fear[ed] that the grants of aids and taxes might turn to a bondage to them and their heirs" (*PP 1610* 2:239). James's actions, Nicholas Fuller argued in the Commons, unsettled the relation between *lex* and *rex* that guaranteed the English people's special freedoms: "by the laws of England the subjects have such property in their lands and goods as that without their consent the king can take no part thereof from them lawfully by any kind of imposition or otherwise without act of parliament" (*PP 1610* 2:152). According to Thomas

Hedley, the MPs were bound to resist James because English identity itself was at stake: "take away the liberty of the subject in his profit or property and you make a promiscuous confusion of a freeman and a bound slave, which slavery is as repugnant to the nature of an Englishman as allegiance and due subjection is to his own proper and peculiar" (*PP 1610* 2:192).

Fitzwilliam, Wentworth, Finch, Fuller, Hedley, and many other Elizabethan and Jacobean MPs feared that a monarch with absolute power over the scope of parliamentary debate or the subject's property would turn the free English into slaves, and they looked to the representatives of the people to curb monarchic encroachments on the subject's liberties. Near the end of the greatest of all political plays, the fate of a "rumorer" we never see suggests that Shakespeare feared that the representatives of the people might be oppressive masters rather than guardians of liberty.

Epilogue: Losing Power, Losing Oneself

The Third Citizen and Tragedy

The most tremendous thing which has been granted to man is: the choice, freedom. And if you desire to save it and preserve it there is only one way: in the very same second unconditionally and in complete resignation to give it back to God, and yourself with it.

Søren Kierkegaard, *Journal*

We have power in ourselves to do it, but it is a power that we have no power to do.

The Third Citizen

In the very first moments of *Coriolanus,* a company of lowly Roman "garlic-eaters" debate whether or not they should kill Coriolanus, Rome's greatest warrior and the darling of her patrician oligarchs:

FIRST CITIZEN: First, you know Caius Martius is chief
enemy to the people.
ALL: We know't, we know't.
FIRST CITIZEN: Let us kill him, and we'll have corn at our
own price. Is't a verdict?
ALL: No more talking on't, let it be done. Away, away.
(1.1.7–12)

There is, in fact, a little more "talking on't": the Second Citizen raises several possible defenses of Coriolanus's conduct (27–28, 38–40), but he does not shake the resolve of his fellow plebeians, who all agree to "proceed especially against Caius Martius" (24–26). The audacity and self-possession of these Roman mechanicals must have electrified at least some of the garlic-eaters in Shakespeare's audience.

When we next see our band of citizens, they are preparing to enjoy the fruits of their rebellion: armed now with voices rather than weapons, the newly enfranchised people await the arrival of Coriolanus, who must solicit their suffrages for the consulship. They are changed men: the same citizens who resolved to storm the Capitol and murder Coriolanus now patiently wait for him to descend from the Senate House to the marketplace. The Third Citizen, scrupulously obedient to the new order, carefully rehearses for his fellow initiates the still unfamiliar customs of electoral politics: "We are not to stay all together, but to come by him where he stands by ones, by twos, and by threes. He's to make his requests by particulars . . . I'll direct you how you shall go by him" (2.3.42–47).[1]

The stunning transformation of "mutinous citizens" into docile political subjects is felt most profoundly when the citizens briefly debate their proper role in the consular election. When the play begins, the citizens sit in judgment over Coriolanus's life; now they wonder if they have the right to deny him their own voices. Although the people have been taught the forms of representational politics, they remain uncertain of the precise nature of their new powers. The First Citizen insists that the plebeians must yield their voices to Coriolanus, but the Second Citizen claims that they may withhold their voices "if [they] will" (2.3.3). The Third Citizen manages to take both positions:

> We have power in ourselves to do it, but it is a power that we have no power to do. For if he show us his wounds and tell us his deeds, we are to put our tongues into those wounds and speak for them; so if he tell us his noble deeds, we must also tell him our noble acceptance of them. (2.3.4–9)

The political marketplace the Third Citizen imagines here is hardly free; he conceives of the people's actions as *necessary* reactions to Coriolanus's offers: "if he show us his wounds and tell us his deeds, we are to put our tongues into those wounds and speak for them"; "if he tell us his noble deeds, we must also tell him our noble acceptance of them."[2]

But the Third Citizen does not think of himself as powerless; rather, he imagines himself simultaneously powerful and powerless: that is, quite literally a vessel of power ("we have power in ourselves") and yet incapable of exercising the power he possesses ("it is a power that we have no power to do").[3] The Third Citizen recognizes (believes) that he has a power, but he also recognizes (accepts as legitimate) that he cannot exercise that power. This double recognition constitutes a misrecognition: if the Third Citizen believes that he can exercise power only by yielding it, he will always be powerless or, put another way, he will be powerful only at the instant he makes himself powerless. In the Third Citizen's misrecognition, Shakespeare registers if not the birth of ideology per se, then the birth of a new kind of ideology. The Fable of the Belly grossly misrepresents the real conditions of production and consumption, but Menenius does not aim to convince the subordinate Members that they are actually the governing Belly. The preachers who situated early modern England's social hierarchy within a divine chain of being did not suggest to those at the bottom of the ladder that they were in fact at its summit. These primitive ideologies rationalize, naturalize, and mystify the cultural production of poverty and powerlessness. By contrast, the (fully subjected) subject of political representation believes himself or herself to be empowered by the very political arrangements that render him or her powerless. The (misrecognized) sign of power in the culture of representational politics is the absence of power.

Shakespeare stages the improbable efficacy of the new ideology by lifting its mystifying veil from the citizens' eyes for a few moments. Immediately after they give their voices to Coriolanus, the Second and Third Citizens perceive that something is amiss:

> THIRD CITIZEN: But this is something odd.
> SECOND CITIZEN: An 'twere to give again—but 'tis no matter.
> (2.3.82–83)

In the Third Citizen's vague "something odd," we see a moment of apprehension rather than comprehension—an incomplete agitation of the rational against false consciousness. A little later, as they try to explain their actions to Brutus and Sicinius, the people fully awaken from their dream.

> SECOND CITIZEN: To my poor unworthy notice
> He mocked us when he begged our voices.
> THIRD CITIZEN: Certainly. He flouted us downright.
> FIRST CITIZEN: No, 'tis his kind of speech. He did not mock us.
> SECOND CITIZEN: Not one amongst us save yourself but says
> He used us scornfully. He should have showed us
> His marks of merit, wounds received for's country.
> SICINIUS: Why, so he did, I am sure.
> ALL THE CITIZENS: No, no; no man saw 'em.
> THIRD CITIZEN: He said he had wounds which he could show in private,
> And with his hat, thus waving it in scorn,
> "I would be consul," says he, "Aged custom

> But by your voices will not so permit me.
> Your voices therefore." When we granted that,
> Here was "I thank you for your voices, thank you.
> Your most sweet voices. Now you have left your voices
> I have no further with you." Was not this mockery?
> (2.3.158–73)

The Third Citizen, who was so deeply under the spell of the new ideology of power, now attains a Rousseauian clarity: "Now you have left your voices / I have no further with you." (Cf. Rousseau, *Du contrat social,* 190: "Le peuple anglais pense être libre, il se trompe fort: il ne l'est que durant l'élection des membres du parlement; sitôt qu'ils sont élus, il est esclave, il n'est rien.") Shakespeare allots the Third Citizen this belated penetration of the ideology that had blinded him not to suggest its fragility but rather to reveal its power.

The citizens' calm, lucid recognition of their folly should shape our reaction to their subsequent devolution into an irrational mob. When news of Coriolanus's imminent sacking of Rome spreads through the city, the people seem to indulge themselves in an hysterical, almost incoherent rewriting of history:

> FIRST CITIZEN: For mine own part,
> When I said "banish him" I said 'twas pity.
> SECOND CITIZEN: And so did I.
> THIRD CITIZEN: And so did I, and to say the truth so did very many of us. That we did, we did for the best and though we willingly consented to his banishment, yet it was against our will.
> . . . .
> FIRST CITIZEN: The gods be good to us! Come, masters, let's home. I ever said we were i'th'wrong when we banished him.
> (4.6.148–54, 162–64)

The people's seemingly childish refusal to own their actions—"When I said 'banish' him I said 'twas pity"; "though we willingly consented to his banishment, yet it was against our will"—is not an accurate representation of the banishment, but it is continuous with the confusion that enabled both the banishment and the election itself: the confusion, that is, that political representation both produces and requires for its reproduction.

Let me try to explain precisely what I mean by "confusion" by suggesting that the people's repeated disowning of the words they spoke in the marketplace is not entirely unreasonable. The tribunes did, after all, supply the people with their lines:

SICINIUS: . . . in the name o'th' people,
And in the power of us the tribunes, we
E'en from this instant banish him our city
In peril of precipitation
From off the rock Tarpeian, never more
To enter our Rome gates. I'th' people's name
I say it shall be so.
ALL THE CITIZENS: It shall be so, it shall be so. Let him away.
He's banished, and it shall be so.
(3.3.103–11)

The people, we recall, initially called for Coriolanus's death; if they thought the penalty of banishment "'twas pity," it wasn't for reasons that would win them any favor with Coriolanus. The sentence of banishment does indeed originate not with the people but with their tribunes. Do the people, then, own their words when they exclaim "He's banished, and it shall be so."? For Hobbes, of course, it is the political representative who has no property in the words he speaks: "Of Persons Artificiall, some have their words and actions Owned by those whom they represent. And then the Person is the Actor; and he that owneth his words and actions, is the AUTHOR" (*Leviathan* 218). In the banishment scene, by contrast, the people's words—"it shall be so. . . . He's banished"—are authored by the tribunes: the people, then, are the artificial persons through whom the tribunes speak and act.

My purpose here is not to mitigate the irrationality of the people's account of their role in the banishment but instead to recover their irrationality as, in part, an effect of political representation. As Coriolanus bears down on Rome, the people do not, in fact, deny that they pronounced and willed his banishment: "I said 'banish him'"; "we willingly consented to his banishment"; "we banished him." Rather, they claim that they were alienated from their own voices and wills: "When I said 'banish him' I said 'twas pity"; "we willingly consented to his banishment, yet it was against our will"; "I ever said we were i'th'wrong when we banished him."[4] The people's representation of their unwilling willing of Coriolanus's banishment is thus consistent with their subjective state at the moment they elect Coriolanus: "we willingly consented to his banishment, yet it was against our will"; "We have power in ourselves to do it, but it is a power that we have no power to do." The particular form of the people's panicked reaction to Coriolanus's march on Rome leads us back to what Shakespeare represents as the fundamental irrationality of representational politics:

> THIRD CITIZEN: Here he comes, and in the gown of humility. Mark his behaviour. We are not to stay all together, but to come by him where he stands by ones, by twos, and by threes. He's to make his requests by particulars, wherein every one of us has a single honour in giving him our own voices with our own tongues. Therefore follow me, and I'll direct you how you shall go by him.
>
> ALL THE CITIZENS: Content, content.
>
> (2.3.41–48)

Several Whig critics see the Third Citizen's belief in the "honor" of "giving one's voice, casting one's vote" as a celebration of "the ratifying act of democracy," but it seems to me a moment of tragic confusion.[5] The Third Citizen believes it will be an honor to empower Coriolanus because he will give his own voice with his own tongue. The Third Citizen's investment in self-possession is moving, of course, because he simultaneously believes that it is honorable to dispossess oneself of power. But this is a delusion of possession, because the Third Citizen also believes he does not have the power to deny Coriolanus his voice: the thing he claims to own is never within his power to withhold.

The Third Citizen is, of course, only a minor character in *The Tragedy of Coriolanus.* Coriolanus's tragedy, in the eyes of many critics, is a tragedy of bad timing. Coriolanus's "whole delicately constructed masculine identity," as Janet Adelman argues in a beautiful essay about Volumnia and her son, depends on a fantasy of absolute self-sufficiency (133). But in the new order, even the great must depend on and ask the people for their honors and their offices. Coriolanus, then, suffers his tragic fate in part because his profound psychic investment in the notion that one achieves honor through action per se—rather than the people's recognition of actions as honorable—costs him the consulship. What name, then, should we give to the dramatic fate of the Third Citizen, who, when we meet him in act 1, is in possession of himself and, perhaps, on the brink of wresting power from the patricians but who soon believes that he can win honor only by recognizing honor in others, that he can ennoble himself only by conferring nobility on others, that he can make his voice heard only by letting others speak for him, that he can be powerful only by making himself powerless?

At the end of his brilliant, epochal study of Elizabethan power and the Second Tetralogy, Stephen Greenblatt famously echoes Kafka: "There is subversion, no end of subversion, only not for us" ("Invisible Bullets" 65). There is no subversion for us, Greenblatt argues, because the monarchic doctrines and institutions Shakespeare's plays potentially unsettle have no place—still less any legitimacy—in our own culture: they are, as it were, always already subverted and unreal. Our recognition of subversion in the absence of subversiveness is a function of the difference between our republican culture and Shakespeare's monarchic culture. We might, however, read the final sentence of Greenblatt's essay as a lament about the possibility for subversion in contemporary America, as a lament historically appropriate to the culture of political representation—a political structure that Shakespeare figures precisely as the systematic containment of subversion, as the institutionalization of popular misrule. Read this way, Greenblatt's echo of Kafka for me echoes the Third Citizen's conundrum in *Coriolanus:* "We have power in ourselves to do it, but it is a power that we have no power to do." We have power, no end of power, but it is not (quite) for us. In Shakespeare's representation of the Third Citizen's tragic misrecognition, there is subversion, no end of subversion, and it is now, thanks to the movement of history, especially for us.[6]

Notes

Introduction

Epigraphs: Rousseau, ed. Grimsley 190: "The English people thinks it is free; it is greatly mistaken, it is free only during the election of Members of Parliament; as soon as they are elected, it is enslaved; it is nothing. The use it makes of its freedom during the brief moments it has it fully warrants its losing it" (trans. Gourevitch 114); Madison: "The Same Subject Continued: The Union as a Safeguard Against Domestic Faction and Insurrection," published under the pseudonym Publius in the November 23, 1787, edition of the *New York Packet.* See http://thomas.loc.gov/home/histdox/fed_10.html (accessed March 22, 2006).

1. Yelverton contributed several scenes to *The misfortunes of Arthur* (1588) and wrote the epilogue to Gascoigne's *Jocasta* (1566). In the closing oration he drafted for his friend John Puckering in 1584, Lord Burghley felt no need to dress up the analogy between Elizabeth's legislative role and divine power in poetic paganism: "your Majesty shall do no less than perteyneth to the authorite which yow have lyk to God almighty, who as he gyveth lyff and being to all his creatures gret and small, so your Majesty shall gyve lyff and contynuance to the fruites of our consultations . . . without which your royall assent by your own breath, the same shall become without liff and sence" (*PPE* 2:24).

2. By "representationalism," as unlovely a word as might be imagined, I mean those practices and discourses that establish the claim to represent as the positive condition of a discrete form of political power and legitimacy.

3. In Elizabethan England, "hearsay" distinguished rumors and secondhand reports from the articulation of personal experience, but the *OED* does not recognize "hearsay evidence" as a legal term until 1753 (2b). As Bacon's defense of Heanage's report of Clifford's speech makes clear, however, the inadmissibility of reported speech in many legal proceedings was already a firmly established rule of evidence in 1593.

4. Unless otherwise noted, all references to and quotations from Shakespeare's works follow the Oxford edition (ed. Stanley Wells et al.).

5. While their counterparts in history departments "read the modern Parliament back into history" (Elton, *Parliament,* ix), Whig literary critics read contemporary sociopolitical liberal values back into literary history. The Whig project reaches its logical, self-reflexive conclusion in the discovery that Shakespeare was

himself a Whig critic: "I take the position that Shakespeare was one of our first cultural critics, in the sense of being capable of profound, structural analysis. I assume that he, as well as we, was capable of grasping . . . the function of all those practices that for want of precise definition we loosely denote as aspects of 'culture'" (*SPV* 9–10). Thus, Shakespeare validates the work of the cultural critic, and, in return, the cultural critic demonstrates that Shakespeare was misunderstood by his contemporaries and earlier scholars. For Shakespeare's favorable representation of popular politics "was prophetic, in a way that we are only now, perhaps, fully able to appreciate" (ibid., 3). If only we are fully able to appreciate Shakespeare's prophetic republicanism, what value can Shakespeare's progressive meditations have held for his contemporaries? Alan Liu has argued that new historicists tend to identify the critical "we" with the historical "them" (746). Whigs take this identification so far that their Shakespeare is more than "our contemporary": he is our colleague.

6. The author of *The Federalist* 52 (1788)—Hamilton or Madison—essentially concurs: "The scheme of representation, as a substitute for a meeting of the citizens in person, being at most but very imperfectly known to ancient polity, it is in more modern times only that we are to expect instructive examples" (http://thomas.loc.gov/home/histdox/fed_52.html [accessed March 22, 2006]).

7. An election per se does not establish the person elected as a representative: the president and vice president of the United States, prom kings and queens, and so on, are not representatives.

8. Using the phrase "public opinion" and discussing the Habermasian public sphere in relation to Elizabethan and Jacobean parliamentary politics is a tricky business: the *OED*'s first instance of "public opinion" dates from 1735 (I.3.a); Habermas does not recognize a public sphere in England prior to the 1660s and claims that "public opinion in the strict sense" does not figure in parliamentary politics prior to 1792, when published reports of proceedings became widely available. I am not arguing that Habermas's "classical" bourgeois public sphere—a "public sphere in the political realm evolved from the public sphere in the world of letters" (30–31)—was already functioning in Shakespeare's England, but certain crucial features of a "public sphere in the political realm" emerged in England far earlier than Habermas, not always the best historian, realizes.

Habermas claims not simply that "public opinion" is absent from the Elizabethan and Jacobean vocabulary but that the *concept* of "'vulgar opinion' [is] still completely lacking in Shakespeare" and his time (90). In fact, Habermasian "vulgar opinion" very clearly corresponds to sixteenth-century characterizations of the opinions of the common people: "They whiche commyt them selfe to the opinion of the common people, [have] ben oppressed with great myserye" (Anonymous, *Tales and quicke answeres,* [c. 1535], 54); "It was talked amongst the Popes Secretaries, that those men who framed their lyfe after the opinion of the common people, were in a miserable bondage" (Blague, *A schole of wise Conceytes,* [1569], 205); "it is the common opinion of the vulgar people, that where there is no riches, there is no nobilite" (Painter Si[v]). In Chapter 3, I demonstrate that many Elizabethan and Jacobean MPs recognized themselves as the addressees and subjects of *political* opinion articulated and sometimes circulated in print by private persons who collectively constituted a public.

9. See Zeeveld 5–6 for examples of the Tribune/MP analogy and *PP 1610* 2:xix for the plebeian/commons analogy. The most widely disseminated comparison of the Republic and England's mixed estate may have been Thomas Smith's claim, in his oft-reprinted *De republicum Anglorum* (1583), that "all that ever the people of Rome might do either in *Centuriatis comitiis* or *tributis* the same may be done by the Parliament of England" (78). William Harrison, perhaps cribbing from Smith, similarly argues that "whatsoever the people of Rome did in their *centuriatis* or *tribunitiis comitiis,* the same is and may be done by authority of our Parliament House" (150). Efforts to elaborate comprehensive analogies between England's mixed estate and the late Republic always yielded odd gaps: the MP Robert Cary, for example, suggested that the Speaker was analogous to the consul (Loach 155), but if the Speaker is the consul, are the MPs senators? If so, who are the tribunes? And, where, Elizabeth might have asked, did the monarch fit in? A similar set of questions attends the dedication of Thomas Scott's *Vox Coeli, or Newes from Heaven* (1624) to the House of Commons: "great Brittaines greatest Palladines and Champions; to you the invincible Bulwarke of our King and his Royal progeny, and the inexpugnable Cittadell and Acrocorinth of our Estate: To you I say the Conscript Fathers of our Supreamest Senate" (A1[r]).

10. The first session of Elizabeth's fourth Parliament opened in May 1572; the third and final session closed on March 18, 1581: the 1575 and 1578 by-elections in Warwickshire were called to fill the seats of sitting knights who had died between sessions. I have given a very conservative reckoning of John Shakespeare's franchise: although he seems to have run into financial difficulty in 1578 and began to sell off property, his remaining holdings were likely of a sufficient value to qualify him for the county franchise in 1578, 1584, 1586, 1588, 1593, 1597, and 1601. However, John stopped attending meetings of the Stratford corporation in 1576 (*CDL* 39), and it seems best to assume that he did not participate—if he ever had—in shire elections after that date.

11. I cannot prove that Shakespeare ever voted in or witnessed a parliamentary election, discussed parliamentary affairs with his associates, or read tracts and books about Parliament—but I strongly believe he did all of these. Here's what we do know: in 1611, Shakespeare and seventy-one other Stratford residents contributed to a fund to help promote a highway improvement bill in the House of Commons. Shakespeare signed the funding petition (*WS,* 48–49). Shakespeare's double life as Warwickshire property owner and one of London's leading theatrical professionals complicates the biographer's attempts to fix his whereabouts at any particular moment but also makes for a wide circle of acquaintances and business partners. Shakespeare knew MPs in both the town and the country. In 1602, Shakespeare purchased 107 acres from "William Combe of Warricke . . .

Esquire" and his nephew John Combe (*WS*, 42–43). William Combe represented Warwickshire as the junior knight in 1601. Though we have no record of an earlier acquaintance between Shakespeare and William Combe, Shakespeare had known John for many years, and it is almost certain that he knew William before and during his term as an MP. In 1605, Shakespeare purchased from Ralph Huband a half-interest in a lease of tithes for corn and grain in Old Stratford, Welcombe, and Bishopton (*WS*, 44; *CDL*, 246). The contract was witnessed by William Huband. Shakespeare's business associates were relatives of a John Huband who was elected junior knight for Warwickshire in 1571 and again in the by-election of 1575. There is no evidence that Shakespeare knew John Huband, but his connection to the Huband family indicates that news about Parliament might well have circulated in Shakespeare's Warwickshire orbit. In London, Shakespeare's acquaintances may well have included many MPs, and he certainly knew Henry Wriothesley, who, as earl of Southampton, sat in the House of Lords. Rather than speculate about other possibilities, I will simply remark that Shakespeare knew Jonson and Jonson knew everyone.

12. Members of the clergy who did not sit in the House of Lords were represented in Convocation; they could also vote in parliamentary elections, although they could not serve as MPs.

13. See *HC* 47–49 and Hirst 228.

14. Many election contests emerged out of rivalry within the elite rather than conflict between the elite and their inferiors. During such contests, however, the common voters may well have felt a rush of power and importance: after all, the hopes of great gentlemen who had fallen out now lay in their hands. In 1597, behind-the-scenes maneuverings in Yorkshire could not sort out a dispute between Sir John Saville and Sir John Stanhope over the position of senior knight: when the undersheriff asked the thousands of voters to shout the names of their choices, "[c]ries of 'Stanhope and Hoby,' 'Saville and Fairfax' filled the castle yard" (Kishlansky 53). After two hours, the undersheriff could still not make a determination, and the two camps of supporters were separated. "[A] number of indifferent triers . . . [took] the view" and declared Saville and Fairfax the winners (53). The archbishop of York had personally tried to arrange a "ticket" of Stanhope and Saville; thousands of nameless voters forged a different settlement of the tiff. To understand early modern political culture and representationalism, we must register the *experience* of popular participation in parliamentary politics—of voting, of shouting a candidate's name, of seeming power—but we must also put it in context: most of the voters in York were the tenants of men who were allied with one of the candidates; those landlords exercised considerable influence over their tenants (see *HC* 25 and 70).

15. Even Andrew Hadfield, who believes that Shakespeare was deeply interested in republicanism, scarcely mentions the House of Commons or parliamentary politics in his work on Shakespeare and republicanism: see his *Shakespeare and Renaissance Politics*, "Shakespeare and Republicanism," and "'Tarquin's Everlasting Banishment.'"

16. For a very interesting study of Elizabethan parliamentary oratory, see Mack.

17. If the MPs' claims to represent the people of the realm sometimes vexed the monarch, they could also be turned to account: Burghley himself added the words "the universall state of [her] whole people of all degrees" (*PPE* 2:245) to the petition for Mary's execution.

18. For a fine account of the Elizabethan uses of the divine right of kings, see Sommerville "Richard Hooker," esp. 234–42.

Chapter 1 "An epitome of the whole realme"

1. The 1624 woodcut is in the Lemon Collection at the Society of Antiquaries of London; the 1628 engraving is in the Print Room of the British Library. I am grateful to both the British Library and the Society of Antiquaries for permission to reproduce these items from their respective collections. See Kyle 91–95 for a fine discussion of the symbolic import of the Commons' acquisition of a home of its own.

2. Prior to 1547, the Commons met in various halls and buildings, including the chamber that would eventually become the Blackfriars Theatre. For an interesting history of the Commons' many temporary homes, see Hawkyard.

3. See Hasler 3:513–15 for a sketch of Topcliffe's disgraceful life.

4. "Every person of the Parlement," according to Hooker's *Order and usage,* "ought to keep secret and not to disclose the secrets and things spoken and doon in the Parlement house" (187).

5. Prior to 1571, for example, the Commons had never claimed a right to secret debate (Russell, *Parliaments and English Politics,* 222). Ronald Butt, however, has found in accounts of Commons proceedings from the reign of Edward III evidence that the MPs pledged to each other that they would keep their debates secret (339–40).

6. My critique of the early modern House of Commons does not anachronistically apply the standards of modern representative democracy to Elizabethan and Jacobean parliamentary representation (see pp. 18–19 above).

7. See, e.g., Haigh 15–20.

8. What Davis and Hexter perceive as the global realization of freedom in our time provides them with an irresistible confirmation of Whig historiography: "The series needs no retrospective justification drawn from the startling and moving events that at the end of the 1980s swept from China to Eastern Europe to Latin American and South Africa, but those events provide an important perspective on this history [of freedom] and have given a new authenticity to the working definitions that underlie it" (v). Revisionists such as Elton and Christopher Haigh have suggested that Cold War anxieties seemed to find expression in Neale's idealization of the Elizabethan House of Commons and its pursuit of liberties (see

Haigh 13). The collapse of communism appears to have inspired Neale's Whig inheritors to conflate the historical analysis and the ideological celebration of representative institutions unabashedly.

9. In 1610, motions were made to publicize the proposal for the Great Contract and to give the members leave to "take intelligence" in "their several countries" (*PP 1610* 2:292). The motion failed, but see *CJ* 427 and *PP 1610* 2:366.

10. "Parliament," James I allowed, "is the honourablest and highest judgement in the land (as being the Kings head Court) if it be well used, which is by making of good laws in it" (*Political Writings* 59).

11. Elizabeth once referred to the MPs as "restles heades, in whose braines the neadeles hammers beate with vaine judgment" (*PPE* 1:95).

12. Elton, Sharpe, Munden, Russell, and many other revisionists are far too quick to adduce opposition to particular crown policies and initiatives as evidence of the pettiness and selfishness of the MPs, and cavalierly to judge what seem to be well-reasoned political positions as incompetence or childish pique. Among the "idle heads" who served in the Commons during Shakespeare's lifetime were many of England's greatest poets, statesmen, antiquarians, Puritan leaders, soldiers, legal scholars, philosophers, explorers, political theorists, jurists, orators, and, for want of a better term, Renaissance men.

13. The early modern House of Commons did, in fact, consider both public and private bills, and although some private bills were instruments used to accomplish what we would consider public works (road repair, dam modifications, and so on), many other private bills pursued strictly personal ends. To take one example among hundreds: on May 27, 1572, Francis Alford, the important London MP, introduced a bill to settle a disputed real estate deal in his favor (*PPE* 1:291–93). For the role of private bills in the Commons, see Dean 543, 545. J. D. Alsop has argued that because Elizabethan MPs never contested or even seriously debated the crown's requests for supply, the Commons could focus its energies elsewhere and function as "a forum where private interests could achieve realization of their own priorities" (100).

14. I quote here from a very early printed copy of the "Petition," included by an anonymous editor in *Record of some worthy Proceedings . . . in the late Parliament*, 16. The MPs composed the document after James I publicly declared that he could establish impositions by prerogative and then sought to restrain debate on the matter. See *PP 1610* 2:371.

15. Hexter rightly notes that the Apology of 1604, like many other landmark Commons documents, was designed to secure freedom of speech *in the House of Commons* rather than throughout the realm (44).

16. Coke may very well have been referring to John Hooker's 1572 translation of the *Modus*. The *Modus* was often figured as a sacred authority on parliamentary history and procedure. In 1610, for example, Heanage Finch argued the Parliament's antiquity—one of the Commons' most important ideological claims—by appealing to the *Modus,* which miraculously bears witness to the Commons' and

its own existence from time immemorial: "parliaments are as ancient as the law and a part of the fundamental constitutions of the common law. . . . And however ignorant chroniclers write that Henry the First was the first king that called a parliament, 'tis apparently false and may appear . . . by the book of *Modus tenendi parliamentum,* extant in many hands, which was presented to William the Conqueror" (*PP 1610* 2:231). Perhaps Arthur Hall's devastating claim in 1576 that the Commons was a comparatively novel institution generated unprecedented interest in the *Modus* and in parliamentary history. For Hall's attack, see his *Admonition* B4[r] and D3[v]–D4[v]. Jennifer Loach suggests that arguments for the House of Commons' antiquity gained a kind of institutional home in 1586 when William Camden founded the Society of Antiquaries, which included, among many other MPs, Sir Robert Cotton, Robert Beale, Thomas Lake, James Ley, William Hakewill, and James Whitelocke (152).

17. Both Whigs and revisionists give far too much credence to the Commons' protests over the crown's access to their proceedings: for Whigs such protests count as fiery opposition; for Revisionists, they demonstrate the Commons' fear of and subservience to the crown.

18. For the role of patronage in parliamentary elections, see Kishlansky 37–48; Gruenfelder, *Patronage;* and Neale, *HC,* 276–88. Many MPs, it must be noted, were powerful men in their own right. The House was, for example, well stocked with members of the Privy Council and the sons of great lords. Indeed, Chamberlain gestures at the potential for generational conflict between the fathers and older brothers of the Upper House and the younger sons of the Lower (108).

19. Cf. Speaker Wray's entirely untroubled report to the House in 1571 that "the Queene's Majestie had in plaine wordes declared unto him that she had good intelligence of the orderly proceedings amongst us, whereof shee hadd as good likinge as ever shee had of any parliament since shee came unto the crowne" (*PPE* 1:238).

20. In 1610, for example, a man named Taverner wrote to William Trumball that James's ready access to the Commons' proceedings "hath brought so base a fear amongst" the MPs that "no man dareth speak freely" (*PP 1610* 2:46). On the other hand, no one expressed any alarm when Francis More in 1601 suggested that the speaker convey an apology to the queen because "divers Speeches have been made extravagantly in this House, which doubtless have been told her Majesty, and perhaps all ill conceived by her" (D'Ewes 654).

21. When the lords expressed displeasure with Robert Snagge's remarks about the Upper House, Wentworth declared that the "freedome of the House [was] taken away by tale tellers" and called for an investigation to determine who in the Upper House had received the intelligence and who in the Lower House had provided it (*PPE* 1:403). Perhaps we should take Wentworth's use of the term "tale teller" seriously, for the members often complained not about leaks per se but about the accuracy of these reports to the crown and lords. On another occasion in 1572, for example, Wentworth "toke occasion to speke, and toochinge the lyberties

and pryveleges of the Howse inveighed agaynst certeyne members of the Howse that had enformed the Quene *untrewly* of a . . . mo[c]ion mad[e] in this Howse by Mr Bell . . . namyng [Sir Humphrey Gilbert] a flatterer, a lyer and a naughtie man" (*PPE* 1:248; emphasis added). Thomas Cromwell recalls that "Mr. Recorder declared in the House that Flower and Thompson for carrying tales out of the House were committed to the Tower" (Lambarde 93). The MPs institutionalized their anxiety about being misrepresented: as early as 1559, the speaker's ritual requests of the monarch at the opening of parliament included the plea that the crown allow that any report of the Commons' proceedings might be mistaken (see *PPE* 1:42–3).

22. This was Hall's maiden speech and it gives ample evidence of the rashness that so frequently enraged his colleagues. For a brief summary of Hall's career, see Hasler 2:240–42; for an extended study, see Wright.

23. We must remember that some MPs were very keen on demonstrating that the Commons had the authority to advocate—if not, perhaps, to legislate—Mary's death: "Warninge hath alredy ben given [Mary] by statut," Snagge warned, "and no good folowed of it, and therfore the axe must give the next warninge" (*PPE* 1:324).

24. The Commons, to be sure, also censored members solely for speech *within* St. Stephen's. Such restrictions on speech were quite often a function of the Commons' fear of offending the monarch. But a fine article by J. P. Sommerville suggests that the Commons' censoring of its own members did not decline as the body asserted greater independence from the crown. Thus, while the MPs sent Sir Christopher Piggot to the Tower after he spoke in 1607 *against* James's cherished Union plans, the members of 1624 voted to strike from the record Serjeant Higham's speech *in favor of* James's right to levy impositions (see Sommerville, "Parliament," 75).

25. Cf. the position of Edward Fenner, whose "infinite . . . estimation of liberties" (*PPE* 1:361) and desire for "libertie of speech without restraint" (*PPE* 1:355) moved him to urge that Hall not be punished at all but instead "held as a mad man" (*PPE* 1:361). Francis Knollys, vice chamberlain and treasurer of the Household, concurred with Fenner's diagnosis: "His father before him some what inclined to madness. By his own confession appeareth to be subiect to passions. He would have him condemned for a rashe head and foole" (*PPE* 1:366). Thomas Wilbraham, by contrast, was the sole MP offended principally by the *content* of Hall's speech: "Would have him charged, not whither he spake the wordes but whither if he or any other had spoaken them, whither he thinketh [them] to be evill, rashlie and foolishelie spoaken" (*PPE* 1:366).

26. An anonymous journalist records a similar version of this scene: Hall pleads that "the presence of the place maketh him astonied. . . . He confesseth not the articles, wherwith he was charged, but saith it might be he forgat himself in his speach, for his interruption moved color in him, and so mad him speake, he now forgetteth what" (*PPE* 1:330).

27. Gordon Zeeveld construes the Commons' business as "public" because a few well-placed gentry discuss it in letters (4). Notestein and Relf's careful discussion of publicity in and before 1629 shows that before 1621 the circulation of manuscripts of Commons speeches and proceedings was limited (50–75). Moreover, the circulation lists for such reports were quite exclusive: "Members of Parliament, important country families, great nobles, politically affected clergymen, ambassadors from foreign states, Privy Councilors and less important people" (59). It is telling that no examples are given to justify the inclusion of "less important people" in this list. See, also, Tittler 275–83 and Sharpe, "Communication," 331–45.

28. It is also entirely possible that *Record of some worthy Proceedings . . . in the late Parliament* was printed in London: English printers and booksellers seeking to avoid censorship or persecution occasionally falsified the place of publication.

29. The MPs had raised the issue in 1593 and 1597, and Elizabeth was acutely aware that monopolies were not popular in the Lower House.

30. See Richard Martin's speech on the effects of monopolies on the fourth estate (*PPE* 3:375).

31. Perhaps Cecil let his rhetoric boil over during this extended scolding of his colleagues, but, in the *private* notes he compiled after the parliamentary session of 1610, Thomas Egerton, Lord Ellesmere, worried that if the Commons "be suffered to usurp and encroach too far upon the regality, it will not cease (if it be not stayed in time) until it break out into democracy": "the popular state ever since the beginning of his Majesty's gracious and sweet government hath grown big and audacious, and in every session of parliament swelled more and more. And if way be still given unto it (as of late hath been) it is to be doubted what the end will be" (*PP 1610* 1: 276).

32. As we shall see in Chapter 5, Coriolanus similarly conflates public *discussion* of politics and popular *participation* in governance. According to Coriolanus, the people will gain political power simply by subjecting the Capitol to publicity:

> They'll sit by th' fire, and presume to know
> What's done i'th' Capitol, who's like to rise,
> Who thrives and who declines; side factions and give out
> Conjectural marriages, making parties strong
> And feebling such as stand not in their liking
> Below their cobbled shoes.
> (1.1.189–94)

Once the people have gained access to the business of the Capitol, they will exercise power to "prosper those" whom they favor.

33. This is perhaps a good place to acknowledge that I frequently speak in this chapter of *the* ideology or *the* rhetoric of the House of Commons; there were, of course, many ideologies and rhetorics in play in the Commons. The members pursued diverse agendas, had diverse interests and loyalties, and held very different ideas about their own institution's role in contemporary political culture. At one

extreme, we have the Wentworths and Snagge; at the other, members of the Commons who were also paid officers of the crown. I have focused here principally on ideas, practices, and ideologies that were widely endorsed by Elizabethan and Jacobean MPs. In this chapter and in Chapter 2, however, I do occasionally attend to disputes within the Commons about the nature and proper function of political representation.

34. During the debate over impositions in 1610, for example, many members, sensing that the financial burden would be unpopular, suggested that the knights and burgesses return to "their several countries" to "take intelligence" (*PP 1610* 2:292). To this end, Sir William Twysden prepared an argument based on precedent from Edward III's reign to prove that the MPs could "go into the country and receive a resolution from them [the voters]" (*PP 1610* 2:366). Cf. *CJ* 427. While there was never a formal, authorized canvassing of popular opinion, Sir John Holles later reported that he had consulted the people of Nottinghamshire (see *PP 1610* 2:xix)

35. Doyley's mistake is not as implausible as it might at first seem. "The Second Parte of Jack of Dover" may refer to the final section of *Iacke of Dover, His Quest of Inquirie, or his privy search for the veriest Foole in England* (London, 1604). I have not found an earlier edition of this text, but the tale of Jack of Dover was already well worn, and some earlier version of the 1604 text must have been the book that so excited poor Doyley. The anonymous author's eponymous hero has been judged "the Foole of all Fooles" (A2^{r}) and seeks to divest himself of this unhappy distinction. At a great feast, he enlists "a whole Iury of pennilesse *Poets*" (A2^{r}) to designate his replacement. Finding many other candidates insufficiently foolish, one poet-juror proposes to his fellows that the "veriest Foole" is surely to be found among themselves and that they should band together: "therefore we thinke fit to have a *Parliament of Poets,* & to enact such Lawes and Statutes, as may proove beneficiall to the Commonwealth, of *Iacke* of *Dovers* Mottley coated Fooles" (E3^{r}). The ensuing session of "the penniles Parliament of thread-bare Poets" (E3^{v}), set off from the preceding pages by a decorative border and announced in large type, might well be called "The Second Parte of Jack of Dover." (It is possible that an entirely discrete sequel was printed, but I can find no trace of it.) Considering how easily Elizabethan and Jacobean MPs took offense, we can only assume that neither Doyley nor any of his colleagues bothered to examine the text itself, in which the poet-MPs gravely debate and pass bills stipulating that "long bearded men shal seldom proove the wysest" (E3^{v}), that "it is lawfull that those Women, that every morning taste a pint of Muskedine with Egges . . . chide as well as they that drinke small Beere all the Winter" (E4^{r}), "that a Mince pie is better than a Musket" (G1^{r}), and so on.

36. For a concerted and serious exercise in political and literary censorship, see Chrimes's account of the Commons' successful campaign to suppress John Cowell's *The Interpreter.* Cowell's book, as Hoskins told his colleagues, figured the MPs as "slaves by reason of the Conquest" (*PP 1610* 2:33).

37. The officers of the House were especially jealous of their "dignity." In 1610, "Mr. Speaker complained that Sir Edward Herbert did use him disgracefully by popping his mouth with his finger in scorn of Mr. Speaker, meeting him upon the stair as Mr. Speaker was going down and again as Mr. Speaker came on his foot-cloth this morning to the House he rid close by him and staring upon him, did the like" (*PP 1610* 2:385). Herbert was brought before the House and tellingly tried to extricate himself by assuring the MPs that "he meant no offense to the House" (*PP 1610* 2:385). "Urged that he should say he meant no scorn to Mr. Speaker, he said at last that he had no intent to scorn the Speaker."

38. Habermas is interested almost exclusively in the literate public sphere, which finds its home in coffeehouses and newspapers. Habermas argues, unconvincingly, that the positive conditions for either a literate or plebeian public sphere were lacking in early modern England. According to the *OED,* the first instance of the phrase "public opinion" dates from 1735 (*OED* I.3.a), but Habermas claims that the *concept* of "'vulgar opinion' [is] still completely lacking in Shakespeare" and his time (90); on this point, he is wrong (see Introduction n. 7 above). Habermas does consider the possibility that the Tudor-Stuart theater was a forerunner of the public sphere but dismisses it on the grounds that the "'ranks' . . . paraded themselves, and the people applauded" at the theater (38). Elizabethan and Jacobean antitheatricalists, of course, routinely reviled the theater precisely because seating *did not* correspond to social rank and because humble playgoers thought that their own judgments of plays were every bit as good as those of their betters (see Chapter 4).

39. For a concise narrative of the evolution of the Commons from its origins up to the reign of Henry VIII, see Elton, "Body," 2–49. Historians of Parliament have long been interested in the question of whether medieval MPs should be regarded as representatives. The MPs did bind the people of the realm to laws; and the principle, well established by the early 1300s, of *quod omnes tangit ab omnibus approbari debet* (what touches all must be approved by all) seems to imply some notion of representation—the approval of all was given by MPs rather than by the people themselves. On the other hand, medieval MPs seldom claimed to speak for the people and seldom figured themselves as guardians of the people's liberties. I would argue that medieval MPs are best understood as legal representatives; prior to the reign of Henry VIII, MPs do not seem to have understood themselves as political representatives. For a variety of views, see Clarke 278–347; Monahan 97–126; Roskell, "The English Monarchy"; and Tierney, "Some Recent Work," 622–25.

40. In *Henry VI, Part 2,* the poor petitioners of Lancastrian England desperately seek out Good Duke Humphrey of Gloucester, the great lord protector of England (1.3.1–9). In the age of Shakespeare, petitioners—poor and prosperous, illiterate and educated—increasingly appealed to the knights and burgesses of the Lower House.

41. In 1614, several MPs became very agitated when a few of their colleagues

seemed willing to let off lightly an intruder named "Bukeley," who claimed that he "came only to see" (*PP 1614* 237). Sir Thomas Hoby wanted "him futher punished" (237); Sir Jerome Horsley argued that he should be "further examined" and ordered to "pay Mr. Serjeant's fees" (237). Sir Richard Tichborne objected that he knew Bukeley to be "simple," but Sir John Savile had "never heard any man in this case dismissed without censure" (237). In the end, Bukeley was committed for a time and then made to kneel at the bar for admonition (238).

42. For the detention of "strangers" in the Ward and the Gatehouse, see the cases of Charles Johnson, Charles Morgan, Richard Robinson, and Roger Dodswell (D'Ewes 248, 334, and 565). For other cases of intruders, see D'Ewes 288–89, 478, 511; *PPE* 1:200; *CJ* 1:83; and *PP 1610* 2:363.

43. In a broadside engraving of the Commons from 1640 (fig. 3), the kneeling figure has been replaced by what I take to be a standing petitioner.

44. Elton argues, with some justice, that while the Commons "may be fairly said to have been an instrument for guarding certain liberties of the subject . . . the liberties it was forever parading around the place were its own, to be most commonly used against the subject" (*Parliament,* 377–8).

45. I can find no codified prohibition on strangers before Hooker's *Order and usage* (1572). I am not, of course, suggesting that pre-Elizabethan sessions of the Commons were open to the public, but strictly excluding strangers seems to have been far more important to Elizabethan MPs: in *The Order and usage,* for example, Hooker mentions the prohibition six times.

46. For a very interesting discussion of the ways in which Sir Thomas Smith's celebration of England's "mixed estate" emerged from his Protestantism and his views on women rulers, see McLaren, "Reading" (esp. 913–20) and Chapter 7 of her *Political Culture.*

47. The committee appointed to draft the "Apology" was large and represented various points of view, but the Commons as a whole did not vote to send the document to James I.

48. See *HC* 413–14; Dean 7; Elton, "Parliament," 88–89; and Loach 40–41.

49. Sir Anthony Cope had called for a deferral of business before Easter, "the House being so small and empty" (Bowyer 250). On April 20, 1607, only 53 MPs were present (Bowyer 253). The Commons' chamber could not hold all 450–482 MPs, but it was large enough for the vast majority of MPs to attend.

50. See also "Observations rules and orders collected out of diverse Journalls of the house of Commons" (1604), British Library, B.L. MS Egerton 3365, 51b.

51. "It is common policy to say upon the Wednesday that the House shall be called on Saturday, and upon Saturday to say it shall be called on Wednesday; and so from day to day by fear thereof to keep the company together" (Lambarde 90).

52. *CJ* 1:291. In 1610, an anonymous MP was similarly outraged that only 100 MPs were present but "moved that it might nowhere be recorded that there was so great a neglect."

53. Bills were frequently passed when only a small percentage of the House was

sitting. According to Jennifer Loach, during the Parliament of 1601 there was not a single division—i.e., a counted vote—in which more than half the members participated (40–41). This figure is all the more striking because divisions were conducted only when important and potentially controversial legislation was at issue.

54. As we shall see in Chapter 2, there was a rival theory of parliamentary representation according to which each MP represented only the residents of the particular borough or shire he represented. Bowyer's account of representation is absolute: each MP is capable of making the entire realm present.

55. The Commons directly and indirectly borrows its figuration of the body politic from theological discourses. Some clerical scholars recognized a nonabsolutist strain in Gratian's *Decretum* (1140) and among the Decretists there was a significant tradition of emphasizing a populist account of religious authority: the whole community of the faithful was infallible and a consensus among them was a sign of the Holy Spirit. The theory of popular power was practically deployed during the Conciliarist movement in the early Renaissance. The Council of Constance (1414) had the unenviable task of trying to choose among rival claimants to the Holy See. In the absence of any traditional procedure for removing a pope from office, the Italian jurist Azo developed sophisticated theories of the primacy of popular power and fashioned a justification for deposing two of the three (would-be) popes. At the Council of Basil (1430s), Bishop Garcia of Burgos, while arguing that the will of the community of believers empowered—and could therefore disempower—any clerical leader, noted that it would be absurd in the secular world to attribute more power to the king than to the whole of his people. (William Prynne quotes Garcia in his 1643 tract on Parliament.) Nicholas of Cues, in 1432, claimed lower magistrates and church officials could resist their superiors if that resistance reflected the will of the people, for the people, he argued, empowered both low and high church officials. Althusius claimed, most simply, that God invested the people with the power of election. There were, of course, secular analogues to all of these arguments; indeed, Brian Tierney has suggested that civic humanism and conciliarism are alternative strategies for developing the principle of communal power.

56. "Be it further enacted, that if at any time it happen that for her sake and in her name ther be raysed or procured any tumult or insurrection within this realme . . . any person or persons [who] shall attempt to dispatche and destroy her . . . shall not be any kinde of wayes troubled or impeached for the same" (*PPE* 1:315).

57. See Fried 1–70.

Chapter 2 Cade's Mouth

1. In the Oxford Shakespeare, *Henry VI, Parts 2 and 3* are restored to their original titles, *The First Part of the Contention of the Two Famous Houses of York and Lancaster* and *The True Tragedy of Richard Duke of York.* For the sake of clarity,

I use the more familiar titles *Henry VI, Parts 2 and 3* and the abbreviations *1HVI, 2HVI,* and *3HVI.*

2. Hall, too, strongly suggests that Gloucester's death spelled Henry's own doom (210).

3. In *Part 3,* Shakespeare again puts pressure on the status of consent in Parliament: outraged over Henry's betrayal of his adoption of York and his sons as heirs to the throne, Warwick fumes to Edward, "He swore consent to your succession, / His oath enrolled in the Parliament" (2.1.172–73).

4. The lords spiritual and temporal could, unlike the monarch, be represented in Parliament by proxies. One of the first orders of business in every session of the House of Lords was the establishment of proxy relations. See, e.g., D'Ewes 1–6

5. The lord chancellor typically addressed a joint assembly of Lords and Commons at the opening and closing of each parliament, explaining on the former occasion why the queen had called her Parliament and assessing on the later occasion the Commons' successes and failures and expressing the queen's gratitude for subsidies granted. In this capacity, John Puckering spoke to the Lords and Commons at the opening of Parliament in 1593: "My Lords all, and yow the knightes and burgesses of the comminalitie, it hath pleased the Queen's most excellent Majestie to charge me (of my self a most unworthie interpreter of so highe and wise a prince, but yet susteyned with the hope of her Majestie's pardone, and assurance of your Lordships' pacience, readie and obedient to take this heavie burden upon me) and to commaunde me to make yow all knowe the only and proper causes of calling and gathering of this noble and great assemblie" (*PPE* 3:14). At the close of Parliament in 1585, Elizabeth felt it necessary to speak for herself: "My lords, and ye of the Lower Howse, my scillence must not iniurie the owner so mocche as to suppose a substitute sufficient to rendar yow the thanks which . . . yowr care apperes so manifest, as for the neglectinge yowre private future perill not regardyng otherway then my present state" (*PPE* 2:31). Cf. *PPE* 2:251.

6. Shakespeare's history of the Wars of the Roses is equally a history of his own present: many of the theories of kingship at play in the first Henriad are Tudor; the theories and practices of political representation that helped shape Shakespeare's representation of the Lancastrian Parliaments are particular to the parliamentary politics of his own time.

7. According to John Hooker's translation of the *Modus,* "The King ought dayly to be present in Parlement" (140). This order seems to have been taken more literally in the medieval parliaments: thus, for example, Grafton reports that Richard II's Parliaments frequently complained about his absences (1:432–33).

8. Cf. Puckering, then speaker of the House, in 1585: "*John Puckering* Serjeant at Law . . . proceeded according to the usual course to desire her Majesty to give Life to such Laws by adding her Gracious Allowance unto them, as had passed either House, and remained as yet but as a dead Letter" (D'Ewes 327). See also *PPE* 1:189–90 and *PPE* 3:174, 199, and 242.

9. In 1593, an inexperienced MP carefully recorded the moment at which the queen-in-Parliament gave life to new laws: "The manner is the Clarke of the Crowne reading the title of every act that hath passed both the Houses, the Clarke of the Higher House hath a paper signed by the Queen, and to every generall bill that passeth after the title read he sayeth, '*La Royne elle veult.*'" If the queen had withheld her consent from a particular bill, the Lords' clerk would respond, "*La Royne s'advisera*" (*PPE* 3:174; cf. *PPE* 3:242). Although these formulae of assent and rejection were articulated by the clerk, Elizabeth had signed the bills and her presence in Parliament guaranteed that the clerk accurately reported his text.

10. "Mystical body" is Coke's term for the monarch's body politic (see Kantorowicz 15). Edmund Plowden identified the body politic and a royal office "consisting of Policy and Government, and constituted for the Direction of the People, and the Management of the public weal" (qtd. in Kantorowicz 17).

11. The concept of the monarch's two bodies was quite familiar, in various forms, to Elizabethan knights and burgesses. Thus, for example, Robert Atkinson, in a 1563 speech against a bill for the Oath of Supremacy, "agree[d] to the saying of Bryan where he saith that a great doctor of law once told him that a priest . . . might be impleaded in the kinge's temporall court *quia rex est persona unita ex sacerdotibus et laicis,* because the kinge is mixte of priesthood and laitie" (*PPE* 1:97). At the close of Parliament in 1567, Speaker Onslow told the joint assembly that "the prince serveth God 2 waies, as a man and as a kinge: in that as he is a man he ought to live and serve God as one of his good creatures; and in that he is king, and so Gode's speciall creature, he ought to make lawes wherby God may be truly worshipped" (*PPE* 1:169).

12. Despite his brothers' warning that his decision to cast off Bona and marry Lady Grey will enrage Warwick, Edward remains firm: "I am Edward / Your king and Warwick's, and must have my will" (*3HVI* 4.1.15–16).

13. Scholars long ago established that some aspects of Shakespeare's representation of the Cade rebellion of 1451 are modeled on chronicle accounts of the 1381 rising led by Wat Tyler and Jack Straw: see, e.g., Cairncross 123n, Caldwell 19, Pugliatti 472, and Stirling 58. For a fine reading of the cultural significance of Shakespeare's simultaneous invocation of both the 1381 and the 1451 risings, see *SPV* 38–41. For contemporary accounts of literacy and the Revolt of 1381, see Dobson 133–34, 155–57, 184.

14. Several other articles address the king's interference in parliamentary elections and legislation: see, e.g., articles 15 and 17 in Grafton (1:474). See Butt 437–58 for Parliament's role in bringing down Richard II.

15. Cf. Grafton 2:474 and Holinshed 3:524.

16. G. R. Elton argues that the sovereignty of the king-in-Parliament emerged near the end of Henry VIII's reign. As late as 1520, Henry claimed that he possessed an "absolute power . . . above the laws" (Elton, *"Body of the Whole Realm,"* 18–19), but in 1543, in the presence of the other estates of the realm, he gave a quite

different account of his relation to the law: "we at no time stand so highly in our royal estate as in the time of Parliament, wherein we as head and you as members are conjoined and knit together into one body politic" (18).

17. One of the affronts to Elizabethan orthodoxy that Arthur Hall was forced to recant was his suggestion that the queen could make law outside of Parliament:

> And where I am chardged to have practised to discredit the aucthoritie of the lawes and proceedinges of the Parliament . . . I doo from the bottome of my harte reverence the lawes and procedinges in the Parliamentes in bothe the Howses and Counsells, and doe allowe of the auntient aucthoritie of that Common Howse wherin the Third Estate of the whole Realme is dewly represented. . . . and doe affirme to my poore understanding that there cannot be anie better order by wytt of man devised for the making, abrogating, or chaunging of lawes to governe the Realme and everie particuler member, from the hiest to the lowest, then is alredie provided for and of auntyent tyme hath been practised in this Realme, by calling and assembling the three Estates of the Realme, as they are called, to geve advise, councell and aydes to the Quenes Majestie as the head of the whole Realme in all causes propounded in the behaulf of the Realme; and I doe likewise acknowledge that the Assemblie in the Common Howse hathe aucthority to assent unto or denye suches lawes as shalbe concluded in Parliamentes. (*APC* 11:10–11)

18. The sheer chance of Elizabeth I's gender made the concept of the monarch-in-Parliament especially useful to the crown. The polemicists who defended Elizabeth against attacks on female rulers sometimes conceded that anxieties about a woman ruler might indeed be justified if the English monarch were capable of legislating alone. Such anxieties, John Aylmer argued in *An Harborowe for Faithful and True Subjects,* were unfounded: "The Queen ruleth but the laws. . . . She maketh no statutes or laws but in the honourable court of Parliament . . . What may she do alone wherein is peril? She may grant pardon to an offender, that is her prerogative. . . . If . . . all hanged upon the king's or queen's will and not upon laws written; if she might make and decree laws alone, without her senate . . . you might peradventure make me to fear the matter more" (Gii^{v}) Because Elizabeth's legislative power is circumscribed and limited by her (all male) Parliament, her male subjects have nothing to fear.

19. See, e.g., *PPE* 1:75, *PPE* 2:26, 54, and *PPE* 3:241.

20. I suspect that some readers will find the arguments I'm pursuing here rather Whiggish in certain respects. I am indeed asserting that when the knights and burgesses made invidious comparisons between their own capacity to represent and the lords' and monarch's nonrepresentativeness, they did so in part to establish their own power.

21. The residency information for the remaining nine members is uncertain.

22. "By the 1580s," according to Mark Kishlansky, "only a handful of knights of the shire were selected for counties in which they did not hold a landed estate"; by contrast, only a small minority of burgesses actually lived in the boroughs they represented (25). J. E. Neale claims that carpetbagging and its attendant notion that MPs didn't necessarily represent only their local constituency are almost as old as the Commons itself, but "it was in the sixteenth century that 'carpet-bagging' overwhelmingly and irrevocably established itself" (*HC* 14). The issue of carpetbagging, however, remained a matter of debate throughout Elizabeth's and James's reigns. See, e.g., *PPE* 2:121 and 3:448. I should note here that many boroughs were quite happy to let local power brokers choose their burgesses for them: it saved time and often meant that the sponsor or the new burgess himself, rather than the borough corporation, paid the customary parliamentary wages of the town's representatives.

23. The construct of the king's two bodies and other aspects of monarchic theory potentially enabled very grand claims about the relation of the monarch to the nation. The body politic, according to Edmund Plowden, could be understood as an incorporation of the king and his people: "he and his subjects together compose the Corporation . . . and he is incorporated with them, and they with him, and he is the Head, and they are the Members, and he has sole Government of them" (qtd. in Kantorowicz 13).

24. See, e.g., Stirling 50 and Richard Wilson, *Will Power,* 27–28. For an astute critique of Wilson, see Patterson, *Shakespeare and the Popular Voice,* 36–37. Rackin (218–19) and Leggatt (18) argue that Shakespeare ultimately rejects Cade's rebellion, but they do not see Shakespeare as an enthusiastic enemy of the people. Laroque (77), Weimann (240), Bristol (89), and Hattaway (18–20) argue for Shakespeare's sympathetic treatment of the revolt. Bernthal recognizes the sophistication of the rebels. See Helgerson for a subtle account of the ways in which Shakespeare renders the Cade rebellion both dangerously radical and safely absurd (207).

25. To emphasize the way Cade's stinking breath imprints itself in the laws that come out of his mouth is to read the scene of Cadeian legislation as a parody of artificial personhood and political representation. Joanna Picciotto has pointed out to me that that Cade's palpable breath also stands in a complex relation to the quasi-divine breath early modern MPs solicited from the monarch at the closing of Parliament. In Parliament, the monarch's invisible spirit is breathed into the dead matter of parliamentary bills that the MPs have, like Pygmalions or carpenters, fashioned in stone or wood (see *PPE* 2:317). Cade doubly unsettles the spirit/matter distinction because his breath is continuous with his body and with legislation (there is never a moment when Cade's dead laws await his quickening breath). One might take a juxtaposition of Cade's breath and Elizabeth's as the point of departure for a consideration of the way in which Shakespeare's parody of artificial personhood in the first tetralogy is often simultaneously a parody of the topos of the monarch's two bodies.

26. For a very interesting discussion of the representation of the Commons in Holinshed, see Zaller and Chapter 6 of Patterson's splendid *Reading Halinshed's Chronicles.*

27. Cf. Hall 130–38, 248, 249.

28. For the Commons' actions against Richard's favorites and councilors, see Fabyan 265.

29. See also Grafton 1:678; Hall 217–19; and Daniel 2:99–114, 3:2–19.

30. Cf. Patterson's analysis of Richard Woods's 1615 account of Kett's uprising in Norfolk: "the text makes its law-and-order motives unmistakable. . . . The common people are described as 'desiring . . . not only to lay open the common Pastures, inclosed by the injurie of some men, but to powre foorth their ungodly desires against the Commonwealth' . . . And pour them fourth, thanks to the hegemonic historian, they do" (*SPV* 42). Patterson then quotes a long passage in which Woods reports the people's grievances. Conflating the most scrupulous and seemingly unmotivated account of popular speech and the lost speech itself seems risky enough, but trusting persons engaged in political, social, or religious debate to represent the positions they oppose is still riskier.

31. Until Mary's execution, the House of Commons repeatedly expressed its concern for Elizabeth's safety, and some MPs, like the commoners of Bury, argued that if Elizabeth would not protect herself, then they would. See, e.g., *PPE* 2:225, 230, 233–38, 241–42, 246, 263, 267.

32. In the First Folio, Warwick and Salisbury are actually present when Margaret, Beaufort, York, and Suffolk ordain Gloucester's murder; in the quarto, they leave the Parliament with Henry.

33. William Carroll notes that "Suffolk's act of enclosure is Shakespeare's invention" (43). Carroll's subtle essay reconstructs the surprisingly complex status of enclosure in Shakespeare's England and its importance to *Henry VI, Part 2.* Carroll's discussion of Cade's communistic rhetoric is also excellent (42–43).

34. It seems reasonable to surmise that Warwick and Salisbury have reported Gloucester's death to the commoners.

35. For a very interesting discussion of Cade as a representative of the people, see Cartelli 56.

Chapter 3 "Their tribune and their trust"

1. For those readers who do not have *Titus* at their fingertips, I offer this abbreviated summary of the bloody plot: Titus sacrifices Alarbus, eldest son of Tamora, Queen of the Goths; Titus enables Saturninus to become Rome's emperor; Saturninus's brother Bassianus prevents the marriage of Saturninus and Lavinia by asserting his own prior claim to Lavinia's hand; Saturninus marries Tamora; Chiron and Demetrius, Tamora's sons, rape and maim Lavinia and murder Bassianus; Titus's sons Martius and Quintus are executed for the crimes; Titus kills Chiron

and Demetrius and bakes them in a pie, later served up to their mother; Titus kills Lavinia; Titus kills Tamora; Saturninus kills Titus; Titus's son Lucius kills Saturninus; Lucius becomes emperor.

2. In *Shakespeare and the Uses of Antiquity,* Charles and Michelle Martindale argue that *Titus* should not be grouped with the Roman plays because it lacks their "alert political intelligence" (142). For the Martindales, *Titus* is a classical play only because it is Ovidian (47).

3. Indeed, the first election scene is, according to some scholars, sufficiently disjointed from the rest of the play as to raise questions of Shakespeare's authorship (Wells 113–15). Spencer is a rare exception: though he doesn't comment specifically on the relation of the elections scenes to the rest of the play, he finds in *Titus* "a consistent dramatic structure which could very well represent the artistry of the young Shakespeare" (11); Heather James also recovers a nexus of issues that Shakespeare develops from the play's opening scene to the final curtain.

4. Thus, the impact of Titus's fall isn't as powerful as Lear's or Hieronimo's because "there is in effect no larger social world within which the outrage takes place, no ongoing business of state and private life within which the isolation and impotence of the injured hero can be presented" (125). Yet Titus himself, as we shall see, is determined to inscribe his own tragedy within political and historical contexts.

For years now, the most provocative readings of *Titus* have located the play's political interest not in Rome's public affairs and institutions but in rape, the family, and literariness (see, e.g., Fawcett, Willbern, "Rape and Revenge," and Goldberg, *Voice,* 75–86).

5. Jed argues that "early Roman annalists required a legend of rape to mark Rome's transition from monarchy to a republican form of government" and to confer "legitimacy upon . . . the foundation of Republican Rome"; hence, "republican laws and institutions also legitimize the conditions of sexual violence" (2). Jed further claims that Renaissance retellings of the Lucrece narrative perpetuate the accommodation of sexual oppression and violence within republicanism. By contrast, I am arguing here that Shakespeare's treatment of the Lucrece narrative—both in *Lucrece* and *Titus*—is a radical critique of the republican rape topos.

6. All quotations from and references to *The Rape of Lucrece* follow Roe.

7. After the death of Tarquinius Priscus, his widow Queen Tanaquil helps her son-in-law Servius Tullius to the crown. Tanaquil thus passes over Lucius Tarquinius, the dead king's own son. Servius solicits popular support and is acclaimed king. Lucius murders Servius and never seeks the people's suffrages to legitimize his rule. Perhaps the succession struggle between Servius and Lucius provided some of the inspiration for the rivalry between Saturninus and Bassianus.

8. In Shakespeare's England, of course, women did not vote in parliamentary elections, but they did occasionally control the votes of their tenants and exercised electoral influence in a variety of other ways. In 1572, for example, the civic leaders of Aylesbury, following a long-standing tradition, delivered their election writ to the lord of the manor, who returned it thus inscribed: "I, Dame Dorothy

Packington . . . lord and owner of the town of Aylesbury . . . have chosen, named, and appointed my trusty and well beloved Thomas Litchfield and George Burden esq. to be my burgesses of the said town" (qtd. in Kishlansky 42). See also Kishlansky 53n13 and Hirst 18. My readings of *Titus* and *Lucrece* do not assume that Shakespeare was an advocate of women's suffrage, though we should not discount such a possibility as "unthinkable." I am arguing that Shakespeare perceived and exploited contradictions in both Roman and English constructions of liberty.

9. For years, Ovid has been central to *Titus* criticism (Leonard Barkan and Eugene Waith are outstanding examples); I am proposing here a shift toward a Livian reading of the play. Heather James has broken new ground, with very fine results, in a different patch of literary-historical ground: she argues for the importance of Virgil to the representation of empire and nation in *Titus* (42–84).

10. Shakespeare ignored "the political and dynastic considerations in the source," say Barber and Wheeler (136), but the "source" in question—*The History of Titus Andronicus,* a prose narrative of Titus's life—is extant only in an eighteenth-century chapbook, which may or may not approximate a sixteenth-century text. Bullough suggests that *The History of Titus Andronicus* may well be a reprint of a 1594 text and concludes that some version of the prose history probably predates Shakespeare's play (3:327). In any event, if the chapbook narrative does represent a source, Shakespeare has expanded and complicated rather than diminished its very spare political plot.

Some scholars have argued for Shakespeare's indebtedness to the poem "Titus Andronicus' Complaint," first registered in 1594; the earliest extant version appears in Richard Johnson's *The Golden Garland of Princely Pleasures* (1620). But almost all scholars agree that the play predates the poem: some posit a play-prose history-poem sequence (see Mincoff), others a prose history-play-poem sequence (see Bullough 3:329). Without rendering an opinion on these matters, let me point out that almost all of the events and issues important to the concerns of this chapter appear *only* in Shakespeare's play: the succession struggle between the brothers; the dispute over Lavinia; the invocations of Lucrece and Virginia; the role of the popular voice in Roman politics; and the election of Lucius.

11. See *OED* I.3b, II.21b, III.24 for these three meanings—all current by 1592—of "to tell."

12. I am relying here not only on the important fact that no one takes up Marcus's cry ("Long live our Emperor Saturnine!"), but also on my reconstruction of the staging of this scene. Who is on stage when Marcus's representative "we" makes Saturninus emperor? The text and stage directions indicate the presence of Marcus, Titus, the two tribunes, an unspecified number of Senators, Saturninus, Bassianus, the Captain, Martius, Mutius, two men bearing a coffin, Lucius, Quintus, Tamora, Chiron, Demetrius, Aaron, Lavinia, "and others as many as can be." Two questions are before us then: how many "others" might there be; and who might these "others" be? If we assume that a company of no more than twenty-seven actors performed the play and that there are only two "Senators," there can

be no more than seven "others" on stage at 1.1.230–33. (I am even assuming here that the actor playing Alarbus rushes back to the stage after he is taken away for execution at 1.1.129.) These "others" enter with Titus, who has *just* returned from his defeat of the Goths (see 1.1.64–69). Perhaps these "others," then, are Titus's soldiers or Gothic prisoners; they cannot be members of the group of people who invest Marcus with their voices *before* Titus and these "others" return to Rome. In short, when Marcus speaks for the people, none of the people for whom he claims to speak can be present on stage.

Titus and Marcus could, of course, address the audience when they solicit popular acclamations: thus performed, the play would juxtapose the presence of the audience to theatrical representation and the tendency of representational politics to make the people absent.

13. One might argue that the audience has no way of knowing whether Marcus accurately represents the people's will. Indeed, we have only Marcus's word on this matter, but the problem of political representation is precisely that the representative's construction of "the people's" will *is* the people's will.

14. Recall Gadamer's account of incarnational representation: "in light of the Christian idea of the incarnation and the mystical body," Gadamer argues, representation "acquired a completely new meaning. Representation now no longer means 'copy' or 'representation in a picture' . . . but 'replacement' . . . what is represented is present in the copy" (513–14n53).

15. As soon as he appears on stage, Marcus, borrowing a familiar locution from the morality play, announces that he "stands for" the people; Shakespeare represents Marcus's displacement of the people from the political field by effacing them from his stage. As we shall see, however, the potential analogies between political and theatrical representation—in both economies, the few stand for the many, those who represent assume artificial identities, and so on—were deeply troubling to Shakespeare.

16. One expects Bourdieu's discussion of "performative magic" to lead to a consideration of Austin, Searle, and Speech Act theory, but Bourdieu quickly passes over Austin, who, he claims, wrongly locates the "efficacy of [official] speech" in "discourse itself—in the specifically linguistic substance of speech, as it were" (*Language,* 109). I am much indebted to Bourdieu's work, but this is a bizarre lapse in scholarship: in *How to Do Things with Words,* Austin returns again and again to the extralinguistic conditions that must obtain in order for performative utterances to have effective force. Consider the example Austin uses to introduce his taxonomy of the "infelicities" that obviate or undermine performative utterances: if a ship's purser, rather than its captain, declares two persons to be married, the "act in question . . . is not successfully performed at all, does not come off, is not achieved" (16). The purser may perfectly rehearse the appropriate words, but because he is not the "appropriate" person—because he lacks the necessary extralinguistic authority—his utterances have no effect. See also 17–24, 34–35, and 42–43, and id., *Philosophical Papers* 236–40.

17. For the purpose of my discussion here, it is important to recognize that Titus's army may well provide some of the muscle behind Marcus's speech acts. Indeed, one might argue that the real power in Roman politics is military: perhaps Titus's army enforces Marcus's declaration and decisively influences Saturninus's decision to pick Lavinia as his empress. Lucius's Gothic army similarly makes his "election" at the end of the play irresistible. The basic premise here is not at all implausible—Shakespeare seems quite well versed in the history of Rome's military strongmen—but such an argument would *complicate* rather than diminish the importance of political representation in Roman politics. If armies constitute the real power in Rome, the rhetoric and practice of political representation provide a necessary ideological mystification of the real conditions of power.

18. Bourdieu tends to treat representation and delegation as virtually synonymous. By rehearsing his use of the terms "delegate" and "delegation," I in no way mean to suggest that I reject the sharp distinctions most political philosophers make between representatives and delegates.

19. Bourdieu's model of representation is a special case of his influential construction of the relation between structure and agency. Rather than adopting either the functionalist and structuralist bias for the determining power of social structure or the volunteerist bias for the unfettered shaping power of the agent, Bourdieu argues that structure and agency are interdependent and recursively generated: "to escape from the *realism of the structure,* which hypostatizes systems of objective relations by converting them into totalities already constituted outside of individual history and group history, it is necessary to construct the theory of practice, or, more precisely, the theory of the mode of generation of practices, which is the precondition for establishing an experimental science of the *dialectic of the internalization of externality and the externalization of internality"* (*Outline,* 72). To study the generation of practices is to study the internalization (by agents) of externality (structure) and the externalization (the production of structure) through agency. The medium of the recursive reproduction of structure and agent, according to Bourdieu, is the "habitus," a system "of durable, transposable *dispositions,* structured structures predisposed to function as structuring structures. . . . [a] durably installed generative principle of regulated improvisation, [which] produces practices which tend to reproduce the regularities immanent in the objective conditions of the production of the their generative principle" (ibid., 72, 78). Put another way, the habitus produces actions that (re)produce the habitus: "the practices produced by the habitus . . . always tend . . . to reproduce the objective structures of which they are the product" (73). The political representative, then, embodies Bourdieu's habitus: he creates the agents who create him.

20. Both the use and the trust raised many thorny legal questions about the precise nature of the relationship between the feoffee or trustee and the property enfeoffed by the *cestui que use* or the *cestui que trust.* The feoffee and the trustee technically owned but reaped no profit from the entrusted property: voting rights and jury service were just two of many civic rights and duties reserved not simply

for property owners but for owners of property that produced a certain amount of profit per annum. The great lawyer and jurist Sir James Dyer argued that, prior to the Statute of Uses (1536), a feoffee, although he "navera forsque nude possession del franktenement, et a null value quant a lui," could sit on the same jury as the *cestui que use* who had enfeoffed the property to him (2:271).

21. The common law did not recognize bequests of land by will; land passed automatically to the eldest son. The use—a legal pact whereby feoffees to uses managed an estate on behalf of and for the profit of the enfeoffing owner—enabled landowners to yield the profits from land held in use to beneficiaries other than eldest sons. Moreover, neither the landowner's death nor the deaths of individual feoffees provided an occasion for the crown to exact feudal dues, because the use lived on in the persons of the surviving feoffees, who now used the property for the profit of the original landowner's designated heirs, the new beneficiaries of the use. Uses might be deployed in other ways: if the *cestui que use* committed treason, the property he had enfeoffed was safe from royal seizure and would continue to produce profits for his heirs; if the *cestui que use* were in debt, his creditors could not seize property he had enfeoffed; "religious houses," F. W. Maitland remarks, used "the same device . . . to avoid the statutes of mortmain" (223). In 1536, in response to these abuses, Henry VIII succeeded in passing the Statute of Uses, which constructed the landowner, rather than the enfeoffees, as the legal owner. Thus, the landowner's estate was liable for the feudal payments due the king. In response, common law lawyers developed the trust, which had essentially the same structure as the use. The Statute of Uses was met with nearly universal fury, and in 1540 the Statute of Wills, accepted by Henry VIII, legitimized property bequests and reduced feudal dues to one-third of the deceased's land, but it also established trustees as legal owners of property.

The development and nature of both trusts and uses are complicated, and I have offered here only the most cursory account. For the relation between uses and trusts, see Kolbert and Mackay 147–51 and Yale 2:88–91; for an introduction to the trust, see Maitland 3:321–404; for an exceptionally lucid explanation of the Statute of Uses and the Statute of Wills, see Gray 177–80; for the perfection of trust law in the late seventeenth century, see Yale 2:87–113.

22. To be sure, MPs often used "trust" to mean "faith," but it is often difficult—and misguided—to distinguish between the technical and nontechnical senses of the word. According to the MPs who wrote the "Apology" of 1604, "the shires, cities, and boroughs of England . . . have free choice of such persons as they shall put in trust to represent them" (qtd. in Tanner 223); in 1576, Peter Wentworth reminded his fellow MPs that they were "chosen of the whole realme of a speciall trust and confidence by them reposed in us" (*PPE* 1:428); "if you discharge your truste well," F.A.'s father suggests, "they are in your debt, and they well may vaunte of the perfection of your execution" (Fi^r; cf. Ei^r): in all of these cases, the fiduciary sense of trust is, at the very least, sharing space with a more general meaning.

23. J. D. Alsop has argued that during Elizabeth's reign, not even an individual

MP, much less the Commons as a body, "ever attempted to refuse a request for taxation" (100). How we define "attempt to refuse" matters here, and one could certainly point to grumblings about subsidies and brief discussions about the distributions of tax burdens, but Alsop's research certainly demonstrates that the Elizabethan Commons was very compliant on this matter. Prior to Henry VIII's reign, English monarchs observed the convention of financing peacetime governance and household expenses through hereditary revenues and poundage and tonnage. In 1529, Henry VIII requested a peacetime subsidy but the Commons balked. Henry had, however, broken the ice and the Commons met his requests in 1534 and 1540; Edward VI and Mary I each requested and received one peacetime subsidy. During Elizabeth's reign, the peacetime subsidy became routine.

24. Cf. Sir Robert Cotton, in 1610, who lamented the Commons' willingness to grant a subsidy in the absence of any guarantee that James, in turn, would approve other statutes the MPs wished to advance: "For if we give one subsidy now without something for it . . . as if we had voices in parliament only to give subsidies or give subsidies to have voices in parliament" (*PP 1610* 2:147). Cf. the earl of Northampton, who dismissed the MPs fears that their constituents would consider them bad trusts if they granted the subsidy (*PP 1610* 1: 273).

25. Revisionist historians have rightly argued that the kind of reciprocity I have briefly described here was significantly neglected in Whig celebrations of a feisty Commons ready to take on Elizabeth and James at every turn. Early modern constituents, like our own electorates, expected their representatives to deliver material benefits to their communities: thus, before the parliamentary elections of 1571, the earl of Warwick recommended Edward Aglionby, "a man," he promised, that "you shall finde veary forward in thadvauncement of any thing that may tend to the comon profit & comoditie of your towne" (*BB* 27), to the officers of Warwick. In my discussion of political trust, I am emphasizing both the crown's and the MPs' material interests in a session of Parliament, but the Commons often took up matters of foreign policy, succession, religion, and other loftier issues.

26. "The Legislative," Locke argues in *The Second Treatise of Government* (1690), has "only a Fiduciary Power to act for certain ends" (367); if the people "find [that] the *Legislative* act contrary to the trust reposed in them . . . the *trust* must necessarily be *forfeited,* and the Power devolve into the hands of those that gave it" (367); "the *Legislative acts against the Trust* reposed in them, when they endeavour to invade the Property of the Subject" (412).

27. Not all bribery, of course, originated with Hall's "great ones." John Hooker's diary of the 1571 session mentions two bribery cases: Thomas Longe, burgess for Westbury-under-the-Plain, was investigated for having bribed local officials for his election (*PPE* 1:251); and "there was mich ado about suche men of the Howse as . . . have receved fees yn the Howse for the preferringe or speking to any byll, of which [Thomas] Norton . . . was charged" (*PPE* 1:255).

28. In "A Treatise of Monarchy," Fulke Greville draws an unflattering analogy

between the economic speculator in the marketplace and the democratic representative in the political field:

> . . . as those persons usually do haunt
> The market places, which at home have least:
> So here those spiritts most intrude and vaunt
> To doe the business of this common beast,
> That have no other means to vent their ill,
> Then by transforminge reall thinges to will.
> (188–93)

Just as the speculator converts material into immaterial capital, so the politician—with no incorporate power—converts the people—real things—into political authority. When he enters the political field, the political speculator has no power of his own—unlike a monarch who theoretically has inherent power—but by doing the political business of the people he becomes powerful. Similarly, Marcus can function as a repository of the people's voices only because those voices—that political capital—have been alienated from the people themselves and transformed into capital.

29. For a perceptive reading of Titus's choice of Saturninus as a sign of his own dynastic ambitions, see Heather James 52–53; Spencer also remarks the politics of Titus's choice (74). Kahn's reading of the exchanges between Titus and Saturninus is especially astute (51).

30. Marcus, then, simultaneously violates the two most sacred principles of any trust: he uses what has been entrusted to him not for the benefit of *cestui que trust* but for the benefit of others; and he conveys what has been entrusted to him—the people's voices—to a party outside the compact.

31. "Convey" and "seize" are technical terms in early modern property law.

32. Most scholars think that Shakespeare wrote *The Rape of Lucrece* after he wrote *Titus Andronicus,* although there are some heretics on this point. It is almost certain that only a year or so separates the composition of these two treatments of the republican rape topos, and it is not at all unlikely that Shakespeare worked on the poem and the play simultaneously. We know that *Titus Andronicus* was performed no later than January 23, 1594 (ed. Waith, 5). Like most recent editors, Waith argues that an early version of *Titus* was on stage by 1592 and that the texts that have been transmitted represent a revision completed by 1593 (4–11). *The Rape of Lucrece* was entered on the Stationers' Register on May 9, 1594.

33. Perhaps Shakespeare was inspired here by the mourning scene in Ovid's *Fasti:* "ecce super corpus communia damna gementes / obliti decoris virque paterque iacent" (2.835–36). Here, the father and the husband share rather than dispute their loss, but "damnus" often designates the loss of property.

Although my larger political interpretation of *Lucrece* departs from previous readings, several critics have discussed the commodification of Lucrece. Jonathan

Crewe, for example, reads the "grieving contest" as a property dispute between the possessive Collatine (145) and "Lucrece's furiously proprietary father" (148). "Rape," Crewe claims, "can mean physical assault on Lucrece's person, but as an act of seizure (*raptus*) it can also be regarded as that which nonexclusively instantiates an originary desire for and crime against private property" (146). See also Lynda Boose's insightful reading of Titus's patriarchal ownership of his daughter.

34. According to many Catholics, of course, Elizabeth and James were tyrants.

35. There were, of course, exceptions: Peter Wentworth's incendiary speeches in 1576 identified Parliament's right to free speech in general and to debate matters of religion in particular as the foundation of English freedom (*PPE* 1:425–34).

36. After Elizabeth promised that she was prepared to eliminate and reform monopolies, More celebrated the subject's emancipation: "seeing it hath pleased her Majesty of her self, out of abundance of her Princely goodness, to set at liberty her Subjects from the thraldom of those Monopolies, from which there was no Town, City or Country free" (D'Ewes 654). See Sacks for a very fine analysis of monopolies and Elizabethan parliamentary politics.

37. When James I publicly declared that he could establish impositions by prerogative and then sought to restrain debate on the matter, a group of MPs responded with "A Petition for the Parliament's Liberty," one of the more stirring Jacobean articulations of parliamentary freedoms (see *PP 1610* 2:371). According to the "Petition," the House of Commons was established "to debate freely al matters, which do properly concerne the subject, and his right, or State: which freedome of debate being once forclosed, the essence of the libertie of Parliament is with all dissolved" (*Record of some worthy Proceedings . . . in the late Parlement,* 16). During the parliamentary sessions of 1614, MPs routinely figured impositions as slavery: James's "liberty" to impose, Edwin Sandys argued, "makes us bondmen, gives us but no propriety. May, by the same reasons, make laws without parliament" (*PP 1614* 147).

38. See Nancy Vickers 209–22 for a persuasive account of the role Collatine's encomium to Lucrece's "sovereignty" plays in the etiology of Sextus's desire. See also Kahn 36.

39. According to Leonard Tennenhouse, rape transforms Lavinia into a metonymical representation of Rome's ruling elite: Chiron and Demetrius's dismemberment of Lavinia reproduces on her body the fragmentation of the aristocratic body of Rome (106–12). Tennenhouse's tendency to understand the theater as an instrument of monarchy perhaps leads him astray here: Lavinia is a figure for the aristocracy because she is associated with "Virginia"—a name that must, despite the resonance of the historical Virginia, stand for Elizabeth I (109). For other political readings of the rape of Lavinia, see Harris (esp. 390–97); Hadfield, "Tarquin's . . . Banishment"; Detmer-Goebel; and Ray.

40. Titus's "wresting" registers the way in which the translation of Lavinia's body into letters is already indistinguishable from a misinterpretation of those letters: "wrest" signifies not only invasive, violent twisting and turning but also the

hostile (mis)representation of language, the twisting and turning of signs. Recent critics have understood Lavinia's body as a textualized site of violence, but they mistakenly attribute that violence not to misrepresentation but to the condition of textuality per se. In a typically original and brilliant reading of *Titus* and literary allusion, Jonathan Goldberg asserts that Lavinia's "body is a text" (*Voice Terminal Echo,* 81)—and a violated text—because Shakespeare inscribes Lavinia within a tradition of literary precedents. Anticipating his later *Writing Matter,* Goldberg assumes that because all writing is "violence and violation" (82), the particular instrumental agent of writing is inconsequential. Mary Laughlin Fawcett similarly argues that Lavinia is a "'map of woe,' whom, like a map, we must learn to read" (265). But treating Lavinia's body as always already textual requires us to attribute the violence of Titus's "wresting" to writing itself. Critics who thus absolve Titus of the agency of textualization tend to argue that Lavinia's "mutilated body 'articulates' Titus's own suffering and victimization" (Green 322). But this is to see Lavinia as Titus's would have us see her. Lavinia's body articulates nothing; it speaks to Titus of his suffering only because, as we shall see, he imposes meaning on it. For a very subtle treatment of Shakespeare's relation to the violence of rape and writing, see Crewe, esp. 141–42.

41. Titus's suggestion that Lavinia commit suicide recalls Chiron's parting advice to the woman he has just raped and maimed: "An 'twere my cause, I should go hang myself" (2.4.9). This echo is only one of several analogies Shakespeare draws between Titus and the demonic others—Chiron, Demetrius, and Aaron—he claims have destroyed Roman culture.

42. Crewe argues that Lucrece does not, in fact, "successfully name Tarquin, but can only manage a repeated 'He, He—'" (148). But the repetition of "He, he" seems to me a kind of virtual speechlessness induced precisely by the wrenching act of naming Tarquin: "Here with a sigh as if her heart would break, / She throws forth Tarquin's name: 'He, he,' she says, / But more than 'he' her poor tongue could not speak" (1716–18). Lucrece "throws forth Tarquin's name," but can then say no more than "He, he": she can name the subject ("Tarquin" or "He"), but she cannot supply the predicate—"raped me."

43. Coppélia Kahn argues that in "giving Lucrece a tongue, Shakespeare perforce works *against* the patriarchal codes that, at the same time, he puts in her mouth" (28). Lucrece's interpretation of the Trojan War might serve as a paradigmatic example of the tension Kahn describes.

44. Kahn's Lucrece recovers her agency by authoring Roman history: "The poem ends with the rout of the Tarquins, carried out by Collatine and his kinsman but authorized by Lucrece's account of the rape and her suicide. Thus she as a woman plays a peculiarly heroic role in the foundation of the Roman republic" (42). Abigail Heald's Lucrece is more complex; see important forthcoming work.

45. Waith suggests that the Lucrece story is "relevant to *Titus Andronicus,* and may in turn have suggested the story of Virginia" (37).

46. The very movement in *Titus* from the identification of Lavinia and Lucrece

to Titus's fatal identification of Lavinia and Virginia suggests that Shakespeare was familiar with the relation between the two heroines in republican historiography.

47. When Appius "perceiv[es] the constancie of Icilius, and that the people were in a great mutine," he defers final judgement (Dii[v]) but awards Marcus temporary custody of Virginia. Icilius protests that he will guarantee Virginia's safety and appearance, and Appius relents.

48. Virginius, emboldened perhaps by the show of popular sentiment, confronts Appius: "I have betrouthed my doughter to Icilius & not to thee Appius. My care in bringyng her yp, was to marrie her, and not to be violated and defloured. . . . I cannot tell, whether the multitude here present, will supporte this enormitie, but I am sure the armed souldiors, and such as carrie armure will not suffer it" (Painter Diii[r])

49. Saturninus may be a tyrant, but he is no Appius: indeed, Bassianus's seizing of Lavinia as his property identifies him with Appius.

50. Aeneas's abandonment of Dido can be understood as necessary to the honorable fulfillment of his epic mission to found the new Troy, but Shakespeare's many references to the tragic conclusion of Dido and Aeneas's romance always take Dido's part. Consider, especially, the allusion in Hermia's great vow: "And by that fire which burned the Carthage queen / When the false Troyan under sail was seen, / By all the vows that ever men have broke / (In number more than ever women spoke), / In that same place thou hast appointed me / To-morrow truly will I meet with thee" (*A Midsummer Night's Dream* 1.1.173–78).

51. Shakespeare's Lucrece is obsessed with Sinon's treachery (1543–46). Anthony Brian Taylor has Lucius's number (see esp. 143–49).

52. Saturninus, Tamora, Aaron, Chiron, and Demetrius are undoubtedly villainous, but Titus's ritual slaughtering of Alarbus and his antipopulist handling of the imperial election are the positive conditions of Rome's disaster and his own family's tragedy.

53. Cf. the "election" of Lucius to the popular empowerment of Scilla—i.e., Sulla—in Thomas Lodge's *The Wounds of Civil War* (1589?):

> FLACCUS: If Scilla's virtue, courage, and device,
> If Scilla's friends and fortunes merit fame,
> None, then, but he should bear Dictator's name.
> POMPEY: What think you, citizens? Why stand ye mute?
> Shall Scilla be Dictator here in Rome?
> CITIZENS: By full consent, Scilla shall be Dictator.
> FLACCUS: Then in the name of Rome I here present
> The rods and axes into Scilla's hand,
> And fortunate prove Scilla our Dictator.
> (5.5.21–29)

Note that, in contrast to *Titus,* the citizens themselves acclaim Scilla dictator. Moreover, Lodge makes this popular acclamation necessary rather than supplemental to Scilla's rule: Scilla is referred to as dictator only after the citizens' "shall" (26) creates him dictator.

54. Jonathan Bate accepts "Marcus" as the proper designation for the first acclamation—though he clearly finds nothing sinister in Marcus's speaking for all of Rome, even at this point in the tragedy—but reassigns the second acclamation to "All Romans." Bate suggests that this second acclamation recalls *Richard III* 3.7 "where first Buckingham acclaims Richard, then 'ALL' respond" (274n). This is a very telling analogy: The second acclamation ("Amen" [231]) clearly belongs where all the quartos put it—in the mayor's mouth; the citizens invariably remain silent when they are asked to acclaim Richard king (see 3.7.1–41, 91–93).

55. Saturninus construes Titus's letter-writing campaign as both mad and savvy: Titus may fancifully address his chronicles of tyranny to the gods—"now he writes to heaven for redress. / See, here's to Jove, and this to Mercury" (4.4.13–14)—and shoot them toward the clouds, but the arrows, Saturninus realizes, "fly about the streets of Rome . . . blazoning our injustice everywhere" (4.4.17–19).

56. Titus's offer to represent the Clown—"by me thou shalt have justice at his hands"—recalls Marcus's earlier act of representation: "the people of Rome, / Whose friend in justice thou hast ever been, / Send thee by me, their tribune and their trust, / This palliament of white and spotless hue" (1.1.182–85).

57. Titus's yoking of letters and weapons literalizes the imaginative relation of writing and violence Shakespeare has been developing throughout the play. Consider, e.g., the encomium Marcus delivers to Titus "hands": "Which of your hands hath not defended Rome, / And reared aloft the bloody battle-axe, / Writing destruction on the enemy's castle?" (3.1.167–69). For a wonderful discussion of Shakespeare's deep punning on "hands," see Barber and Wheeler 140.

58. In the rest of this chapter, I use the phrase "illiterate audience" to designate those members of Shakespeare's audience who could neither read nor write. I do not, of course, mean to suggest that all playgoers were illiterate.

59. In *The Tragical History of Titus Andronicus,* Lavinia reveals her fate by "taking a wand between her stumps" and writing "The lustful sons of the proud Empress / Are doers of this hateful wickedness" (Waith 202). *The Ballad of Titus Andronicus* nearly replicates the prose history here: "For with a staff, without the help of hand, / She writ these words upon that plot of sand: / The lustful sons of the proud Empress / Are doers of this wickedness" (Waith 206).

60. Some of the play's finest recent critics have emphasized both its flashy literariness and its thematizing of literary authority (see, e.g., Goldberg, *Voice,* and Heather James 71–78).

61. In *Menaphon* (1589), Robert Greene expresses his contempt for uneducated "shifting companions, that . . . busie themselves with the indevors of Art, that could scarcelie latinize their necke-verse if they should have need; yet English Seneca read by candle light yeeldes manie good sentences, as Bloud is a beggaer, and so foorth: and if you intreate him faire in a frostie morning, he will affoord you whole Hamlets, I should say handfulls of tragical speaches" (10).

62. For a summary of Dover Wilson's argument and for recent defenses of his handling of 4.3.96–105, see Appendix E of Waith's edition of *Titus Andronicus*, 211–12.

63. Although the body of such a prayer was spoken in English, grace—depending on the one's religious leanings—might well begin and end with a little Latin. Thus, in Heywood's *How a man may chuse a good wife from a bad* (1602), Aminadab asks his friends to pause before a meal: "*Gloria deo,* sirs *proface,* / Attend me now whilst I say grace" (Gi[v]). After an endless enumeration of dishes that certainly seem to require some special divine blessing ("Cow-heels, chitterlings, tripes, and sowse . . . Sheephead and garlick, brawne and mustard"), Aminadab can still praise God: "Benidicanus domino." The assembled guests say "amen" and fall to their trenchers with unaccountable enthusiasm. Cf. William Habington's "To a Friend, Inviting him to a meeting upon promise": "Come therefore blest even in the Lollards zeale, / Who canst with conscience safe, 'fore hen and veale / Say grace in Latine; while I faintly sing / A Penitential verse in oyle and Ling" (25–28).

64. I quote here from the 1551 edition; the text went through dozens of editions in Shakespeare's lifetime.

65. We can now better appreciate the unwitting insight of the Clown's misunderstanding of Titus's question "can you deliver an oration to the Emperor with a grace?" (4.3.98). "Nay, truly sir, I could never say grace in all my life" (99): the Clown construes "grace" not as a modification of "deliver" but as a substantive; but, in fact, the original meaning of "oration" is "a prayer" (*OED* 1).

66. Heather James makes the same point about this "grimly proleptic" malapropism (70). James's passing remark is, to my knowledge, the only recent critical comment on the Clown episode. For an illuminating interpretation of the Clown's Christianity, see the important forthcoming work of J. K. Barret.

Chapter 4 "Caesar is turn'd to hear"

1. Unless otherwise noted, all quotations from Plutarch follow Thomas North's 1579 translation of Jacques Amyot's translation of the *Parallel Lives* (*Les vies des hommes illustres* [1559]). Exactly which edition of North Shakespeare read remains a matter of scholarly debate: both the first edition of 1579 and the revision of 1595 have their champions. I have closely compared all quoted passages with the corresponding passages in the 1595 edition.

2. "The Romans, who were in the grip of famine, chose Pompeius to oversee the corn supply and gave him twenty senators as assistants. . . . By stationing them . . . in the various provinces, he dealt with the problem, and soon filled Rome with plenty of grain, which raised his power and reputation to new heights" (Appian 78).

3. I quote here from Sir Arthur Gorges's 1614 translation of Lucan's *Bellum Civile* (1.284–99). Shakespeare may have read Marlowe's translation, first pub-

lished in 1600 but extant in manuscript many years before the first performance of *Caesar.* Marlowe's blank verse is far better than Gorges's rhymed couplets, but his version of Pompey's retirement from martial enterprises lacks Gorges's Lucanian verve:

> . . . Pompey was strook in years,
> And by long rest forgot to manage arms,
> And being popular sought by liberal gifts,
> To gain the light unstable commons' love,
> And joyed to heare his *Theatre's* applause;
> He lived secure boasting his former deeds,
> And thought his name sufficient to uphold him,
> Like to a tall oak in a fruitfull field,
> Bearing old spoils and conquerors' monuments . . .
> (103–11)

4. See Beacham 78–85 for the bases of these estimates and for a brief account of the building of the theater and its early history.

5. Nash suggests that Pompey constructed the temple in this fashion in order to thwart his rivals' efforts to marshal opposition to a permanent theater: because the rows of seats could be construed as steps to the temple, the entire building was dedicated not as a theater but as a religious structure (2:516).

6. After the rout, Pompey repaired to Egypt to regroup for a new offensive against Caesar's army, but members of Ptolemy's court murdered him in the hope of gaining Caesar's favor. It would be hard to imagine a more profound misunderstanding of *Romanitas,* in general, or of Caesar's character in particular: as soon as he was presented with Pompey's head, Caesar ordered the execution of the assassins.

7. See Fisher 178 and Platner 229–30. Caesar had just broken ground on a new Senate House—the *curia Iulia*—and it may be that he was preparing the *curia Hostilia* for new functions. See Nash 1:142–43.

8. North does better with an earlier mention of "le conclave" (Amyot 2:1058), which he translates as "chapter house" (North 679). The principal usage for "un conclave" in *A Dictionairie of the French and Englishe Tongues* (1611) is tantalizing: "a secret or private roome; and especially that (for it is seldome used but to expresse that) wherein the Cardinalls assemble about the election of a new Pope" (Cotgrave Tiv^{r}).

9. In a characteristically brilliant reading of the play, Jonathan Goldberg figures Caesar's murder as a "drama in Pompey's Theater" (*James* 164; see also 165); John Drakakis claims that Cassius's "metaphorical location in the play . . . is 'Pompey's Theater' . . . significantly, also, the place where Caesar's own death will be staged in accordance with the generic demands of *de cassibus* tragedy" (70).

10. On three occasions, the site of the fateful meeting of the Senate is identified as "the Senate House" (2.2.52, 59; 2.4.1); seven other passages refer to a meeting in "the Capitol" (2.1.201, 211; 2.4.10–11, 20, 26, 28; 3.1.12). According to Lizette An-

drews Fisher, "the Senate House" and "the Capitol" were, in Shakespeare's mind, interchangeable: "Shakespeare conceived of the Capitol as a *building* in which the meetings of the Senate took place" (178); in fact, the "Capitol of Roman antiquity was the temple of Jupiter Capitolinus on the Mons Tarpeius . . . [and] in a wider sense, the whole hill, including the temple and the citadel" (177). But the seeming interchangeability of the Senate House and the Capitol in *Caesar* might just as plausibly suggest that Shakespeare understood that "Senate House" designated a particular building within a larger area designated "the Capitol."

Most Elizabethan and Jacobean authors locate the assassination in the Capitol or the Senate House (see, e.g., Lodowick Lloyd, "Triumphs of Trophes," 57, and "Julius Caesars Death," 3–4; and E.L., *Romes Monarchie,* 13.1), but a few authors more precisely designate Pompey's court (Higgins, *Caius Iulius Caesar*, 336, 343, and 343; *The Tragedies of Caesar and Pompey, or Caesar's Revenge* [1592–96?], 3.6.80, 91, and 106; and Alexander, *The Tragedie of Iulius Caesar* [1607], 5.2.125–26).

11. If Pompey's Theater did not figure in the play at all, attaching much importance to Shakespeare's setting of the murder would be rather speculative. But Shakespeare clearly took very careful notice of North's references to Pompey's Theater and its "porches"; indeed, the passages in North are, to my knowledge, the only possible English source for Shakespeare's references to "Pompey's porch." Shakespeare was, moreover, the first English literary artist even to mention Pompey's Theatre or its portico. Finally, there is no ancient source for the clandestine meeting at Pompey's Theater. There is every reason, then, to treat Shakespeare's topography as highly deliberate.

12. Even the most topographically scrupulous reading of North would place the death scene in "one of the porches about the theatre, in the which there was a certain place full of seats for men to sit in" (1858).

13. It is equally true that some early modern antitheatricalists and hostile political authorities figured the theater as a breeding ground for conspiracies: the performance of a play, they claimed, offered plotters an opportunity to meet without arousing suspicion. Cassius's decision to plot the conspiracy in an *empty* theater is the first of many signs that Shakespeare resists this indictment of the theater.

14. To claim that Shakespeare's critique of Brutus's republicanism is radical rather than conservative is not to claim that Shakespeare endorsed democracy. Similarly, to claim that Shakespeare figures theatrical relations of power as democratic is not to claim that Shakespeare endorses democracy in the world outside the theater. In the epilogue to this book, I briefly address the relevance of Shakespeare's politics to recent criticism and to contemporary Anglo-American political culture.

15. Literate members of the audience, unless they were well educated enough to have read widely in Italian (see n. 17 below), would have been surprised, I think, by a treatment of Caesar's fall that assigned any weight to popular politics. The expectations of the illiterate are harder to guess, though the anonymous *The Tragedies of Caesar and Pompey, or Caesar's Revenge,* which focuses on aristocratic factionalism, may have been performed before 1599 (see Boas xiii).

16. Jan Blits neatly suggests the irony of this scene: "Our first glimpse of Caesar's Rome shows the tribunes, whose ancient office had been established to protect the people against the nobility's arrogance, now apparently forced to defend the Republic against the people themselves" (23; see also 27–28). We should note, however, that in the late Republic, the office of tribune was open to members of the senatorial class (see Appian 13).

Shakespeare certainly had the first scene of *Caesar* percolating in his mind when he conceived the first scene of *Coriolanus* (see p. 208 above). The real question, I think, is whether Shakespeare was already pondering a play about Coriolanus and the origins of European political representation when he wrote *Caesar*. Indeed, Shakespeare's interest in a play about Coriolanus may date from the very beginning of his career. In *Titus Andronicus* 4.4.62–68, Aemilius compares Lucius Andronicus, who is leading a Gothic army against Rome, to Coriolanus leading the Volscians to the gates of Rome. Perhaps the young Shakespeare had simply heard of this event, but unlike Caesar, Brutus, Lucrece, and Virginia, Coriolanus was hardly a star in Elizabethan literary culture: Shakespeare's play of 1608 is the first English drama even to mention him, and he merits only the most cursory treatment in a handful of Tudor poems. I suspect, then, that Shakespeare had already read North's *Life of Caius Martius Coriolanus* or Painter's prose narrative in *The palace of pleasure* (1566) before he wrote *Titus*.

17. Plutarch's Rome, of course, is not the only Rome, but I have not found a single ancient author who claims that Caesar, who had indeed been a great favorite of the plebeian class during long stretches of his career, was popular at the time of his death. In the postclassical world, however, an alternative tradition emerged, especially in Italy. Demonizing Brutus and Cassius was common enough: Dante puts them in Satan's gnashing maw, a pride of place they share only with Judas. But Machiavelli is perhaps the first Renaissance author to suggest that Caesar still enjoyed widespread popular support in 44 B.C.: "But of all the dangers that can arise after the execution of a conspiracy, there is none more certain nor more to be feared than when the people have loved the prince you have killed; against this danger conspirators have no remedy whatsoever and can never secure themselves. As an example there is Caesar, whose death was avenged by the Roman people, who loved him. The reason why the conspirators, subsequently driven out of Rome, were all killed at various times in various places stems from this fact" (*Discourses,* 142). Machiavelli's popular Caesar may be a kind of back-formation, a way of explaining how Antony, Octavian, and Lepidus overcame Brutus and Cassius. Machiavelli may have found the suggestion for such an explanation in Appian: "The people *missed* him more than they had anyone else; they went round hunting for his killers, gave him a funeral in the middle of the forum, built a temple on the site of the pyre, and still sacrifice to him as a god" (3; emphasis added). In any event, a popular Caesar is nowhere to be found in English literature before 1599. This is not, of course, to say that Caesar is always represented negatively; "popularity" was not, after all, a universally prized quality in early modern

England. The English Caesar is rather protean: poets condemned him as a pagan (Richard Lloyd 81), a colonialist oppressor of England (Chester 17; Holme 3.153; Sharrock; 1.13–14), and a tyrannical enemy of his own people (Chester 137). But several English poets celebrated James I's ascension by styling him "Englands Caesar" (Petowe 4; see Rowlands, "Aue Caesar," 11–12).

18. Plutarch records a third serious affront to the people. When the whole assembly of the Senate, the consuls, and the praetors approach Caesar to inform him of new honors granted him by the Senate, he disdains to rise from his special seat in the marketplace: "But he, sitting still in his majesty, disdaining to rise up unto them when they came in, as if they had bene private men. . . . This did not onely offend the Senate but the common people also" (791).

19. See Chapman for an interesting attempt to put the first scene in the context of early modern politics and shoemaking.

20. Cassius posits the same relation between the people and Caesar's power: "What trash is Rome, / What rubbish, and what offal, when it serves / For the base matter to illuminate / So vile a thing as Caesar!" (1.3.108–11). Being a feather on Caesar's wing sounds quite a bit better than being the offal that kindles his spotlight, but in both metaphors the people empower Caesar. Cf. Coriolanus's scathing rejection of popularity: "He that depends / Upon your favours, swims with fins of lead" (1.1.177–78).

21. Wayne Rebhorn, for example, argues that we should "see [*Caesar*] as depicting a struggle among aristocrats—senators—aimed at preventing one of their number from transcending his place and destroying the system in which they all ruled as a class. In this perspective, then, the assassination is not regicide, but an attempt to restore the status quo ante" (78–79).

22. John Kayser and Ronald Lettieri argue that the tribunes "fear an alliance of the plebs with Caesar . . . would undermine the precarious balances of the old mixed regime" (208).

23. Flavius's street-sweeping program resonates with Brutus's recollection of his family's role in the founding of the Republic: "My ancestors did from the streets of Rome / The Tarquin drive, when he was call'd a king" (2.1.53–54). When he invokes Lucius Junius Brutus and his other forbears, Brutus is contemplating ridding Rome of Caesar, but his words closely echo Flavius's determination to "drive away the vulgar from the streets" (1.1.70). Perhaps republican streets can brook neither kings nor people.

Flavius and Marullus's treatment of their constituents is not, I want to insist, a corruption of the tribunate. As I argue in Chapter 5, the original purpose of the tribunate, according to Shakespeare's critique of republican history, is the suppression of popular participation in public life: thus, in *Coriolanus,* Sicinius and Brutus, the first tribunes, reproduce the very condition of their offices—that is, the containment of popular disorder—when they prevent the people from running "about the streets / Crying confusion" (4.6.29–30) and confine them instead to their homes (see 2.1–10) and to "singing in their shops and going / About their functions friendly" (4.6.8–9). When Shakespeare turned his attention to the origins of the tribunate, he fashioned Sicinius and Brutus as the forbears of Flavius and Marullus. *Coriolanus* is a prequel—a dreadful but handy term—to *Julius Caesar.*

24. Barbara Parker's reading of this scene adopts the tribunes' attitude toward the people: thus, the "populace . . . is insolently contemptuous of the law: although it is 'a laboring day,' they have discarded their prescribed working attire and, literally and symbolically, their 'rule' (1.1.3, 7), taking an unauthorized holiday to witness Caesar's triumph" (36). Blits takes a similar view (24–25). But Shakespeare has cooked the chronology of his sources to make Caesar's triumph coincide with an ancient holiday. Several critics have argued that both the people and Caesar are perverting the Lupercalia, but as Marullus himself acknowledges, the day the people have chosen to celebrate Caesar's triumph is, in fact, a holiday (1.1.67).

25. Cassius's political philosophy lies too far outside the principal concerns of this chapter and this book to merit lengthy discussion. I would only suggest that one could plausibly argue that Cassius—despite his failure to express any concern for the common people, despite, indeed, his contempt for the plebeians—believes that the *mere* mortality shared by all human beings makes intolerable the subjection of any person to another: "I cannot tell what you and other men, / Think of this life," he tells Brutus, "but for my single self, / I had as lief not be as live to be / In awe of such a thing as I myself" (1.2.90–95). Cassius may be haughty, but he offers here the most radically egalitarian justification for opposing Caesar's bid for supremacy.

26. Cf. Pechter 67–68.

27. Some critics suggest that the overheard shouts and Casca's report create confusion (see, e.g., Danson 54). Casca himself is very clear about Antony's tentative attempt to crown Caesar and the people's reaction: the people rejoice *because* Caesar refuses the crown. Shakespeare never gives the audience any reason to doubt Casca's interpretation of this event.

28. Casca reports that "Marullus and Flavius, for pulling scarfs off Caesar's images, are put to silence" (1.2.282–83), and Caesar's treatment of the Senate is certainly proprietary and high-handed, but many of Shakespeare's sources detail a vast and systematic assault on republican institutions and liberties.

29. T. S. Dorsch, the editor of the Arden *Caesar,* suggests that Caesar reorients himself because he is, as we learn at 1.2.210, deaf in one ear (9 n.9). But this seems, on two counts, an unlikely reading of what Shakespeare has in mind for the staging of this moment. Caesar has no trouble hearing the Soothsayer, for he immediately, before anyone else reacts, responds "Ha! Who calls?" Moreover, Caesar has been speaking with Calphurnia, Casca, and Antony, so he might be supposed to have his back to "the press."

30. Althusser gives his fullest explanation of "the Other Subject" in a discussion of religious ideology:

> [I]t . . . emerges that the interpellation of individuals as subjects presupposes the "existence" of a Unique and central Other Subject, in whose Name the religious ideology interpellates all individuals as subjects.
>
> All this is clearly written in what is rightly called the Scriptures. "And it came to pass at that time that God the Lord (Yahweh) spoke to Moses in the cloud. And the Lord cried to Moses, 'Moses!' And Moses replied 'It is (really) I! I am Moses thy servant, speak and I shall listen!' And the Lord spoke to Moses and said to him, '*I am that I am.*'" (134)

In the Rome of *Julius Caesar,* the people play the role of Yahweh.

31. In the previous scene, the Soothsayer tells Portia that he is going to the Capitol to beseech Caesar "to befriend himself" and to warn him again of perils of the ides of March (2.4.30). The Soothsayer never really gets a chance to issue his warning because Artemidorus is so busy issuing his (see 3.1.1–12).

32. John Higgins's Caesar in *A Mirror for Magistrates* pays scant attention to the letter because he thinks it *does not* concern him personally:

> There met me by the way a *Romayne* good,
> Presenting mee a scrole of every name:
> And all their whole device that sought my bloud,
> That presently would execute the same.
> But I supposde that for some suit hee came,
> I heedelesse bare this scrole in my left hand,
> And other more, till leasure, left unscand,
> Which in my pocket afterwards they fand.
> (361–68)

33. In *The Description of England,* which appeared in the 1587 edition of Holinshed's *Chronicles,* William Harrison identifies "four sorts" of people in England: "gentlemen, citizens or burgesses, yeomen, and artificers or labourers" (94). Harrison, then, would not have considered the cobbler of 1.1 a "citizen," but the category of citizen was much looser and more capacious in practice than Harrison's neat division would suggest.

34. The bequests in Caesar's will, for example, clearly identify the plebeians as citizens: "To every Roman citizen he gives, / To every several man, seventy-five drachmas" (3.2.242–43). Antony is reading the document to an audience of "plebeians," and he makes it clear that they are the beneficiaries of these bequests: "'Tis good you know not that you are his heirs" (3.2.147; see also 3.2.237–40). In his English histories, by contrast, Shakespeare tends to distinguish citizens from "the people": thus, for example, a messenger warns Henry VI that "Jack Cade hath almost gotten London Bridge; / The citizens fly and forsake their houses; / The rascal people . . . Join with the traitor" (*2HVI* 4.4.48–51).

35. Cassius later enlists Cinna in the plan to fabricate public opinion:

> Good Cinna, take this paper,
> And look you lay it in the praetor's chair
> Where Brutus may but find it; and throw this
> In at his windows; set this up with wax
> Upon old Brutus' statue: all this done,
> Repair to Pompey's porch, where you shall find us.
> (1.3.142–47)

Cassius issues these instructions to Cinna in Casca's presence; thus, we know that these three conspirators consciously act to fabricate public opinion, and we might even surmise that the necessity of forging such notes reveals that they recognize the absence of any widespread public desire for Caesar's death.

36. Alexander Leggatt claims that Cassius's forgeries are not, in effect, forgeries: "The letter-writing campaign is designed to give Brutus the impression that he is surrounded by the approval and expectations of his fellow Romans. As the eagerness of the other conspirators to have him join shows, this is not just an illusion" (143). But the unsigned letters Cassius forges are not designed to convince Brutus that the five men who will soon appear at his door want him to conspire against Caesar; they are designed to create the illusion that Rome wants Brutus to dispatch Caesar.

37. Bourdieu, whose reflexive models are closely related to Althusser's construction of the recursive reproduction of the conditions of production, seems to me to mistake ideology for "the real": what he describes as the truth of political representation is, in fact, an imaginative rendering of the real relation of the representative to the represented and of the real relation of the represented to the representative. In other words, the passage I quote from Bourdieu is both a theory of political representation and an instantiation of the ideology of political representation. For a fuller critique of Bourdieu, see Chapter 3 above (and see also Arnold, "New Historicism," 35–38).

38. Many critics see Brutus as a fine expression of republicanism (see, e.g., Worden 43; MacCallum 233–34, 249; Bloom 92–94). I am not disputing this claim; rather, I am arguing that Shakespeare thinks being a "good" republican means disregarding or misconstruing the general will. For a consideration of Brutus as crypto-monarchist, see Blits 52–53.

39. The topos of the monarch's double nature would seem to be another way to bridge this gap: the execution of Mary might grieve Elizabeth Tudor, for example, but Elizabeth I had to protect the general interests of the realm. In *Basilicon Doron,* James I frequently suggests that the godly ruler makes "the general good" his particular good:

> A good King . . . emploieth all his studie and paines, to procure and maintaine, by the making and execution of good Lawes, the well-fare and peace of his people; and as their naturall father and kindly Master, thinketh his

> greatest contentment standeth in their prosperitie, and his greatest suretie in having their hearts, subjecting his owne private affections and appetites to the weale and standing of his Subjects, ever thinking the common interesse his chiefest particular: where by the contrarie, an usurping Tyran . . . frame[s] the common-weale ever to advance his particular. (20)

James acknowledges a divergence—even a conflict—between the ruler's "private affections and appetites" and the "weale . . . of his Subjects" even as he identifies "the common interesse" as the ruler's "chiefest particular." James's account of the "good King," I suggest, depends on some notion of the monarch's double nature. On the differences between "the king's two bodies" and the representative's two persons, see Chapter 2.

40. See *PPE* 2:90 for the particulars of the bill.

41. In a very fine study of the debate over monopolies in Elizabeth's late Parliaments, David Harris Sacks discusses Martin's performance and points, in particular, to the disjunction between Martin's own circumstances and the downtrodden "poor subjects" he impersonates here (see Sacks 98).

42. As we shall see when we turn to *Coriolanus,* Shakespeare's tribunes typically put their own words into the mouths of the people for whom they speak.

43. My sense of the relation between the imaginary and the ideological owes a very considerable debt both to Althusser and to Stephen Greenblatt's *Hamlet in Purgatory.*

44. Steve Sohmer contends that *Julius Caesar* was the first play performed at the Globe.

45. As I argue in Chapter 1, representative presence begins as a legal fiction that neither requires nor seeks genuine belief but eventually becomes an ideological article of faith. The vulnerability of this myth in the face of sensory experience helps explain why MPs were so anxious to prevent members of the public from entering the House of Commons.

46. Hakewill is, I think, entirely sincere; his record in the Commons, over many Parliaments, is one of consistent concern for the poor. But Hakewill contributes as much—perhaps more—to the development of an ideology that disempowers the people as does a man like Bacon, whose deployment of the myth of representative presence is entirely cynical. I do not discount the possibility that Brutus is, at his best, the Hakewill of Rome.

47. The two clerks of the House of Commons and the serjeant-at-arms were also present in St. Stephen's, but all three were bound by very strict secrecy oaths (see John Hooker 24–27).

48. This entire chapter is indebted to Berger's *Imaginary Audition,* a brilliant book and a wonderfully subtle account of the relation between the theater audience and performance.

49. I borrow the phrase "subjected sovereign" from Foucault (221).

50. Wilson argues that the people actually want Caesar to become king: "Cae-

sar's authoritarian paternalism deflects the vox populi towards the institution of monarchy by the invigilation of the people's private desires" ("'Is this a holiday?'" 40). Cf. Blits 1. But the play offers no evidence that the people want Caesar to be king. The Third Plebeian does, to be sure, exclaim "O royal Caesar" in the Forum, but Caesar is, of course, safely dead by then and, in any event, none of the other plebeians take up this cry.

51. Shakespeare has departed from his sources in order to make the people's refusal to crown Caesar unanimous and unambiguous. In both Appian and Plutarch, the crowd's reception of Antony's attempt to crown Caesar is at least somewhat mixed:

> *Antony* . . . ranne up to *Caesars* seate, and set a crowne on his head, at the which sight few rejoicing, and more lamenting, *Caesar* threw it off. *Antony* set it on againe, but *Caesar* rejected it. The people stoode silent, looking what end this woulde have, and when they saw *Caesar* utterly refuse it, they rejoyced, and highly commended him therefore. (Appian 14)
>
> *Antonius*. . . . came to *Caesar,* and presented him a Diademe wreathed about with laurel. Whereuppon there rose a certaine crie of rejoycing, not very great, done onely by a few, appointed for the purpose. But when *Caesar* refused the Diademe, then all the people together made an outcrie of joy. Then *Antonius* offering it him againe, there was a second shoute of joy, but yet of a few. But when *Caesar* refused it againe the second time, then all the whole people shouted. (North 792)

Transforming Appian's mixture of booing and applauding and Plutarch's succession of weak shouts and great cries of joy into three general shouts, Shakespeare leaves no doubt about the people's desire that Caesar not become king and Brutus's willingness to reject the unanimous will of the people.

52. For conservative critics, the direct expression and exercise of the popular will must always be constructed as anarchy: thus, Leggatt, commenting on this moment, speaks of "the *mob's* offstage shout" (143). Figuring a gathering of people the audience cannot even see as a "mob" is rather revealing; moreover, even Casca, who loathes the people, never says anything to suggest that they are a mob. The people of act 1 can only be construed as a mob if one construes any resistance to any authority and any deviation from tradition as mob rule. Cf. Worden 5.

53. References to the bad breath of the humbler ranks of early modern playgoers are too legion to list here, but consider that Dekker alone makes four such remarks in his *Non-dramatic* works (2:53, 2:203, 4:96, 4:194).

54. Richard Burt assumes that the plebeians are "mistaken" in their belief that "Caesar does not want the crown" (118), but it is just as plausible to claim that the plebeians enjoy Caesar's refusal of the crown in part because they know he wants it but denies himself in deference to them.

55. Critical discussions of the importance of holiday in *Julius Caesar* tend to

focus on the very ancient festival of Lupercalia: "Amid a wealth of speculative hypotheses, the most satisfactory explanation for the ceremony is perhaps that it was a rite of fertility magic combined with purification" (Liebler 77; see also Scullard 76–78); "but whatever the origins, by the time of Caesar the annual ceremony had become a spectacular public sight, with the young men running through the streets playfully and licentiously" (Scullard 78). Some critics see Brutus exploiting the holiday's roots in purgation and foundation myths (see, e.g., Liebler 63–64); others see Caesar refashioning the holiday into a personal, dynastic cult ritual (see, e.g., Drakakis 68 and Wilson, "'Is this a holiday?'" 52). Both arguments are certainly plausible, and Plutarch's *Lives* of Caesar, Antony, Brutus, and Romulus would have provided Shakespeare with the kind of detailed information about the Lupercalia these arguments assume. But it seems to me that the people's celebration of Caesar's triumph over Pompey overwhelms the Lupercalia.

56. Blits, by contrast, claims that "*Caesar* shows [that] . . . Rome's new Caesarian regime. . . . stems from a free and prosperous people's voluntary surrender of their liberty rather than from a tyrant's violent seizure of power through revolution" (1). This is a simplified version of Plutarch's account of Caesarism: "the Romanes inclining to *Caesar's* prosperity, and taking the bit in the mouth, supposing that to be ruled by one man alone, it would be a good meane for them to take breth a little, after so many troubles and miseries as they had abidden in these civil wars; they chose him perpetuall Dictator. This was plaine tyranny, for to this absolute power of Dictator they added this, never to be afraid to be deposed" (789). More to the point, Blits's argument mistakes Shakespeare's Caesar for the "historical" Caesar: in Shakespeare's *fiction* about the historical Caesar, we never see the people surrender their liberty. As I have already suggested, Shakespeare never represents Caesar's oppression of the people's freedoms, and, indeed, the conspirators themselves speak only of Caesar's affronts to the patrician class.

57. For a critique of "theatrical power," see the Introduction.

58. For polemical purposes, I am elaborating an opposition between a monarchic theater and a popular theater, but, of course, the conditions of theatrical production were shaped by popular audiences and the crown, "citizens" and lords, censors and municipal authorities, and so on.

59. Quoted in Chambers 4:256.

60. The first record of the commercial—and thus "common"—connotation of "patron" comes to us from the public theater: Volpone, disguised as the mountebank doctor, addresses his audience of potential customers as "most noble gentlemen and my worthy patrons!" (2.2.34). For the mountebank, as for any participant in the marketplace, nobility is a function of worthiness, and worthiness is exactly commensurate with the size of one's pocketbook.

61. Thomas Dekker, *The Gull's Hornbook* (1609) in *Non-Dramatic Works* 2:246–7.

62. The most familiar analogy between the theater and the courtroom figures jurors as an audience and audience members as a jury. And, in fact, Renaissance

playwrights themselves typically styled their audiences as judges: according to Beaumont, Blackfriars is a court in which "a thousand men in judgment sit" (qtd. in Gurr 22). For other identifications of audiences as juridical bodies, see Gurr 41, 45, 86, and 153.

63. When Jack—the "Second Boy" of the Induction—finally speaks the Prologue, he proudly insists that his author's Muse "shunes . . . popular applause / Or foamy praise, that drops from common jaws,"; but even before a select audience at Blackfriars, Jonson's Muse is subjected to a collective power:

> The garland that she weares, their hands must twine,
> Who can both censure, understand, define
> What merit is: Then cast those piercing rays,
> Round as a crown, instead of honour'd bays,
> About his *poesie;* which, (he knows) affords
> Words above action: matter above words.

64. I haven't come across a Renaissance playwright who was too proud to profit from "car-men" and tinkers who could afford the price of admission, but quite a few railed against having to submit their plays to the aesthetic judgment of "stinkards."

65. Massinger attributed the success *The Roman Actor* (1629) enjoyed at Blackfriars to "the suffrage of some learned and judicious gentlemen" (Epistle Dedicatory).

66. The day after the opening at the Hope theater, *Bartholomew Fair* was presented to James I. A special prologue written for the occasion and addressed directly to the king did not, needless to say, appeal for James's suffrage.

67. The prologue added to the 1641 revival of Chapman's *Bussy D'Ambois* asks the audience to encourage a particular actor in his first assay of the lead role: "As Richard [III] he was liked, nor do we fear / In personating D'Ambois he'll appear / To faint, or go less, so your *free consent,* / As heretofore, give him encouragement" (23–26; emphasis added).

68. From the beginning of Charles I's reign to the closing of the theaters in 1642, playwrights increasingly solicited "votes" from their audiences: see, e.g., the prologues to Brome, *The Novella* (19); Shirley, *The Imposture* (2); Denham, *The Sophy* (3); and Glapthrone, *Wit in a Constable* (26); see also the epilogues to *Wit in a Constable* (14); Glapthorne, *The ladies priviledge* (9); and Shirley, *St. Patrick for Ireland* (11).

69. James refused to license the Canons of 1606 for publication because one Canon held that a ruler who had been established by the popular overthrow of the previous ruler could still command the obedience of his or her (new) subjects (see Kenyon 11n).

70. The king's admonition was delivered to the Commons by the Earl of Salisbury (Kenyon 12).

71. Cf. Hall's description of Jack Cade's rebels: "the kentishmen be impacient

in wronges disdayning of to much oppression, and ever desirous of new chaung, and new fangelness" (219).

72. Wilson somewhat improbably constructs this moment as the fulfillment of Caesar's master plan: "Caesar turns politics into theatre as 'the tag-rag people . . . clap and hiss him, as they use to do the players'. . . . He is the Carnival King, a Lord of Misrule" ("'Is this a holiday?'" 37).

73. See Gruenfelder 55. I discuss early modern parliamentary elections at length in Chapter 5 above.

74. The decorum that now rules theater audiences—yelling out a remark during a performance would mark one out as virtually insane—renders this analogy obsolete, but we must remember that early modern audiences, especially at amphitheaters, rendered judgments during performances (see Gurr 44–48) and occasionally compelled playing companies to bring a play to a premature close or to stop the scheduled performance and put on a different play (Gurr 46 and 255n48).

75. I depart here from the Oxford Shakespeare, where the speech tags for Peto and Bardolph appear as, respectively, Harvey and Russell.

76. Cf. Greenblatt's discussion in *Shakespearean Negotiations* (41–43) of Hal's plan to "falsify men's hopes" (*1HIV* 1.2.208).

77. We find no such calculation in Plutarch's various accounts of the debate over Antony's fate (976 and 1063).

78. In Plutarch, the conspirators, "having their swords bloudy in their handes," go directly to the marketplace (1063).

79. René Girard points out that "the bloody mess" the conspirators make violates "the well-known ritual principle that sacrificers should avoid unnecessary contact with the blood of their victim" (219) but does not address Brutus's notion that the way to obscure the "bloody mess" is with a neat display of blood.

80. Cf. Blits's analysis of Brutus's strategy of emphasizing his personal sacrifice: "What men give up, not what they gain, shows their disinterestedness" (51).

81. Girard argues that Brutus's hope that "immediately after the murder, the conspiracy will dissolve into the restored unanimity of the Roman people, *its* sacrificial unanimity" is "sound" sacrificial thinking (212). I am arguing, by contrast, that Brutus's sacrifice is defective precisely because it seeks unanimity *after* the sacrificial act has already been performed.

82. Pompey's statue was eventually moved to the theater itself, but at the time of Caesar's death it stood in the *curia* (see Appian 19 and 21; North 1061).

83. In his often penetrating reading of the play, John Drakakis argues that "it is characteristic of all the conspirators that they oppose 'truth' to a distinctly theatrical falsity" (69). I am not sure we can comfortably apply this generalization to Cassius's vision of staged reenactments of Caesar's death. Cassius certainly misconceives theater, but, by his lights, a play figuring the conspirators as "the men that gave their country liberty" would be a true representation.

84. Consider, in this context, Ludovico Castelvetro's remarks on the difficulties

that attend a comedy about "the rise of a private person to a throne, of which some instances are recorded in history":

> I reply first that a plot of this kind is appropriate to tragedy and not to comedy . . . and secondly that performances of it would give little pleasure in republics and even less in monarchies: in republics because men who love freedom and are determined to preserve it cannot desire that their fellow-citizens witness the example of a private person usurping a throne, and in monarchies because being jealous of their royal state kings guard against setting before the common people and private citizens examples of actions that might awaken in them the desire to overthrow the monarchy and establish a new order. (152)

85. Richard Burt, by contrast, argues that Brutus and Cassius imagine that by controlling the theater they can control history: "The conspirators assume that the representation of Caesar's assassination inscribes a political effect within it: as often as the act is reproduced, the actors will be called the same thing. It follows for them that control of representation equals political control" (115).

86. Burt rightly claims that the conspirators "stag[e] the assassination as an act of legitimate and necessary sacrificial violence," but his suggestion that "the conspirators [*sic*] use of theatrical metaphors . . . connects their act with the act on Shakespeare's stage" (114) misses the ways in which Shakespearean theatricality persistently undermines the conspirators' appropriations of theatricality.

87. Many critics dismiss Brutus's performance in the Forum as a failure (see, e.g., Girard 68 and Halpern 80–81). Antony's triumph in the Forum may reveal certain defects in Brutus's oration, but Brutus's performance is hardly a failure: when he finishes, after all, the people cheer him wildly and exalt him as the new Caesar. In Plutarch's Rome, where the people envy and hate Caesar, Brutus's success would not be very remarkable, but in Shakespeare's Rome, he is addressing an audience of outraged plebeians who loved Caesar.

88. Antony begins by answering Brutus's indictment of Caesar's self-serving ambition:

> He hath brought many captives home to Rome,
> Whose ransoms did the general coffers fill
> Did this in Caesar seem ambitious?
> When that the poor have cried, Caesar hath wept.
> Ambition should be made of sterner stuff.
> . . . .
> You all did see that on the Lupercal
> I thrice presented him a kingly crown,
> Which he did thrice refuse. Was this ambition?
> (3.2.89–93, 96–98)

Antony's Caesar wants nothing for himself, and the selfless concern for the people that animated his life, Antony later claims, finds its fulfillment in a will that, far from seeking to establish a family dynasty, confers much of Caesar's private property on the public: "he hath left you all his walks, / His private arbors, and new-planted orchards, / On this side Tiber; he hath left them you, / And to your heirs forever: common pleasures, / To walk abroad and recreate yourselves" (3.2.249–53).

89. Antony's skeptical analysis of Brutus's motives, his recollections of Caesar's selflessness, and his claim that the dictator's will names the people as heirs certainly move his audience (3.2.79–147): the Fourth Plebeian calls the conspirators "traitors" (155), and the Second Plebeian charges them as "murderers" (157). When the Second Plebeian decides that the conspirators are murderers rather than sacrificers, we can see that Brutus's enterprise is collapsing, but I would argue that Antony's postmortem is quite distinctly the coup de grâce (or coup de theatre): there is no talk of revenge—and revenge is what Antony seeks—until the people see the body.

90. Before he arrives in the Forum, Antony has already seen the affective power of Caesar's corpse. While he is privately mourning that "bleeding piece of earth" (3.2.254), Octavian's servant enters to deliver a message but the sight of Caesar's body stops up his speech: "[Octavian] is coming, / And bid me say to you by word of mouth— / O Caesar!" (3.2.279–80). Perhaps as he registers the servant's reaction, Antony conceives his Forum strategy. For a fine study of the dramatic and rhetorical use Antony makes of Caesar's "vesture," see McGowan.

91. Wilson argues provocatively that "Antony's anatomy lesson. . . . turns desire in the mob to authoritarian ends" ("'Is this a holiday?'" 40), but Antony's goals in the Forum seem to me more modest.

92. The forming of the ring marks a distinct shift in Antony's oration. Antony has been speaking from the rostrum, but now he asks permission to descend: "You will compel me then to read the will? / Then make a ring about the corpse of Caesar, / And let me show you him that made the will. / Shall I descend? and will you give me leave" (3.2.159–62). "All" respond "come down" (163). This is Antony's Caesarean moment: the future master of half the world asks the people's leave to descend. Once Antony is among the people, the forming of the ring becomes, for several moments, the center of our attention:

FIFTH PLEBEIAN: A ring! Stand round.
FIRST PLEBEIAN: Stand from the hearse, stand from the body.
SECOND PLEBEIAN: Room for noble Antony, most noble Antony!
ANTONY: Nay, press not so upon me; stand farre off.
ALL: Stand back! Room! Bear back:
(3.2.162–66)

93. Perhaps Antony's reference to the people's regenerative tears—see *OED* 6 for this meaning of "gracious"—and Brutus's earlier image of Caesar "bleed[ing] in sport" owe something—something quite complicated—to Thomas Nashe's account in *Pierce Penilesse* (1592) of Talbot's death scene *Henry VI, Part I*: "How

would it have joyed brave *Talbot* (the terror of the French) to thinke that after he had lyne two hundred yeares in his Tombe, hee should triumphe again on the Stage, and have his bones newe embalmed with the teares of ten thousand spectators . . . who, in the Tragedian that represents his person, imagine they behold him fresh bleeding!" (qtd. in Gurr 135).

Chapter 5 "Worshipful mutineers"

1. According to a list of bailiffs appended to *The Black Book* in the seventeenth century, Brookes served as bailiff in 1565, but I have not found a record of his election.

2. The oath of office sworn by all principal burgesses included a secrecy article: "Such things as youe are and shallbe callid to counsaill of towching the said Borough ye shall kepe secrete and not reveale to any person out of the counsaill house or place where the same shalbe by youe and others of the principall burgesses spoken of resolued and determyned" (*BB* 1).

3. Fisher's account of the barn incident alone fills nearly one hundred pages, and this local history beautifully exemplifies the complex diffusion and fragmentation of power in early modern England. John Ray mortgaged the leases for the tithes for Myton to Brookes and soon thereafter charged Brookes with "fraudulent dealing." The Warwick town corporation ordered Brookes to restore the tithes to Ray; he refused. Ray appealed to the Court of Requests, which ordered Brookes to "redeliver to Ray all such writings leaces & bonds as he had of Ray and pay to the said Raye iiij^{xxli} for the corne & hey of the said tithes which the said brookes had taken the two yeres before the decree and that he should deliver quiet possession therof to the said Raye and that Ray should pay to the said Brookes so much mony as by covenant or specialty was due to Brookes" (*BB* 227). Brookes refused. Between Brookes's defiance of the order from the Court of Requests and the end of the story, an astonishing array of institutions and individuals became involved in the dispute over the Myton tithes: the Star Chamber, the sheriff and bailiff of Warwick, Sir Fulke Greville (the poet's father), the jurist Sir John Dyer, the lord chief justice of England, and the earl of Warwick. Richard Brookes was not a powerful landowner and the Myton tithes were not an enormously important or valuable asset. But in Elizabethan England, a relatively humble subject's relationship to great powers was in many ways remarkably personal, and there were many authorities to enlist in one's cause: as soon as Brookes's enemies lodged a complaint in one court, Brookes made a counterclaim in another; as soon as Brookes's enemies appealed to one key local personage, Brookes's wrote a letter to another. So it was that the struggle for the tithes dragged on for two years.

4. John Fisher was one of the leading citizens of Warwick for nearly half a century: he was twice elected bailiff, served as deputy recorder and town clerk, and sat for the borough in the House of Commons (see *BB* xxvii–xxix).

5. An account was read before the assistants, who judged it to be incomplete (*BB* 56).

6. The principle that "what touches all must be approved by all" originates in private law: the Justinian Code of 531 stipulates that a decision affecting the interests of all members of a corporation or joint venture must be approved by all (*"ut quod omnes similiter tangit, ab omnibus comprobetur"*). The principle became one of the foundations of medieval accounts of church governance that limited papal power, and then migrated to constitutional theory and political discourse. For the relation between religious and secular elaborations of *quod omnes tangit, ab omnibus approbari debet,* see Tierney, "Some Recent Works" and "Medieval Canon Law"; for a general introduction to the political uses of the principle, see Monahan 97–111.

7. In 1603, the principal burgesses of Sandwich became so angry with "the mutinous opposition . . . of the meaner sort" in municipal elections that they eliminated their voting rights (Hirst 207).

8. Richard Wilson remarks that "representation is in flux in [*Coriolanus*] as it was in Shakespearean Warwickshire, where notables like the Grevilles warned the gentry that 'You are plebeians / If they be senators; and they are no less'" ("Against the Grain," 127). I don't know which of the Grevilles or what events Wilson is referring to here, but Coriolanus's dire warning to the Senate about the dangers posed by the people and their tribunes does capture Fisher's anxiety:

> . . . You are plebeians
> If they be senators, and they are no less
> When, both your voices blended, the great'st taste
> Most palates theirs. . . .
> . . . .
> . . . . and my soul aches
> To know, when two authorities are up,
> Neither supreme, how soon confusion
> May enter 'twixt the gap of both and take
> The one by th' other.
> (3.1.104–7, 111–15)

9. The members of the common council had hoped not only to retain their full strength but to increase their privileges: "the said company do request that they may have free speche at all tyme & tymes in the counsell house . . . [and] that they may yerely bee callid & made pryvy to the burgesses acomptes as heretofore they have been acustomyd" (*BB* 109).

10. The "libels" also charged that Fisher had promoted a "newe order to be taken w[tn] this towne, that none of the poore Lame olde nor Impotent people shall goe abrode in the towne to gather the good and charytable devocion of good people" (*BB* 324).

11. Any lines we draw in a reconstruction of Warwick's town politics will be

somewhat shaky: in 1576, John Green, one of Brookes's closest associates in the struggles of 1579, had been on the other side of the barn door and had to dodge Brookes's arrows. Thomas Powell, to take another example, aided Brookes but was himself one of the four trustees of the charitable trust established by Thomas Oken.

12. The local oligarchs objected to a proposal to meet in the Shire Hall: the "Balif & Burgesses thought that the Shire Hall was no convenyent place for conferrence, bicause yt was a place very publicke, and where all maner of persons both of the towne and countrey woold thrust uppon them"; instead, they proposed a venue "where they might be more quiet & private" (BB 331). Lucy agreed, but Edward Broughton insisted on the Shire Hall (331–32). In this respect, the burgesses of Warwick were like the officers in most Elizabethan towns. In Shakespeare's Stratford, for example, the town corporation agreed in 1593 to expel any alderman or burgess who discussed the proceedings of the corporation outside the council chamber (Fox 13).

13. There seems to have been some real fire at the bottom of Brookes's smoke: at the very least, the trustees had played rather loosely with their responsibilities. See *BB* 339–41 for several inconsistencies in the administration of the trusts.

14. Neale documents a remarkable range of electoral franchises among Elizabethan boroughs: in King's Lynn, twelve aldermen and eighteen common councilors selected the MP; in Shrewsbury, by contrast, well over 400 inhabitants participated in the 1584 parliamentary elections (*HC* 237; see also 166).

15. The burgesses' protests about carpetbaggers are complicated by the fact that in every parliamentary election they allowed the earl of Warwick to appoint one burgess; they did not, it goes without saying, demand that the great earl choose only Warwick residents.

16. Like his father, the poet-courtier Fulke Greville was a powerful player in Warwickshire and intervened frequently in the municipal politics of both Warwick and Stratford. See Kemp 394 and Fox 123. He also served as a Warwickshire representative in 1586, 1589, 1593, 1597, 1601, and 1621 and as the recorder of Warwick and Stratford from 1608 to 1628.

17. In 1614, the freeholders of Norfolk sent a petition to the House of Commons to complain that when three thousand voters arrived at Norwich Castle, which had been publicly designated the site of the parliamentary election, the sheriff's deputy informed them that the election was in fact taking place at "a place called Swaffor, being about twenty miles of bad way, remote from the same castle at Norwich, at which place of Swaffor the high sheriff was present and went to election of the knights of the shire with some few freeholders being brought thither for the same purpose two young knights were chosen before eight of the clock the same forenoon" (*PP 1614* 46–47). This crude but often effective strategy was not uncommon.

18. Kishlansky underestimates the extent to which Neale himself recognized the social character of the election process: Neale, for example, warns that catego-

ries such as "a right to vote" are not helpful in trying to understand early modern elections, and he presents many case histories in which local magnates worked behind the scenes to stave off potential election contests. See, especially, *HC* 28–29.

19. Derek Hirst, the chief target of Kishlansky's revisionism, counts only thirteen contested elections in 1604 and fifteen in 1614 (13, 216–222).

20. Kishlansky demonstrates that many boroughs were happy to have great patrons choose burgesses, in part because they paid their parliamentary expenses (33–34).

21. The Privy Council intervened, for a range of reasons, in many election contests: for its activities in 1601, for example, see *APC* 32:247–48, 271, 342.

22. Qtd. in Gruenfelder 54. All subsequent excerpts from the borough's election report are quoted from this article.

23. According to the *OED*, the principal contemporary meaning of "to seduce" was "to persuade . . . a servant . . . to desert his allegiance or service."

24. The town officers' reports of this and other unruly elections clearly belong to a particular Renaissance genre of official speech: the discourse of misrule. Cf., e.g., the Gloucester election report with the Privy Council's report on the apprentice riots during the end of Elizabeth I's reign: "on Midsommor evening or Midsommer night or about that time to renew their lewd assembli togeather by cullour of the tyme for some bad mischevious intenciuon, to the disturbance and breache of her Majesty's Peace, and committing some outrage" (*APC* 22:550). I suggest that in the eyes of the Gloucester's officers, elections were potentially a "cullour of the time" for disorder; or, rather, the elections did away with the need for a cloak and simply institutionalized disorder.

25. The elections that I have discussed here were unusual, though hardly unique, because they were publicly contested. But like fairs and holidays, even the quietest elections promised a release from the quotidian: spectacle, food and drink, and the experience of community. Elections were among the very few occasions for gathering together in large groups: only certain fairs and religious activities involved more people on a regular basis; war and riot were infrequent causes of mass gatherings. Moreover, unlike elections in highly developed modern democratic societies, sixteenth- and seventeenth-century elections were highly public affairs. The entire electorate assembled in the same place, at the same time, and voters openly exercised their franchises. The scene of empowerment was quite similar to a theatrical event: candidates very often stood on scaffolds, and the electorate, arrayed around the platform like an audience in an inn yard, almost always expressed their preferences by applauding or shouting at the appropriate moment or by calling out a candidate's name. The modern technology of representational politics has radically diminished the communal aspect of representational politics: citizens vote at different locations within one community; votes are cast at different times over a period of many hours or even days; the secret ballot occludes participation in the elective process; the absentee ballot undermines the communal experience of election. Not surprisingly, these technologies have subtly altered the ideology

and experience of representational politics. Certainly, the isolation of the individual voter and the long delay between an individual's act of voting and the moment at which a successful candidate is recognized—usually by the electronic media—as the elected representative contribute to the electorate's disaffection and sense of powerlessness.

26. Victor Gourevitch translates this passage from "Des députés ou représentants" as follows: "The English people thinks it is free; it is greatly mistaken, it is free only during the election of Members of Parliament; as soon as they are elected, it is enslaved; it is nothing. The use it makes of its freedom during the brief moments it has it fully warrants its losing it" (114).

27. Cf. Patterson's critique of Kishlansky (*SPV* 128–29).

28. See, e.g., MacCallum 470; Huffman (any page will do); and Pettet 38. O. J. Campbell and A. P. Rossiter represent a more moderate view according to which Shakespeare does not revile the common people but thinks them incapable of participation in politics (see Campbell 162 and Rossiter 243).

29. The scholars I mention here have broken very important new ground, but T. J. B. Spencer's seminal early study of Shakespeare's Roman plays demonstrates that there has long been an alternative to the antipopulist reading of *Coriolanus:* "there are many elements in the representation of the mob which are not unflattering, not offensive. In the battle of wits with their social superiors they generally come off honourably if not victoriously" (44).

30. Both Patterson and Barton read the conduct of the people in the first scene as not only a departure from earlier Renaissance representations of the people but also a breakthrough in Shakespeare's own attitude towards the commons: *Coriolanus* "countered [the] skeptical analysis, in *Julius Caesar,* of republicanism in decay" (*SPV* 11); "this play is unique in the canon for the tolerance and respect it accords an urban citizenry" (Barton 117). Cf. Baldo 20–25.

31. For my use of the term "Whig," see Introduction, n. 5, above. Among Whiggish critics of *Coriolanus,* there is considerable diversity: Leah Marcus (203), Shannon Miller, and R. B. Parker (33–43) read *Coriolanus* against an unmistakably Whiggish interpretation of Jacobean political history; Lars Engle develops an economic Whiggism according to which *Coriolanus* endorses "the consensual Roman market" (180) as "a site of hope" for the plebeians," a place "where their voices, like their labor and their wares, are needed" (194); and Anne Barton locates *Coriolanus* within a Whiggish intellectual history.

32. In his analysis of economy in *Coriolanus,* Richard Wilson argues that the First Citizen can discredit the fable because he "grasps . . . the functional relationship between poverty and plenty" ("Against the Grain," 112). Wilson is certainly no Whig: his Shakespeare is a materialistic enemy of the people. I admire the forcefulness of Wilson's unapologetic attack on Shakespeare, but, obviously enough, I think that it is wrong-headed.

33. Scholars have long recognized the Midlands revolts as a context for *Coriolanus:* noting that Plutarch makes "the sore oppression of usurers" the catalyst of

rebellion, Reuben Brower argues that Shakespeare's representation of "the famine as the principal cause for the plebeians' complaints . . . is almost certainly traceable to the unrest in England, more especially to the Midlands revolt of 1607" (36). See also Pettet, Burke, and Spencer, who notes that the revolts reached Shakespeare's own Warwickshire (47). Brian Vickers dismisses any connection between Jacobean unrest and *Coriolanus* (427). For a recent history of the Midlands crisis, see Martin 161–215. See Haigh 131–35 on the ruling elite's misuse of grain during Elizabeth's reign.

34. On Elizabethan and Jacobean analogies between the institutions of Roman republicanism and England's mixed estate, see Introduction, n. 10, above.

35. Patterson, relying too heavily on Thomas Smith's taxonomy of the four estates, underestimates the humbleness of many Elizabethan and Jacobean voters: at the Hertford election of 1624, tanners, tailors, locksmiths, glovers, coopers, gardeners, butchers, and a barber cast votes (Hirst 78); in Essex in 1604, Lord Maynard was disgusted that "fellows without shirts challenge[d] as good a voice as [his]" (qtd. in Kishlansky 61); according to Star Chamber records relating to the Chichester election in 1586, "the meanest and basest sort of the people" voted for James Colbrand (*HC* 256); and in Rutland in 1601, James Harrington's supporters included "'cottiers of cottages,' some of whom were so mean that they worked for twopence a day at threshing and fourpence at other daily work" (*HC* 130). Derek Hirst estimates that the "House of Commons was, in terms of numbers, directly representative of perhaps about one-third of the adult male population" (157). Not all historians agree with Hirst, and one-sixth of the adult male population may be a better, more conservative estimate.

36. For an interesting critique of Patterson, see Cefalu.

37. See George for a short but stinging assessment of the tribunes.

38. Vivian Thomas argues that because the other group of citizens have "forced a constitutional innovation," they are more effective than the citizens we see (185).

39. Anne Barton, by contrast, argues that Shakespeare "looked attentively at the young Roman republic delineated by Plutarch and by Livy, and chose to emphasize what was hopeful, communal and progressive in it" (129). It is impossible to square this reading with Shakespeare's treatment of source materials: Livy's and Plutarch's tribunes are not without blemishes, but they are hardly the scheming antipopulists we find in Shakespeare's play.

40. Michael Platt, like many other critics, argues that "the belly fable . . . pacifies the city" (73). It is the tribunate that pacifies the city. The Whig emphasis on Menenius's Belly Fable is misplaced in many respects. To begin with, the plebeian demystification of paternalistic ideology signals a radicalism novel to neither Shakespeare nor early modern England. The Belly Fable and its ideology are, in fact, pretty fat and familiar targets. For example, Francis Trigge's *The humble petition of two sisters* (1604), a polemic against enclosures, insists that greedy landowners are rich enough and increase their own wealth only at the expense of the poor: "If Inclosers would be content with the auncient apparrell, and houses and dyet of

their ancestors, as they were ashamed of their lands, they neede never raise rents, nor improve their lands" (C4[r]). Moreover, in Shakespeare's earlier—indeed earliest—plays, the poor generally know they are being sold a bill of goods when the rich tell them that their society is just and natural and that they, in fact, are really better off than gentlemen and gentlewomen. (See, e.g., the discussion between Henry and Williams in *Henry V* and, especially, Cade's rebels in *2HVI,* who know that their own deprivation is a function of elite comfort.)

41. In a compelling essay on *Julius Caesar,* John Drakakis notes in passing that the plebeians in *Coriolanus* are "simultaneously empowered and disempowered" (72). See, also, Spotswood, especially 64–65.

42. Cecil's and Coriolanus's anxieties reveal a subtle dimension to Habermas's seemingly banal observation that "whatever was submitted to the judgment of the public gained *Publizitat* [publicity]" (26). Both Cecil and Coriolanus conflate public *discussion* of politics and popular *participation* in governance.

43. The plebeians do indeed get some corn "gratis" (3.1.45), but they themselves have already defined this corn as a mere "superfluity" of aristocratic wealth (1.1.14–16).

44. Capital is the "wealth . . . stocke . . . principall or chief substance" that enables enterprise (Randle Cotgrave, *A dictionairie of the French and English tongues* [1611]).

45. Reproaching the tribunes (and himself), Menenius confirms Coriolanus's indictment of the patricians: "We loved him, but like beasts and cowardly nobles / Gave way unto your clusters, who did hoot / Him out o'th' city" (4.6.129–31).

46. See Bristol for a very astute analysis of the tensions between Coriolanus and the senators.

47. Patterson, by contrast, argues that the perfecting of the republic enables "the popular will, institutionalized by creation of the tribunate, to intervene in the affairs of state" (*Fables,* 119).

48. Plutarch devotes several pages to the patricians' furious reaction to Coriolanus's banishment. We see no evidence of this in Shakespeare's Rome: even Menenius acknowledges that Coriolanus's absence has brought peace to the city. In act 4, scene 3, a Roman in the Volscian camp reports that "There hath been in Rome strange insurrections, the people against the senators, patricians, and nobles" (14); "the nobles receive so to heart the banishment of that worthy Coriolanus, that they are in a ripe aptness to take all power from the people, and to pluck from them their tribunes for ever" (19–20). This report is, of course, worth remarking, but we never see any other sign of this patrician plot against the tribunes.

49. Perhaps when Brutus, reacting to the intelligence that Coriolanus is marching on Rome, exclaims "Would half my wealth / Would buy this for a lie" (4.6.167–68), we should ponder the source of that wealth.

50. Shakespeare's inspiration for the whipping of the slave does, however, derive from Plutarch's *Life of Coriolanus.* After describing the meeting of Coriolanus and Aufidius in Antium, Plutarch shifts his scene back to Rome. Plutarch begins to discuss the bad blood between "nobilitie" and "commonalitie" in the wake of

Coriolanus's banishment (trans. North 539), but he then launches a long digression: the senate has become preoccupied with reports of a man who dreamed that Jupiter told him to warn the senators that he would punish them for "caus[ing] a verie vile lewd dancer to go before the procession" (539). Upon investigation, the senators discover that the "lewd dancer" was, in fact, a slave whose master had had him "whip[ed] . . . up and down the market place"; "whipping him cruelly," the master's other bondmen "did so martyr the poor wretch that for the cruel smart and pain he felt he turned and writhed his body in a strange and pitiful sort" (540). The slave's writhing has been mistaken for suggestive dancing. The senators consult the "priests," who conclude that Jupiter is angry not because a procession has been desecrated but because a slave has been mistreated: "For the Romans at that time did use their bondmen very gently, because they themselves did labor with their own hands and lived with them and among them" (540).

51. Shakespeare's characterization of the tribunes may have been inspired by Livy, who represents Sicinius as a provocateur (2.3–2.6). However, while Livy's tribunes may be ambitious, they certainly never plot and scheme behind the people's backs as Shakespeare's do. Ambitious representatives are, of course, a traditional problem in representational politics. Yet a case can be made that the representative who preserves his or her own interests—even by selling out to great ones—necessarily serves the interests of those he or she represents. In *Coriolanus,* for example, the tribunes recognize that if Coriolanus attains the consulship their "office may, / During his power, go sleep" (2.1.219–20). The tribunes then plot Coriolanus's "sure destruction" (2.1.240) for entirely selfish reasons: "so it must fall out / To him," warns Brutus, "or our authority's for an end" (241–42). Perhaps Brutus and Sicinius protect the people's interests by protecting their own: there is, after all, every reason to believe that Coriolanus would abolish the people's political rights and the tribunate.

The tribunes' effort to save their very offices—and thereby the people's political power—is a sort of primal instantiation of what Pierre Bourdieu theorizes as the enabling structure of representational politics. According to Bourdieu, we can usefully compare "political life to a theater" once we recognize the "truly symbolic relation between . . . *representatives* providing a *representation* and the agents, actions and situations that are represented. The congruence between . . . representative and the represented . . . results . . . from the homology between the structure of the political field and the structure of the world represented, between the class struggle and the sublimated form of this struggle which is played out in the political field" (182). The homology between the political and social fields effectively neutralizes the self-interest of the representative class: "by pursuing the satisfaction of the specific interests imposed on them by competition within the field," political representatives "satisfy in addition the interests of those who delegate them: the struggles of the representatives can be described as a political mimesis of the struggles of the groups and classes whose champions they claim to be" (*Language,* 182). Thus, even though representatives merely *claim* to be the people's champions, they protect the people's interests in spite of themselves (cf. ibid., 169). Political representation works, in other words, because the political is a representation of "the real." But why are the fields homologous? Here, again, we must assume the tautological economy of recursivity and representation: there is a homology between the fields because representation works; and because there is a homology, representation works. For Bourdieu, representativeness is organic rather than artificial; the political field necessarily represents the social field because the two fields are derived from each other. The political field mirrors the social field because the represented group and the representing agents have recursively produced each other in the first place—they always already represent each other. The ideology of political representation is, in this respect, continuous with the theory of recursivity.

52. Many critics have remarked that the tribunes have almost as much contempt for the people as does their enemy Coriolanus: see Martindale and Martindale 150; Rabkin 206; and Brian Vickers 415.

Epilogue. Losing Power, Losing Oneself

Epigraph: Kierkegaard 189.

1. Popular participation in consular elections in fact predated the creation of the tribunate, but Shakespeare makes the election of Coriolanus an aspect of the new order.

2. Lars Engle, by contrast, argues that the "consensual market" (180) is free and promising: "For the plebeians . . . the marketplace is a site of hope, where their voices, like their labor and their wares are needed" (194).

3. Jonathan Dollimore develops a provocative Brechtian reading of the citizens' debate about their power: "disunity prevents [the oppressed] from actualising their potential power, while the cause of that disunity is the very oppression which power, if actualised, could overcome" (223).

4. Consider another moment when the people seem to be puppets rather than "natural persons." After the people resolve to revoke the consulship, Brutus and Sicinius send them to the Capitol to announce their decision to the senators. The tribunes themselves would prefer not to deliver this vexing news to the patricians: "To th' Capitol, come," Sicinius advises Brutus after the people have left the stage, "We will be there before the stream o'th' people; / And this shall seem, as partly 'tis, their own, / Which we have goaded onward" (2.3.260–63). The decision to revoke the vote will both seem to be and be the people's own decision. Sicinius is, of course, acting in bad faith, but his theory that the people both own and only seem to own the decision is entirely consistent with a political ideology in which the people are always alienated from their own voices and power. See Danson 144–45 for a very keen reading of "voice" in *Coriolanus.*

5. Patterson, *Shakespeare and the Popular Voice,* 131; cf. Engle 178.

6. This book ends where it began—with inspiration from Stephen Greenblatt's remarkable work.

Works Cited

An A.B.C. wyth a Cathechisme, that is to saye: an instruction to be learned of everye chylde before he be brought to be confyrmed of thee Byshoppe. Sette forth by the kinges Majestye. Whereunto is also ioyned the Letany and Suffrages with certayne Graces to be sayde at dyner and supper. London, 1551.

Adelman, Janet. "Feeding, Dependency, and Aggression in *Coriolanus.*" In *Representing Shakespeare: New Psychoanalytic Essays,* ed. Murray M. Schwartz and Coppélia Kahn, 129–49. Baltimore: Johns Hopkins University Press, 1980.

Agnew, Jean-Christophe. *Worlds Apart: The Market and the Theater in Anglo-American Thought, 1550–1750.* Cambridge: Cambridge University Press, 1986.

Alexander, William, earl of Stirling. *Recreations with the Muses.* London, 1637.

———. *The Tragedie of Iulius Caesar.* London, 1607.

Alsop, J. D. "Parliament and Taxation." In *The Parliaments of Elizabethan England,* ed. D. M. Dean and N. L. Jones, 91–116. Oxford: Basil Blackwell, 1990.

Althusser, Louis. "Ideology and the Ideological State Apparatuses (Notes Towards an Investigation)." In id., *Lenin and Philosophy, and Other Essays,* trans. Ben Brewster. London: New Left Books, 1971.

Appian, of Alexandria. *Shakespeare's Appian: A Selection from the Tudor Translation of Appian's "Civil Wars."* Edited by Ernest Schanzer. Liverpool: Liverpool University Press, 1956.

Arnold, Oliver. "Der New Historicism und die Ideologie der Zustimmung." In *Historismus am Ende des 20. Jahrhunderts: Eine internationale Diskussion,* ed. Gunter Scholtz, 23–39. Berlin: Akademie-Verlag, 1997.

Austin, J. L. *How to Do Things with Words.* Cambridge, Mass.: Harvard University Press, 1975.

———. *Philosophical Papers.* Edited by J. O. Urmson and G. J. Warnock. Oxford: Clarendon Press, 1979.

Aylmer, John. *An Harborowe for Faithfull and Trewe Subjectes agaynst the late blowne Blaste, concerninge the governmnt of Wemen.* Strasbourg [i.e. London], 1559.

Baldo, Jonathan. *The Unmasking of Drama: Contested Representation in Shakespeare's Tragedies.* Detroit: Wayne State University Press, 1996.

Barber, C. L., and Richard P. Wheeler. *The Whole Journey: Shakespeare's Power of Development.* Berkeley: University of California Press, 1986.

Barish, Jonas. *The Antitheatrical Prejudice.* Berkeley: University of California Press, 1981.

Barkan, Leonard. *The Gods Made Flesh: Metamorphosis and the Pursuit of Paganism.* New Haven: Yale University Press, 1986.

Barrow, Henry. *The Writings of Henry Barrow, 1590–1591.* Edited by Leland H. Carlson. Elizabethan Nonconformist Texts, vol. 5. London: George Allen & Unwin, 1966.

Barton, Anne. "Livy, Machiavelli, and Shakespeare's *Coriolanus.*" *Shakespeare Survey* 38 (1985): 115–29.

Bate, Jonathan. See under Shakespeare, *Titus Andronicus.*

Beacham, Richard. *The Roman Theater and Its Audience.* Cambridge, Mass.: Harvard University Press, 1992.

Bentley, Gerald Eades. *Shakespeare: A Biographical Handbook.* New Haven: Yale University Press, 1961. Cited as *WS.*

Bernthal, Craig. A. "Jack Cade's Legal Carnival." *Studies in English Literature, 1500–1900* 42 (2002): 259–74.

Berger, Harry, Jr. *Imaginary Audition: Shakespeare on Stage and Page.* Berkeley: University of California Press, 1989.

Blague, Thomas. *A schole of wise Conceytes, Wherin as every Conceyte hath wit, so the most have much mirth, Set forth in common places by order of the Alphabet.* London, 1569.

Blits, Jan H. *The End of the Ancient Republic: Essays on "Julius Caesar."* Durham, N.C.: Carolina Academic Press, 1982.

Bloom, Allan David. With Harry V. Jaffa. *Shakespeare's Politics.* New York: Basic Books, 1964.

Boas, Frederick S., ed. *The Tragedy of Caesar's Revenge.* 1607. Oxford: Oxford University Press, 1911.

Boose, Lynda E. "Scolding Brides and Bridling Scolds: Taming the Woman's Unruly Member." *Shakespeare Quarterly* 42 (1991): 179–213.

Booth, Stephen. "The Shakespearean Actor as Kamikaze Pilot." *Shakespeare Quarterly* 36 (1985): 553–70.

Bourdieu, Pierre. *In Other Words: Essays Towards a Reflexive Sociology.* Translated by Matthew Adamson. Stanford: Stanford University Press, 1990.

———. *Language and Symbolic Power.* Edited by John B. Thompson. Translated by Gino Raymond and Matthew Adamson. Cambridge, Mass.: Harvard University Press, 1991.

———. *Outline of a Theory of Practice.* Translated by Richard Nice. Cambridge: Cambridge University Press, 1977.

Bowyer, Robert. *The Parliamentary Diary of Robert Bowyer, 1606–1607.* Edited by David Harris Willson. Minneapolis: University of Minnesota Press, 1931.

Brinklow, Henry. *The complaynt of Roderyck Mors, somtyme a gray fryre, unto the parliament howse of Ingland his natural cuntry for the redresse of certen wicked lawes, evel customs a[n]d cruell decreys.* Strasbourg, 1542.

Bristol, Michael D. "Lenten Butchery: Legitimation Crisis in *Coriolanus.*" In *Shakespeare Reproduced: The Text in History and Ideology,* ed. Jean E. Howard and Marion F. O'Connor, 207–24. New York: Methuen, 1987.

Brockman, B. A., ed. *Shakespeare: "Coriolanus." A Casebook.* London: Macmillan Press, 1977.

Brome, Richard. *The Novella.* In *The Dramatic Works of Richard Brome.*, vol. 1. Edited by R. H. Shepherd. London: J. Pearson, 1873.

Brower, Reuben. *Hero and Saint: Shakespeare and the Graeco-Roman Heroic Tradition.* New York: Oxford University Press, 1971.

Bullough, Geoffrey, ed. *Narrative and Dramatic Sources of Shakespeare.* 8 vols. New York: Columbia University Press, 1957–75.

Burke, Kenneth. "*Coriolanus* and the Delights of Faction." In *Language as Symbolic Action.* Berkeley: University of California Press, 1966.

Burt, Richard A. "'A Dangerous Rome': Shakespeare's *Julius Caesar* and the Discursive Determinism of Cultural Politics." In *Contending Kingdoms,* ed. Marie-Rose Logan and Peter L. Rudnytsky, 109–30. Detroit: Wayne State University Press, 1991.

Burt, Richard A., and John Michael Archer, eds. *Enclosure Acts: Sexuality, Property, and Culture in Early Modern England.* Ithaca, N.Y.: Cornell University Press, 1994.

Butt, Ronald. *A History of Parliament: The Middle Ages.* London: Constable, 1989.

Cairncross, Andrew S. See under Shakespeare, *King Henry the Sixth: Part Two.*

Caldwell, Ellen C. "Jack Cade and Shakespeare's *Henry VI, Part 2.*" *Studies in Philology* 92 (1995): 18–79.

Campbell, Oscar James. *Shakespeare's Satire.* London: Oxford University Press, 1943.

Carroll, William C. "'The Nursery of Beggary': Enclosure, Vagrancy, and Sedition in the Tudor-Stuart Period." In Richard A. Burt and John Michael Archer, eds. *Enclosure Acts: Sexuality, Property, and Culture in Early Modern England,* 34–47. Ithaca, N.Y.: Cornell University Press, 1994.

Cartelli, Thomas. "Jack Cade in the Garden: Class Consciousness and Class Conflict in *2 Henry VI.*" In Richard A. Burt and John Michael Archer, eds. *Enclosure Acts: Sexuality, Property, and Culture in Early Modern England,* 48–67. Ithaca, N.Y.: Cornell University Press, 1994.

Castelvetro, Ludovico. *Castelvetro on the Art of Poetry.* Edited and translated by Andrew Bongiorno. Binghamton, N.Y.: Center for Medieval and Renaissance Texts and Studies, 1984.

Cefalu, Paul. "'The End of Absolutism': Shakespeare's *Coriolanus* and the Consensual Nature of the Early Modern State." *Renaissance Forum: An Electronic Journal of Early Modern Literary and Historical Studies* 4 (2000).

Chamberlain, John. *The Chamberlain Letters: A Selection of the Letters of John Chamberlain Concerning Life in England from 1597 to 1626.* Edited by Elizabeth McClure Thomson. New York: Putnam, 1965.

Chambers, E. K. *The Elizabethan Stage.* 4 vols. Oxford: Oxford University Press, 1923.

Chapman, Alison A. "Whose St. Crispin's Day Is It? Shoemaking, Holiday Making, and the Politics of Memory in Early Modern England." *Renaissance Quarterly* 54 (2001): 1467–94.

Chapman, George. *Bussy D'Ambois: A tragedie.* 1607. 2nd ed. London, 1641.

Chester, Robert. *The Strange Birth, honourable coronation, and most unhappie Death of famous Arthur King of Brytaine. Loves martyr.* London, 1601. In *The English Poetry Full-Text Database.* CD-ROM. Cambridge: Chadwyck-Healey, 1992.

Chrimes, S. B. "The Constitutional Ideas of Dr. John Cowell." *English Historical Review* 64 (1949): 461–87.

Clarke, M. V. *Medieval Representation and Consent.* London: Longmans, Green, 1936.

Clopper, Lawrence M., ed. *Records of the Early English Drama: Chester.* Toronto: University of Toronto Press, 1979.

Cohen, Walter. "Political Criticism of Shakespeare." In *Shakespeare Reproduced: The Text in History and Ideology,* ed. Jean E. Howard and Marion F. O'Connor, 18–46. New York: Methuen, 1987.

Cook, Ann Jennalie. *The Privileged Playgoers of Shakespeare's London.* Princeton: Princeton University Press, 1981.

Cotgrave, Randle. *A dictionairie of the French and English tongues.* 1611. Facsimile edn., ed. William S. Woods. Columbia: University of South Carolina Press, 1950.

Crewe, Jonathan. *Trials of Authorship: Anterior Forms and Poetic Reconstruction from Wyatt to Shakespeare.* Berkeley: University of California Press, 1990.

Cromwell, Thomas. *Certain Statutes and Precedents* (1587). In William Lambarde, *Notes on the procedures and privileges of the House of Commons* (1584), ed. Paul L. Ward, 90–94. London: H.M. Stationery Office, 1977.

Daniel, Samuel. *The Civil Wars.* Edited by Laurence Michel. New Haven: Yale University Press, 1958.

Danson, Lawrence. *Tragic Alphabet: Shakespeare's Drama of Language.* New Haven: Yale University Press, 1974.

Davidson, Clifford. "*Coriolanus:* A Study in Political Dislocation." In *Shakespeare Studies IV,* ed. J. Leeds Barroll, 263–74. Dubuque, Iowa: William C. Brown, 1968.

Dean, D. M. "Public or Private? London, Leather and Legislation in Elizabethan England." *Historical Journal* 31 (1988): 525–48.

Dean, D. M., and N. L. Jones. "Introduction: Representation, Ideology and Action in the Elizabethan Parliaments." In *The Parliaments of Elizabethan England,* ed. D. M. Dean and N. L. Jones. Oxford: Basil Blackwell, 1990.

Dee, John. *To the honorable Assemblie of the* COMMONS *in the present Parlament.* London, 1604.

Dekker, Thomas. *Non-Dramatic Works.* Edited by Alexander B. Grosart. 5 vols. New York: Russell & Russell, 1963.

Denham, John. *The Sophy.* London, 1642.

Detmer-Goebel, Emily. "The Need for Lavinia's Voice: *Titus Andronicus* and the Telling of Rape." *Shakespeare Studies* 29 (2001): 75–92.

D'Ewes, Simonds. *The Journals of all the Parliaments during the Reign of Queen Elizabeth, both of the House of Lords and House of Commons.* 1682. Facsimile ed. Shannon, Ire.: Irish University Press, 1973. Cited as D'Ewes.

Dobson, R. B. *The Peasants' Revolt of 1381.* New York: St Martin's Press, 1970.

Dollimore, Jonathan. *Radical Tragedy: Religion, Ideology and Power in the Drama of Shakespeare and His Contemporaries.* 1984. 2nd ed. New York: Harvester Wheatsheaf, 1989.

Dollimore, Jonathan, and Alan Sinfield, eds. *Political Shakespeare: New Essays in Cultural Materialism.* Ithaca, N.Y.: Cornell University Press, 1985.

Drakakis, John. "'Fashion it thus': *Julius Caesar* and the Politics of Theatrical Representation." *Shakespeare Survey* 44 (1992): 65–73.

Dyer, Sir James. *Reports from the Lost Notebooks of Sir James Dyer.* Edited by J. H. Baker. 2 vols. London: Selden Society, 1994.

E.L. *Romes Monarchie.* London, 1596.

Elton, G. R. *"The Body of the Whole Realm": Parliament and Representation in Medieval and Tudor England.* Charlottesville: University Press of Virginia for the Jamestown Foundation of the Commonwealth of Virginia, 1969.

———. "Parliament." In *The Reign of Elizabeth I,* ed. Christopher Haigh, 79–100. Athens: University of Georgia Press, 1987.

———. *The Parliament of England, 1559–1581.* Cambridge: Cambridge University Press, 1986.

———. "The Points of Contact: I. Parliament." *Transactions of the Royal Historical Society* 24 (1974): 183–200.

———, ed. *The Tudor Constitution: Documents and Commentary.* 1960. Reprint. Cambridge: Cambridge University Press, 1982.

Engle, Lars. *Shakespearean Pragmatism: Market of His Time.* Chicago: University of Chicago Press, 1993.

Fabyan, Robert. *The New Chronicles of England and France.* 1516. Reprint. Edited by H. Ellis. 2 vols. London, 1809.

Fawcett, Mary Laughlin. "Arms/Words/Tears: Language and the Body in *Titus Andronicus.*" *English Literary History* 50 (1983): 261–77.

Field, John, and Thomas Wilcox. *An Admonition to the Parliament.* London, 1572.

Fisher, Lizette Andrews. "Shakespeare and the Capitol." *Modern Language Notes* 23 (1907): 177–82.

Fletcher, John. *The Dramatic Works in the Beaumont and Fletcher Canon.* 10 vols. Edited by Fredson Bowers. Cambridge: Cambridge University Press, 1966–96.

———. *The Humorous Lieutenant.* 1619. In id., *Dramatic Works,* vol. 5.

———. *The Loyal Subject.* 1618. In id., *Dramatic Works,* vol. 5.

Fortescue, Sir John. *On the Laws and Governance of England.* Edited by Shelley Lockwood. New York: Cambridge University Press, 1997.

Foster, Elizabeth Read, ed. *Proceedings in Parliament, 1610.* 2 vols. New Haven: Yale University Press, 1966. Cited as *PP 1610.*

Foucault, Michel. *Language, Counter-Memory, Practice: Selected Essays and Interviews.* Translated by Donald F. Bouchard and Sherry Simon. Edited by Donald F. Bouchard. Ithaca, N.Y.: Cornell University Press, 1977.

Fox, Levi, ed. *Minutes and Accounts of the Corporation of Stratford-upon-Avon and Other Records.* Vol. 5. Hertford, Eng.: Stephen Austin and Sons, 1990.

Frey, David L. *The First Tetralogy: Shakespeare's Scrutiny of the Tudor Myth: A Dramatic Exploration of Divine Providence.* The Hague: Mouton, 1976.

Fried, Michael. *Absorption and Theatricality: Painting and Beholder in the Age of Diderot.* Chicago: University of Chicago Press, 1980.

Gadamer, Hans-Georg. *Truth and Method.* 1960. Translated by Garrett Barden and John Cumming. New York: Crossroad, 1988.

George, David. "The Tribunes' Envy: *Coriolanus,* I.I.245–260." *Notes and Queries* 50 (2003): 56–57.

Girard, René. *A Theater of Envy: William Shakespeare.* New York: Oxford University Press, 1991.

Glapthorne, Henry. *The Ladies Priviledge.* 1640. In id., *Plays and Poems,* vol. 2.

———. *The Plays and Poems of Henry Glapthorne.* 2 vols. Edited by J. Pearson. London, 1873.

———. *Wit in a Constable.* 1640. In id., *Plays and Poems,* vol. 1.

Goldberg, Jonathan. *James I and the Politics of Literature.* 1983. Reprint. Stanford: Stanford University Press, 1989.

———. *Voice Terminal Echo: Postmodernism and English Renaissance Texts.* London: Methuen, 1986.

———. *Writing Matter: From the Hands of the English Renaissance.* Stanford: Stanford University Press, 1990.

Gorges, Arthur. *Pharsalia, containing the Civill Warres betweene Caesar and Pompey, written in Latine heroicall verse. Translated into English verse by Sir Arthur Gorges.* London, 1614.

Grafton, Richard. *A Chronicle at Large and Meere History of the Affayres of England and Kinges of the Same.* 1569. Reprint. Edited by H. Ellis. 2 vols. London, 1809.

Gray, Charles M. "Parliament, Liberty, and the Law." In *Parliament and Liberty from the Reign of Elizabeth to the English Civil War,* ed. J. H. Hexter, 155–200. Stanford: Stanford University Press, 1992.

Great Britain. Parliament. House of Commons. *The Journals of the House of Commons.* London, 1742. Cited as *CJ.*

———. Parliament. *Rotuli Parliamentorum; ut et Petitiones, et Placita in Parliamento.* 6 vols. London, 1767–77.

———. Parliament. *Statutes of the Realm.* 11 vols. London, 1810–28. Cited as *SR.*

———. Public Record Office. *Acts of the Privy Council of England, 1542–1631.* New series. Edited by J. R. Dasent et al. 46 vols. London: H.M. Stationery Office, 1890–64. Cited as *APC.*

Green, Douglas E. "Interpreting 'her martyr'd signs': Gender and Tragedy in *Titus Andronicus.*" *Shakespeare Quarterly* 40 (1989): 317–26.

Greene, Robert. *Menaphon.* Edited by G. B. Harrison. Oxford, Basil Blackwell, 1927.

Greenblatt, Stephen. *Hamlet in Purgatory.* Princeton: Princeton University Press, 2001.

———. "Invisible Bullets: Renaissance Authority and Its Subversion." *Glyph: Textual Studies* 8 (1981): 40–61. Revised version in id., *Shakespearean Negotiations.*

———. "Murdering Peasants: Status, Genre, and the Representation of Rebellion." In id., *Learning to Curse: Essays in Early Modern Culture.* New York: Routledge, Chapman & Hall, 1992.

———. *Shakespearean Negotiations.* Berkeley: University of California Press, 1988.

Greville, Fulke, Lord Brooke. *The Remains: Being Poems of Monarchy and Religion.* Edited by G. A. Wilkes. Oxford: Oxford University Press, 1965.

Gruenfelder, John K. "Gloucester's Parliamentary Elections, 1604–40." *Bristol and Gloucestershire Archaeological Society Transactions* 96 (1978): 53–59.

———. *Influence in Early Stuart Elections, 1604–1640.* Columbus: Ohio State University Press, 1981.

Gurr, Andrew. *Playgoing in Shakespeare's London.* Cambridge: Cambridge University Press, 1987.

Habermas, Jürgen. *The Structural Transformation of the Public Sphere: An Inquiry into a Category of Bourgeois Society.* Translated by Thomas Burger. Cambridge, Mass.: MIT Press, 1989.

Habington, William. "To a Friend, Inviting him to a meeting upon promise." 1635. In id., *Castara.*

———. *Castara.* 2nd edition. London, 1635.

Hadfield, Andrew. *Shakespeare and Renaissance Politics.* London: Thomson Learning, 2004.

———. "Shakespeare and Republicanism: History and Cultural Materialism." *Textual Practice* 17 (2003): 461–83.

———. "Tarquin's Everlasting Banishment: Republicanism and Constitutionalism in *The Rape of the Lucrece* and *Titus Andronicus.*" *Parergon: Journal of the Australian and New Zealand Association for Medieval and Early Modern Studies* 19 (2002): 77–104.

Haigh, Christopher, ed. *The Reign of Elizabeth I.* Athens: University of Georgia Press, 1987.

Hall, Arthur. *An Admonition by the Father of F.A. to him being a Burgesse of the Parliament, for his better Behaviour therein.* Printed with *A letter sent by F.A, touchyng the proceedings in a private quarell . . . betweene A.H., and M. Mallerie.* London, 1576.

Hall, Edward. *The Union of the Two Noble and Illustre Families of Lancaster and York.* 1548. Reprint. London: J. Johnson, 1809.

Halpern, Richard. *Shakespeare Among the Moderns.* Ithaca, N.Y.: Cornell University Press, 1997.

Harris, Bernice. "Sexuality as Signifier for Power Relations: Using Lavinia, of Shakespeare's *Titus Andronicus.*" *Criticism: A Quarterly for Literature and the Arts* 38 (1996): 383–406.

Harrison, William. *The Description of England.* 1587. Edited by George Edelen. 1968. Reprint. New York: Dover Publications, 1994.

Hartley, T. E., ed. *Elizabeth's Parliaments: Queen, Lords, and Commons, 1559–1601.* New York: Manchester University Press, 1992.

———. *Proceedings in the Parliaments of Elizabeth I.* Vol. 1: *1558–1581.* Wilmington, Del.: Michael Glazier, 1981. Vol. 2: *1584–1589* and vol. 3: *1593–1601.* London: Leicester University Press, 1995. Cited as *PPE.*

Harvey, I. N. W. *Jack Cade's Rebellion of 1450.* Oxford: Clarendon Press, 1991.

Hasler, P. W., ed. *The House of Commons, 1558–1603.* 3 vols. London: H.M. Stationery Office, 1981.

Hattaway, Michael. "Rebellion, Class Consciousness, and Shakespeare's *2 Henry VI.*" *Cahiers Elisabethains: Late Medieval and Renaissance Studies* 33 (1988): 13–22.

Hawkyard, Alistair. "From Painted Chamber to St. Stephen's Chapel: The Meeting Places of the House of Commons at Westminister Until 1603." *Parliamentary History* 21 (2002): 62–84.

Helgerson, Richard. *Forms of Nationhood: The Elizabethan Writing of England.* Chicago: University of Chicago Press, 1992.

Hexter, J. H., ed. *Parliament and Liberty from the Reign of Elizabeth to the English Civil War.* The Making of Modern Freedom series. Stanford: Stanford University Press, 1992.

Heywood, Thomas. *How a man may chuse a good wife from a bad.* London, 1602.

———. *The rape of Lucrece a true Roman tragedie.* London, 1608.

Higgins, John. *The first parte of the Mirour for magistrates containing the falles of the first infortunate princes of this lande: from the comming of Brute to the incarnation of our saviour and redemer Iesu Christe.* London, 1574.

Hirst, Derek. *The Representative of the People? Voters and Voting in England Under the Early Stuarts.* Cambridge: Cambridge University Press, 1975.

Hobbes, Thomas. *A Discourse upon the Beginning of Tacitus.* 1620. In *Three Discourses: A Critical Modern Edition of Newly Identified Work of the Young Hobbes,* ed. Noel B. Reynolds and Arlene W. Saxonhouse. Chicago: University of Chicago Press, 1995.

———. *Leviathan.* Edited by Richard Tuck. New York: Cambridge University Press, 1991.

Holinshed, Raphael. *The Chronicles of England, Scotland and Ireland.* 2nd edition. 1587. Reprint. 6 vols. London: J. Johnson, 1807–8.

Holme, Wilfrid. *The fall and evill successe of Rebellion from time to time.* London, 1572.

Holmes, Christopher. "Time for the Plebs in *Julius Caesar.*" *Early Modern Literary Studies: A Journal of Sixteenth- and Seventeenth-Century English Literature* 7 (2001): 1–32.

Hooker, John. *The Order and usage of the keeping of a Parlement in England.* 1571. Reprinted in John Snow, *Parliament in Elizabethan England.* New Haven: Yale University Press, 1977.

Hooker, Richard. *Of the Laws of Ecclesiastical Polity.* Edited by Arthur Stephen McGrade. Cambridge: Cambridge University Press, 1989.

Howard, Jean E., and Marion O'Connor, eds. *Shakespeare Reproduced: The Text in History and Ideology.* New York: Methuen, 1987.

Huffman, Clifford Chalmers. *"Coriolanus" in Context.* Lewisburg, Pa.: Bucknell University Press, 1971.

Hulse, S. Clark. "Wresting the Alphabet: Oratory and Action in *Titus Andronicus.*" *Criticism* 21 (1979): 110–27.

Jacke of Dover, His Quest of Inquirie, or his privy search for the veriest Foole in England. London, 1604.

James, Heather. *Shakespeare's Troy: Drama, Politics, and the Translation of Empire.* Cambridge: Cambridge University Press, 1997.

James I, king of England. *The* Basilicon Doron *of King James VI.* 2 vols. Edited by James Craigie. Edinburgh: W. Blackwood and Sons, 1944–50.

———. *Political Writings.* Edited by Johann P. Sommerville. Cambridge: Cambridge University Press, 1994.

Jameson, Fredric. "Marxism and Historicism." In *The Ideologies of Theory: Essays, 1971–1986.* Vol. 2: *Syntax of History (Ideologies of Theory).* Minneapolis: University of Minnesota Press, 1988.

Jansson, Maija, ed. *Proceedings in Parliament 1614 (House of Commons).* Philadelphia: American Philosophical Society, 1988. Cited as *PP 1614.*

Jed, Stephanie H. *Chaste Thinking: The Rape of Lucretia and the Birth of Humanism.* Bloomington: Indiana University Press, 1989.

Johnston, Alexandra F., and Margaret Rogerson, eds. *Records of the Early English Drama: York.* 2 vols. Toronto: University of Toronto Press, 1979.

Jonson, Ben. *Bartholomew Fair.* 1614. In id., *Complete Plays,* vol. 3.

———. *The Complete Plays of Ben Jonson.* 4 vols. Edited by G. A. Wilkes. New York: Oxford University Press, 1981–82.

———. *Cynthia's Revels.* 1600. In id., *Complete Plays,* vol. 1.

Kahn, Coppélia. *Roman Shakespeare: Warriors, Wounds, and Women.* New York: Routledge, 1997.

Kantorowicz, Ernst Hartwig. *The King's Two Bodies; a Study in Mediaeval Political Theology.* Princeton: Princeton University Press, 1957.

Kastan, David Scott. "'The *King* Hath Many Marching in His Coats': Or, What Did You Do in the War, Daddy?" In *Shakespeare Left and Right,* ed. Ivo Kamps, 241–58. New York: Routledge, 1991.

Kayser, John R., and Ronald J. Lettieri. "The Last of All the Romans: Shakespeare's Commentary on Classical Republicanism." *Clio* 9 (1980): 197–227.

Kemp, Thomas, ed. *The Black Book of Warwick.* Warwick, Eng.: Henry T. Cooke and Son, 1898. Cited as *BB.*

Kenyon, J. P., ed. *The Stuart Constitution, 1603–1688.* Cambridge: Cambridge University Press, 1966.

Kezar, Dennis. "*Julius Caesar* and the Properties of Shakespeare's Globe." *English Literary Renaissance* 28 (1998): 18–46.

Kierkegaard, Søren, *The Journals of Kierkegaard.* Edited and Translated by Alexander Dru. New York: Harper, 1959.

Kishlansky, Mark A. *Parliamentary Selection: Social and Political Choice in Early Modern England.* Cambridge: Cambridge University Press, 1986.

Klausner, David N., ed. *Records of the Early English Drama: Herefordshire, Worcestershire.* Toronto: University of Toronto Press, 1990.

Kolbert, Colin Francis, and N. A. M. Mackay. *History of Scots and English Land Law*. Berkhamsted, Eng.: Geographical Publications, 1977.

Kyle, Chris R. "Parliament and the Palace of Westminster: An Exploration of Public Space in the Early Seventeenth Century." *Parliamentary History* 21 (2002): 85–98.

Lambarde, William. *Notes on the procedures and privileges of the House of Commons.* 1584. Edited by Paul L. Ward. London: H.M. Stationery Office, 1977.

A Lamentable Complaint of the Commonality, by way of supplication to the High Court of Parliament, for a learned ministry. London, 1585.

Laroque, François. "The Jack Cade Scenes Reconsidered: Popular Rebellion, Utopia, or Carnival?" In *Shakespeare and Cultural Traditions,* ed. Tetsuo Kishi, Roger Pringle, and Stanley Wells, 76–89. Newark: University of Delaware Press, 1994.

Lee, Maurice, ed. *Dudley Carleton to John Chamberlain, 1603–1624*. New Brunswick, N.J.: Rutgers University Press, 1972.

Leggatt, Alexander. *Shakespeare's Political Drama: The History Plays and the Roman Plays*. 1989. Reprint. London: Routledge, 1992.

Lehnhof, Kent. "'Rather Say I Play the Man I Am': Shakespeare's *Coriolanus* and Elizabethan Anti-Theatricality." *Shakespeare and Renaissance Association of West Virginia: Selected Papers* 23 (2000): 31–41.

Levin, Carole. *The Heart and Stomach of a King: Elizabeth I and the Politics of Sex and Power*. Philadelphia: University of Pennsylvania Press, 1994.

Liebler, Naomi Conn. "'Thou Bleeding Piece of Earth': The Ritual Ground of *Julius Caesar.*" *Shakespeare Studies* 14 (1981): 175–96.

Littleton, Thomas. *Littleton tenures in englishe.* London, 1574.

Liu, Alan. "The Power of Formalism: The New Historicism." *English Literary History* 56 (1989): 721–71.

Livy. *Livy, Books I–X.* Edited by J. R. Seeley. Oxford, The Clarendon Press, 1874.

Lloyd, Lodowick. *Certaine Englishe verses.* London, 1586.

———. "Juius Caesars Death." In id., *Certaine Englishe verses.*

———. *The Marrow of History, or, The Pilgrimage of Kings and Princes.* London, 1573.

———. "The Triumphs of Trophes." In id., *Certaine Englishe verses.*

Lloyd, Richard. *A briefe discourse of the most renowned actes and right valiant conquests.* London, 1584.

Loach, Jennifer. *Parliament Under the Tudors.* Oxford: Oxford University Press, 1991.

Loades, David. "Politics and the 'Men-of-Business' in the Tudor Parliaments." *Parliamentary History* 12 (1993): 73–77.

Locke, John. *Two Treatises of Government.* Edited by Peter Laslett. Cambridge: Cambridge University Press, 1997.

Lodge, Thomas. *The Wounds of Civil War.* Edited by Joseph W. Houppert. Lincoln: University of Nebraska Press, 1969.

Logan, Marie-Rose, and Peter L. Rudnytsky, eds. *Contending Kingdoms.* Detroit: Wayne State University Press, 1991.

Lucan. *Pharsalia.* Translated by Arthur Gorges. London, 1614.

MacCallum, Mungo William. *Shakespeare's Roman Plays and Their Background.* London: Macmillan, 1910.

Machiavelli, Niccolò. *Discourses on Livy.* Translated by Harvey C. Mansfield and Nathan Tarcov. Chicago: University of Chicago Press, 1996.

Mack, Peter. "Elizabethan Parliamentary Oratory." *Huntington Library Quarterly* 64 (2001): 23–61.

Maitland, Frederic William. *The Constitutional History of England.* Edited by H. A. L. Fisher. 1908. Reprint. Cambridge: Cambridge University Press, 1979.

———. "Trust and Corporation." In *The Collected Papers of Frederic William Maitland,* ed. H. A. L. Fisher, 3:321–404. Cambridge: Cambridge University Press, 1911.

Marcus, Leah S. *Puzzling Shakespeare: Local Reading and Its Discontents.* Berkeley: University of California Press, 1988.

Marlowe, Christopher. *The Complete Poems and Translations.* Edited by Stephen Orgel. Harmondsworth, Eng.: Penguin Books, 1971.

Marston, John. *Jacke Drums entertainment: or The comedies of Pasquill and Katherine.* London, 1601.

Martin, John E. *Feudalism to Capitalism: Peasant and Landlord in English Agrarian Development.* London: Macmillan, 1983.

Martindale, Charles, and Michelle Martindale. *Shakespeare and the Uses of Antiquity: An Introductory Essay.* London: Routledge, 1990.

Massinger, Philip. *The Emperor of the East.* 1631. In id., *The Plays and Poems,* vol. 3.

———. *The Plays and Poems of Philip Massinger.* Edited by Philip Edwards and Colin Gibson. 5 vols. Oxford: Clarendon Press, 1976.

Maxwell, J. C., ed. *Titus Andronicus.* 1953. Reprint. London: Methuen, 1985.

McGowan, Margaret M. "Caesar's Cloak: Diversion as an Art of Persuasion in Sixteenth-Century Writing." *Renaissance Studies* 18 (2004): 37–48.

McLaren, A. N. *Political Culture in the Reign of Elizabeth I: Queen and Commonwealth, 1558–1585.* Cambridge: Cambridge University Press, 1999.

———. "Reading Sir Thomas Smith's *De republica Anglorum* as Protestant Apologetic." *Historical Journal* 42 (1999): 911–39.

Miller, Shannon. "Topicality and Subversion in William Shakespeare's *Coriolanus*." *Studies in English Literature, 1500–1900* 32 (1992): 287–310.

Mincoff, Marco. "The Source of *Titus Andronicus*." *Notes and Queries* 216 (1971): 131–34.

Miola, Robert S. *Shakespeare's Rome.* Cambridge: Cambridge University Press, 1983.

Modus tenendi Parliamentum. Translated by John Hooker. 1572. Reprinted in John Snow, *Parliament in Elizabethan England.* New Haven: Yale University Press, 1977.

Monahan, Arthur P. *Consent, Coercion and Limit: The Medieval Origins of Parliamentary Democracy.* Montreal: McGill-Queen's University Press, 1987.

Mullaney, Steven. *The Place of the Stage: License, Play, and Power in Renaissance England.* Chicago: University of Chicago Press, 1988.

Munden, R. C. "James I and 'the growth of mutual distrust': King, Commons, and Reform, 1603–1604." In *Faction and Parliament: Essays on Early Stuart Culture,* ed. Kevin Sharpe, 43–72. 1978. Reprint. London: Methuen, 1985.

Nash, Ernest. *Pictorial Dictionary of Ancient Rome.* 2 vols. London: A. Zwemmer, 1961–62.

Neale, J. E. *The Elizabethan House of Commons.* 1949. Reprint. Harmondsworth, Eng.: Penguin Books, 1963. Cited as *HC.*

———. *Elizabeth I and Her Parliaments.* Vol. 1: *1559–1581.* Vol. 2: *1584–1601.* London: Jonathan Cape, 1953–57. Cited as EJ.

North, Sir Thomas. See Plutarch.

"Observations rules and orders collected out of diverse Journalls of the house of Commons." 1604. British Library Egerton MS 3365.

Orgel, Stephen. *The Illusion of Power: Political Theater in the English Renaissance.* Berkeley: University of California Press, 1975.

———. "Making Greatness Familiar." In *The Power of Forms in the English Renaissance,* ed. Stephen Greenblatt, 41–48. Norman, Okla.: Pilgrim Books, 1982.

Owens, Margaret E. "The Many-Headed Monster in *Henry VI, Part 2.*" *Criticism: A Quarterly for Literature and the Arts* 38 (1996): 367–82.

Painter, William. *The palace of pleasure beautified, adorned and well furnished, with pleasaunt histories and excellent novelles, selected out of divers good and commendable authors.* London, 1566.

Palliser, D. M. *The Age of Elizabeth: England Under the Later Tudors, 1547–1603.* 1983. Reprint. New York: Longman, 1992.

Parker, Barbara L. "'A Thing Unfirm': Plato's Republic and Shakespeare's *Julius Caesar.*" *Shakespeare Quarterly* 44 (1993): 30–43.

Parker, Patricia, and Geoffrey Hartman, eds. *Shakespeare and the Question of Theory.* New York: Methuen, 1985.

Parker, R. B. See under Shakespeare, *Coriolanus.*

Patterson, Annabel. *Censorship and Interpretation: The Conditions of Writing and Reading in Early Modern England.* Madison: University of Wisconsin Press, 1984.

———. *Fables of Power: Aesopian Writing and Political History.* Durham, N.C.: Duke University Press, 1991.

———. *Reading Holinshed's "Chronicles."* Chicago: University of Chicago Press, 1994.

———. *Shakespeare and the Popular Voice.* Cambridge: Basil Blackwell, 1989.

Pechter, Edward. "*Julius Caesar* and *Sejanus:* Roman Politics, Inner Selves, and the Powers of the Theatre." In *Shakespeare and His Contemporaries: Essays in Comparison,* ed. E. A. J. Honigmann, 60–78. Manchester: Manchester University Press, 1986.

Petowe, Henry. "His Maiestes Most Royall Coronation." In *Englands Caesar. His Maiesties most Royall Coronation.* London, 1603.

Pettet, E. C. "*Coriolanus* and the Midlands Insurrection of 1607." *Shakespeare Survey* 3 (1950): 34–42.

Petyt, William. Jus parliamentarium: or, the ancient power, jurisdiction, rights and liberties, of the most high court of Parliament, revived and asserted. London, 1739.

Platner, Samuel Ball. *The Topography and Monuments of Ancient Rome.* Boston: Allyn & Bacon, 1911.

Platt, Michael. *Rome and Romans According to Shakespeare.* 1976. Rev. ed. New York: University Press of America, 1983.

Plutarch. *The lives of the noble Grecians and Romanes compared together by that grave learned philosopher and historiographer, Plutarke of Chaeronea translated out of Greeke into French by James Amyot . . . and out of French into Englishe* by Sir Thomas North. London, 1579.

———. *Les vies des hommes illustres, grecs et romains, comparées l'une avec l'autre par Plutarque de Chaeronée.* Translated by Jacques Amyot. 1559. Paris: François Gueffier, 1565. Edited by Gérard Walter as *Les vies des hommes illustres.* 2 vols. Bibliothèque de la Pléiade, 43–44. Paris: Gallimard, 1951.

Pugliatti, Paola. "'More than history can pattern': The Jack Cade Rebellion in Shakespeare's *Henry VI, Part 2.*" *Journal of Medieval and Renaissance Studies* 22 (1992): 451–78.

Puttenham, George. *The Arte of English Poesie.* Edited by G. D. Wilcock and A. A. Walker. Cambridge: Cambridge University Press, 1936.

Rabkin, Norman, "*Coriolanus*: The Tragedy of Politics." *Shakespeare Quarterly* 17 (1966): 195–212.

Rackin, Phyllis. *Stages of History: Shakespeare's English Chronicles.* Ithaca, N.Y.: Cornell University Press, 1990.

Ray, Sid. "'Rape, I Fear, Was Root of Thy Annoy': The Politics of Consent in *Titus Andronicus.*" *Shakespeare Quarterly* 49 (1998): 22–39.

Rebhorn, Wayne A. "The Crisis of the Aristocracy in *Julius Caesar.*" *Renaissance Quarterly* 43 (1990): 75–111.

A Record of some worthy Proceedings in the Honourable, wise and faithful Howse of Commons in the late Parliament. Amsterdam (?), 1611.

Rose, Mark. "Conjuring Caesar: Ceremony, History, and Authority in 1599." *English Literary Renaissance* 19 (1989): 291–304.
Roskell, J. S. "The English Monarchy, Powers and Limitations, in the Middle Ages." In *Parliament and Politics in Late Medieval England,* 1: 1–4. London: Hambledon Press, 1981.
Rossiter, A. P. *Angel with Horns and Other Shakespeare Lectures.* Edited by Graham Storey. London: Longmans, 1961.
Rousseau, Jean-Jacques. *Du contrat social.* Edited by Ronald Grimsley. Oxford: Clarendon Press, 1972.
———. *The Social Contract and Other Later Political Writings.* Edited and translated by Victor Gourevitch. Cambridge: Cambridge University Press, 1997.
Rowlands, Samuel. "Aue Caesar; God saue the king." 1603. In vol. 2 of *The Complete Works of Samuel Rowlands, 1598–1628.* 3 vols. Glasgow: Printed for the Hunterian Club, 1880.
Russell, Conrad. *The Crisis of Parliaments: English History, 1509–1660.* Oxford: Oxford University Press, 1971.
———. "Parliamentary History in Perspective, 1604–1629." *History* 61 (1976): 1–27.
Sacks, David Harris. "Parliament, Liberty, and the Commonweal." In *Parliament and Liberty from the Reign of Elizabeth to the English Civil War,* ed. J. H. Hexter, 85–121. Stanford: Stanford University Press, 1992.
Schoenbaum, Samuel. *William Shakespeare: A Compact Documentary Life.* 1977. Rev. ed. New York: Oxford University Press, 1986. Cited as *CDL.*
Scott, Thomas. *Vox Coeli, or Newes from Heaven.* London, 1624.
Scullard, H. H. *Festivals and Ceremonies of the Roman Republic.* Ithaca, N.Y.: Cornell University Press, 1981.
Shakespeare, William. *The Complete Works.* Edited by Stanley Wells, Gary Taylor, John Jowett, and William Montgomery. Oxford: Clarendon Press, 1986.
———. *Coriolanus.* Edited by R. B. Parker. Oxford: Oxford University Press, 1994.
———. *King Henry the Sixth: Part Two.* Edited by Andrew S. Cairncross. New York: Routledge, 1990.
———. *The Poems.* Edited by John Roe. Cambridge: Cambridge University Press, 1992.
———. *Titus Andronicus.* Edited by Jonathan Bate. New York: Routledge, 1995.
———. *Titus Andronicus.* Edited by Eugene M. Waith. Oxford: Oxford University Press, 1984.
———. *Titus Andronicus.* Edited by John Dover Wilson. 1948. Reprint. Cambridge: Cambridge University Press, 1968.
Sharpe, Kevin. "Crown, Parliament and Locality: Government and Communication in Early Stuart England." *English Historical Review* 101 (1986): 321–50.

———. "Introduction: Parliamentary History 1603–1629: In or out of Perspective?" In *Faction and Parliament: Essays on Early Stuart Culture,* ed. Kevin Sharpe, 1–42. 1978. Reprint. London: Methuen, 1985.

Sharrock, John. *The valliant actes and victorious Battailes of the English nation.* London, 1585.

Shirley, James. *The Coronation.* In id., *Dramatic Works and Poems,* vol. 3

———. *Dramatic Works and Poems.* 5 vols. New York: Russell & Russell, 1966.

———. *The Imposture.* 1640. In id., *Dramatic Works and Poems,* vol. 5.

———. *St. Patrick for Ireland, Part I.* 1640. In id., *Dramatic Works and Poems,* vol. 3.

Smith, Irwin. *Shakespeare's Blackfriars Playhouse.* New York: New York University Press, 1964.

Smith, Marion B. *Casque to Cushion: A Study of "Othello" and "Coriolanus."* Ottawa: Canadian Federation for the Humanities, 1979.

Smith, Sir Thomas. *De republica Anglorum.* 1583. Edited by Mary Dewar. Cambridge: Cambridge University Press, 1982.

Sohmer, Steve. "12 June 1599: Opening Day at Shakespeare's Globe." *Early Modern Literary Studies: A Journal of Sixteenth-and Seventeenth-Century English Literature* 3 (1997): 1–46.

Sommerville, Johann P. "Parliament, Privilege, and the Liberties of the Subject." In *Parliament and Liberty from the Reign of Elizabeth to the English Civil War,* ed. J. H. Hexter, 56–84 Stanford: Stanford University Press, 1992.

———. "Richard Hooker, Hadrian Saravia, and the Advent of the Divine Right of Kings." *History of Political Thought* 4 (1983): 229–45.

Sorge, Thomas. "The Failure of Orthodoxy in *Coriolanus.*" In *Shakespeare Reproduced: The Text in History and Ideology,* ed. Jean E. Howard and Marion F. O'Connor, 225–41. New York: Methuen, 1987.

Spencer, T. J. B. *Shakespeare: The Roman Plays.* London: Longmans, Green, 1963.

Spotswood, Jerald W. "'We are Undone Already': Disarming the Multitude in *Julius Caesar* and *Coriolanus.*" *Texas Studies in Literature and Language* 42 (2000): 61–78.

Stirling, Brents. *The Populace in Shakespeare.* New York: Columbia University Press, 1949.

Tales and quicke answeres, very mery, and pleasant to rede. London, 1534.

Tanner, J. R. *Constitutional Documents of the Reign of James I, 1603–1625.* Cambridge: Cambridge University Press, 1930.

Taylor, Anthony Brian. "Lucius, the Severly Flawed Redeemer of *Titus Andronicus.*" *Connotations: A Journal for Critical Debate* 6 (1996–97): 138–57.

Tennenhouse, Leonard. *Power on Display: The Politics of Shakespeare's Genres.* London: Methuen, 1986.

Thomas, Vivian. *Shakespeare's Roman Worlds.* New York: Routledge, 1989.

Thomson, Elizabeth McClure, ed. *The Chamberlain Letters.* New York: G. P. Putnam's Sons, 1965.

Tierney, Brian. "Medieval Canon Law and Western Constitutionalism." *Catholic Historical Review* 52 (1966): 1–17.

———. "Some Recent Works on the Political Theories of the Medieval Canonists." *Traditio* 10 (1954): 599–612.

Tittler, Robert. "The Elizabethan Towns and the 'Points of Contact: Parliament.'" *Parliamentary History* 8 (1989): 275–88.

The Tragedies of Caesar and Pompey, or Caesar's Revenge. See under Boas.

Trigge, Francis. *To the King's most excellent Majestie. The humble petition of two sisters; the Church and Commonwealth: for the restoring of their ancient Commons and liberties*. London, 1604.

Vickers, Brian. *Appropriating Shakespeare: Contemporary Critical Quarrels*. New Haven: Yale University Press, 1993.

Vickers, Nancy J. "'The blazon of sweet beauty's best': Shakespeare's *Lucrece*." In *Shakespeare and the Question of Theory*, ed. Patricia Parker and Geoffrey Hartman, 95–115. New York: Methuen, 1985.

Waith, Eugene M. See under Shakespeare, *Titus Andronicus*.

Weimann, Robert. *Authority and Representation in Early Modern Discourse*. Baltimore: Johns Hopkins University Press, 1996.

Wells, Stanley, and Gary Taylor, with John Jowett and William Montgomery. *William Shakespeare, A Textual Companion*. Oxford: Clarendon Press, 1987.

Wentworth Papers, 1597–1628. Edited by J. P Cooper. Camden Fourth Series. Vol. 12. London: Royal Historical Society, 1973.

Willbern, David. "Hyperbolic Desire: Shakespeare's *Lucrece*." In *Contending Kingdoms,* ed. Marie-Rose Logan and Peter L. Rudnytsky, 202–24. Detroit: Wayne State University Press, 1991.

———. "Rape and Revenge in *Titus Andronicus*." *English Literary Renaissance* 8 (1978): 159–82.

Williams, Penry. "The Crown and the Counties." In *The Reign of Elizabeth I,* ed. Christopher Haigh, 125–46. Athens: University of Georgia Press, 1987.

———. *The Tudor Regime*. New York: Oxford University Press, 1979.

Wilson, John Dover. See under Shakespeare, *Titus Andronicus*.

Wilson, Richard. "Against the Grain: Representing the Market in *Coriolanus*." *The Seventeenth Century* 6 (1991): 111–44.

———. "'Is this a holiday?': Shakespeare's Roman Carnival." *English Literary History* 54 (1987): 31–44.

———. *Will Power: Essays on Shakespearean Authority*. Detroit: Wayne State University Press, 1993.

Worden, Blair. "Shakespeare and Politics." *Shakespeare Survey* 44 (1992): 65–73.

Wright, H. G. *The Life and Works of Arthur Hall of Grantham, Member of Parliament, Courtier and First Translator of Homer into English*. Manchester: Manchester University Press, 1919.

Yale, D. E. C., ed. *Lord Nottingham's Chancery Cases*. 2 vols. London: Bernard Quaritch for the Selden Society, 1961.

Zaller, Robert. "King, Commons, and Commonweal in Holinshed's *Chronicle.*" *Albion* 34 (2002): 371–90.

Zaret, David. *Origins of Democratic Culture: Printing, Petitions, and the Public Sphere in Early-Modern England.* Princeton: Princeton University Press, 2000.

Zeeveld, Gordon W. "*Coriolanus* and Jacobean Politics." *Modern Language Review* 57 (1962): 321–34.

Index